Hoods and Shirts

The

Extreme Right

in Pennsylvania,

1925–1950

The
University
of North
Carolina Press
Chapel Hill &
London

and Shirts

Philip Jenkins

© 1997
The University of
North Carolina Press
All rights reserved
Manufactured in the
United States of America

The paper in this book
meets the guidelines for
permanence and durability
of the Committee on
Production Guidelines
for Book Longevity of
the Council on Library
Resources.

Library of Congress
Cataloging-in-Publication Data
Jenkins, Philip, 1952–
Hoods and shirts : the extreme right
in Pennsylvania, 1925–1950 / by
Philip Jenkins.
p.   cm.
Includes bibliographical references
and index.
ISBN 0-8078-2316-3
1. Right-wing extremists —
Pennsylvania — History — 20th
century.   2. Pennsylvania — Race
relations.   3. Pennsylvania — Ethnic
relations.   I. Title.
F160.A1J46   1997
322.4'2'0974809041 — dc20
96-25437
                              CIP

01 00 99 98 97   5 4 3 2 1

TO LIZ

Contents

Tables

Acknowledgments

In undertaking the research on which this book is based, I have received the assistance of the Institute for the Arts and Humanistic Studies at the Pennsylvania State University and the Office for Research and Graduate Studies in the College of the Liberal Arts at the same institution, under its head, Dean Ray Lombra. I would also like to thank the Pennsylvania Historical and Museum Commission for their kindness in appointing me as a scholar-in-residence in the summer of 1995 and, specifically, for the help of Bob Weible at that agency. As always, the Anti-Defamation League of B'nai Brith was generous in providing information.

It would be hopeless to attempt a comprehensive list of the individuals who have helped me complete this project, so I will confine myself to thanking my wife, Liz Jenkins, and my colleagues Gary W. Gallagher, Baruch Halpern, Kathryn Hume, William Pencak, and Gregg Roeber. I also appreciate the helpful advice received from Lew Bateman at the University of North Carolina Press, from Leo P. Ribuffo, and from an anonymous reviewer of the manuscript. The mistakes are all mine.

Note on Usage

Throughout this book I often refer to the German American Bund and its Bundist members. The difficulty here is that simple reference to the Bund can cause confusion with the respectable Jewish Socialist organization of that name, whose members were likewise known as Bundists. Partly to avoid this confusion, contemporary enemies of the pro-Nazi Bund referred to its supporters as Bunders or Bundsters, on the analogy of "gangsters." In the present work, the terms "Bund" and "Bundists" should invariably be taken to imply the German American group.

Also in terms of definition, in Chapter 1 I explore the many problems encountered in the correct use of the terms "fascism" and "fascist." Throughout the book these words are used with an upper-case "F" to refer to the Italian and Italian American movements of that name. The generic political creed will be referred to in lower case.

Hoods and Shirts

MUST AMERICA GO FASCIST?

In the decade before the attack on Pearl Harbor, the United States possessed a number of activist organizations that were commonly described as fascist or Nazi in their political orientation. The best known was the German American Bund, but other "shirt" groups proliferated. In 1940 the leftist news-sheet *The Hour* typically claimed that "scores of new and old terrorist organizations — Silver Shirts, Black Legion, Christian Front, Mobilizers — sprout overnight like toadstools."[1] Fears about a fascist danger were focused in two periods; in each, observers perceived analogies between domestic conditions and the circumstances that had brought dictators to power in other nations. Each period was marked by an outpouring of exposé literature and by congressional investigations that in turn fueled media investigation.

The first wave of concern occurred at the worst of the Great Depression, between about 1932 and 1934, at a time when the media were giving extensive coverage to the collapse of German democracy and Hitler's seizure of power with the assistance of reactionary industrial interests. The 1932 Bonus March to Washington showed how mass discontent could potentially be harnessed

for a direct challenge to the nation's political and industrial establishment.[2] This movement inspired imitation by aspiring leaders
seeking to mobilize the unemployed and desperate. Father Cox of
Pittsburgh used another such march to lay the foundations for his
Blue Shirt army, while Art Smith's Khaki Shirts aimed to seize
power through a ludicrous March on Washington in 1933.

In these same years the United States acquired a number of
extremist groups that acknowledged their ideological debt to the
Nazis: the Silver Shirts of William Dudley Pelley, the Association of the Friends of the New Germany, and the Order of 76.
All used anti-Semitic rhetoric, which was brought into the public
arena by the activities of Pennsylvania congressman Louis McFadden. The world of the shirts was publicized by the McCormack-
Dickstein congressional committee of 1934–35, which investigated
"Un-American Activities."[3] These organizations were exposed in a
number of magazine articles and pamphlets published during 1934,
especially John L. Spivak's investigative series in *New Masses*.[4]
This influential account portrayed an extensive network of hate
groups, closely linked to foreign intelligence agencies and domestic reactionaries.

America seemed to have acquired the components of a German-
or Italian-style dictatorship that required only the appropriate
strong man to consolidate into a threatening movement. Many
felt that Huey Long had the potential to play such a role, while
after his assassination in 1935, populist and anti-Semitic activism was continued by his associates and admirers such as Gerald
L. K. Smith and Father Charles Coughlin. A 1935 study of these
leaders was ominously titled *Forerunners of American Fascism*.[5] In
the same year, Sinclair Lewis's novel *It Can't Happen Here* portrayed a fascist takeover in the United States under the demagogic
Buzz Windrip and his paramilitary MMs, or Minutemen.[6]

Fears revived at the end of the decade. Between 1938 and 1941
a flood of books and periodical articles regularly made extreme
claims about the vast and imminent danger posed by American
fascists, and papers such as *Equality*, *American Appeal*, and *The
Hour* devoted themselves to exposing the "Nazi menace." This
was the age of books such as Stefan Heym's *Nazis in USA*, George
Britt's *The Fifth Column Is Here*, Harold Lavine's *Fifth Column*

in America, John L. Spivak's *Secret Armies*, and Donald Strong's *Organized Anti-Semitism in America.*[7]

The "fascist exposé" genre depicted ultra-Right movements as a vast menace threatening armed revolt and civil disorder within the United States.[8] In this view, groups were sponsored and supported by foreign intelligence agencies, working through diplomatic missions and consulates, and the subversive activities of the far Right extended to plotting "fifth column" and treasonous behavior in the event of American entry into the European war.[9] In 1943 John Roy Carlson's best-selling book *Under Cover* exposed "the development of a nativist, nationalist, American Nazi or American fascist movement which, like a spearhead, is poised to stab at Democracy."[10]

Sayers and Kahn's book *Sabotage: The Secret War against America* provides a characteristic example of the far-reaching rhetoric offered: "By 1939 the Christian Front had assumed the proportions of a subversive army numbering some 200,000 members, many of whom were secretly drilling with rifles and other military equipment. Working closely with the German-American Bund, the Christian Mobilizers, the Silver Shirts and similar gangs, the Fronters made American cities the scenes of violent anti-Semitic agitation."[11] By 1940 George Britt could claim in *The Fifth Column Is Here* "the first complete revelation of a foreign army within the United States—four times as large as the regular US Army . . . a million Fifth Columnists—and that is cold official estimate based on investigation."[12] The federal prosecutor charged with investigating pro-Axis sedition in the years leading to war saw a systematic plan: "They talked in terms of legal means and counter-revolution. Their legal means, however, consisted of underground armies of Storm Troopers, Silver Shirts, White Knights, Christian Mobilizers, Christian Fronters, marches on Washington, appeals to army officers to be disloyal, pogroms, and finally a nationalist dictatorship."[13]

Charges acquired national visibility following a series of incidents which implied that America contained within its borders groups that were aspiring to the same role played by other seditionists in Madrid, Vienna, or the Sudetenland. Three domestic events had a particular impact, including a massed Bund rally at Madison Square Garden in February 1939. Ostensibly a patriotic celebration of the birthday of George Washington, this gathering of 20,000 faithful bore an unsettling resemblance to a Nuremberg Party Day rally. In January 1940 the arrests of the Christian Front leadership in New York City for allegedly planning a putsch raised public fears about the military potential of the far Right and their conduct in the event of war. The following August this threat was reinforced by a joint rally of Bund paramilitaries and Ku Klux Klansmen at Camp Nordland in New Jersey, an incident that reflected growing unity among the diverse sects and ideologies. Meanwhile the parade of extremist leaders before the revived Un-American Activities Committee chaired by Martin Dies offered a thorough review of the nation's would-be dictators and pogrom organizers.

In retrospect the charges made against the far Right seem ludicrously exaggerated, at least as much as the accusations made against leftist and Communist infiltration in the decade after 1945. However, in both eras, there was some basis for the hysteria in that the specific groups named did exist, and they genuinely did have a political base, some following in particular classes, regions, and ethnic groups. Rightist sects really did discuss or advocate violent or subversive activities, and on occasion they formed links with the governments or intelligence agencies of hostile regimes. They preached racial terrorism, and in some urban areas their activities excited widespread tension and fear. To pursue the Red analogy, the fact that the anti-Communist crusades of the Truman era involved hysteria and wild exaggeration does not mean that the American Left was not a real presence, or that the Communist Party and its affiliates were not connected to Soviet interests and policies.

As in later years, however, claims about a subversive menace must be placed in their proper political context, specifically the intense political polarization of the late 1930s, when the threat from the Right acted as a potent ideological weapon to promote unity on the Left. In the most benevolent view, anti-fascist observers and critics were likely to focus attention on the most violent, bigoted, and bellicose statements of their opponents and portray them as typical. More seriously, the question arises whether seditious or fifth column allegations might be wholly invented. Questions about authenticity and bias abound. One of the most influential platforms for these views was Albert Kahn's *The Hour*, which ran from 1939 to 1943. However, the paper's editors were committed to a political agenda that was not merely left wing but solidly pro-Soviet. Their charges of Nazi sabotage plans in the United States thus drew heavily on material from the Soviet purge trials of the late 1930s, a source to which few later commentators would give any credence whatever.[14]

Like the far Left, the Roosevelt administration had much to gain from portraying American fascism as a genuine subversive menace. Robert E. Herzstein suggests that by 1938 at the latest the White House was deliberately orchestrating a campaign to link the far Right to foreign espionage and potential subversion. This was achieved both through the FBI and through friends and assets in the mass media, through broadcasters such as Walter Winchell.[15] The emphasis on the rabid anti-Semitism of the Right served both foreign and domestic policy goals in linking racial bigotry to political disloyalty and Hitlerism. The Nazi and anti-Semitic agitation of 1939 and 1940 proved a godsend for the administration in stirring public fears at a time when the intervention debate was reaching a crescendo.[16]

To this extent the Brown Scare, the fifth column scare, was a socially and politically constructed phenomenon, in which an ideological superstructure was built around a less impressive core of objective reality. On the other hand, this does not mean that there was no underlying reality, that the fascist and Nazi groups were invented by their political opponents, or that they may not have enjoyed much influence. Even in the extreme case of subversion and conspiracy, we should not necessarily dismiss out of hand all the allegations made. Germans and Italians used overseas sympathizers to undertake assassinations and sabotage activities in Europe, and it was not improbable that they would try to use such tactics in North America. Italian Fascists carried out violent acts in the United States, and the Germans forged alliances with overseas dissident groups like the Irish Republican Army (IRA).[17] The fact that something resembles conspiracy paranoia does not mean that it is not objectively true, however lurid the terms in which it is framed.

There never were a million fifth columnists, but there were dozens of extremist groups on the far Right, forming an interlocking network that looked to the same core of leaders and theorists and that shared common facilities for the manufacture and dissemination of propaganda. While the terminology is controversial, at least some of these movements can legitimately be described as Nazi or fascist.

STUDYING AMERICAN FASCISM

Rightist extremism of this era has attracted a good deal of distinguished modern scholarship. The Bund has provided the basis for three major studies, and Father Charles Coughlin has attracted a number of biographical studies, though his followers have been poorly served.[18] Appropriately enough, given the political context, the literature often focuses disproportionately on the ideas and activities of the leaders rather than the led. However, several writers have placed the various movements in the broader tradition of American nativist and racist agitation and fringe religious activity.[19] Scholars such as Geoffrey S. Smith and Charles Higham have studied the wider networks, the interplay between the different groups that gave such apparent plausibility to charges of national conspiracy.[20] The diplomatic and propaganda role of the pro-Axis movements has been placed in a broader political context by Herzstein and in other work on the isolationist campaign.[21]

There are also real lacunae in recent research. Much of the most valuable material on this period is found in unpublished dissertations, and this includes the best accounts of the Silver Shirt movement as well as the best case study of the Christian Front movement and Schonbach's pioneering survey of the whole spectrum of "native fascism."[22] While dissertations are relatively accessible, at least to an academic audience, there is a lack of modern scholarship in other large areas of concern. Apart from the Germans, other ethnic fascist movements have been poorly served, and Diggins's key work on Italian Fascism pays only limited attention to party organization and activism at the level of the streets and local communities.[23] Ukrainian and other Slavic groups remain unstudied, and whole movements such as the Christian Front, the Christian Mobilizers, the White Shirts, and the Khaki Shirts have yet to find their historians. The same is true of the Ku Klux Klan revival in the 1930s, despite the huge volume of work that has appeared on that group in its heyday before 1928.[24] With a few notable exceptions, biographical studies are lacking for most of the leaders and propagandists of these years. Without case studies of the specific movements, it is impossible to estimate the success of rightist campaigns, the numerical scale of the membership, and the wider audience. A circular argument might be at work here: as the movements are so little studied, they appear to be of no great historical significance, and therefore they attract few researchers.

Another dark area concerns the fate of the rightist groups after Pearl Harbor. Such accounts as do exist concentrate on the late 1930s and the isolationist movements, with the implicit suggestion that the groups faded away on the outbreak of war, presumably in response to official intervention and a radically altered public mood. This perception conceals the continuing activity of some organizations and individuals, who occasionally remained active in rightist causes through the McCarthy era. Observing this continuity draws attention to the Mothers' movements that were pivotal to extremist campaigns in the 1940s, and which have been studied by Glen Jeansonne.[25]

LOCAL STUDIES

By far the greatest omission lies in the area of local studies of rightist movements in the depression era, of the sort that have revolutionized our understanding of the Ku Klux Klan in the 1920s. Such accounts are lacking for the 1930s, except to the extent that virtually every major examination of a national rightist movement focuses chiefly or entirely on one locality, New York City.[26] We thus know a great deal about the Bund and the Italian Fascists in this region, and this is the one center where there exists a detailed picture of the Christian Front.[27] Activities elsewhere are mentioned in passing, but there is an implicit suggestion that activism was largely a metropolitan phenomenon, with some spillover into nearby cities like Boston and Philadelphia.

The absence of local research increases the likelihood that the New York experience will be seen as normative for other cities and communities, both on the East Coast and, more perilously, nationwide. These generalizations are often unsafe. To take one example, most rosters of extremist parties include the Christian Mobilizers headed by Joe McWilliams as one of the most powerful factions, and this is usually listed alongside such major groups as the Bund and the Christian Front.[28] This may have been true in New York City, but the group had a negligible presence elsewhere, and

McWilliams was a local phenomenon, in contrast to widely active national leaders such as James B. True or George Deatherage. Conversely, New York-based writers pay little attention to movements with little impact in the northeastern United States—groups such as George W. Christians's White Shirts, which flourished in the South and West in the early 1930s, or the still more active Silver Shirts. Chicago and Detroit spawned movements like the American Vigilant Intelligence Federation, which enjoyed great success in the Midwest while penetrating little to either the West or East Coasts. The regional character of most extremist movements of these years deserves emphasis.

In the absence of local studies, it is scarcely possible to speak about the relationships between the various rightist groups. At the time, antifascist campaigners confidently depicted a tightly organized Brown Front, a degree of unity that seems questionable in retrospect, but there was certainly overlap between sects. German and Irish groups in particular were so closely aligned that it is futile to study any given group without taking account of the several others with which it shared an often transient membership. To study a particular organization, such as the Bund or the Silver Legion, is to impart to it a solidity and continuity that might prove illusory when considered against the local situation. Furthermore, the traditional New York emphasis again leaves many unanswered questions about the relationship between new groups such as the Bund and the older political traditions or networks of a particular area. Did new movements coopt and absorb older patriotic or racist clubs, or did they simply provide ideological cover for activities that were already in progress?

Also at issue are the relationships between the extremist movements and the social or political mainstream. To take the Klan analogy, there had in the 1920s been cities and entire states where the endorsement of the Invisible Empire was required for election to public office. While movements of the 1930s never exercised such influence, this does not mean that these groups were ostracized to the extent of their modern counterparts. In Pennsylvania there were two U.S. congressmen who were at least fellow travelers of extreme rightist and anti-Semitic sects, as well as others who were prepared to appear on their platforms. The far Right enjoyed close contacts with many "respectable" organizations, including cultural, fraternal, patriotic, and veterans' groups, all of which would be critical to the mobilization of rightist sentiment during the 1930s.

To varying degrees extreme right-wing groups operated as a recognized presence within the "normal" landscape of social and political life, and in a few cases, above all the Italian Fascists, they dominated the activities of a particular ethnic community. The far Right had its familiar bastions of support in certain cities and in sections of those communities, customarily designated by ethnicity, class, and religion. Like so much else, this political geography can only be explored on the basis of local case studies that place the extremist movements in the context of a particular city or state. Further research on the far Right of the 1930s must of necessity be locally based.

PENNSYLVANIA

Once the value of a case-study approach is granted, then Pennsylvania offers obvious advantages. This was an important and populous state with almost 10 million people in 1940, with about two-thirds of its residents in urban areas. It was an industrial powerhouse, with a bitter record of labor conflict. Pennsylvania was and remains socially and politically diverse, with Philadelphia and other communities heavily influenced by movements and ideas from New York City, while Pittsburgh and the western industrial cities looked to the Midwest. The state had its distinctive political and cultural traditions. Most valuably for present purposes, Pennsylvania in the first half of the century offered an ethnic mosaic as rich as any outside New York City itself, with proportionately some of the largest American communities of Germans, Italians, Irish, Jews, and Slavic groups as well as an African American presence in Philadelphia and Pittsburgh. In 1990 a survey of the ethnic heritages claimed by Pennsylvanians suggested that of the dozens of nationalities mentioned, by far the largest groupings were those citing some German ancestry, with over 28 percent, followed by 15 percent Irish, 9 percent Italian, and 8 percent English.

Pennsylvania therefore contained within itself all the features that might have been expected to give rise to rightist extremism in the depression era, and this expectation was richly fulfilled. Between 1933 and 1941 both Philadelphia and Pittsburgh had flourishing branches of the German American Bund, the Silver Shirts, the Ku Klux Klan, the Italian Blackshirts, and the Christian Front. There were also purely local anti-Semitic groupings that at various times aligned with national structures, such as Philadelphia's Anti-Communism Society (ACS), the American Christian League, or the National Blue Star Mothers. Philadelphia was a national center for far-Right political activism and provided the publishing base for several extremist newspapers.[29] It had local celebrities like Bessie R. Burchett, whose incendiary remarks on the subject of democracy, President Roosevelt, and the Jewish question often provided good copy for the press. Lancaster had its Bund, York and Uniontown their Klan lodges, and Wilkes-Barre had both Klansmen and Ukrainian fascists. Reading had branches of the Bund and the Italian Fascists, while sections of the city's corporate elite demonstrated unequivocal pro-Nazi sentiments. Well-connected individuals such as Paul M. Winter of Shavertown (near Wilkes-Barre) belonged to a network of extremists, anti-Semites, and alleged fifth columnists, a group of what we can only describe as fascist militants with both national and international connections.

The extensive nature of far-Right activism in this period can be illustrated from the experience of Philadelphia in 1939, probably the high point of fascist and anti-Semitic organization in the present century. In March a rally organized by local patriotic societies was addressed by General Van Horn Moseley, the would-be dictator of the United States.[30] His talk included threats of military resistance to the Roosevelt administration and unsubtle calls for Philadelphia citizens to prepare for a local putsch. Around this time German and Italian paramilitary units celebrated Washington's birthday in the presence of current and former U.S. military personnel, who appeared sympathetic to the flagrant Nazi symbolism and regalia. The German American Bund, then at the height of its notoriety, was particularly active in the city and was friendly with the new U.S. representative from the Fifth District, Fritz Gartner. The city's Bund leader was about to succeed as the new national *Bundesleiter*.

In March, attacks on meetings advocating racial and religious tolerance announced the appearance of the new Christian Front, which targeted Jews and political leftists. There followed a long, hot summer characterized by acts of assault and vandalism by the "bands of Nazi hoodlums who are ranging the city," the violence being especially intense in Irish working-class neighborhoods such as Kensington and West Philadelphia. Meanwhile thousands of protesters regularly picketed those radio stations that refused to carry the broadcasts of the Front's inspiration, Father Coughlin. In July, 7,000 to 8,000 supporters packed two Philadelphia halls to hear his voice transmitted from Detroit; in August, Front militants were organizing weapons training and discussing the acquisition of several thousand rifles. In the fall, war fears and calls for isolationism intensified far-Right agitation, culminating in mass meetings by the Christian Front and a German Day celebration at which the state's Republican senator was heiled for his anti-intervention stance. Irish nationalist gatherings provided another mass forum for the expression of isolationist and pro-Axis views.

The plethora of rightist organizations was expanded by the revival of the Ku Klux Klan, which made Philadelphia a base for a new organizational drive. Extremist groups collaborated in joint military training. Uniformed squads of various nationalities trained at rural camps in Pennsylvania and New Jersey, where German Bundists exercised with their Italian, Ukrainian, and Irish counterparts. The year ended with a leafleting campaign aimed at persuading Philadelphians to "Buy Christian" and to boycott Jewish-owned businesses. These activities caused enormous concern. The city's Protestant churches warned of "signs of minority conflicts here that could seriously impair not only the peace of Philadelphia, but what we consider the principles of democratic government." [31] Leftist and Jewish groups warned more succinctly of a "reign of terror" by "Nazi thugs," while West Philadelphia was a "stronghold of Fascism." [32] In the national antifascist press, *Equality* presented an exposé titled "Swastika over Philadelphia," while *The Hour* reported a "fascist boom in Philadelphia." [33]

NUMBERS

Assessing the scale of ultra-Right activities, the so-called fascist boom, is extraordinarily difficult. Because extremist groups are regarded as beyond the acceptable spectrum of opinion, supporters are sometimes reluctant to express their views openly for fear of stigmatization or retaliation. Movements also have good reason to fear persecution or sabotage by political rivals or agents of law enforcement. Quantifying the adherents of the far-Right groups is complicated, and examining broader support is all but impossible. The distinctive nature of the American electoral system also had its impact. Unlike most Western democracies, political success in the United States has usually required at least notional conformity to one of two broad parties, thus discouraging serious third party activism. Third parties have rarely enjoyed much success at either the presidential or the congressional level during the present century, and with few exceptions ultra-rightists generally chose to support candidates within the existing partisan framework. This makes it hard (though not impossible) to employ such customary tools of political analysis as voting patterns.

We can judge the numerical strength of a given party at a specific time, though with the caveat that this would not include the penumbra of lapsed members, fellow travelers, and general sympathizers. Some of these might well be associated with party-affiliated groups, including fraternal orders and veterans' clubs. Nor does the fact of party membership necessarily say much about the relative strength of ideological commitment. We encounter the question made painfully familiar by the McCarthy era, of how far a person's political outlook can legitimately be deduced by membership in a series of front groups not officially connected with an organized party. Italian Fascist numbers are perhaps the most difficult of all to approach, given the movement's thorough penetration of the Italian fraternal societies. Only a tiny proportion of those enrolled in the Fascist-dominated Order of the Sons of Italy (OFDI) or the war veterans' societies were politically committed to the Fascist cause. Extremist groups also tended to burn out rapidly. Of perhaps 250,000 Pennsylvanians who joined the Ku Klux Klan at its height in the mid-1920s, fewer than 1,000 retained this commitment a decade later. The meteoric rise and collapse of the Khaki Shirt movement occurred entirely within one year.

The relationship between party affiliation and broader sympathy is suggested by the German American Bund, whose peak Philadelphia membership of a few hundred was the tip of an iceberg of metropolitan "influence" that the FBI assessed at some 8,000. We are on somewhat firmer ground with the followers of Father Coughlin, whose Social Justice clubs in Philadelphia comprised about 400 members in late 1939. However, his followers could muster between 5,000 and 10,000 supporters for several major rallies during 1939, among the largest rightist gatherings in that city during the depression era. Even on the coldest January and February days, 1,000 to 2,000 boosters regularly turned out for picket duty. It is reasonable to estimate the Coughlin movement around this time at several thousand in the Philadelphia area alone, though this figure included many individuals who should simultaneously be counted as part of the Bund support.

Combining the Bund, the Coughlin groups, the Italian Fascists, the Klan, and the smaller ad hoc movements, a plausible estimate would place the active membership of extreme rightist organizations in the Philadelphia metropolitan area at perhaps 2,000 between 1938 and 1941, with some 20,000 supporters and associates. Assessing support becomes even harder outside Philadelphia, though the Bund was stronger in Reading than in Philadelphia itself, and the movement's rallies in Berks County dwarfed anything in the metropolis. Pittsburgh contributed several hundred more activists, with a strong contingent of ethnically based movements of Eastern European origin.

Though these numbers may not sound impressive, rightist strength was quite comparable to that of the better-known and more intensely studied Communist Party. Philadelphia was a noted Communist center. Eastern Pennsylvania and Delaware formed part of District Three in the party's structure, with an average membership of 3,000 at any given point between 1936 and 1948.[34] Though party strength was concentrated in the greater Philadelphia region, this total would also include members in several other cities and industrial regions. The average party strength in Philadelphia proper would have been around 2,000 in the late 1930s, roughly equal to that of the far Right.

Rightist and especially Coughlinite demonstrations in Philadelphia drew attendance at least comparable to anything the Left could accomplish, and the audience of 7,000 to 8,000 who listened to a Coughlin remote broadcast in mid-1939 compared with the 4,000 who heard the Communist Earl Browder speak some months later.[35] By another standard, barely 55,000 Pennsylvanians supported Henry Wallace's Progressive Party in 1948, when it attracted solid Communist backing. This compared with 67,000 for Coughlin's populist movement in 1936. Of course, Coughlin's Royal Oak Party at this stage had not acquired the extreme Right tinge that would characterize it in later years, but there was some continuity. In Philadelphia, Wallace's vote of 21,000 was only slightly above that of the earlier Coughlin-linked candidate, while in Allegheny County (Pittsburgh) the Royal Oak far outpolled the later Progressive ticket. While rightist membership in a city like Philadelphia was concentrated in certain sections and ethnic groups, Communist strength was equally focused in particular strongholds, especially in Jewish areas. The far Right was concentrated in only eight or nine of the city's fifty wards, just as Communist strength was focused in a similar number of its particular territories. If the local history of the extreme Left is deemed worthy of historical attention, the same is true for the opposite political fringe.

THE DARK FIGURE

The vigor and militancy of the extreme Right in Pennsylvania is surprising in view of the virtual neglect of these movements in recent historical writing on this state. Despite the fear they caused, movements such as the Bund and the Christian Front are rarely mentioned in modern studies of depression-era Pennsylvania, even in those concerned with topics that one would expect to bear very closely on the theme.[36] Accounts of Pennsylvania politics customarily emphasize moderate traditions, a middle-of-the-road mainstream Republicanism, albeit existing alongside a radical industrial heritage that stretches from the Molly Maguires through the Congress of Industrial Organizations (CIO), the Socialists, and the Mineworkers Union. Figures such as Paul Winter and Bessie Burchett remind us of a very different tradition, a radical nativist, racist, and antidemocratic element that found its most advanced expression in the shirts and the street violence of 1939.

It is not difficult to understand why the extreme Right has been so relatively ignored. After 1945 the tradition appeared so thoroughly extinct as to have little contemporary relevance, while academics of liberal or leftist disposition were more attracted to the rich veins of labor and ethnic history in Pennsylvania, to women's history or the development of urban communities, and the whole tradition of "history from below." However, the rightist movements attracted a substantial activist support, and for much of their existence they were at least as familiar and "respectable" as their left-wing opponents. What gives the rightists their peculiar importance is that they represent the "dark figure," the unexplored portion of many more popular topics of research. In Pennsylvania's ethnic history, one can search at length in the accounts of the major communities without appreciating that, at least for a few years, some of the most important groups maintained a lively dialogue with the far Right. Antiunion or anti-Semitic extremists are occasionally mentioned in the history of leftist parties and labor organizations, but with little sense of their identity or real significance.

HOW DO WE KNOW?

Clandestine movements of whatever political shade pose unusual problems for the historian, and the groups about which most can be known are not necessarily those that were most significant at the time. During the 1930s some extremist groups and leaders received intense attention from media and official agencies, while others were scarcely mentioned. This variation owed something to media perceptions of newsworthiness but also reflected the power and influence of the group in question and the likelihood that an exposé might lead to retaliation or loss of public sympathy. While we are well informed about German-oriented Nazi groups, relatively little is available for domestic or Slavic shirt groups, little on African American anti-Semitism, and next to nothing about the vital Catholic networks.

The historical attention paid to German American fascists is partly explained by the accessibility of the organization's records, seized by the federal government at the outbreak of war.[37] The Bund also dominated contemporary coverage. At least from 1933, Hitler and his followers were rarely far from the international headlines, and any suggestion of parallel developments within the United States was likely to attract public attention, either for political activists or journalists. Jews naturally saw Nazism as a primary threat and expressed far more concern about the dictatorship in Germany than for comparable events in any other European or Asian state.

As early as 1934 the McCormack-Dickstein committee was specifically charged with exploring "Nazi propaganda activities."[38] It produced abundant evidence of pro-Nazi sympathies within the United States and of linkages between the German-oriented groups and other domestic activists, so that groups like the Silver Shirts acquired a transferred stigma from the Nazi link. In 1938–39 the Un-American Activities Committee held well-publicized hearings on the Bund, including an embarrassing interrogation of *Bundesleiter* Fritz Kuhn. The congressional privilege accorded to interviews and exhibits allowed them to be reported without fear of libel proceedings, so the Dies Committee effectively declared open season on the Bund.[39]

Other ideological trends were less likely to be observed, or if they were noticed, they were dismissed as merely a new manifestation of ethnic politics and traditions that were scarcely understood. Italian Americans offer a classic example. By any measure, the influence of pro-Mussolini groups within the Italian community in North America was at least equal to the parallel pro-Hitler movement among their German counterparts. Italian Fascist groups were founded earlier and lasted far longer. They attained hegemony over large sections of the Italian American media and business community and enjoyed real success in staking a claim to be the authentic representatives of Italian culture and political interests. Their success exceeded the wildest dreams of the Bund within the German American community.

Blackshirts, however, were never viewed as a threat remotely as serious or pernicious as the Nazis. The relative mildness of Italian anti-Semitism contributed to this image, while Italian American political groups constituted a powerful and sensitive voice in the urban political machines critical to the New Deal coalition. The McCormack-Dickstein Committee ignored Italian Fascist activities altogether, in part because of Representative Dickstein's close ties to Italian American political organizations in New York City.[40] In consequence, congressional investigations into un-American activities had little to say about Italian aspects of the problem and offered little in the way of privileged material for the newspapers to reproduce and pursue.[41] The neglect of Italian American Fascism was paralleled among other ethnic communities regarded as still less familiar or comprehensible to the mainstream. The internal factional wars of the Ukrainians and Croats were fought out in languages understood by few outsiders.

As a general rule, the degree of public attention devoted to a given movement was proportionate to the amount of public concern and fear that a group incited and the consequent intensity of conflict. Coverage was a function of public perceptions rather than of any intrinsic qualities of the groups themselves, so that organizations regarded as well integrated into a particular community did not attract opposition and thus escaped attention. Materials on Nazi supporters in Philadelphia are so abundant precisely because they had so many enemies there and excited so much antipathy; comparable sources on, for example, Reading Nazis or Italian Fascists anywhere in Pennsylvania are scarce because these ideological strands were not regarded as particularly shocking or deviant within those communities.

The degree of attention paid to groups or incidents reflected both the political priorities of congressional committees and the concern of newspaper owners and editors for their own safety and comfort. By the late 1930s, reporting Nazi or Ku Klux Klan activities was a low-risk enterprise, in that both groups suffered from widespread public hostility or ridicule. Other groups had powerful connections in the political mainstream and virtually escaped public investigation. By far the most prominent example was Father Coughlin, in 1939–40 the most visible anti-Semitic and pro-Axis leader in the nation.[42] However, the media said little about the activities of his numerous followers, lay and clerical, or about predominantly Catholic anti-Semitic groups such as the Christian Front. In consequence, the Front and its related movements remain the least reported and examined component of the rightist network.

This restraint was symptomatic of a general media reluctance to offend the Catholic church. Throughout these years, newspapers were well aware of the reprisals that could befall any paper or radio station viewed as anti-Catholic, and that label adhered to those who accurately depicted actual crimes or misdeeds by Catholic clergy.[43] Media reluctance to report on the Coughlinites was reflected in official investigations. While the Dies Committee heard many references to Coughlin, he never faced the kind of intensive examination received by leaders such as Kuhn, Pelley, and Moseley. A public move against Coughlin might alienate Catholics, who would rally to defend a priest subjected to pillorying or prosecution, thereby turning the father into a potential martyr.

Coughlin escaped numerous snares. In 1940 the rounding up of the New York putschists was greeted on the Left as a perfect opportunity to investigate the subversive activities of the movement, presumably leading to the father himself. However, J. Edgar Hoover made the remarkable declaration that "the Rev. Charles E. Coughlin, radio priest, had no connection with the Christian Front," and no attempts were made in subsequent trials to explore the wider connections of the movement. Even though his newspaper *Social Justice* was suppressed in 1942, Coughlin avoided indictment in the wartime sedition investigations.[44]

The priest's role as the most distinguished un-person in official discussions of the extreme Right was exemplified by the House Committee on Un-American Activities hearings on anti-Semitic extremism in Philadelphia.[45] Following two years of specific warnings and denunciations about potential fifth columnists, in January 1942 the committee finally subpoenaed fourteen of the city's activists, including all the most visible leaders of the ACS and its allies and of the Christian Front: figures of such local notoriety as Bessie Burchett, Joseph Gallagher, Philip M. Allen, Catherine V. Brown, and the Blisard family.[46] The hearings provided a rhetorical tour de force, in that extensive interrogations of the Coughlinite organization in Philadelphia scarcely mentioned either Coughlin or the Christian Front. In contrast the committee spent much time vainly pursuing connections with minor German American figures and with nonexistent Japanese contacts. The affair illustrates the partial and political nature of the congressional hearings and the media reports derived from them.[47]

REPORTING EXTREMISM

While some groups were more or less likely to be covered than others, it was generally true that many major newspapers had little incentive to report on the doings of the radical Right because of the degree to which the Brown threat had become a partisan issue, a defense of the New Deal, or a reason for foreign interventionism. By the late 1930s the activities of anti-Semitic or shirt groups were most likely to be taken seriously in leftist or liberal publications and dismissed as irrelevant posturing by conservatives. In the case of Pennsylvania this political context severely limited the opportunities for investigation or exposé, as few major media outlets were

predisposed to New Deal sympathies. In Pittsburgh two of the three major papers belonged to strongly conservative chains, the
Hearst *Sun Telegraph* and Paul Block's *Post-Gazette*, which com-
bined to destroy most of their smaller rivals. While the Scripps-
Howard *Pittsburgh Press* was relatively liberal, its proprietor Roy
Howard had long been hostile to Roosevelt.[48] In Philadelphia similarly, the Annenbergs' *Philadelphia Inquirer* was the "Bible of Republicanism," while the *Public Ledger* was denounced for strikebreaking and antilabor practices. Outside the two main cities the
local papers were often so diehard conservative as to verge on parody.[49] In covering rightist extremism these papers would report
major riots or other incidents, but they rarely initiated proactive investigations or drew attention to local movements other than those
currently making national headlines.

There was one crucial exception that provides extensive evidence about the doings of the far Right and thereby illustrates
the nature of media taboos. The *Philadelphia Record* was owned by
J. David Stern, a maverick press lord who resigned from the conservative publishers' cartel, the American Newspaper Publishers
Association, and who consistently supported the New Deal in the
region. Together with his financial backer Albert Greenfield, Stern
was one of the leading figures in the Democratic Party at both the
state and the city level.[50] Throughout the 1930s the *Record* was
the only paper in the city and sometimes in the state that published stories seen as too difficult by other proprietors. In 1936,
for example, Stern was the only publisher to report a widespread
department store strike that led to violence and a "miniature revolution" in Philadelphia.[51]

Stern's determined liberalism gave the *Record* a tradition of investigative reporting rarely paralleled outside New York City. In
1934 and 1935 his papers were the only media outlets to give serious and sympathetic attention to Smedley Butler's claims about
the alleged coup d'état plotted by domestic corporate interests.[52]
The *Record* investigated local anti-Semitic activities and from 1937
onward regularly published exposés on the local Bund and the
ACS.[53] However, even Stern found the Catholic church too difficult an enemy to challenge.[54] At the height of anti-Semitic agitation and violence by Irish Catholic Coughlin supporters in 1939,
the *Record* reported and denounced the incidents as fully as pos-

sible, though without once noting the religious or ethnic identity of the culprits, who are generally characterized as "Nazis" or "Bund supporters."

Treatment of Catholic anti-Semitism was complicated by the structure of the Philadelphia press, in which both the major chains were dominated by Jewish magnates, respectively Moe Annenberg of the *Inquirer* and Stern of the *Record*. While both were sensitive to the growth of anti-Semitic activism, neither publisher could risk charges that their papers' editorial views reflected the interests of a Jewish media conspiracy or cartel. In this context any confrontation with the Catholic church would be uniquely perilous.

Apart from the religious issue, the *Record* had to respect ethnic sensibilities. While crusading so tirelessly against Nazi activity, the paper had next to nothing to say about Italian Fascism and successfully covered Irish anti-Semitic movements without ever once noting their members were either Irish or Catholic, an elision achieved by generous use of the term "Nazi." These absences were also motivated by the desire to avoid placing unnecessary strain on the new city and statewide Democratic coalitions in which Stern and Greenfield played so powerful a role, and which depended on harmony between Irish, Italian, and Jewish leaders. One did not have to probe too far into the support of both Irish and Italian rightist extremism to find involvement by prominent clergy, politicians, and elected officials, a fact that, if exposed, could lead to bitter controversy and possibly to the collapse of the Democratic Party in Pennsylvania.

For all its omissions, the existence of the *Record* is a major boon for research in the history of the Pennsylvania Right, as the availability of local journalists and archives permitted contemporary writers to include substantial case studies of the city in their accounts of particular movements. There are few cases where a national story about the far Right in Philadelphia cannot be traced back to the *Record*. In turn the publicity accorded in journalistic sources led to further investigation by official and congressional agencies, which has left a rich vein of material on the leading militants in that city. However, the relative abundance of Philadelphia references should not therefore lead us to conclude that a lack of similar material for other cities, notably Pittsburgh and Reading, reflected a smaller degree of extremist organization there.

While there are obvious difficulties in studying the extreme Right in Pennsylvania, the state does offer an unusually rich volume of evidence for a surprisingly broad range of movements. Apart from the internal archives of groups such as the Klan and the Bund, the activism of figures like Stern permits us to reconstruct with some confidence the history and development of the ultra-Right.

WERE THEY FASCISTS?

The organizational structure of the far Right exhibited far less stability or continuity than the Communist Party, and there was, if anything, an even stronger tradition of evanescent front groups and structures that existed solely on letterhead. This makes it difficult to define the scope of the study. If they did not all belong to a common party, how far is it legitimate to bracket together members of distinct organizations, which at least on paper accepted sharply divergent ideologies? Is it possible to approach the rightist groups under a blanket term such as "fascist," in the same way that the pro-Soviet Left can be categorized as Communist?

Many of the groups discussed in this study were described by contemporaries as fascist or Nazi, but the terminology is sometimes inaccurate and polemical. In such an ideologically charged atmosphere there was no shortage of leftist or liberal literature dismissing a particular rival group with loaded words that were already acquiring the stigma that has since become quite overwhelming. In the Roosevelt years, "fascist" was a label regularly applied to antilabor corporations, to isolationists, and to militant opponents of the New Deal, above all the Liberty League.[55] Republicans were fascist, steel bosses and mineowners were fascist, the American Legion was fascist, and conservative "Tory" Democrats were fascist. The rhetorical goal of the smear is suggested by the 1945 speech of liberal congressman Adolph Sabath in which he demanded the "naming of outstanding American fascists, such as the Duponts, the Pews, the Girdlers, the Weirs, Van Horn Moseley, H. W. Prentis junior, Merwin K. Hart and others."[56] Corporate magnates and ultraconservative politicians were listed alongside anti-Semites and Axis supporters in a tactic similar to the rightwing portrayal of all liberals and socialists as tools of Stalin.

In contemporary left-wing literature the Pennsylvania movement most frequently discussed as a "forerunner of American fascism" was the Johnstown Citizens' Committee of 1937. Described by *New Republic* as "America's most openly fascist organization," this militant antiunion group had elements of vigilantism but lacked virtually all the attributes of Continental fascism.[57] The following year the *Philadelphia Record* attacked the leader of the Republican machine in Delaware County as "McClure—Our Own Hitler."[58] A left-wing meeting in Chester was told that "Fascism is gaining a foothold in America through such men as Republican leaders John J. McClure and Joseph N. Pew."[59]

The tactic of guilt by association is illustrated by the comment of Benjamin Stolberg in 1938:

> Today there are innumerable shirt organizations, nightgown rackets, the Black Legion, the Friends of New Germany, the Americaneers, the Committees of 100, of 200, of one million, the Women's National Association for the Preservation of the White Race. . . . There are literally hundreds of such outfits. And this spirit reaches into the darker corners of the DAR, the ROTC, the American Legion, the Veterans of Foreign Wars, the Chamber of Commerce, the Lions, the Elks, the Eagles, the Moose, and the rest of the zoo of the small-time Babbitry. It's all very dreadful and the Lord knows where it's leading to.[60]

There is nothing here that is demonstrably false, as antidemocratic sentiments are located in the "darker corners" of the various groups, but the common perception on the Communist Left in particular was that most of these groups were as really or potentially fascist as the Black Legion and the shirts.

Conversely, ultra-rightists and anti-Semites such as Gerald L. K. Smith and Louis McFadden depicted the Roosevelt White House as the main purveyor of fascism in the United States, with the suggestion that this was an undesirable fate.[61] In 1941 the pro-Nazi German newspaper *Philadelphia Herold* argued against war on the disingenuous grounds that the required centralization of authority would make Roosevelt a dictator and thereby bring fascism to the United States.[62] Repeatedly, ultra-rightists attacked official attempts to suppress their propaganda as the work of a "Jewish Gestapo." When expedient, even fascists denounced fascism.

Not all those named as fascists deserve the designation; but the usage was not inaccurate in all cases, and historians have been too reluctant to see the American far-Right groups as part of a common international phenomenon, with parallels in Europe, Latin America, and the Middle East.[63] Herzstein is unusual in his straightforward discussion of "the rise of American fascisms."[64] Donald S. Strong chose the more complex term, "national radical revolutionary" anti-Semitic movements.[65] David H. Bennett's superb account of American nativism and rightist extremism describes the groups of the 1930s as "quasi-fascists," a distinction explained by the mystical-apocalyptic tendencies of the American groups and their strong inheritance from the older Protestant nativism.[66] Geoffrey S. Smith uses the still more restrained term "counter-subversives" to characterize the likes of Pelley and Coughlin, ironically given the accusations that these individuals and their followers were authentically subversive rather than the reverse.[67] While these approaches are perhaps overcautious, they are valuable in forcing us to seek an accurate definition of the controversial term "fascist."

Definition is far from easy, and only in retrospect does the Nazi obsession with anti-Semitism appear so ideologically central. Not until 1938 did Italian Fascism adopt racial laws vaguely comparable to those of Germany, and these were never applied with anything approaching the same vigor. Most historians would agree on certain core elements, including right-wing authoritarianism and demagoguery, hostility to organized labor, totalitarian state organization and corporate economic structure, and an exaltation of military and paramilitary methods. White Shirt leader George W. Christians admired "the Fascist idea of personal leadership, unity, force, drama and nationalism." The oath taken by Italian American Fascists included a pledge to "serve with loyalty and discipline the Fascist idea of society based upon Religion, Nation and Family, and to promote respect for law, order and hierarchy, and of the tradition of the race." Some historians emphasize the crucial role of "anti-ism," defining the fascist tradition in terms of what it opposed. Juan J. Linz offers a complex definition:

We define fascism as a hyper-nationalist, often pan-nationalist, anti-parliamentary, anti-liberal, anti-Communist, populist and therefore anti-proletarian, partly anti-capitalist and anti-bourgeois, anti-clerical or at least non-clerical movement, with the aim of national social integration through a single party and corporative representation not always equally emphasized; with a distinctive style and rhetoric, it relied on activist cadres ready for violent action combined with electoral participation to gain power with totalitarian goals by a combination of legal and violent tactics.[68]

This approach prevents us from applying the fascist label on the strength of one or two characteristics. It was not sufficient to preach or practice anti-Semitism, to urge action of the most violent kind against industrial unionism, or to sympathize vociferously with the cause of the Axis powers in conflicts such as those in Spain or Ethiopia. Nor was it enough to adopt some of the trappings of European fascism at a time when shirt movements and rhetoric were "in the air." In Pennsylvania, radical Catholic priest Father James Cox sought to institutionalize his mass unemployed movement in the form of a Blue Shirt Jobless Party, which in the context of the early 1930s obviously had Continental implications. He denounced union "racketeers," urged that Roosevelt establish a dictatorship, and warned that the nation must face a choice between "my party and Communism." He even tried to mobilize veterans' organizations to support his social crusade.[69] On the other hand, the priest denounced Mussolini as early as 1932, at a time when many liberals viewed the dictator as essentially progressive. Cox retained his left-wing and pro-labor affiliations throughout, and at the end of the decade emerged as an aggressive critic of Catholic anti-Semitism.

The problem of definition is complicated by the issue of public self-identification. In the case of the Left, recognition as "Communist" or "socialist" was quite respectable in many social circles. Many people joined parties or societies that adopted these names and can easily be given these political labels, although not every particular member fully shared every aspect of the given ideology. Conversely, "fascism" never achieved anything like the same degree of public acceptability, although there were groups and theorists who were unabashed about their beliefs. Lawrence Dennis wrote *The Coming American Fascism*, and there were minuscule splinter groups such as the American Fascists; but the word usually suggested a specifically pro-Italian bent.[70] Even its correct pronunciation required the distinctive Italian *sc* sound, an exotic note that caused political difficulties for ultra-rightists in other English-speaking nations (British adherents such as Sir Oswald Mosley favored the pseudo-native-sounding "fassist").[71]

The organizations most enthusiastic about European Nazism or fascism rarely included these provocative terms in their titles. The main pro-German organization was successively known as the Friends of the New Germany and the German American Bund rather than anything more avowedly National Socialist. After 1929 the Italian Fascist League of North America (FLNA) was replaced by more discreet substitutes, such as the deliberately obscure Lictor Federation. From the late 1930s the terms "Christian" and "Nationalist" were the favored code words for the far-Right sentiments: "Christian" referred less to specific theological concepts than to a denial of Judaism, while "Nationalist" implied opposition to the cosmopolitan doctrines of Jews and Communists. Both also echoed the rightist movements of the Spanish Civil War.

Caution about the fascist label was desirable because the far Right had such a strong vested interest in stirring American patriotic or xenophobic sentiment against the "alien creed" of Communism, a rhetoric that would be contaminated by reference to the foreign principles of Mussolini or Hitler. This consideration ruled out European affectations such as national "socialism" or "syndicalism," which raised sensitive economic concerns. It was precisely the liberal New Deal state condemned by the far Right that was instituting so many of the corporatist and dirigiste measures that in a European context usually had fascist overtones. Even if the phrase were acceptable, totalitarian ideas of "national socialism" were anathema to the public rhetoric of the American Right, which presented itself as the voice of a modified form of free enterprise capitalism.

The antitotalitarian stance was all the more essential when congressional investigations and federal grand juries threatened to impose severe sanctions against the friends of the Axis powers. A denial of fascism was phrased as part of a general rejection of any foreign theories, in the commonly used sentiment that "I am against every '-ism', except Americanism," the wording used by Coughlinite militant Catherine V. Brown. When a Pittsburgh Christian Front organizer asserted, "We're against Communism," her liberal critic responded, "Fine! So am I. But are you against fascism too?," only to receive the typical answer, "Oh, yes. . . . We are against all the -isms. We are for America." [72] Ku Klux Klan propaganda leaflets boasted that the movement would "banish from our country every foreign -ism, Nazi-ism, Communism, Fascism." Extreme right-wing figures rarely admitted adherence to fascism as such in a public setting and hedged on specific beliefs that might confirm this diagnosis. Even when Father Coughlin had by 1939 accepted most of the elements of a fascist theory and strategy (his Franco Way), he still affected to reject the street activists who fanatically supported him.

The ideological dilemma can be illustrated by examining some specific groups and individuals whom contemporary opinion universally assigned to the far Right. For example, it has been objected that the fascist label can only with difficulty be applied to the Silver Shirt movement. Pelley's social and economic theories were at variance with either German or Italian models, and mystical/religious ideas predominated more clearly than in most European counterparts. [73] On the other hand, these ideological distinctions seem tenuous when set alongside the anti-Semitic demagoguery of Silver Shirt orators, the group's paramilitary organization, and their exaltation of the "Beloved Chief." This orientation is confirmed by the Silver Shirts' intimate collaboration with the Bund and their enduring role as a central component of local coalitions of extreme Right groups. Moreover, leaders explicitly identified with Hitler's theories and policies. This was not merely an example of a fringe religious or social movement chancing to adopt the shirt imagery then in vogue. The *Pittsburgh Press* was not far from the mark when it characterized the movement in 1938 as "a Hitler movement in miniature. Its principles are those of Nazi Germany." [74]

Critical here is the diversity of international fascism, in which there was no single norm: if Mussolini's Italy was the only true orthodoxy, then Hitler's Germany was not fascist, and vice versa. Pursued to its logical conclusion, this approach can reach the bizarre conclusion that fascism never existed except as the imaginary construct of a paranoid Left. In reality, fascism was polychromatic rather than monotone, and different movements developed an impressive range of attitudes and activities. The religious quirks of the Silver Shirts were eccentric by the standards of Italian or British Fascists or Spanish Falangists, but they were no odder than the war-god neopaganism of Hungarian, Scandinavian, and some German extremists. If the Coughlin movement was dominated by clergy, so were the Croat Ustashi. If some American rightists were hazy about the orthodoxies of the fascist economic order, so were their Blue Shirt counterparts in Ireland, who like the early Coughlin, drew far more from the social thought of the popes than the dictators. If the American far Right was an unstable mixture of diverse linguistic and ethnic groups, so were the extremist parties of Canada and Belgium. Yet in each case at least some historians are prepared to view as part of a fascist spectrum groups such as the Rexists, the Ustashi, and the Blue Shirts. Why, then, the qualms about the followers of Pelley or Coughlin? If the Silver Shirts and like American groups were not fascist, then neither were many of the European movements that are customarily so described by the historians of their respective nations.[75]

BESSIE BURCHETT AS FASCIST

Perhaps the best-known extreme rightist in Philadelphia was Bessie R. Burchett, whose outrageous remarks and activities were much reported in the local press and in national leftist publications in the late 1930s. Her political positions lacked the corporatist economic theories or the *Führerprinzip* of continental fascism and were not explicitly totalitarian. On the other hand, they combined most of the remaining components of quite an advanced fascist theory, including thoroughgoing elitism and antimodernism, opposition to democracy and socialism, antiproletarianism, a belief in paramilitary activism, and advocacy of anti-Semitic violence, all ideas that Burchett carried to extremes. Moreover, she encouraged her followers to pursue these goals through physical confrontations in the streets and meeting halls.

Burchett would have described herself as a staunch Republican and an anti-Communist whose 1935–36 campaign to expose Communist influence in the public schools received widespread support on the conservative Right. Many respectable figures echoed her position that "we must continue to look to private enterprise for the efficient conduct of our business," and some shared her fears that anti-Communist Americans would have to arm and organize to meet the potential threat of violence from the Left. If "Two-Gun Bessie" had still been active in the different political atmosphere of the McCarthy era, she would have been close to the ideological mainstream of the Republican Party of that day. Nor was her position that "the Anglo-Saxon race is supreme in most respects" far removed from mainstream conservative opinion, any more than the notion that American heroes such as George Washington represented "Nordic" virtues and physique.[76]

Where she departed from mainline conservatism was in her elitist and implacably antidemocratic views, and she was quoted denouncing democracy as "one of the most inefficient, terrible means of government we know. . . . It doesn't work."[77] In her view the U.S. Constitution was designed to create a constitutional representative republic rather than a democracy, and so it had remained until the dark year of 1932.[78] She believed that education should be confined to "a select few white Protestant Americans of high IQ."[79]

Burchett also rejected conventional views about race and religion, including the most basic ideas about religious tolerance. She believed that the government had neither the duty nor the right to tolerate religions that were "wicked," a view she illustrated by the case of Mormonism. If the government prohibited polygamy, then it could regulate other antisocial or criminal practices, including sexual improprieties or nudism. In what was probably an oblique reference to the anti-Jewish blood libel, she asserted that the government would certainly have the right to suppress a religion that sacrificed its children to Moloch.[80] As an intellectual argument this was by no means absurd, and the U.S. Supreme Court today still wrestles with the balance between religious liberty and the enforcement of criminal law. These opinions traveled beyond the limits of legal debate in her conviction that the Jewish race and religion represented an utter evil, to be eliminated. While extermination was not consistently advocated, Burchett threatened or fantasized about extreme anti-Jewish violence, including Hitler bombing New York Jews, or America's problems being solved by hanging millions of Jews on lampposts. Jews and Communists were not only to be exposed; they were to be directly confronted

and combated, by activist cadres denounced by their opponents as "storm-troopers."

Though ostensibly rejecting Nazism and Fascism as foreign ideologies, Burchett found their confident nationalism incomparably superior to the meaningless "democratic" ideology espoused by Roosevelt "or of those for whom he is the golden mouthpiece." [81] She cooperated with the German American Bund, spoke at the group's meetings, and identified with Nazi symbolism and regalia enough to give the Hitler salute at rallies. In this case, surely, we have moved far beyond "Americanism" or "quasi-fascism."

We are unusually well informed about Bessie Burchett because she was a controversial figure whose views were often reported by the media and who was the subject of a lengthy interrogation by the House Un-American Activities Committee, while she expounded her opinions at length in her 1941 book *Education for Destruction*. But enough evidence exists about her colleagues and allies to indicate that her views were unusual neither in their orientation nor in their vigor but in the frank and systematic nature of their presentation. Burchett and her political circle can properly be described as fascist in all essentials, an integral component of a network that included the Bund, the Silver Shirts and the Italian Fascists, and the militant Coughlinite groups collectively known as the Christian Front. Similar sentiments can be located in sections of other movements, especially the Ku Klux Klan, though this group was sharply divided over the pro-Axis enthusiasm of some of its members. All these groups fall within the scope of the present study, which is concerned with extreme right-wing, authoritarian, antidemocratic, paramilitary, racist movements: a circumlocution that can justifiably be replaced with the concise term "fascist."

THE PRESENT BOOK

These caveats and qualifications should be borne in mind when considering the extremist groups that form the subject of the present study. Specifically, fascist and Nazi groups must be situated in the larger context of the extreme Right and of militant anti-Communist and antilabor movements that were not fascist by any reasonable definition. Rightist extremism would probably have flourished in Pennsylvania regardless of the partisan alignment of the government at the national or the state level, given the critical economic circumstances of the time and the impression created by European fascist movements. However, rightist militancy was enhanced by the political circumstances of the mid-1930s and the industrial crises of 1937–38. Conservative fears concentrated on the labor militancy of the CIO, commonly viewed on the Right as the industrial arm of Communism, foreign and domestic.

Fear of Communism was by no means a new force in the 1930s, but conflicts were intensified by the likelihood that the Left might come to power with the assistance of the federal government. A radical left-wing regime might thus result from a revolution directed and manipulated from above, in alliance with mass popular movements. Roosevelt and his Democratic allies in Pennsylvania might be naively permitting a Red triumph or covertly aiding it, but in either case the prospects for civil peace seemed poor. Chapter 2 describes the political environment that encouraged conservatives to view government as a clandestine tool of Communism and to seek extralegal solutions to industrial turmoil. In reaction to this threat, corporate interests supported private vigilante or paramilitary groups, which in some cases adhered to the ideologies of the extreme Right.

Chapter 3 describes the Ku Klux Klan, the movement that historically benefited from such industrial crises and Red scares, and that in the 1920s gained a major bastion in Pennsylvania on the strength of fanatical anti-Catholic sentiment. There were many analogies between the Klan and contemporary European fascist movements. Like the Fascisti or the Brown Shirts, the Klan flourished in reaction to the failed radicalism of 1919–20, offering veterans the chance to relive wartime comradeship and solidarity. The Klan too advocated a return to tradition, military virtues, and paramilitary structure and assumed all the familiar ritualistic trappings of authoritarian movements. It advocated the rights of native labor in partnership with capital, against an insidious foreign foe. In some cases, notably Paul Winter himself, we can trace a direct continuity from the superpatriotic "American Nationalism" of the 1920s to an advanced pro-Nazi sentiment a decade later.

While Klan lodges survived and enjoyed some revival in the late 1930s, they were dwarfed by newer ideological strands that were overtly influenced by contemporary European events. Chapter 4 describes the first such ethnically based campaign to win mass support, the Italian Fascist cause that also inspired local imitators such as the Khaki Shirts. Like the Klan, the American Fascisti of the 1920s can be viewed as a precursor of the later movements. They established a new political vocabulary, an innovative range of symbols and techniques on which later groups could draw. Though initially hated by nativists as a foreign and Catholic intrusion, the shirt tradition became far more popular after 1933 because of its symbolic identification with the cause of anti-Semitism, discussed in Chapter 5. Increasingly, shirts supplanted "hoods."

European fascism had a dual impact on American extremism, both in exciting a desire to emulate the achievements of Hitler or Mussolini and in causing racial persecutions that threatened to create a flood of Jewish emigrants to the New World. This would have reopened the mass immigration that had given the Klan such huge support and that had been terminated by the 1924 Immigration Act. Anti-Communist fears of the mid-1930s coincided with and became linked to an upsurge of anti-Semitism, an equation that encouraged extremists to identify with the German form of fascism rather than with any competitor. Beneficiaries included the emerging Silver Shirt movement but also a number of small ad hoc bodies; the best-known group in Pennsylvania was the Philadelphia ACS, founded by Bessie Burchett.

In the late 1930s the political development of the extreme Right focused on the "German Question" as decisively as an earlier generation of leftists had responded to the ideological challenge of the new Soviet Union and its Communist allies. The central importance of Germany in international affairs consolidated the prestige of Nazi political and rhetorical models and made the German American Bund the stereotypical face of the American extreme Right. Chapter 6 describes the successes of the Bund and related movements in Pennsylvania and their penetration of existing German cultural and fraternal structures. In turn, opposition to Hitler's local supporters and apologists gave an organizational fillip to the Pennsylvania Left. Philadelphia in particular illustrates the role of the federal government in coordinating anti-Nazi activities at the local level and granting carte blanche to its officials to undertake counterpropaganda among the German American community.

With the growing likelihood of war and the increasingly controversial nature of Bund activities, the organization affected to dissolve itself in 1939 and continued its operations through a catena of front groups. This did not indicate a diminution of militancy, especially given the critical issue of isolationist sentiment, which promised to unite the rightist constituency against such familiar foes as Roosevelt, the Jews, the Communists, and the British. During 1939, rightist organization concentrated on the formation of a Christian Front coalition. Originally a Catholic term, this was now expanded to include all willing "Christians" (Gentiles) in the struggle against Jews and, by extension, Communists. The coalition was even prepared to collaborate with African Americans, who were courted by Nazi and anti-Semitic propagandists. Chapter 7 describes this period, perhaps the most active and violent phase of direct action in the history of the far Right. The traditional strength of German and Irish political groupings in Pennsylvania gave the movement a particular resonance in the state.

Chapter 8 examines the Pennsylvania far Right in the two years prior to the outbreak of war, and their attempt to form a broad isolationist coalition to avert the ultimate disaster of war against the Axis powers. Rightists focused their activism on new forms of organization, including the ostensibly neutralist Mothers' movement, and they tried to penetrate the America First organization. Their achievements were distinctly mixed. While rightists cooperated sufficiently to allow us to speak of a network of shared propaganda and activism, this was never close enough to constitute the united Brown Front attacked by leftist critics, or the Nationalist crusade vaunted by anti-Semitic leaders themselves. Such a picture arose from the hostile propaganda of the Roosevelt administration as much as from the exalted dreams of the rightist leadership. The limits of rightist unity were emphasized by the failure of the great sedition trial in which federal authorities sought to expose supposed fascist plotting in the United States.

After 1945, fears of subversion shifted to the Left, with Moscow rather than Berlin viewed as the ultimate enemy, and evidence of far-Right or fascist activism declines precipitously. This reflects a genuine decline in rightist organization, due in large part to the massive rightward shift in the political mainstream during the anti-Communist purges of these years. However, Chapter 9 suggests that a continuing strand of fascist and anti-Semitic politics can be traced through the 1950s and 1960s, in some cases involving the familiar groups and individuals from the earlier period. Though this tradition was confined to the further reaches of political discourse, we can find some examples of continuity from the debates of the 1930s to the contemporary concerns of the nonracist religious Right.

Chapter 10 summarizes the lessons of this state-based study for the history of the extreme Right at the national level and suggests some areas in which the Pennsylvania experience may have been untypical. Even so, this geographically limited history indicates how much remains to be discovered about this period—about the relationship between extremist sects and the established fraternal or patriotic societies, about the diverse ethnic appeal of the far Right, and about the degree to which mainstream politicians courted or tolerated extremist supporters. These questions can only be approached by a series of local studies in other states and regions, and not until these are available can a national synthesis be undertaken to describe the American encounter with fascism and fascisms.

2 | Red Years
Political and Industrial Conflict

xtremism is a relative concept. Extreme political ideas can only be defined as such with reference to other opinions that are regarded as moderate or mainstream, and the relationship between the respective bodies of thought may and must change over time. Ideas that appear mainstream or moderate for one political generation may appear unacceptably daring or extreme in another, and vice versa. The time taken for such a transformation will vary depending on circumstances, but in eras of political or social revolution, extreme ideas might enter the mainstream in a period of a few years or even months. In order to understand the appeal of the extremist groups of the depression era, it is necessary to locate their ideas and rhetoric on the broader political spectrum, and in so doing we find that many of these beliefs were not that far removed from those of quite respectable sections of the political community.

By the late 1930s one did not have to travel far across the spectrum to find political rhetoric of quite startling violence, ideas of all-out warfare between "Americanism and Communism," of American national survival hinging on "exterminating" the "crackpots and political gangsters" who had inflicted the New Deal on an unfortunate nation. The phrase about extermination stemmed not from a fringe group or shirt leader, but from G. Mason Owlett, a prominent representative of Pennsylvania's business interests. He was a leader of a dominant faction within the state's Republican Party who organized a plausible campaign for the U.S. senatorial nomination in 1938. This not untypical example of inflammatory anti-Roosevelt activism suggests how far to the Right the enemies of the New Deal had drifted at both national and state levels.[1]

For most American states the mid-1930s were a time of social turmoil and political reconfiguration. Pennsylvania experienced both a radical transformation of the relationship between labor and employers and the simultaneous overthrow of a long-standing political regime in state and city government. Taken in conjunction with the federal New Deal, these events could be viewed as part of a true revolution, the reaction to which might necessitate extraordinary and perhaps even extralegal measures. The sweeping scale of the Democratic victories caused a reshaping of Republican coalitions and a swing to the reactionary Tory tradition, anti–New Deal, antilabor, anti-Communist. Themes of confrontation and conspiracy became fundamental to the rhetoric of the respectable conservative Right, arousing public fears and expectations.

For the true extremists of the paramilitary Right, the Klan and the Bund, the Silver Shirts and Christian Front, this shift was useful in popularizing ideas, issues, and terminology on which they could subsequently build and employ as a basis for recruitment. More direct links with the far Right are more controversial. Leftist observers often alleged sinister sponsorship of ultra-Right groups by great corporations and conservative politicians, and these links were an essential component of the Marxist analysis of the origins and functions of fascism. A leftist commonplace saw fascism as "the steel hoop that will try to bind together the rotting barrel of capitalism." While rejecting the view that domestic extremism was in any sense a simple creature of big business, some conservative groups did give political and financial backing to groups that can properly be described as fascist. Industrial struggles gave rightist groups such as the Klan and the Bund the opportunity to establish footholds in local communities, which they were able to exploit for years afterward.

Gains by the political Left and by organized labor were all the more telling in a state where Republicans had recently held a one-party monopoly. Pennsylvania had long lacked a true Democratic opposition in one of the few industrial regions where Republican dominance at the state level was not countered by Democratic machines in the cities.[2] The Democrats elected no U.S. senators between 1875 and 1934 and no state governors between 1890 and 1934, and the party lost ninety-five of ninety-six statewide elections between 1893 and 1931.[3] In consequence, political conflicts were fought by factions within the Republican Party.[4] Though alliances shifted frequently, this never damaged the overwhelming power of the Republican interest.[5] In 1926 the Republican candidate for U.S. senator defeated his Democratic rival by a margin of three to one, and that after long infighting within his own party (see table 2.1).

In the 1920s the party was divided between several main groups, each with a foundation in either a corporate interest or a local party machine. Factions included the Mellon family, with their vast industrial and financial resources and power in the Pittsburgh machine (the "Mellon Patch"), and the Vare machine, which dominated Philadelphia through electoral manipulation and a stranglehold on the city's patronage resources. The Vares benefited from their alliance with the Pennsylvania Railroad. Other players included Joseph R. Grundy, founder and president of the Pennsylvania Manufacturers' Association (PMA), the "king of lobbyists" and a master fund-raiser for favored candidates.[6] There was also Gifford Pinchot, a remarkably radical social reformer who had run for the U.S. senate in 1914 on the progressive Washington Party ticket and who, with his brother Amos, was a leading exponent of a humane progressivism.[7] Gifford Pinchot's two terms as governor (1923–27 and 1931–35) foreshadowed many aspects of the New Deal at the national level. He was sympathetic to labor, defended civil rights, and was the first Pennsylvania governor to raise a woman to a position of real power in his cabinet.

Republican supremacy was crippled by the depression, which hit Pennsylvania as hard as any industrial state.[8] Between 1929 and 1935 the number of factories operating in Pennsylvania fell by 22

TABLE 2.1. *Pennsylvania Senators and Governors, 1922–1954*

Year of Election	Senator 1	Senator 2	Governor
1922	George Wharton Pepper (R)	David A. Reed (R)	Gifford Pinchot (R)
1926	William Vare (R); (but Vare denied election, so Joseph R. Grundy (R.) took the seat in 1929)		John Fisher (R)
1928		David A. Reed (R)	
1930	James J. Davis (R)		Gifford Pinchot (R)
1932	James J. Davis (R)		
1934		Joseph Guffey (D)	George Earle (D)
1938	James J. Davis (R)		Arthur James (R)
1940		Joseph Guffey (D)	
1942			Edward Martin (R)
1944	Francis J. Myers (D)		
1946		Edward Martin (R)	James H. Duff (R)
1950	James H. Duff (R)		John Fine (R)
1952		Edward Martin (R)	
1954			George Leader (D)

Source: *Pennsylvania Manual.*

percent, the industrial workforce shrank by 16 percent, manufacturing wages fell by 39 percent, and the value of industrial products went down by over 40 percent. Coal production fell from 142 million tons in 1929 to 91 million in 1935. By March 1933 there were almost 1.5 million unemployed workers, some 40 percent of the labor force, and economic collapse crippled the relief system. Civil disorder broke out in New Kensington and Uniontown, with extensive fears of generalized disorder throughout the southwestern part of the state by 1933.[9] In 1932 a May Day demonstration in Philadelphia was met by brutal police intervention. In August a mass demonstration by the unemployed led to a confrontation with Philadelphia police in the "Battle of Reyburn Plaza."[10] Communist influence among the unemployed was said to be growing steadily.

The economic facts were grave enough, but the ruling party

suffered from its callous response and the insistence on fiscal responsibility in the face of social calamity. In Philadelphia, Mayor J. Hampton Moore consistently rejected allegations that a depression even existed and refused federal assistance at a time when *The Nation* was headlining "Mass Misery in Philadelphia" and the city government was laying off thousands of workers.[11] The state's Republican senator was David A. Reed, whom Gifford Pinchot denounced as an "errand boy of the Mellons" and the steel industry. Reed, like Grundy, belonged to the diehard conservative wing of the party, which regarded even Herbert Hoover as perilously liberal. Franklin Roosevelt was anathema, and by 1936 Reed was sufficiently desperate to halt FDR that he pressed the Republicans to form an electoral coalition with disaffected Democrats and even to run a Democrat on the Republican ticket.[12]

In Harrisburg, however, the Republican state government was far more flexible, and the second Pinchot administration was comparatively radical. As early as 1930 Pinchot had campaigned against exploitative utilities and the selfish interests of city machines and giant corporations. He favored an active federal role to assuage the relief crisis and won the praise of John L. Lewis as perhaps the most "advanced" governor in the United States.[13] By 1934 he had declared support for Roosevelt and his "fight for the forgotten man" and was not far from open defection. His wife, Cornelia, a political figure in her own right, was an outspoken New Deal advocate. The 1934 elections deeply divided the Republican Party in Pennsylvania. Pinchot's bid for the Republican senatorial nomination resulted in a bruising primary contest, in which Pinchot supporters weakened the Mellon interests in Pittsburgh. Though he lost that struggle, it seemed likely that Pinchot would run on the Democratic ticket. His defeat ensured that for a decade the Republican Party would be largely free of those progressive and liberal elements that had played so significant a role since the time of the first Roosevelt. The death of William Vare later that year removed another pillar of the Pennsylvania party. Through internal conflict and attrition the party fell into the hands of Joseph Grundy and his conservative allies, but at the cost of maintaining Republican power over state politics.

These elections marked a tectonic shift in party allegiance.[14] Joseph Guffey became the first Democratic U.S. senator in

twentieth-century Pennsylvania, while George Earle was the first
Democrat to be elected governor since 1890, and the party gained control of the state house. Earle himself was a wealthy Main Line patrician and a recent defector from the Republicans, but he was a vigorous liberal whom Pennsylvania loyalists saw as a likely heir to FDR. His rhetoric was fiercely populist, depicting Republican elected officials taking their orders from a corporate clique "like so many trained bird dogs." The obstinacy of these "puppets" threatened to steal the food from 600,000 desperately poor Pennsylvanians and to provoke a revolution on the Russian model.[15] In a 1936 speech to the Pennsylvania American Legion, he condemned the "men of great wealth [who] send us on a wild goose chase after so-called radicals while they continue to plunder the people," and who branded as Communists "everyone who dared contradict the opinions of Wall Street."[16]

Earle's radicalism won popular support, and 1934 only marked the beginning of greater things. Pittsburgh fell to the Democratic Party headed by David Lawrence in the electoral revolution of 1936, the year that FDR became the first Democratic presidential candidate to carry the state since before the Civil War.[17] He also carried every Pittsburgh ward. Democratic success was based on an electoral realignment that had begun with the Al Smith campaign of 1928 and which under FDR created a statewide coalition of "city dwellers, organized laborers, Catholics, Jews, Negroes and the poor."[18] Blacks and recent immigrants swung decisively to the Democratic Party between 1934 and 1936, a transition that decided many elections over the next half-century.

Philadelphia did not pass entirely into Democratic hands until the late 1940s, but there were major gains even here. Before 1933 the Democratic interest in the city had been virtually nonexistent, in the sense that Republican boss William Vare not only controlled the Democratic Party machinery, but he even paid the rent on its headquarters. In 1931 the Democratic candidate for mayor had received under 10 percent of the vote, and until 1934 there was never any question that the Republicans would hold all seven of the city's congressional districts with massive margins. In 1933, however, a local insurgency secured the party's independence. In 1935 S. Davis Wilson was elected mayor as an independent Republican who initially sought to "repudiate" the New Deal, but his later career paralleled Pinchot's.[19] Distancing himself from the Republican Party, he moved inexorably toward a coalition with the Democrats, to the extent of seeking the senatorial nomination on that ticket in 1938. He was instrumental in bringing the 1936 Democratic convention to the city.[20] His political ambitions were thwarted by a series of corruption scandals that effectively destroyed his administration, but by this point there was every reason to believe that Philadelphia would soon be a firm part of the new Democratic hegemony.[21] In 1936 FDR carried all but seven of the city's fifty wards, and all seven of the city's U.S. representatives were Democrats. Between 1931 and 1939 the number of registered Democratic voters in Philadelphia had grown from 34,000 to 447,000.[22] This contributed to a substantial expansion of the electorate statewide: 2.2 million people cast votes in the presidential election of 1924 and around 4.1 million in 1936 and 1940. The electorate in the Roosevelt era was far more numerous and much more diverse in ethnic and religious terms (see table 2.2).[23]

The new regime was consolidated through the patronage opportunities offered by the Works Progress Administration (WPA), a bastion for the liberal and prolabor elements of the party. In Philadelphia alone some 40,000 citizens were working for the WPA by 1936.[24] Under firm Democratic domination, between 1935 and 1937 the state executed a series of radical measures collectively known as the Little New Deal, which dealt with issues as varied as minimum wages, hours of work, teacher tenure, workmen's compensation, the regulation of sweatshops, factory inspection, the employment of minors, stream pollution, and restrictions on coal and iron police. A Little Wagner Act promoted the rights of labor.[25] The Earle regime began a massive public works campaign, which among other things built the new Pennsylvania Turnpike. Many of these ideas had formed part of a progressive platform for two or three decades, but they were now made law within one tumultuous gubernatorial term.

The durability of this power was uncertain, tied as it was to events on the national scene, and problems in Roosevelt's second term raised Republican hopes that their eclipse might be short lived. In 1938 ideological divisions within the Democratic Party allowed Republicans to elect a vociferously probusiness governor in Arthur James, who promised to "make a bonfire of all the laws

TABLE 2.2. *Pennsylvania Popular Votes in Presidential Elections, 1912–1940 (millions of votes)*

Year	Republican	Democrat	Other[a]
1912	0.27	0.4	0.44
1916	0.7	0.52	
1920	1.22	0.5	
1924	1.4	0.41	0.32
1928	2.06	1.07	
1932	1.45	1.3	
1936	1.69	2.35	
1940	1.9	2.17	

Source: *Pennsylvania Manual.*

a. This takes account of major third-party candidates earning at least 100,000 votes in the state in a particular year. Only two parties succeeded in attaining this level of support in the period discussed: Theodore Roosevelt's movement in 1912, and Robert M. LaFollette's Progressives in 1924.

passed by the 1937 Legislature."[26] Incumbent James J. "Puddler Jim" Davis defeated George Earle's bid for the U.S. Senate. However, the 1940 election was a triumph for the Democrats, showing that the days of the one-party Republican state were gone forever. Even in the favorable circumstances of 1938 the Republicans could take only the fifth and seventh U.S. congressional districts in Philadelphia, and in 1940 they retained only the seventh. Of five seats in the Pittsburgh area, the Democrats held a monopoly from 1934 through 1940, except for the short-lived loss of two districts in 1938. Following the 1944 election there was even a brief period when both U.S. senators were Democrats, the only time that such a conjunction has occurred in the last century.

THE INDUSTRIAL CRISIS

Political realignment coincided with a profound revision of the economic role of government, a phenomenon that was most apparent in the divisive labor disputes of the mid-1930s. In itself labor violence was neither novel nor surprising, as the state had a long reputation as a pivotal battleground of industrial conflict, from the time of the Molly Maguires and the Homestead Strike to the steel strike of 1919 and the series of great coal stoppages between

1922 and 1927.[27] However, the conflicts of the New Deal era were sharply different from earlier events, so that industrial struggle was brought firmly into the realm of party politics. Federal and state governments now became decisively involved in the shaping of disputes, and it was no longer possible to assume that the forces of the state would be committed to the defense of business and property.

The changing role of the state is illustrated by the question of union organization. Until the 1920s the critical issue facing the labor movement was the achievement and defense of the right to unionize, in the face of aggressive antiunion attitudes by Pennsylvania employers. Resistance to labor organization was enhanced by structural changes that placed unionized industries at an economic disadvantage. In the coal industry long-established union representation was repeatedly challenged during the 1920s in response to competition from nonunion southern coalfields and to the rise of new energy sources. Grueling strikes crippled the industry but failed to guarantee the permanent position of the unions. In other industries, especially steel, union organization was much more rudimentary, despite prolonged struggles in 1892 and 1919.

Since the 1870s, state involvement in strikes and lockouts had been limited in nature, and when it did occur, it was virtually always in support of the employers.[28] The state devolved extensive policing functions to employers, and Richard Mellon had asserted that "you can't run a coalmine without machine guns."[29] In 1910 a transit strike in Philadelphia was marked by appalling excesses by the private detectives and strikebreakers imported by the Philadelphia Rapid Transit Corporation (PRT): "Never before were there such systematic, willful, brutal, unprovoked assaults upon an unoffending populace in an American city."[30] When even these resources proved inadequate, state agencies assisted the defeat of labor movements. In 1905 labor unrest in the state led to the creation of the State Police, a widely imitated paramilitary constabulary unit that applied to Pennsylvania the counterinsurgency lessons learned in the Philippines.[31] The State Police—the "Cossacks"—provided organized labor with a litany of martyrs and massacres in which strikers and protesters had been killed by the forces of authority: at Mount Carmel in 1906, McKees Rocks in 1909, and Bethlehem in 1910. During the 1919 steel strike local police had regularly collaborated with thugs hired by the companies and permitted the mobbing and assault of union organizers.[32] The courts assisted employers by sweeping antiunion injunctions that if observed literally would have all but prohibited any form of activism by organized labor. In 1935 a coal strike in Luzerne County led to a "reign of terrorism" by "the moneyed citizens, state and local police, the magistrates, the courts, the better citizens, and the industrial powers."[33]

The role of government changed substantially under the governorship of Gifford Pinchot, who viewed his role in industrial disputes as that of an honest broker. He earned a prolabor reputation by his mediation of a strike in the anthracite region in 1923, and in his second term (1931–35) he attacked the devolution of police powers to private companies. He described the coal and iron police as "gunmen, thugs, felons and professional troublemakers."[34] In 1933 Pinchot ensured that National Guard intervention in a major coal strike was limited to its ostensible goal of neutral peacekeeping. Predictably Pinchot's behavior attracted conservative charges about his alleged Communist sympathies. These local trends foreshadowed more significant events at the federal level, when the New Deal administration showed itself likely to be evenhanded or even to favor unions.

Labor relations were revolutionized by the National Industrial Recovery Act (NIRA) and the Wagner Act and the subsequent creation of the National Labor Relations Board. Federal law now assumed some form of right to labor organization, giving an incentive to union organization in industries hitherto little affected by these trends. In Pennsylvania the new laws permitted unionization in what had once been regarded as the most harmonious and paternalistic companies, including the Hershey chocolate industry and the Reading knitting mills. Both were the setting for prolonged labor confrontations in 1936 and 1937 when government played a role in shaping the conflicts that would have been inconceivable a decade previously (see below).

The changed environment was equally apparent in Philadelphia, which had long been a stronghold for the traditional craft unions of the American Federation of Labor and was a notoriously difficult city for other forms of labor organization.[35] In 1934 a strike by hosiery workers initiated several years of intense labor struggle, and 1937 was marked by numerous sit-down strikes led and won by the CIO. In April a sit-in resulted in a union victory at the Artcraft Silk Hosiery Mill, which in turn inspired the bitterest single struggle of the year, at the Apex Hosiery mills in northeastern Philadelphia. Five thousand workers stormed the Apex plant, beating managers and guards while police allegedly stood by, and 250 sit-in demonstrators held the mill for six weeks.[36] Meanwhile a CIO union threatened to displace the company union in the PRT.[37] By the end of the decade Philadelphia had become the strong union town that it would remain for the next half-century.

The Earle administration was allied to labor and especially the CIO, which was becoming a potent political presence in the state. Earle's lieutenant governor, Tom Kennedy, was the secretary-treasurer of the United Mineworkers and was moreover the first Catholic ever to hold high state office in Pennsylvania. In the summer of 1936 Kennedy attracted controversy when a mass demonstration by unemployed supporters of the Workers' Alliance caused the suspension of the state senate in Harrisburg.[38] Conservative mythology stated that Kennedy, then chairing the body, had permitted the radical takeover by failing to clear the demonstrators.[39] As with the police inaction in the Apex strike, this was taken to prove the Democrats' preference for mob action over constitutional government. And Kennedy was known to have gubernatorial ambitions himself in 1938.[40]

The value of having a prolabor state administration was amply demonstrated by the Johnstown steel strike of 1937, a crucial event in both the political and industrial history of Pennsylvania between the wars. In 1936 the Steel Workers' Organizing Committee used federal legislation as a charter to organize the Little Steel companies, resulting in a series of strikes and lockouts over the following year. In Pennsylvania this movement had its sharpest impact in Johnstown, where threats of mass marches and rioting culminated that June in rumors that 40,000 miners were on the point of invading the city. Governor Earle responded in traditional style by sending in the State Police, but on this occasion their mandate was to close the Johnstown mill complex, in effect accomplishing the union's goals.[41] The plant reopened within a few weeks, but the closure had enduring effects in still further polarizing state politics. Following the hunger march on Harrisburg and the labor struggles at Hershey, Philadelphia and Reading (all reaching a climax during that spring), the events at Johnstown permitted the administration to be painted as a menace to business and property. For Pennsylvania, 1937 looked like a year of incipient Red revolution.

TORY REACTION

Between 1936 and 1938 Republicans found themselves facing the prospect of years in the political wilderness and in the unaccustomed role of a party in opposition. Moreover, this impotence coincided with a period of apparent Red revolution across the state. In response the party swung sharply to the political right. Purged of the progressive heresy after the bloodletting of 1934, the party over the next decade was dominated by two major factions, each representing violent opposition to the New Deal and respectively headed by Joseph Grundy and Joseph N. Pew, vice-president of Sun Oil. Grundy's power base lay in the PMA, which represented 7,000 or so of the state's smaller business interests.[42] A high representation of textile manufacturers ensured a strong antilabor streak to the movement, as this industry represented the storm front of CIO pressure for militant unionism, with several bitter strikes between 1933 and 1937. Though ostensibly nonpartisan, the manufacturers' group remained a focus of anti-Roosevelt sentiment, and its views gained impact because of its critical role in funding Republican candidates. Successive PMA presidents such as Grundy, G. Mason Owlett, and John M. Flynn determined that this strand of business opinion remained at the heart of state politics. The Grundy-Owlett machine strenuously opposed any progressive tendencies within the party as a climbdown in the face of the Red New Deal.

The other faction represented very large Wall Street moneyed interests, since the Pews were, together with the Mellons and the Pitcairns, among the dozen or so wealthiest families in the United States. In 1936 the Pews and the Mellons were among the largest contributors to the Republican National Committee, and in 1940 Pew was a principal backer of Wendell Willkie.[43] Within the state, Joe "Mr. Money Bags" Pew contributed huge sums to secure control over the party machinery, and he developed a particular hold over the reviving Philadelphia organization, where he allied with the Annenbergs of the *Inquirer*.[44] In 1938 Arthur James won the governorship as a Pew ally.[45] Politically the Pew interests were, if anything, even less sympathetic to the Roosevelt administration than Grundy was, and Joseph N. Pew was "one of the fiercest anti-Roosevelt crusaders in the country."[46] His brother J. Howard Pew was one of the primary backers of the Republican Party at the national level as well as of right-wing pressure groups such as the American Liberty League.

In 1936 Governor Earle dismissed the Republicans as "protectionists," "protecting the interests of Joe Pew, Joe Grundy and Andy Mellon and the other financial angels of the Republican gang," the "men of vast wealth."[47] In 1938 the pro-Roosevelt *Philadelphia Record* published a cartoon, "The Gang's All Here," depicting a similar view of the "Tory" Republican coalition. Joseph Pew was shown with steel magnate Ernest T. Weir and other figures representing "Grundyism," "Reaction," and "Opposition to Labor."[48] While blatantly partisan, such analyses offer a reasonable portrait of the party at this stage. With the backing of Grundy, Owlett, and Pew, it is not surprising that the Republican administrations of Arthur James and Edward Martin were both strongly antilabor and sought to reverse the Little New Deal. In 1941 the state legislature permitted the prompt termination of subversive and un-American teachers, in language clearly directed against the Left rather than fascist activists, while an unsuccessful series of bills sought to implement loyalty oaths for public employees.[49]

As Republicans tried to interpret their plight, their political rhetoric developed a vehement tone that drew heavily on traditions of conspiracy politics, denouncing opponents as not merely incompetent but also actively criminal or seditious. From the mid-1930s organized labor was pilloried as a chief foe of traditional American values, with the CIO as a sinister and Communist-influenced component of the Roosevelt coalition. In 1936 the Republican campaign in Pennsylvania was firmly founded on Red-baiting. State Republican chairman (and Grundy ally) M. Harvey Taylor asserted that the "un-American doctrines" of the Democratic Party were adorned with "Russian whiskers." G. Mason Owlett argued that the Democrats had ceased to exist and the name had been appropriated by "a conglomeration of Communists, Socialists and job-holders."[50] Extravagant charges accused Roosevelt of seeking to abolish marriage and religion.[51] This Jacobin-Bolshevik plot was founded on the WPA, which created a docile army of helots whose livelihood depended on the unquestioning support of the New Deal system.[52] In 1938 Senator Davis depicted the relief system as "a wicked exchange of bread for votes."[53] In 1940 state Republican leader Jay Cooke warned that if Roosevelt obtained his third term, America would become a dictatorship indistinguishable from Nazi Germany.[54] Edward Martin described the CIO's Political Action Committee simply as an arm of the Communist Party.[55]

The vigor of anti-Roosevelt and anti-Red sentiment among die-hard Republicans can be illustrated by the experience of Kern Dodge, who served as Philadelphia's director of public safety under Mayor J. Hampton Moore in 1932–33. He was responsible for ordering the savage police attack on leftist protesters in Reyburn Plaza in 1932, at which time he fulminated against "the Communist attempt to overrule constitutional authority . . . to substitute mob rule."[56] "This lawless class of Communists," usually aliens, were responsible for sedition and probably for much of the city's street crime. He defended the police against the accumulating barrage of allegations of corruption and brutality.[57] Though Dodge was out of office in the mid-1930s, his numerous connections in the police and the fire department gave added force to his criticisms of the pro–New Deal administration of Davis Wilson.[58] He gravitated to the ultra-Right ACS, founded by Bessie Burchett, whom he found closely attuned to his elitist and nativist stance. He blamed the spread of Communist subversion on the ignorance and apathy of the masses who had been permitted to vote and the nefarious influence of immigrants.[59] At one of the society's gatherings in 1939, he declared that "radicals have ideas which are being fostered by President Roosevelt, that the lower classes are entitled to a more abundant life."[60] By this time Dodge was involved with anti-Semitic activism and possibly the Christian Front movement, and he was accused of sponsoring the "bombing" of the city with anti-Semitic propaganda leaflets.[61] Dodge later served alongside other strongly anti-FDR Republicans on the governing committee of Philadelphia's America First Committee.

Militant opinions were reflected by Pennsylvania's diminished but still powerful Republican delegation in Congress, which included some extremely conservative members. One was J. William Ditter, from the staunchly conservative Seventeenth District, in Montgomery County. His diatribes against the New Deal were

quoted approvingly by Father Coughlin's *Social Justice* in 1939–
40, at a point where that periodical had turned stridently anti-
Roosevelt and anti-Semitic. Ditter also published material in work
produced by the far-Right National Republic movement, where he
was in the very conservative company of politicians such as Carl
Mundt and John E. Rankin of Mississippi. Another Pennsylvania representative was James Van Zandt, whose violently anti–New
Deal opinions were cited by extremists like James B. True. In 1939
Van Zandt was scheduled to appear on a Philadelphia platform
alongside such extreme rightists as General Moseley and Father
Curran.[62]

THE PMA

The papers and speeches of the PMA demonstrate the Manichaean critique of the New Deal. In this view both organized
labor and recent social reforms were manifestations of the ultimate evil of Communism, which threatened to destroy the values
of fairness and freedom summarized by the emotive and much-
used term "Americanism." In 1945 Owlett offered his summary of
recent American history as a simple struggle between democracy
and state socialism, the "preachings of Karl Marx and Nikolai [*sic*]
Lenin," and cited as a primary goal the derailing of the "disaster-
bound Communistic trend of the New Deal."[63]

The New Deal illustrated incompetence, mismanagement, and
outright treason. Senator David Reed described the whole scheme
as "poison from which it will take decades to recover. . . . The
troubles that will come from it will overwhelm us."[64] Edward
Martin dismissed the national program as simply "un-American,"
while the state's own Little New Deal was "unsound, unhealthy
and unwarranted class legislation."[65] Senator Davis rejected the
"raw radicalism of New Deal excesses."[66] In 1943 the *Monthly
Bulletin* of the "non-partisan" PMA wrote,

> The history of the Roosevelt administration shows that it has
> taken sadistic delight in attacking and dissipating the nation's
> industrial resources. It has sought to perpetuate its political
> power on a preposterous dole system or vote catch-all which has
> helped undermine public morale and discourage personal initia-
> tive. Free enterprise has become the favorite whipping post of

starry eyed planners and enraptured visionaries who in the fury
of bureaucratic controls and regimented panaceas have tried to
break down every constitutional bulwark and strip the federal
government of all its elemental human decencies.[67]

These crimes were wrought in alliance with "the overlords
of labor—money-hungry, dues-chasing opportunists,"[68] "arrogant
parasitic racketeers."[69] These sinister enemies were guilty of the
near-destruction, the "martyrdom" of the businessmen who had
built the country and who were now hapless victims of "the
clutching hand of mono-party arrogance."[70] In 1943 Mason Owlett
complained that for the last decade, "every demagogue, every op-
portunist, every crackpot, was able to picture the doers and the
builders as those to blame for their plight."[71] True Americans
should respond forcefully to this subversion. In his presidential
address to the 1944 PMA convention Owlett asserted, "Political
morons, who couldn't find their way out of a revolving door, have
sat in judgment and rendered decisions affecting all industry. If we
are to survive as a nation, we must exterminate the crackpots and
political gangsters now living off the people. . . . We must exterminate the fleecy minded cloud dwellers who say that we must not be
concerned with the public debt because we owe it to ourselves."[72]

BOILED SHIRT VIGILANTISM, 1936–1937

Leftist writers accused the Republican Party of flirting with fascist ideas or collaborating with extremist leaders at the local level.
With occasional exceptions such as Kern Dodge, such charges are
greatly exaggerated, as an ideological gulf separated the conservatives from fascist ideologies. Republican leaders such as Grundy,
Owlett, Reed, and Pew rejected any form of corporatism in favor
of a traditional orthodoxy based on monolithic fiscal conservatism,
laissez-faire economics, and an unrestricted labor market. However, the Republican crisis did contribute to the development of
extremist ideas in popularizing the notion of New Dealers as sinister foes of uncompromising "Americanism." Polarization was at
its height during Roosevelt's second term, and it was intensified
by the industrial conflicts of these years.

The New Deal regime could not be defied outright, but the affected corporations themselves devised new techniques and strate-

gies to cope with labor insurgency. Company unions were one obvious weapon that could be used in the short term to indicate at least apparent compliance with legality. If police and courts could no longer be counted on to defeat strikes, then business could return to the traditional concept of private law enforcement and detectives, but now coupled with networks of citizen vigilantes. The new organizations were united by an antiradical Americanist ideology of community solidarity and class collaboration. There was a powerful recent precedent for this in the American Protective League of the First World War, a vigilante alliance of local employers and businessmen, supported by professional detective and security firms, pledged to root out any leftist or alien sentiment that could threaten the war effort.

In 1937 the steel employers mounted a campaign to persuade employees to return to work. This was organized by employee associations, in alliance with Citizens' Committees, "often composed of anti-union businessmen and professionals with close ties to the steel companies."[73] These groups were sponsored by the three major Little Steel firms, National, Republic, and Bethlehem, with their powerful executives Tom Girdler, Eugene Grace, and E. T. Weir, all firmly ensconced in the demonology of organized labor.

"The most formidable of the vigilante movements" was formed in the Johnstown conflict of that year as part of a conservative protest against Earle's intervention.[74] A citizens' committee was led by the secretary of the local chamber of commerce, assisted by a number of local businessmen, civic leaders, and clergy. The movement was heavily funded by employers' groups, R. T. Mellon, and the National Association of Manufacturers in addition to Bethlehem Steel. The Johnstown committee was militantly partisan, announcing its violent opposition to FDR, George Earle, and John L. Lewis, and it claimed that U.S. government policy was now firmly in the hands of the CIO. Speakers before the committee were described by terms such as "a vitriolic and rabble rousing anti-union crusader and demagogue."[75] In a pamphlet titled *It Can't Happen Here? It Did Happen Here*, local parson John H. Stanton argued that Earle had allied with the CIO to trample the rights of business and private property and impose a leftist tyranny.[76] However, the citizens' committee fell well short of the "fascist" interpretation so often presented by its opponents and, at least at its inception, drew widely on the local middle class, recruited through fraternal groups such as the Elks, Kiwanis, Rotary, and Lions. Members included Protestants, Catholics, and Jews, and a rabbi served until he resigned over growing antiunion extremism.[77]

In June 1937 the Johnstown committee sought to nationalize its cause, summarizing grievances in a widely printed newspaper advertisement titled "We Protest." The flood of letters this called forth amply shows how this local conflict focused national hostility against the New Deal and the supposed Communist peril. Extremist groups offering their services included the Americaneers, George Washington's Body Guard, and the pro-Mussolini American Vigilant Intelligence Federation.[78] Royal Scott Gulden of the Order of 76 praised "the real old-fashioned American stand that you and your committee have taken to protect your homes and country from the Red aliens and the renegade politicians and traitors now in political power."[79] Even Republican senator Davis urged the critical need for the state government to respect legality.[80] The committee attracted right-wing speakers from across the nation, including figures such as Michigan representative Clare Hoffman.[81] In July Johnstown was the setting for a national convention of citizens' committees, chambers of commerce, and vigilante groups, who combined to form a new Citizens' National Committee under Stanton. The new group noted that as unworthy public officials had failed to observe their oaths "to protect American citizens in their inalienable constitutional rights to work without molestation," these rights must be restored by a new "nationwide organization" which would combat "activities which are un-American, Communistic and destructive to the welfare of our nation."[82]

The ideological tone of the citizens' committees and employer-sponsored organizations is equally apparent from the outpouring of propaganda designed to oppose the unions in the Berks County knitting mills. The County Manufacturers' Association denounced Communist plotting in the United States, while the citizens' committee denounced outsiders who subverted the harmony of Berks County and declared that "we stand foursquare for the peace, contentment and prosperity of our community." The employee associations, the company unions, noted that the fundamental principle of life should be "cooperation—cooperation among ourselves; cooperation with the manufacturers who employ us," but that the

Roosevelt administration threatened this tranquility. "The suspicion has often been advanced in the newspapers that the National Labor Relations Board is a part of the CIO." Local employers supported a strident antiunion newspaper, *The Spectator*, "dedicated to the exposé of the labor racketeer and the publishing of the facts about the union racket." In 1935 the antiunion campaign coalesced with the Red-baiting tradition that the Reading area had developed in response to the electoral successes of the Socialist Party in the city government. The "Fusionist" (anti-Socialist) campaign unleashed a series of newspaper advertisements and posters, some sponsored by patriotic groups such as the Minutemen of Berks County. These typically asked, "Do we desire a handlebar mustachioed Stalin regimenting all of us? Do we want a red flag to replace Old Glory at City Hall?" [83]

Taken together, the various antiunion strategies offered the potential for large companies to meet the challenge of the CIO and its political friends. However, the new alignment of probusiness forces also had implications for conservative and far-Right political organizations, which cast their fortunes with the array of company unions, citizens' committees, and vigilante squads. In turn the members of such ad hoc groups identified themselves with explicitly rightist causes and provided fertile recruiting ground for the parent movements. This symbiosis is illustrated by the prominent role played by rightist groups in three of the largest strikes that occurred in 1937, respectively at Johnstown, Hershey, and Reading.

THE AMERICAN LEGION

The link between industrial vigilantism and the far Right was especially apparent in the case of the American Legion, a popular movement that had over 1 million members nationwide in 1930 and that maintained an average membership of 800,000 through the 1930s.[84] In Pennsylvania alone, by 1930 there were 73,000 members organized in 567 posts, not counting auxiliaries; in 1944 there were over 100,000 members in 675 posts, with 50,000 more in the auxiliary.[85] In 1937 Philadelphia alone had 12,500 legionnaires.[86] The organization was far from monolithic, and individual posts represented a wide range of ethnicity, religion, and political opinion. Many legionnaires were themselves prolabor or active unionists, and by 1940 there were fifteen African American posts in the state.[87] The legion as a whole was also deeply suspicious of Nazism and Hitler's revival of German military power. The group condemned the display of Nazi uniforms or symbols, and legionnaires engaged in violent confrontations with the German American Bund.[88] The *Philadelphia Record* cited no less than four separate occasions on which Bund leader G. W. Kunze had been beaten up by legionnaires, including incidents in Philadelphia and Pittsburgh.[89] In 1938 the executive committee of the Pennsylvania legion recorded advocating "a firm stand against Communism, Nazism and Fascism, and Commander Smith delivered another of his now famous attacks on subversive groups."[90]

For all its anti-Nazi militancy, the political tone of the legion leadership was well to the Right, and the group became a primary exponent of a conservative and nativist view of Americanism. The national legion established its Americanism Commission in 1919, and between the wars this body struggled against radicalism in the factories, streets, and schools. In 1922 the Pennsylvania state convention was reminded that "we have more aliens in the state . . . than in any other state with one exception, the state of New York. . . . There is no need to emphasize the importance of the work of instilling American ideals here."[91] In 1927 the legion's role as self-appointed guardian of Americanism led to a scandal when the legion secured the dismissal of two professors at West Chester State Normal College, who in addition to their affiliation with the American Civil Liberties Union had also attacked U.S. policies in Nicaragua.[92] The *Philadelphia Inquirer* remarked that the publicity "bid fair to make this a case about as prominent as the Scopes trial."[93]

Defending Americanism also took the form of combating leftist political movements. In 1919 and 1920 Pennsylvania legionnaires disrupted radical gatherings. In the Socialist stronghold of Reading, some 5,000 legionnaires gathered to denounce radical (and German) leader James Maurer.[94] In 1924 a Lenin commemoration in Wilkes-Barre was disrupted at the point of rifles wielded by veterans from the legion post, who forced the radicals to salute the American flag.[95] The local mayor granted the legion the de facto right to veto any future meetings, by force if necessary.[96]

This political stance remained constant through the next decade. In 1938 the state convention of the legion was reminded of "subversive forces and influences operating to overthrow the government by force and violence in Pennsylvania."[97] The legion leadership demanded severe measures against Bund and fascist activism in the state but at the same time warned of Bund infiltration within the legion itself.[98] Meanwhile the convention experienced controversy over an alleged incident in which the mere mention of Governor Earle's name attracted jeering from some legionnaires.[99] The following year the convention called for restrictions on "undesirable" aliens in terms that would have meant the deportation of every person in the United States who was not an American citizen, some 8 million individuals.[100]

The legion in these years earned a reputation as a mass lobby group subsidized by big corporations and the National Association of Manufacturers, with the primary goal of combating strikes and labor unions.[101] "Through the twenties and through most of the thirties, the Legion became increasingly identified in the public mind with strike breaking and vigilantism."[102] In the steel regions in the southwest of the state, the legion provided foot soldiers for opposition to the Steel Workers' Organizing Committee.[103] In 1934 Aliquippa police chief Michael Kane led 200 armed men, mainly legionnaires, against steel strikers in the town of Ambridge, resulting in the death of one man and the gassing or wounding of hundreds of others who were picketing the Jones and Laughlin steelworks.[104] Antiunion forces, many of whom appeared in legion uniforms, were called out by the post commander, who was an employee of Jones and Laughlin; the sheriff who authorized the action was a former chief of the same company's coal and iron police.[105]

In 1935 Michael Kane reappeared as the leader of a new organization called the Constitutional Defense League, described as an offshoot of the legion's National Americanism Commission. It is unclear whether Kane was an isolated extremist or if in fact he was implementing an emergency scheme designed by the legion at the national level.[106] Kane himself urged that union organizers be hanged or "taken for a ride," but the legion also used a subtler propaganda campaign with its Harmony Ads of 1936, which opposed the efforts of the CIO by urging collaboration between labor and capital.[107] As labor tension rose the following year, the legion was again drafted for physical confrontation. In Johnstown "the mayor deputized the local Legion post commander as a special policeman, saying 'That deputizes the entire membership of the American Legion post in Johnstown.' "[108] Three hundred legion-naires were thus given full police powers.[109] *The Nation* complained that the vigilantes of the American Legion constituted a "fascistic" organization in western Pennsylvania and presented Kane's group as an iniquitous manifestation of "Fascism in Pennsylvania."[110]

Legion vigilantism was evident in other strikes of these years, respectively at Hershey and Reading. In Hershey a sit-down strike that began in April 1937 was crushed by a movement organized through the company-sponsored Loyal Workers Club, in alliance with local farmers and college students. They were supported by company police and private detectives from the innocuously named Railway Audit and Inspection agency. Mass parades were organized by the local American Legion, which led the storming of the plant and the eviction of the strikers.[111] The legion post's Drum and Bugle Corps was active in a final assault by 2,000 vigilantes, who forced the defeated strikers to run a gauntlet. "Local farmers, some of them Legionnaires, supplied the factory with more than 800,000 quarts of milk a day."[112] With the unionization campaign in ruins, the "Loyalist" club became the nucleus of a procompany Independent Chocolate Workers Union. That summer, Hershey was the setting for a Convention of Independent Workers, to serve as a counterweight to the CIO.[113]

THE BERKS COUNTY CONFLICT

The Reading hosiery industry presented a somewhat similar picture. In 1933–34 the Wyomissing Berkshire Delta Mills pro-vided one of the earliest cases heard by the National Labor Board created by the NIRA. The company resisted unionization by the promotion of a company union headed by a loyal employee named Fred Werner, and this organization fervently opposed a campaign that culminated in a thirteen-month strike by the American Fed-eration of Hosiery Workers in 1936–37.[114] With the failure of the "Berky" strike, the company union retained its position in close alliance with a rightist political organization. In this case, however, the outside support came not from the American Legion but from the German American Bund, for which the strike opened unpar-alleled opportunities in the Reading area.

The Bund identified the CIO as one of its chief enemies, and members were ordered to combat strikes where possible, if only by crossing picket lines and patronizing strikebound businesses. In Reading the Bund was permitted to recruit within the workforce, in exchange for supplying members to combat potential strikes and labor disturbances.[115] The new company union operated as a showcase for anti-CIO labor organization. There were contacts between the Berkshire union and the Independent Chocolate Workers at Hershey as well as rightist political sects such as the Constitutional Educational League. In 1937 Werner congratulated the Johnstown Citizens' Committee on their resistance to the "un-American tactics" of Governor Earle and personally visited the group to share his experiences.[116]

The Bund's political outlook was largely shared by the circle of German American magnates who dominated the Berks County textile firms of Textile Machine, Berkshire Knitting Mills, and Narrow Fabric, the family nexus based on Ferdinand Thun and Henry Janssen.[117] Their partner Gustav Oberlaender (died 1936) became a vigorous Hitler supporter who made several visits to the Reich and who drew unfavorable comparisons between the industrial situation in the two countries: "There has been less disorder in Germany than in the United States, where strikes are everywhere. Hitler believes no state can exist where one class is pitted against another. For that reason, he has forbidden strikes. . . . Hitler is doing wonderful work. Germany has no strikes, nor prospects of any. When radicals try to start trouble of that sort, the government gets after them and they are soon taken care of. But in the United States, we just let them run loose."[118] His wife observed in 1937 that Josef Goebbels "has a charming face and is a wonderful orator."

In 1931 Oberlaender gave $1 million to the Carl Schurz Foundation to establish the Oberlaender Trust to promote cultural relations between the United States and Germany. This benevolent philanthropic foundation distributed money to many worthy causes, and its recipients included prestigious scholars, artists, and archaeologists as well as numerous Pennsylvania teachers and academics.[119] Nor was the trust an uncritical supporter of the "New Germany," in that by 1938 it was giving generously to assist exiled scholars gain new livelihoods in the United States; even Albert Einstein shared its largesse.[120] However, the promotion of cultural links in the Nazi era inevitably had political overtones. In 1937, for example, the trust sponsored a German trip by the head of Philadelphia's German American Broadcasting Company in order to secure "cultural material for radio programs."

On a local basis Oberlaender attempted to preserve the Reading area from future disorder by disseminating German tactics and practices. Following the first great Berkshire strike in 1934, his trust began funding Reading city officials to travel to Germany to study social and industrial policies. Beneficiaries included the school superintendent, the city engineer, the city forester, the hospital superintendent, and the superintendent of recreation. The city forbade further visits following an outcry against children "being Hitlerized on public playgrounds," but the trust's work further reinforced rightist and pro-German sentiment in the Reading area.[121]

HOODS AND SHIRTS

Other groups received a degree of sponsorship from employers and their organizations. Among the Italian communities of Philadelphia there were attempts to create Fascist-oriented labor movements to inspire harmony between employers and workers. By 1928 the city had a chapter of the Longshoremen's Federation of North America, a classic Fascist "syndicate."[122] In the clothing industry that was so critical to Italian American economic life, there were recurring conflicts between leftist unions and Fascist militants.

The Ku Klux Klan also benefited from the new vigilantism. In the Midwest, employers' organizations supported a Klan revival in the form of the Black Legion, and some Pennsylvania industrial communities experienced a similar phenomenon in mid-decade. During the coal strike of 1933 the Klan sponsored docile company unions in an attempt to divide the labor movement.[123] In the bituminous coal district of Fayette County during 1936 a spate of Klan recruitment literature urged the movement's familiar remedies: the deportation of illegal aliens, the suppression of Communism, the restoration of constitutional government, the separation of church and state, a Buy American policy, and white supremacy. The Fayette Klan achieved wide support through the enthusiastic cooperation of the local mineowners, the Frick Coal Company, who now found "a homemade illegal union-wrecking machine." Rituals were carried out at a local cemetery, where "masked and equipped with police maces and riot whistles, the traffic directors at the cemetery are either Frick deputies or Uniontown police." [124] By 1938 Fayette had the largest number of Klansmen of any county in Pennsylvania, including Philadelphia. Klavern #128 (Uniontown) grew from 52 members in 1933 to 101 in 1936 and retained 48 of these by 1940. Klavern #345 increased its active membership from 40 in 1933 to 66 in 1936 at a time of a precipitous decline in Klan activity in the rest of the state.

The Silver Shirts played a similar role in the steel districts of Ohio and western Pennsylvania, and the Dies Committee was told of meetings between Republic Steel's Tom Girdler and Ohio Silver Legion leader Spencer J. Warwick, who was also active in Pennsylvania steel communities such as Sharon.[125] The proposed meeting may also have involved other Silver commanders. In Cleveland in 1937, leftist newspapers alleged the formation of a "Vigilante Coalition," a "United Front of Tom Girdler, Silver Shirts, Strikebreakers and Nazis." [126]

The clearest overlap between "boiled shirt vigilantism" and the new fascist sects came from Pittsburgh, where in 1938 Charles B. Swift headed the Constitutional Defense Committee of the American Legion in Allegheny County, a direct parallel to Michael Kane's group in neighboring Beaver County.[127] According to Dies Committee investigators, Swift was a reserve naval officer who developed an impressive private intelligence network. The investigator stated, "He has in his possession large Naval Intelligence files, and . . . he also obtains information and cooperation from the Military Intelligence in Pittsburgh. I learned that he has access to information of the Military Intelligence Service, and that he has built up, apart from that, a sort of espionage organization of his own among citizens of a patriotic character who apparently have been duped into believing that in serving Mr. Swift they are serving the United States Naval Intelligence Service." The intelligence presence in the city reflected the crucial importance of firms such as Westinghouse in naval production. Swift, an employee of Duquesne Light, denied all the charges and derided the investigation. He accused committee investigators of making him "everything from soup to nuts, from being Kaiser Bill on down to Hitler."[128]

In October Swift invited thirty Pittsburgh businessmen to the Pittsburgh Athletic Association for "a secret meeting or a sort of vigilante meeting" of the kind the American Legion had so often sponsored in recent years. This proved to be a Silver Shirt gathering in which T. Roy Zachary delivered "a violent anti-racial, anti-religious and anti-government attack," endorsing Hitler. According to the House Committee on Un-American Activities, in inviting his audience Swift was able to cite his American Legion connections, but he also "flashed a Naval Intelligence card." One police contact had requested the Pittsburgh police chief to give him credentials so that Swift would not be bothered by "snooping policemen."[129] He declared that he was "planning to call a number of other meetings under the so-called auspices of the American Legion" and that his other proposed guests included George Deatherage, the anti-Semitic leader of the Knights of the White Camellia.[130] The following year an American legionnaire administered the oaths for the Christian Front organization in Pittsburgh, the leadership of which included a U.S. army reserve officer.[131]

THE REVOLT OF THE CONSERVATIVES

The group most often criticized as a conduit for corporate support for the far Right was the American Liberty League, founded in mid-1934 with the announced goal of preserving American freedoms from the Communist-inspired New Deal. This right-wing group received large donations from industrial families such as the DuPonts and from Pennsylvania magnates like Raymond Pitcairn, Andrew Mellon, J. Howard Pew, and Ernest T. Weir. Former U.S. senator Reed served on the league's National Advisory Council and its Lawyers' Committee.[132] The Liberty League was denounced as a vehicle for fascist plotting, and some leaders did employ extreme rhetoric. Reed was eloquent in his praise of Mussolini and saw him as a possible model for resolving American social difficulties. A 1936 investigation of lobbying activities found that large donations had passed from these magnates to an anti-Semitic league subsidiary called the Sentinels of the Republic, which stressed the "Jewish-Communist menace" of the New Deal.[133] Raymond

Pitcairn served as national chairman, and his family had given $100,000 to the group.

Also in Pennsylvania, smaller donations came from J. Howard Pew and former Republican senator G. Wharton Pepper. Pew's generosity extended to other conservative, isolationist, and anti-union groups such as the Campaign to Uphold Constitutional Government, the Farmers' Independence Council, and the Minute Men and Women.[134] This last group attracted notoriety in 1937 when vigilantes fired tear gas bombs at union organizers active in the Apex Hosiery strike. Subsequent investigation by the *Philadelphia Record* showed that the activists had been armed and instructed by the Minute Men and Women.[135] In 1944 Pew associates were accused of sponsoring a campaign of anti-Semitic postcards directed against union leader Sidney Hillman.[136]

During his time as U.S. minister to Austria in 1933–34, George Earle had witnessed fascist insurgency at first hand.[137] As governor of Pennsylvania in 1936, he cited these personal observations to argue that ultraconservatives were creating disturbing precedents in the United States: "The money-changers and the great industrialists behind the Liberty League and the present Republican party leadership cannot escape responsibility for this creature of their malicious, shameless propaganda against the government of the United States. The Black Legion is the first fruit of their campaign for Fascism."[138] Far from being an objective analysis, this was in fact the mirror image of the Republican tendency to stigmatize enemies by portraying them as Communist extremists. However, a perceived need to derail the New Deal did lead some Pennsylvania conservatives to flirt with extreme right-wing ideas and to support movements with an ambivalent attitude toward democratic practice.

Earle's remarks were accurate in stressing the effects of the antigovernment rhetoric of the mid-1930s. If so many respectable legislators were prepared to denounce the state government as perilously radical, who could criticize Father Coughlin when he warned in 1939 that the Reds were planning to turn Philadelphia into "another Barcelona"? If Republicans alleged that President Roosevelt and Governor Earle were in alliance with the CIO to subvert democracy, it was a short step to identifying the more sinister forces manipulating them and to arguing for the reality of Jewish plots. And who could question the necessity to organize paramilitary or vigilante responses against these threats, if so many mainstream business and political interests were mobilizing citizens' committees? If New Dealers and Communists were supporters of a subversive "Zinoviev Front," were not the Coughlinites justified in responding with their Christian Front? [139]

3 | The White Giant
The Ku Klux Klan

he growth of extremist organizations between the world wars was a direct response to the economic consequences of the depression and the political effects of the New Deal. However, the emerging far Right drew on older traditions of ethnic hostility, tensions that can be traced to the nativist movements of the mid-nineteenth century and that grew dramatically following the mass immigration at the turn of the century. Resentment at the new ethnic pluralism was expressed in religious terms, in the anti-Catholicism mobilized by groups such as the American Protective Association of the 1890s and the Ku Klux Klan refounded in 1915.[1] Though its original goal was the reassertion of white supremacy in the South, the second Klan spread rapidly in northern states by exploiting the religious issue. In Pennsylvania, hostility to Catholics, immigrants, and blacks made the Klan a true mass movement by the early 1920s. As in many industrial states, the battles of political reaction were fought in terms of ethnic and religious confrontation long before anti-Semitism developed as a central theme. The Ku Klux Klan was a protofascist movement, which provided the essential foundation for many later developments on the far Right. By the

late 1930s the Klan participated directly in the upsurge of extremist and anti-Semitic militancy.

ETHNICITY

In the mid-nineteenth century, ethnic rivalries in Pennsylvania mainly involved conflicts between Irish Catholic immigrants
and native-born white Protestants. The resulting religious confrontations were a primary fact of Pennsylvania politics and occasionally resulted in serious civil disorder.[2] Tensions increased at
the end of the century with the rapidly growing diversity of the
state's population. By 1910 the proportion of foreign-born Pennsylvanians was 19 percent (see table 3.1). By 1920 over one-fifth
of Pittsburgh's population was foreign born, the largest groups of
non-English speakers using, respectively, Yiddish, Polish, Italian,
and German. Similar concentrations of foreign-born populations
were found in neighboring industrial districts; in cities such as
Aliquippa, McKeesport, New Castle, Sharon, and Johnstown; in
anthracite mining areas such as Scranton, Hazleton, Wilkes-Barre,
and Nanticoke; and in eastern steel towns like Bethlehem.[3]

Philadelphia's population doubled between 1870 and 1920 and
became far more diversified. Of almost 2 million residents in 1930,
only 1.36 million were native-born whites, some 70 percent of
the whole, the remainder comprising 220,000 blacks and 370,000
foreign-born whites. Catholics made up half of the city's population, chiefly Irish, Italian, and Polish, while Jews comprised perhaps 15 percent. Of foreign-born Philadelphians, 82,000 reported
Yiddish as their mother tongue; 69,000, Italian; 52,000, German;
and 25,000, Polish. As immigrant groups tended to be younger
than native communities, their birthrates were accordingly higher,
raising the prospect that the "ethnic" share of the population
would steadily increase. In 1930 only 59 percent of children in the
Philadelphia school district had an American-born father.[4]

By 1940 fifty Pennsylvania newspapers were directed at a specific ethnic group and written largely or entirely in the appropriate language.[5] At least twelve languages were represented in the
Pittsburgh media, eight in Philadelphia. Half of the foreign language papers were aimed at Slavic nationalities, the Poles being
best represented with eleven titles. The Slavic press was active

TABLE 3.1. *National Origins of the Largest Foreign-Born Populations in Pennsylvania, 1930 (thousands)*

Italy	226
Poland	167
England/Scotland/Wales	132
Russia	116
Germany	111
Czechoslovakia	111
Ireland[a]	98
Austria	50
Yugoslavia	40
Lithuania	37
Hungary	34
Other	118
Total	1,240

Source: U.S. Census 1930.

a. Includes both Irish Republic and Northern Ireland.

in the anthracite country as well as Pittsburgh and Philadelphia. Several periodicals served distinctive fraternal and secret societies, and Pittsburgh alone produced magazines in Croat, Slovak, and Polish. Other major components of the ethnic press included the Germans and Italians (eight newspapers each statewide) as well as many less-numerous groups.

For native-stock residents, the ethnic and religious changes symbolized by this abundant diversity were largely negative and portended the destruction of all that was authentically American. The cities, always havens of immorality and foreign ways, now appeared utterly strange and polyglot. In Pennsylvania as elsewhere the Klan emerged from the anti-alien movement that culminated in the restrictive Immigration Act of 1924. James J. Davis, later the state's U.S. senator, commented at this time that "the United States was in danger of sliding into the hands of descendants of such poor human stock . . . that the ideals of our founders will not have the ghost of a chance to remain dominant in the Republic."[6]

There were also newer racial rivalries, though it would be some years before black-white conflicts became as widespread or as venomous as religious issues. Pennsylvania had an established African

American community, but the numbers increased dramatically in the early part of the century with the northward black migration that reached a climax in the First World War era. Between 1910 and 1920 the black population of Philadelphia increased by 59 percent;[7] the figure for Pittsburgh in the same years was 47 percent.[8] The state as a whole had 190,000 blacks in 1910 and 430,000 by 1930. Between the wars, more prosperous blacks moved into areas outside the traditional urban cores, in the face of growing white antipathy. In Philadelphia in the 1920s and 1930s there was strong resistance to black expansion north of Lehigh Avenue, into areas of Germantown and North Philadelphia that were already subject to what would later be termed "white flight."

Blacks were not numerous outside the two great metropolitan areas, and only in Chester was a moderately visible minority present in a smaller or middle-sized city. However, the use of black strikebreakers had left a heritage of racial antipathy in the industrial areas, in consequence of a deliberate policy of fomenting conflict among the workforce. This had been an explosive issue in the bituminous coalfields of western Pennsylvania during the great strikes of 1922 and 1927, in counties such as Fayette and Somerset. Otherwise radical mineworkers' leaders such as Philip Murray had denounced the interlopers as threats to white womanhood and public order. In 1923 the city of Johnstown effectively ordered its industries to expel all black workers, an edict that affected several hundred persons.[9] Local racial conflicts enhanced the plausibility of Klan assertions of a pervasive threat to white supremacy.

THE KLAN IN PENNSYLVANIA

We are unusually well informed about Klan activities and membership in Pennsylvania. A 1936 book by Emerson H. Loucks was a pioneering political study, while in 1940 Klan infighting accidentally exposed the internal archives of the movement.[10] The Klan organization split over the appropriate relationship to the Nazi-oriented anti-Semitic groups, and a "patriotic" faction led a wholesale defection. In the ensuing controversy, persons unknown stole the entire state archives covering the previous two decades and eventually donated the whole to the State Police, making them available for intelligence and countersubversion activities.[11]

The movement enjoyed an extremely high media profile. Dur-

ing the 1920s the Klan gained over 5 million members nationwide, and its Pennsylvania membership alone is credibly estimated
at over a quarter of a million. What gives this figure plausibility
is the fact that local Klan authorities were often in controversy
with national headquarters in Atlanta over the issue of dues (taxes)
owed, and these were assessed on the basis of membership. It benefited the state organizations to understate membership rather than
to make excessive claims, and the national organization expressed
skepticism at claims as suspiciously low as 250,000. Many Klan
members joined and paid dues only briefly, so these vast numbers
would not have applied for any substantial period, but the organization was very popular in the state between about 1923 and 1925.[12]

In these peak years the Klan made frequent appearances in the
Pennsylvania newspapers, both for regular rituals and parades and
for increasingly frequent acts of violence and confrontation. Some
of their gatherings attracted impressive numbers, often exceed-
ing the religious camp meetings on which they were modeled. On
Independence Day 1924, 10,000 Klansmen and -women met at
Huntingdon, including members "from towns between Williamsport, Harrisburg, Johnstown and the Maryland state line." The
figure did not include guests and family members: "22,000 dinner
tickets were sold. Fourteen hundred members, it is said, were initiated tonight under the light of fiery crosses. Three young couples
were joined in matrimony according to Klan rites."[13]

Aggressive Klan demonstrations and anti-Catholic protests led
to conflict with Catholic groups, and in 1923 and 1924 riots led
to bloodshed in the western towns of Carnegie, Scottdale, and
Lilly. One such fight gave the Klan a celebrated hero in Tom Abbott, the "martyred Klansman" of pamphlet and legend.[14] In July
1924 a still-controversial incident at Haverford College, in Delaware County, left two policemen shot, one of whom (a Catholic)
was killed. Though the press and public opinion generally blamed
the Klan, the organization itself presented the incident (for once,
accurately) as an attack by its enemies, part of a systematic persecution.[15] In response to the continuing violence, the Klan formed
a paramilitary corps of "klavaliers," and the surviving application
forms for this movement are informative about the social and geographical appeal of the Klan.[16]

Like its southern models, the Klan attacked blacks both as communities and as individuals. The Haverford cross-burning in 1924 was intended specifically "to have frightened the Negroes and others out of the section." At Beaver, Klansmen killed a black victim in one of only a handful of lynchings known in the whole history of the state.[17] However, Catholics were overwhelmingly the major targets of hatred and fear. In this view the Catholic church represented tyranny, paganism, immorality, persecution, and every anti-Christian force. The Klan rehearsed the ancient charges of American nativism about Catholic evils, including the Inquisition, the allegedly seditious secret oaths taken by the Knights of Columbus, and the conspiratorial nature of the Jesuit order.[18] Throughout the 1920s there was a substantial industry in lecture tours by purported ex-nuns who revealed the sexual exploitation said to be rampant within the church. They told of the murder of infants and of political plotting undertaken through the Knights of Columbus.[19]

Catholic "aggression" was expressed in the Catholic marriage laws, which denied the validity of Protestant marriage and family life, and in the sectarian schools, which created and sustained a whole alternative society and cultural life.[20] Surging Catholic power threatened to overwhelm American society and values. In the previous century the church in the United States had grown from 50,000 adherents and 35 priests to 20 million faithful with a vast network of clergy, schools, and seminaries.[21] By the 1920s there was a "general staff"—perhaps a provisional government?—in the form of the elaborate bureaucracy of the National Catholic Welfare Council. The nightmare was that all Americans would someday be subjected to this tyranny and that a Catholic would someday attain the presidency. Catholic strength was founded on "Alienism," "the unassimilated hordes of Europe," which threatened American racial purity.[22]

In 1928 Pennsylvania Klan leader Paul Winter published in *What Price Tolerance?* a systematic statement of anti-Catholic ideology that in its basic principles would have been familiar to members of the Know-Nothings or the American Protective Association of the previous century. Soon an apocalyptic struggle would commence between "traditional Americanism and the religious and political invasion of the United States by the champions of European institutions and ideals."[23] "America's Armageddon" would be physical as well as moral, as Catholics had so often showed themselves the masters of subversion and conspiracy.[24] In Philadelphia, for example, the new church of St. Charles Borromeo was being built with very thick walls that appeared suitable for fortification. Was a Catholic putsch imminent? Against the clear menace to the republic, patriotic forces were stirring, naturally including the Klan, but also a number of other groups that collectively comprised what Winter terms "American Nationalism." This coalition included faithful Protestant clergy untainted by ecumenical temptations, and the network of fraternal and patriotic orders, most powerfully the Freemasons. The model for nationalist action was found, ironically, in Mexico, where a determined anticlerical and anti-Catholic social movement had overthrown papal tyranny.[25]

On the national stage the Klan's chief concern was to forestall the further growth of Catholic power and to combat "the great amount of Roman Catholic propaganda being disseminated through the medium of Press, the stage and the movies."[26] At the state level, Klan supporters tried to pass laws restricting Catholic practices, encouraging the Protestant habit of reading the Bible in the public schools, and generally opposing Catholic interests wherever possible. The Pennsylvania Klan supported the efforts of the Anti-Sectarian Appropriations Association, which condemned the grant of state money to Catholic schools and charities.[27] The Klan was above all a Protestant movement whose events were accompanied by well-known hymns such as "The Old Rugged Cross" and "Onward Christian Soldiers." Protestant clergy were prominent in the leadership of this "crusade," "consecrated beneath the fiery cross of militant Protestant Christianity."[28]

The issues motivating the movement were summarized by its most familiar slogans: "America for Americans," "The Open Bible," "We support one school, the free public school," and "Separation of Church and State."[29] In 1928 Winter summarized the basic Klan beliefs as those principles on which nine-tenths of all true Americans would agree: "immigration [control], enforcement of the eighteenth amendment, non-entanglement abroad, farm relief, public education, etc." The movement adhered firmly to the Protestant panacea of Temperance, and it was observed that "Prohibition made the Klan." Klan policies were invariably dressed in the language and rhetoric of pure patriotism, and klaverns or lodges bore patriotic historical names—American Defender, Pride of America, Old Glory, and Lincoln, for example. Klan celebrations were coordinated with patriotic holidays, especially Independence Day.[30]

The Klan recruited heavily through the Freemasons and other fraternal orders. Masonic hostility to the Catholic church was in part a predictable response to the denunciations of the order in the Catholic press, which condemned Masonry as absolutely anti-Christian.[31] Paul Winter termed the Masons "a constant champion of the spirit of liberty and freedom."[32] Other members were drawn from the many societies that had supported the nationalist campaign against foreign immigration, including the Patriotic Order, Sons of America (POS of A), and the Odd Fellows. Philadelphia and Pittsburgh also had lodges of the Orange Order, originally serving immigrants from Ulster and Scotland, but which by the 1920s was attracting an enthusiastic American membership.[33] Throughout these years Pennsylvania Orangemen celebrated great occasions such as the Battle of the Boyne, and in 1939 the Philadelphia gathering attracted over 5,000 supporters.[34] There were also what Winter terms the "traditionary" groups, patriotic organizations whose membership claimed descent from earlier generations of heroes and soldiers, such as the Sons and Daughters of the American Revolution, Colonial Dames, and Grand Army of the Republic.[35] The application forms of potential Klansmen often boast lengthy lists of memberships in fraternal and secret orders as well as traditionary groups.

Partly to appeal to these fraternal and semimystical bodies, the Klan offered a rich mythology and heraldry, with all the mystique implied by its hierarchy of "Hydras, Great Titans, Furies, Giants, Exalted Cyclops, Terrors." The Klan offered a complete language, "kodes" for codes, and an elaborate system of signs and countersigns. The "K" theme extended to place names, so that the Invisible Empire in Pennsylvania came to include regions such as "Krawford Kounty" and "Klarion Kounty."[36] A full klavern required an elaborate hierarchy, with at least a dozen officers from the presiding Cyclops down through his klaliff (deputy), kludd (chaplain), kligrapp (secretary), and klabee (treasurer).

CENTERS OF SUPPORT

Pennsylvania was a realm, under its grand dragon, and was further divided into provinces, each under a great titan. In 1929 the eight regions were respectively headed by titans based at Erie, Wilkinsburg, Punxsutawney, Williamsport, Somerset, York, Slatington, and Philadelphia. By 1936 each of the state's sixty-seven counties constituted its own province.

At its height the Klan achieved remarkable popularity in virtually all parts of the state, but some regions were peculiarly susceptible. Of the 423 klaverns founded between 1923 and 1935, at least one was located in every county except the mid-state rural areas of Snyder and Union. Though lodges varied greatly in size, some were immense. By 1925–26 about sixty klaverns claimed 500 or more members, and even this represented a decline from a year or two previously (see table 3.3).

In the social composition of its Klan members, Pennsylvania amply confirms the evidence from other states about the broad cross-class appeal of the Klan movement. Leonard Moore aptly summarizes the older stereotype of Klan members as "religious fundamentalists, small town bumpkins and ignorant, economically marginal individuals," "unwashed members of society," but correctly notes that many members derived from solid middle-class or skilled working-class households. They were "a wide cross-section of white Protestant society." Furthermore, adherents were motivated by far more than ignorant prejudice, in that Protestant nativism was commonly a vehicle for the populist expression of underlying social and political grievances, focused chiefly on rapid social change and a perceived decline of moral values. In Pennsylvania as in other northern states, Klan support was strong in both large and small communities, but it was especially concentrated in the largest conurbations and in industrial regions. As in Indiana, it could fairly be said of Pennsylvania Klan members that "they were average citizens." [37]

The imperial heartland was to be found in the steel and coal regions of southwestern Pennsylvania, within a fifty-mile radius of Pittsburgh. Allegheny and four contiguous counties accounted for

TABLE 3.2. *Klan Lodges (Klaverns) in Pennsylvania, 1922–1935*

Number of Klaverns	Number of Counties
Over 30	1 (Allegheny, 33)
20–30	2 (Philadelphia, 20; Westmoreland, 21)
10–19	7 (Armstrong, 15; Clearfield, 14; Fayette, 13; Indiana, 10; Luzerne, 13; Schuylkill, 11; Washington, 17)
6–9	19
1–5	36
0	2
Total	67

Source: Klan Archives, Pennsylvania State Archives.

ninety-nine klaverns, some 23 percent of the whole, or 60,000 Klan members in the peak years (the other four counties were Westmoreland, Armstrong, Fayette, and Washington). "Especially strong units were organized in Pittsburgh, New Kensington, Homestead, Mount Pleasant, Johnstown, and Altoona. Many of the klaverns had a membership above five hundred, and few indeed did not enroll more than a hundred members." [38] In 1925 Blair County, with a population of 140,000, had nine klaverns with a combined membership of some 4,500. Armstrong County had fifteen active lodges and 2,543 Klan members out of a population of barely 80,000. Gatherings in this area could be huge affairs, and an Armstrong County rally at West Kittaning drew 25,000 followers. [39] The movement attracted the support of elected officials, including Armstrong County's district attorney. [40]

This regional concentration reflects the lingering ethnic tensions resulting from earlier industrial conflicts, when employers had exploited rivalry between native workers and newer immigrants or blacks. [41] In Allegheny County the great steel strike of 1919 was predominantly undertaken by unskilled immigrants, often Catholics, while the native labor force remained at work. [42] Cambria County steel workers were relatively united, but blacks were recruited to break the strike. There was thus great potential for a movement that affected to represent the native workers against foreign and un-American labor and the alien ideologies they epitomized. By

TABLE 3.3. *Largest Klaverns in Pennsylvania, ca. 1925–1926*

County	Klavern #	Membership	Location
Blair	117	2,805	Altoona
Delaware	350	2,155	Chester
Montgomery	239	1,831	Conshohocken
Cambria	89	1,775	Johnstown
Lawrence	25	1,630	New Castle
York	304	1,518	York
Allegheny	7	1,500	Pittsburgh
Dauphin	263	1,320	Harrisburg
Venango	140	1,235	Oil City
Philadelphia	380	1,216	Germantown
Armstrong	62	1,146	Kittanning
Jefferson	27	1,120	Punxsutawney
Clearfield	53	1,053	Dubois
Allegheny	63	1,005	South Hills
Allegheny	47	970	Pittsburgh
Luzerne	311	929	Wilkes-Barre
Luzerne	292	922	Kingston
Westmoreland	3	919	Greensburg
Philadelphia	359	917	West Philadelphia
Jefferson	60	856	Brookville
Lycoming	205	837	Williamsport
Dauphin	284	823	?
Allegheny	54	828	Homestead
Fayette	128	817	Uniontown
Franklin	119	817	Chambersburg
Cambria	121	815	Barnesboro
Allegheny	73	794	Wilkinsburg
Allegheny	32	791	Pittsburgh
Lackawanna	319	753	Carbondale

Source: Klan Archives, Pennsylvania State Archives.
Note: Only lodges with 750 or more members are included.

1926 Allegheny County had at least 15,000 Klan members, Cambria had 4,000, and membership lists often show the importance of skilled workers and foremen as well as petit bourgeois groups such as shopkeepers.

Religious conflict also masked the struggle of older, established
immigrant groups such as the British and the Germans to preserve their privileged employment position in the face of newer groups. For the Germans there was the additional incentive of publicly reasserting their American loyalism, which had been under attack in the war years. Though Klan membership was reserved for native-born Americans, naturalized individuals from these favored Protestant groups could join the affiliated order of American Krusaders.[43]

These conditions also applied in the anthracite region in eastern and northeastern Pennsylvania, where there were long traditions of conflict between older Protestant groups such as the Welsh with Catholics like the Irish, Poles, Slovaks, and Italians. Fifty-seven of the state's 423 klaverns were located in the eight anthracite counties centered on Scranton, Wilkes-Barre, Pottsville, and Hazleton. At its height this may have represented 30,000 to 40,000 members. Luzerne County was a local stronghold, with no less than thirteen klaverns, while Schuylkill had eleven, so that these two counties alone had 10,000 members between them by 1924. Loucks describes Luzerne, Carbon, Lehigh, and Schuylkill Counties as a major regional center of Klan activity, an eastern parallel to the Pittsburgh region. The anthracite country became one of the eight provinces of the Invisible Empire.

Within the industrial areas, the movement exercised a broad appeal. In Westmoreland County the klavalier enlistment forms of 124 individuals between 1924 and 1926 show that the Klan appealed to both unskilled labor (twenty-two laborers) and skilled industrial workers.[44] There were two draftsmen, six carpenters, and four electricians. All the major industries were represented: steel, coal, textiles, and aluminum. Laborers apart, the largest single categories were clerks and cashiers (thirteen), followed by truck drivers (twelve). There were independent tradesmen (eight butchers, bakers, and blacksmiths) and two farmers. There were also a few foremen and managers, and one student. Similar figures emerge from other counties, the exact balance depending on the economic focus of the area in question. In Indiana County, seventeen of twenty-four klavalier applicants were from the mining industry, but we also find a student and a principal. In Carbon County the railroad was clearly the major source of support among the fifty-seven applicants. We find five trainmen, two railroad engineers, two firemen, a motorman, and a railroad clerk in addition to the normal range of trades, skilled and unskilled, including fourteen laborers.

I have suggested that the appeal of the Klan should be located in hostility or fear toward those ethnic and religious groups that appeared to challenge white Protestant hegemony, especially in the industrial context. This rather traditional view contradicts the argument of Moore and others that the Klan found its most intense support in solidly native-stock areas where the direct minority challenge was very slight. While the Pennsylvania Klan was indeed strongest in native communities, these did indeed have some plausible reason to fear incursions or pressure from minorities and the foreign born, either in the form of strikebreaking or of changing residential patterns. It could genuinely be argued that Philadelphia and other cities had witnessed a vast increase in the influence of new ethnic groups who required only somewhat improved coordination to achieve political control, and these examples were naturally disturbing to the residents of neighboring cities or regions. Though ethnic and religious rivalries may often have represented symbolic crusades against other social problems, this does not mean that those tensions were merely superficial.

DECLINE

The heyday of the Klan was between 1923 and 1925, but the organization's success was short lived. Devastating scandals crippled the national leadership, and membership plummeted. According to Loucks, Pennsylvania membership fell from a quarter of a million in 1924 to perhaps 20,000 by 1928, and under 5,000 by 1930.[45] There was a brief revival in 1928, in "the battle to prevent the Roman hierarchy from seating Mr. Al Smith in the presidential chair,"[46] but this had little lasting effect. In John O'Hara's fictional version of Pottsville, the 1928 election caused a number of Klansmen to declare themselves publicly, but to no avail.[47] Loucks argues that the Klan's enthusiasm in this campaign may actually have bolstered the Democratic vote by galvanizing Catholic electoral strength.[48]

The depression was a severe blow, drying up any spare income that might once have been available for robes and membership

dues. At Titusville in Crawford County, klavern #208, Colonel
Drake, had eighty-eight members in 1926. In 1932 the lodge's report lamented that it "has been hard hit by the Depression since the several small industries at Titusville have been closed up most of the time. Some of the good Klansmen have moved away and there are only about four or five left as a nucleus to start with." Many klaverns disappeared altogether, even some that had claimed a thousand members in 1925. Shrinking numbers were a particular problem because Klan rituals were quite labor intensive, and in order to be fully operative a klavern required at least a dozen members to fill the various offices. When a group fell significantly below this figure, continued existence was imperiled, and by the early 1930s many of the existing klaverns were reduced to three or four dues-paying members. The most noticeable change was in the greater Pittsburgh area, where only a handful of anemic cells survived. Of the fifty-four klaverns in Allegheny and Westmoreland Counties, only two remained by 1938, with some twenty-six members in total. In 1936 the titan of Reading-based province six reported "no activities in the province during the year. Only a handful and nothing to work with. . . . Plenty of talk, no action."[49]

THE 1930S

Some Klan lodges remained, in parts of the southwest, in Philadelphia, and in the anthracite country. By 1933 there were traces (often ghostly) of perhaps 140 klaverns in the state, perhaps a third of the original total. Ten of these could mobilize forty or more members in good standing, and a number of other lodges retained the loyalty of a respectable hard core. The impressive figures for Fayette County and other mining regions suggest how closely Klan fortunes had become linked to antiunion movements, and it was generally believed that coal country klaverns were sponsored by the mineowners. By 1930 Pennsylvania reported the largest Klan membership of any state.

That the Klan did not fade away overnight is suggested by the experience of Philadelphia County, where twenty lodges were founded during the 1920s. In 1925 fourteen of these had memberships in excess of 300, and #380 (Robert Morris) exceeded 1,000. Even by 1933 there were still at least sixteen active klaverns, with a total of 700 to 800 members. The William Penn klavern in West

TABLE 3.4. *Largest Klaverns in Pennsylvania, 1933*
(excluding Philadelphia)

County	Klavern #	Membership	Location
Westmoreland	29	26	Turtle Creek
Allegheny	63	20	South Hills
Franklin	119	70	Chambersburg
Fayette	128	52	Uniontown
Lycoming	205	42	Williamsport
Lehigh	210	23	Schnecksville
Montgomery	234	25	Ardmore
Schuylkill	236	44	Schuylkill Haven
Montgomery	239	26	Hickory Hill
Schuylkill	277	27	Tower City
York	304	55	York
Luzerne	311	23	Rescue
Fayette	345	40	Fort Mason
Northampton	365	28	Easton
Fayette	422	46	Rowes Run

Source: Klan Archives, Pennsylvania State Archives.

Philadelphia, "mother Klan of Philadelphia," was probably the largest in the state at this point. This does not take account of substantial suburban membership in the counties of Delaware and Montgomery. There were several concentrations of influence, especially in traditional white Protestant suburbs north of the central city, in Germantown, Manayunk, Roxborough, Olney, Frankford, and the northeast, in the Fifth and Seventh congressional districts. These sections were concerned about the northward spread of nearby "alien" communities, whether Catholic, black, or Jewish. In West Philadelphia too, Klan activity can be seen as a response to black and Jewish dispersal from the city's traditional core.[50]

There would be a long continuity of rightist movements in these areas. In the late 1930s the drills and rallies of the German American Bund usually occurred in the area of 6th Street and Erie Avenue, a few blocks from the gathering place of two klaverns, Spirit of 76 and Penn Treaty, and conveniently close to the old Ben Franklin. In 1933 the Khaki Shirts would also be based nearby, at

Klavern #	Name	Meeting Place, 1933
289	Liberty Bell	2634 N. 34th St.
290		Comly and Cottage, Frankford
358	Cradle of Liberty	2849 Frankford Ave., Kensington
359	William Penn	62nd and Jefferson, West Philadelphia
360	Warren G. Harding	2214 Germantown Ave.
362	George Washington	Broad and Federal, South Philadelphia
375	Paul Jones	52nd and Girard, West Philadelphia
378	Daniel Webster	205–7 East Tioga, Kensington
379	Independence	POS of A Hall, Roxborough
380	Robert Morris	6656–58 Germantown Ave., Germantown
382	Nathan Hale	1345 Clearfield St.
383	Spirit of 76	Germantown and Erie Aves.
385	Old Glory	71st and Woodland, West Philadelphia
404	Loyalty	23rd and Ridge
406	Ben Franklin	Rising Sun Ave., Olney
420	Penn Treaty	Germantown and Erie Aves.

Source: Klan Archives, Pennsylvania State Archives.

Broad and Blavis in Hunting Park.[51] These northern areas included the last bastions of Republican electoral strength at the height of the New Deal era. In 1936 the northwestern sections of Germantown and Manayunk (wards 21 and 22) were two of only seven wards in the city to vote heavily Republican. In what was otherwise a dreadful year for the party, these two populous wards gave the Republicans 55 percent of the local vote, while the Democrats carried the city by a three-to-two margin. In 1940 the Seventh District (to the northwest) provided the city's only Republican congressman, out of seven, and the area voted overwhelmingly for Wendell Willkie in another year that Roosevelt carried Philadelphia convincingly. In 1938 the Fifth District in northeastern Philadelphia elected a Bund ally, Fred C. Gartner, to the U.S. House of Representatives.

Though a pallid reflection of its earlier strength, the Klan in 1933 could hope for better days. Its organizational structure remained intact, if battered, while the continuing significance of ethnic and racial tensions gave it the potential to survive as a pressure group in both urban and small-town politics. Anti-Catholicism remained a sensitive political issue throughout the decade and was easily mobilized against the Democrats. This issue won the 1935 Philadelphia mayoralty election for the Republicans.[52] In 1938 three of the four major contenders for the Democratic gubernatorial nomination were Catholic, and Senator Guffey was nervous about the potential of an electoral backlash (the three were Margiotti, Kennedy, and Lawrence). Even Harold Ickes was worried that the Pennsylvania Democratic Party was "too predominantly Catholic." In 1938 a Klan handbill noted the religious composition of the candidates for office in Allegheny County: thirty-three of forty Republican candidates were Protestant, but only nine Democrats, sustaining charges of a "Romanized Democratic party in the North." Not until 1944 did a Catholic represent Pennsylvania in the U.S. Senate. Republicans regularly smeared their opponents by associating them with Italian and Jewish organized crime syndicates, emphasizing their foreign and un-American character.[53]

THE CRISIS

Continued anti-Catholic sentiment could not save the Klan. Membership continued to shrink in the mid-1930s, so that by 1938 there were barely 400 active klansmen in the whole of Pennsylvania, organized in twenty-five active klaverns. No fewer than ten of these had memberships in the single digits, confirming the general picture that this was a movement on the verge of extinction. Red Star klavern at Ardmore, Montgomery County, had twenty-five members in 1934 and could fill all necessary ritual offices. It had five members by 1938 and ceased to be recorded by 1940. Watsontown in Northumberland County fluctuated between two and six members throughout the decade, but it too had given up the struggle by 1940. Remaining support elsewhere in the state was at best patchy, with strong units only in Fayette County, with its 117 members, and with the active groups in York (#304) and Chambersburg (#119).

Most Philadelphia klaverns collapsed in these years. Even including the two adjacent counties of Montgomery and Delaware, there were barely a hundred Klansmen left in the whole of south-

TABLE 3.6. *The Decline of the Philadelphia Klan, 1933–1940*

Klavern #	Name	Active Members[a]		
		1933	1938	1940
289	Liberty Bell	?		
290		?		
358	Cradle of Liberty	32	26	15
359	William Penn	79	11	6
360	Warren G. Harding	?		
362	George Washington	50	6	
375	Paul Jones	?		
378	Daniel Webster	?		
379	Independence	41	9	
380	Robert Morris	34	16	24
382	Nathan Hale	?		
383	Spirit of 76	?		
385	Old Glory	16	11	8
404	Loyalty	?		
406	Ben Franklin	10		
420	Penn Treaty	29		

Source: Klan Archives, Pennsylvania State Archives.
a. Blank cells indicate Klavern no longer in existence or cannot be traced.

eastern Pennsylvania by 1938 (see table 3.6). In 1936 an already battered organization suffered renewed stigma from the exposure of the pseudo-Klan terrorist group known as the Black Legion, which operated in the Midwest. The last new Pennsylvania klavern was founded in 1935, in Harrisburg, and the following year Loucks's book looked distinctly like an obituary.

THE KLAN REVIVAL, 1938–1940

In the late 1930s the national Ku Klux Klan sought to resuscitate itself by participating in the general growth on the far Right. In order to achieve this, the movement now affected to mute traditional anti-Catholic prejudice and to emphasize instead the evils of "Communism and the CIO." [54] In 1939 former imperial wizard Hiram W. Evans was present at the dedication of a Catholic cathedral in Atlanta, where he shook the hand of Philadelphia's Cardinal

Dougherty.[55] The irenic policy was developed under Evans's successor J. A. Colescott, who urged the Klan to shift its emphasis to the unions. Followers were to "get into every local, every department, division and plant. . . . The UAW and CIO leaders are all Reds—we must Americanize them through Kluxing every white, Protestant, Gentile American." [56]

Catholic authorities remained unimpressed by the apparent change of heart, and the Philadelphia *Catholic Standard and Times* noted sarcastically how the Klan had taken "the old platform of saving the country from the kike, koon and katholic, and has added kommunism." [57] But the antilabor focus was realistic, given the movement's traditional roots in what had become the battlegrounds of CIO organization. The Klan could also hope to benefit from anti-immigration sentiment. By 1939 a recruitment leaflet listed the organization's key beliefs: "Ku Klux Klan Rides Again! Pro-Protestant, Christian, White, militant organization—believes we should register and fingerprint all aliens. Stop immigration for ten years. Deport all aliens and undesirables. . . . Protect the public school. Keep America Protestant. Put none but Americans on guard. Do you believe in Protestant Christian America?"

Nationwide the Klan revival enjoyed some success, claiming an increase in membership of 30 percent in the year following mid-1939.[58] In Pennsylvania, too, there were signs of new life, based on the activism of the state's grand dragon Samuel Stouch, who also ruled the Invisible Empire in Delaware and New Jersey (he adopted the nom de plume "Deljerpen"). He headed klavern #380 and briefly arrested its decline. Stouch mounted a membership drive, contacting former Klan officials from the 1920s and urging them to resume their activities.[59] The revived Klan attracted some support in German areas, in upstate counties "where English is by no means the daily language of the countryside." [60] His correspondence suggests that the prospective klansmen now targeted were not the industrial workers of the 1920s but small businessmen and contractors, who usually had a lengthy record of membership in fraternal orders and societies. "The Klan is concentrating on recruiting members among city and state officials, particularly in the police department, the school system and the courts." [61]

By 1940 it was remarked that "Kluxers in every part of the country have a high respect for Stouch, not only because of the manner in which he has reorganized the Klan in Pennsylvania, but also because he is an intimate friend of J. A. Colescott." [62] In early 1940 Philadelphia was reportedly the setting of a secret weekend convention of East Coast Klan leaders, in which Colescott urged a return to "moralistic" themes, advocating law and order, combating immorality and underage drinking, and urging new coalitions based on a revival of the white Protestant interest.[63]

THE PROTESTANT INTEREST

These points closely foreshadowed the actual course of Stouch's revival campaign in Philadelphia, where he placed the Klan at the head of a renewed Protestant nativist movement. Anti-Catholic prejudice had diminished since the terrifying confrontations of the mid- and late nineteenth century but had never entirely vanished. In 1935 even the anti-Semitic tinge of Davis Wilson's mayoral campaign had not prevented him from garnering a majority of Jewish voters, who joined Protestants in a curious coalition against the Catholic John B. Kelly.[64] Fears of Catholic intolerance were kept alive by sporadic confrontations between the local media and the archdiocese, headed by the authoritarian figure of Cardinal Dougherty, who campaigned tirelessly to ensure that no motion picture or news story ever came close to offending delicate Catholic sensibilities.

In 1939 the rise of the Coughlinite Christian Front added a new edge to the Catholic danger, and in March Catholic activists disrupted a religious tolerance meeting sponsored by leading Protestant clergy. In response to this and similar episodes, the Protestant clergy of the Philadelphia Federation of Churches initiated a number of political groups, including the League for Protestant Action, which sought to "arouse the Protestant constituency of metropolitan Philadelphia." [65] The group carefully mapped the city's wards and Protestant churches with a view to mobilizing electoral strength. The leadership included some powerful ministers, including Daniel A. Poling, one of the city's most respected civic leaders. A Baptist and editor of *Christian Herald*, he ran for mayor on a reform ticket in 1951. It is therefore remarkable to find such individuals in a group viewed by the Catholic archdiocese as a "new Anti-Catholic society." [66]

Despite its impeccable credentials, the league attracted the support of anti-Catholic militants, including the Orange lodges, and Stouch served on the Executive Committee.[67] The league became one of several anti-Catholic groups in which he was active, including the Protestant Cooperative League and the American Protestant Defense League, with its newspaper, *American Protestant*.[68] In the 1940 election Stouch supported the league's efforts to coordinate the Protestant vote in the Republican cause, in opposition to those "racial and sectarian groups . . . ascendant in our political life of today."[69] It is ironic that a group that began as a response to perceived acts of intolerance was so coopted by the Klan.[70]

In Pittsburgh, too, the activities of Father Coughlin were blamed for the fact that "ancient fears of the Inquisition, hangings and burnings and living in caves and dens in the Scotch mountains, racial memories of the hideous Thirty Years War, are stirring again in Protestant breasts."[71] The failure of the Catholic hierarchy explicitly to condemn Coughlin raised the fears of even liberal Protestants about "Catholic power" and the possibility of a future president of that faith. For Klan followers past and present, the Coughlin episode was a vindication of their darkest prophecies.[72]

FAILURE

In the spring of 1940 Catholic and antifascist newspapers reported an apparent revival of the Klan in northeastern and midwestern states, and Catholic papers published cartoons of robed Klan figures starting conflagrations labeled simply "Hate."[73] However, this was to give the Invisible Empire too much credit, for the Klan's new visibility was not reflected in the membership figures. *The Hour* reported Klan claims of 90,000 members in the state, but in reality membership in mid-1940 had fallen below 250 men (membership of the women's lodges in more difficult to assess).[74] This was perhaps one-thousandth of the figure in the Coolidge era. There were now only seventeen klaverns in good standing, and only a handful had twenty or more dues-paying male members. Apart from the familiar center of Uniontown, the most intense activity was in Stouch's immediate vicinity, in Philadelphia. The new map of Klan activities shows that the movement had ceased to function in several traditional heartlands, including the counties of Jefferson, Clearfield, Lancaster, and Delaware. These losses were not compensated by new or reformed klaverns.

TABLE 3.7. *The Pennsylvania Klan, 1938–1940*

Klavern #	County	Name	Members[a] 1938	1940
1		Provisional		22
3	Westmoreland		14	
27	Jefferson		9	
34	Jefferson		8	
63	Allegheny	South Hills	12	15
119	Franklin	Mount Parnell, Chambersburg	27	18
128	Fayette	Uniontown	62	39
160	Fayette	Francis Marion Clelland, Vanderbilt	14	7
187	Clearfield		3	
205	Lycoming	Calvin R. Butler, Williamsport	11?	7
225		Lester C. Kiser		16
234	Montgomery		5	
236	Schuylkill		10	
239	Montgomery	Hickory Hill	9	10
256	Chester	Bonnie Brae	21	16
260	Chester		10	
293	Northumberland		5	
304	York		25	13
311	Wilkes-Barre	Rescue		14
336	Lancaster		12	
342	Delaware		6	
345	Fayette	Fort Mason	41	13
358	Philadelphia	Cradle of Liberty	26	15
359	Philadelphia	William Penn		6
362	Philadelphia		6	
365	Northampton		6	
379	Philadelphia		9	
380	Philadelphia	Robert Morris	16	24
385	Philadelphia	Old Glory	11	8
423	Dauphin	John Harris	18	6

Source: Klan Archives, Pennsylvania State Archives.
a. Blank cells indicate Klavern not in evidence at this date.

Moreover, these figures reflect the situation in August 1940, before the Klan undertook paramilitary exercises with the German American Bund and incited predictable schisms and desertions. The Ku Klux Klan in Pennsylvania was virtually eradicated before the outbreak of war.

THE KLAN INHERITANCE

The continuous decline of the Pennsylvania Klan after 1930 does not mean that the movement ceased to exercise influence in these years. The Klan served as a vehicle for disseminating ideas and theories that would be important for later groups, and some continuity can be traced in both individuals and communities. In terms of ideology the dominant anti-Catholicism of the 1920s mutated as the Klan shrank to an activist hard core. From the early 1930s surviving Klan members evinced more interest in European political and racial theories, and anti-Semitism came to the fore. The chief nightmare was no longer the loss of American liberties in the face of papal aggression but the "mongrelization" of American racial stock by alien races, and the movement early expressed its admiration for Hitler.[75] When Samuel Stouch's archives and library were stolen in 1940, they contained a substantial corpus of overtly Nazi material, much printed in Germany, as well as the newspapers and pamphlets of domestic anti-Semitic groups.

Stouch's anti-Semitism is indicated by his political correspondence. One Klan friend was G. Harry Davidson, who wrote in 1940 that German Jews might be only 1 percent of the population but they "had stolen 95 percent of Germany's law, medicine and educational practice, besides a corner of mercantile and finance, a strangled press, and a state within a state, *as they have almost complete here in America.*"[76] By this point Jews had become the major targets of the charges that fifteen years previously had been levied against the Catholics about their sinister and secretive practices, their lust for dictatorship, and their craving to destroy American liberties. The Communist Party came to occupy a role similar to that of the Knights of Columbus as the clandestine arm of the particular religious conspiracy in question.[77]

The Klan's growing anti-Semitism caused ideological difficulties, especially since so many of the potential allies on the far Right were either Catholic or linked to unpopular foreign rulers.

Stouch continued to subscribe to a number of militant Protestant and Orange publications for whom Hitler, Mussolini, and above all Franco were loathsome dictators subservient to the church of Rome, and who persecuted the Masonic order. However, neither he nor other Klan militants found this an insuperable objection to cooperation with newer fascist groups or to even closer relationships. The White Shirts, for example, were anti-Catholic and anti-Communist, but not anti-Jewish, while the Silver Legion had an anti-Catholic streak.[78]

Though Pelley himself was not anti-Catholic, some of his subordinates failed to share his relative tolerance. In Philadelphia Paul Von Lilienfeld-Toal was uncertain whether Catholics could join without renouncing the Pope and swearing allegiance "to the Silver Legion and our beloved chief." One of the national leaders of the Silver Shirts was Harry F. Sieber from Wynnewood, Pennsylvania, who was an active Klan organizer in the Philadelphia area and Delaware and a frequent correspondent of Stouch, while other Philadelphia Silver Shirts can be identified as former Klansmen. In Pittsburgh, Silver Shirt organizer Charles B. Swift combined traditional themes when in 1938 he denounced the leftist Catholic priests who were supporting the "Damnable reds" of the CIO, specifically "Communist Papist" union boss Philip Murray.[79]

PAUL M. WINTER

A few Klansmen became associated with the most extreme fascist and anti-Semitic movements. The most important was Paul Meres Winter, who from the early 1920s emerged as one of the Klan's most effective evangelists and who served as the personal representative of Hiram W. Evans in the wealthy Philadelphia klaverns. In a striking portent of his later political allegiance, Winter earned notoriety by forming a personal elite bodyguard and enforcement squad known as the Super-Secret Society, the SSS (at this early date the similarity of name to the German SS is assuredly coincidental). The Night Riders of this "Black-Robed Gang" beat and intimidated opponents who questioned Winter's financial dealings. Winter's tactics included the public exposure of the Klan membership of his opponents, seeking thereby to attract boycotts and demonstrations against them by Catholics and other hostile groups.[80] His critics accused him of "building up a far more autocratic organization than Rome ever dared to build." In 1925–26 the Philadelphia Klans were riven by violence, lawsuits, and spectacular mutual expulsions. One "banishment" alone involved the whole strength of the Warren G. Harding klavern, some 550 members.

In light of his later associations it is noteworthy that Winter absolutely rejected Italian Fascism as un-American. In 1928 he identified the movement as an arm of the Romanist cause, both in Mussolini's regime and in the Italian American groups enjoying such a vogue in the contemporary United States, and his excoriation of the "Black Shirts in America" is as thorough as that of any socialist or anti-Fascist source at the time.[81] "To the Nordic Nationalists, the organization of posts of *Fascisti* in the United States is an attempt on the part of Benito Mussolini, Dictator of Italy, to spread the dark tentacles of the *Fascisti* spider around the Italians of America."[82] Like his papal masters, Mussolini represented tyranny, brutality, and international aggression: "Bolshevism and Fascism are apparently the two militant ideals of European political turmoil, which America has inherited from the alien invasion."[83] At this stage, moreover, his anti-Semitism was not particularly marked, and when Jews were denounced, it was usually in the context of being party to Catholic abuses. For example, Jews conspired with the Catholic hierarchy to dominate the motion picture industry.

Despite this, Winter's book *What Price Tolerance?* gives a few signs of the author's later political development. His worldview is founded on a stark conflict between "American Nationalism" and the conspiracies of "Political Romanism," which also involve "alienism, Bolshevism, internationalism, political debauchery and lawlessness."[84] American democracy was under threat from the machinations of the "three international capitals—Rome, Moscow, and Wall Street," though even here the sin of Wall Street is that it is pro-Catholic rather than subservient to Jewish interests. Also, Winter is well versed in racial theories. Both he and his movement are "Nordic" and therefore opposed to "anything emanating from the Latin countries."[85] "America is fundamentally Nordic and Anglo-Saxon"[86] and as such needed to rediscover the Nordic heritage concealed by the Catholic historians. This land is in truth *Amt-Erica*, the land found and named by the Viking Eric the Red rather than the Latin Catholic impostor and plagiarist Columbus.[87]

By this stage Winter's fears were clearly taking more account of
Communist subversion, a tendency encouraged by the upsurge of
radical sympathy during the Sacco-Vanzetti case.[88]

In the next decade Paul Winter's American Nationalism took a
decided anti-Semitic and pro-German slant. He moved to Shavertown, near Wilkes-Barre, where he led klavern #311, Rescue, in
Wilkes-Barre and was presumably the chief activist of the anti-
Semitic Civil Intelligence Bureau reported active there in 1940.[89]
There is a striking portrait of the Shavertown circle in Carlson's
book *Under Cover*. While under cover as an Italian Fascist, Carlson interviewed Winter, "a Legionnaire . . . and distributor of
Nazi pamphlets direct from Berlin."[90] Winter's closest political
associates included well-known anti-Semitic propagandist Elizabeth Dilling and Edwin Flaig, a German who lived at Millvale
near Pittsburgh. Flaig claimed personal acquaintance with Göring,
Frick, and other Nazi leaders. A pronounced anti-Semite, he had
attended Hitler rallies in Germany and looked forward to the day
when Hitler would use mustard gas against New York City.[91] He
was involved in gunrunning and boasted of the existence of armed
Nazi groups in the Pittsburgh area, often disguised as rifle or sporting clubs. After all, "Jew hunting is going to be pretty good soon,
and we are practicing."[92] "The boys" would "dynamite Detroit,
Pittsburgh, Chicago—paralyze transportation and isolate whole
sections of the country. . . . A blood bath is the only way out."
Flaig's Hunter's Lodge at Millvale was described as the operational
base of "American Nazi-dom's traveling emissary," Olov Tietzow,
leader of the American Guard.[93] Flaig was also in touch with the
Silver Shirts.[94]

Another Winter contact was James B. True, whom Flaig reported meeting at Shavertown in 1939 and who had bought some of
Flaig's firearms. True was an anti-Semitic fanatic of national reputation who denounced "the Jew Communism which the New Deal
is trying to force on America." He attempted to patent a type of
billy club under the title of "Kike Killers" and published the anti-
Semitic news-sheet *Industrial Control Reports* (Stouch was a sub-
scriber).[95] He wished "to return the United States from a Talmu-
dic dictatorship to its original republican form of government."[96]
Another friend of both Winter and True was Robert E. Edmondson, publisher of the Nazi *American Vigilante Bulletin*, which at-

tacked J. Edgar Hoover as too liberal and leftist.[97] Like most members of this circle, he also believed that Roosevelt was a Jew. Edmondson was originally based in New York City, but in 1939 his Edmondson Economic Service moved to the remote Luzerne County community of Stoddartsville, from which he published his *American Vigilante* bulletins. This choice of refuge is difficult to explain without assuming the importance of proximity to Winter.[98]

The cases of Stouch and Winter suggest how far the older Klan ideology of Protestant Americanism had been attached to newer theories based on anti-Semitism and ultimately to be subsumed by these approaches. During the 1930s nativist politics were transformed under the influence of shirt ideologies that ultimately stemmed from European movements, the most significant of which was originally Italian Fascism. Ironically the American far Right was thus reshaped by a movement whose adherents represented all that the Klan feared and condemned, who were not only aliens of Mediterranean stock, but Catholics.

hough not remotely as notorious at the time, Italian Fascist groups developed in the United States in almost exactly the same years as the Klan and enjoyed a similarly explosive growth from about 1922 onward. However, they retained their influence long after the White Giant had become a discredited joke.

Pro-Fascist organizations developed in the United States shortly after Mussolini's seizure of power in 1922. The controlling body was the FLNA, and by 1923 a Fascist Central Council was based in New York City.[1] This central command was soon coordinating the activities of some 120 individual *fasci*, or party units. American movements were closely affiliated with the Fascist Party hierarchy in Italy, despite halfhearted pretenses to the contrary. In October 1925, for example, the first American convention of the American *fasci*, in Philadelphia, proclaimed the national autonomy of American Fascism.[2] However, the convention was chaired by a member of the national directorate of the Fascist Party in Italy, and contacts remained close over the years.

Italian intervention in American affairs became controversial in the late 1920s and was denounced by both nativists and liberals.[3] There were thousands of protests against the admission to the United States of Fascist organizer Ignazio Thaon di Revel, while the U.S. government was pressed to refuse naturalization to any member of the FLNA. In 1929 *Harper's* magazine published an influential exposé that portrayed Italian Americans being subjected to a whole invisible empire controlled from Rome, complete with Fascist courts, schools, and even taxes—an ironic echo of the traditional rhetoric of anti-Catholicism.[4] The ensuing diplomatic conflict might have been worse if both countries had not been distracted by growing economic woes. In the event, this campaign forced Italian authorities to play down the overtly Fascist nature of their propaganda and in 1930 to replace the FLNA with the more discreet Lictor Federation. (This was a thin enough disguise, given that the name *lictor* referred to the Roman official who carried the *fasces*). Thereafter, Fascist efforts were concentrated on the cultural and fraternal societies, which became vehicles for their ideology and propaganda. Affiliates of the Lictor Federation or United Front included the Italian Historical Society, the Dante Alighieri Society, the Federation of Italian World War Veterans (Combattenti and disabled Mutilati), the Dopolavoro clubs, and individual *circoli* named after Italian heroes.[5]

As with the German American Nazis, American Fascists acted in concert with a foreign government and intelligence service, in this case Mussolini's secret police, OVRA.[6] Activity was coordinated through the Bureau of Italians Abroad, the success of which may have inspired later German equivalents such as the Auslands-Organization and the Gau Ausland. Except for the 1929 controversy, though, this particular brand of foreign dabbling in American life never excited the concern attracted by the German groups.[7] Italian American Fascism remained a flourishing tradition at least until the American entry into war.

The general tolerance of Italian American Fascism reflected the ambiguous attitude toward the Mussolini regime in the international context. In the 1920s the Fascist government won American friends by its staunch anti-Communism combined with experiments in social progressivism and technocracy. Though Mussolini was discredited in the 1930s by association with Hitler and his aggressive policies in Ethiopia and Spain, it appeared probable up to 1939 that the Italian dictator might serve as an essential counterweight to German expansionism.

Pro-Fascist sentiments were expressed by groups and individuals who by no means shared a wholehearted ideological commitment to the movement.[8] In a comparison that would long haunt the movement, American Legion chief Alvin Owsley declared that "the *Fascisti* are to Italy what the American Legion is to the United States," and Mussolini was invited to address the legion's national convention.[9] In 1932 Pennsylvania senator David Reed announced that "I do not often envy other countries their governments, but I say that if this country ever needed a Mussolini it needs one now."[10] The following year he explained that "Signor Mussolini has given Italy a particularly strong and stable government; he has restored order where once chaos ruled; he has increased productive capacity of Italy and has conferred happiness upon all classes, high and low, the rich and the poor."[11] In 1929 Philadelphia mayor Harry A. Mackey praised "the Duce of new and inspired Italy. Your illuminated statesmanship has added many glorious pages to the history of the Eternal City."[12]

With powerful admirers beyond the Italian community, it is not surprising that Fascism attracted at least the sympathy of many Italian Americans. Among the extremist movements of these years, only the Klan succeeded in establishing itself as firmly in the political mainstream, and even that organization could retain this position for only a few years, far less than the two-decade-long reign of the Fascists. Fascist leaders and organizations never experienced the same massive stigma that subsequently attached to their Klan or Nazi counterparts. Long after the death of Mussolini and the elimination of Fascism in Italy itself, the individuals who dominated American Fascism retained their powerful social positions and political offices. If only for its success in avoiding purges and ostracism, Italian Fascism should perhaps be regarded as among the most successful extremist movements in American history.

THE FASCISTI IN PENNSYLVANIA

With its strong Italian American presence, Pennsylvania naturally contained many of the centers of Fascist activism. In 1930 226,000 Pennsylvanians had been born in Italy, making this the largest Italian American community outside the state of New York, and Philadelphia probably had around 200,000 people of Italian descent, around a tenth of the whole.[13] There were 69,000 foreign-born Italian speakers in Philadelphia and 5,600 more in the neighboring New Jersey city of Camden, with which Philadelphia had close social and economic affinities. Eighteen thousand claimed Italian as the "mother tongue" in Pittsburgh, 4,000 in Scranton, and 3,000 in Erie. Aliquippa, New Castle, Altoona, Hazleton, Norristown, and Reading all boasted between 2,000 and 3,000 residents in this category. By 1940 Philadelphia had three Italian-language papers, Pittsburgh had two, and there was one each in the counties of Berks (Reading), Bucks (Bristol), and Westmoreland (Greensburg).

Italians were especially likely to live in close-knit neighborhoods, such as the Pittsburgh communities of Bloomfield and East Liberty or the enclaves in anthracite communities such as Pittston, Old Forge, and Hazleton.[14] Philadelphia's Italian Americans demonstrated a degree of residential segregation rivaled only by blacks, creating in South Philadelphia a self-contained Italian city in miniature clustered around its Catholic churches. Apart from the parishes, a complex social network was based chiefly on fraternal orders such as the OFDI. This community looked to Charles Baldi as "*padrone* or feudal lord," "undisputed leader of the Italian colony in Philadelphia." By the 1920s his Italian Federation of Societies had some thirty-one constituent organizations in the state, including religious, regional, fraternal, and mutual aid clubs.[15]

Mussolini's success was greeted in these circles as a reaffirmation of national pride, the salvation of the nation from anarchy and irreligion. The achievement buoyed the morale of Italian Americans, who perceived themselves as victims of a dual assault from the Ku Klux Klan and the anti-immigration campaign. After the Fascist seizure of power, "Nobody called us wops."[16] In the 1920s the lawyer Michael Angelo Musmanno boasted in the *Pittsburgh Press* of "the heroic work of the Fascisti in driving Bolshevism from the country, when the *Fascisti* began their purification of Italian soil."[17] Musmanno was a law student in Rome in the 1920s, when he interviewed the Duce personally, and attended lectures by great Italian criminologists who proved scientifically that Lenin and other Communists bore criminal personalities.[18] In the following decade, as a Pennsylvania judge, he was celebrated as a liberal

New Dealer and a supporter of organized labor who campaigned to outlaw the coal and iron police. However, he never lost his loathing for Communism or his taste for sweeping and authoritarian solutions to this social menace.[19]

Others retained their early enthusiasm more consistently and supported the emerging Fascist movement in North America. Philadelphia's *fascio*, or party unit, was founded in 1921, even before the March on Rome, and by 1924 the *fascio* announced that it was operating "according to directions issued by the central headquarters at Rome."[20] By the late 1920s *fasci* had been established in Pittsburgh and Camden, and in 1934 Pennsylvania *fasci* were well represented in the New York celebrations of the "Birthday of Fascism."[21] Reading sent a telegram to "greet in a Fascist fashion" both the consular authorities and old party leaders such as Thaon di Revel, concluding, "We swear loyalty to *Il Duce*."

The most significant Fascist leader in the state was Philadelphia-based attorney Giovanni (John) DiSilvestro, acting Italian consul in the city and subsequently legal adviser to the consulate. He succeeded to much of the local influence held by Baldi prior to the latter's death in 1930. As with Mussolini, DiSilvestro's political odyssey had carried him from the extreme Left to the diametrically opposite pole, so that he became a fanatical exponent of "Fascism, in which are identified the Italian Nation and its people."[22] DiSilvestro held a vital institutional status as supreme venerable, or national head, of the OFDI from 1921 to 1935.[23] This position permitted him to intervene in pre-Fascist Italian politics and subsequently to mobilize American support for Mussolini. He was "more than ordinarily zealous in his championing of the dictatorship of his friend, the Italian Premier, Benito Mussolini."[24] As first president of the Fascist General Council in North America, Di Silvestro also pledged the support of 300,000 Sons of Italy to the man whose "rise as the ruler of the Fatherland will give back to the Nation her old faith and the spiritual discipline necessary to dare and to succeed."[25] Mussolini accepted this allegiance, "wishing that all the Sons of Italy may feel the new born spirit of the motherland presiding over their manifestations."[26] Fascism also won the support of other community leaders such as Charles Baldi and, through them, of the Italian political machines in Philadel-

phia and elsewhere. In Pittsburgh, state senator Frank Zappala was
a distinguished friend of the Mussolini regime.[27]

ANTI-FASCIST VIOLENCE

Fascist activities in Pennsylvania often enter the public record
in consequence of one of the many violent encounters with Italian
American leftists and anti-Fascists, who were strong in the labor
organizations. The labor and radical presence in the Italian steel
and coal communities restrained Fascist expansion in these areas.[28]
In 1931 a bomb addressed to the publisher of a Fascist newspaper exploded in Easton, killing three mailmen.[29] Philadelphia
was another scene of confrontations. A banquet in honor of a visiting Italian aviator turned into a "brick-throwing riot" when rival
factions clashed.[30] In 1927 bombs exploded at the South Philadelphia homes of two of the most active Fascist leaders in the city,
the brothers Giovanni and Giuseppe DiSilvestro.[31] The most spectacular attack occurred in January 1933, when a bomb destroyed
the house of Giovanni DiSilvestro at 1619 South Broad Street,
killing his wife, Elizabeth, and injuring several of his children.
About the same time DiSilvestro was the target of another assassination attempt, this time by rifle.[32] In the Pennsylvania press this
outrage dominated the headlines and virtually excluded such apparently transient foreign stories as Hitler's accession to power in
Germany.

This record of confrontation and violence might suggest that
Fascism remained on the unpopular fringe of the Italian American
community in Pennsylvania, while in reality it came close to being
the central core of that history. While the loss of innocent life in
the DiSilvestro bombing inspired public horror for the terrorists,
the contemporary news coverage suggests the enormous political
strength of the Fascist leadership and the family's role as the un-
crowned royalty of Italian Philadelphia. DiSilvestro was universally portrayed as a distinguished community leader, and his wife's
funeral attracted a massive outpouring of grief and sympathy for
the family both from Italian American leaders from many parts of
the United States and from Italian politicians and cultural figures.[33]
Mussolini sent a personal telegram of condolence.[34] DiSilvestro
received devoted pledges of loyalty and assistance from powerful political friends in Philadelphia, including Judge Eugenio V.

Alessandroni, state senator Joseph C. Trainer, and Assistant U.S. Attorney C. James Todaro—an impressive roll call of the local Republican elite. Todaro used the crime to make a political statement against those "scandalous criminals" who are "against Mussolini. . . . They are allowed by the magnanimity of this country's laws to live here and then they do this sort of thing." The Sons of Italy offered a $15,000 reward to aid in solving the crime and announced a "war" on the groups responsible.[35]

The circumstances of the crime remain unclear, and there were rumors at the time that the act might have been connected with factional or business-related rivalries. Giovanni's financial dealings were not above suspicion, and corruption charges apparently caused his sudden withdrawal from political activity in 1935.[36] In the aftermath of the bombing, however, the consensus was that the perpetrators must have been outsiders, perhaps from anti-Fascist or anarchist circles in New York City, as it was inconceivable that a local could have struck at so respected an individual.[37] Judge Alessandroni commented that "there has been little if any anti-Fascist feeling noticeable either in the Philadelphia community or throughout the Order [of the Sons of Italy], and we are loath to look for a motive in that direction."[38] The police agreed that "the *anti-Fascismo* element in Philadelphia is comparatively small and unorganized."[39] This is in contrast to later bombing or arson attacks directed at German Nazi targets in Philadelphia, in which the main issue facing authorities was to decide which of countless local groups might have been responsible. The *Philadelphia Inquirer* denounced "the grimy hand of anarchy, seeking to undermine Italian Fascism by terrorizing Fascist sympathizers in America," "a diabolical plot," and the paper condemned "the hirelings of an Anti-Fascismo movement."[40] It was in fact *anti*-Fascism that was now defined as alien, violent, and subversive. In turn, the martyrdom of Elizabeth DiSilvestro enhanced the position of the Fascists as the embattled defenders of the Italian community against "red barbarism." She was "immolata, vittima innocente come Cristo . . . una martire." Fifty thousand attended her funeral, at which an honor guard of Italian war veterans gave the Fascist salute.[41]

By the early 1930s the Fascists had gained hegemony over the network of Italian American institutions in Pennsylvania. Fascists dominated the Italian American Union and the Italy-America Society. They operated through numerous front groups and organizations, including mutual aid societies. The process of assimilation, what the Nazis termed *gleichschaltung*, is illustrated by the influential OFDI, which dated to 1905 and which in 1920 was recognized by the Italian government as the official representative of the emigrant community.[42] In 1913 a grand lodge had been founded in Pennsylvania, with lodges at Philadelphia (four units), Easton (three), Pittsburgh, Reading, Renovo, Lock Haven, and Williamsport. The Pennsylvania grand lodge soon became the "strongest, best-organized and richest" in the United States.[43] The OFDI gradually displaced older groupings, such as the Italian Federation, after the death of Charles Baldi, and by 1941 there were some 30,000 to 40,000 Sons in the state.[44] The organization maintained its distinctive charitable enterprises, such as the Dante orphanage at Concordville, in Delaware County.

A period of dissension within the order in the 1920s was followed by Fascist domination at both the national and the local levels in the next decade, and the group maintained an office in Rome. The movement's national head was Giovanni DiSilvestro, whose regime was marked by intense pro-Fascist activism and who explicitly claimed that "the Order of the Sons of Italy in America was the forerunner of the Italian *Fasci*."[45] The order's terminology was significant. Not only was it controlled by a Grand Council, but the order's leaders were the *Gerarchi*, both terms familiar from the Italian Fascist Party.[46] Salvemini cites many examples across the United States where OFDI lodges and personnel overlapped extensively with those of the new *fasci*, and this picture is amply confirmed in Pennsylvania. The cooptation of the OFDI by the Fascist cause was amply illustrated by the group's 1928 pilgrimage to Italy, which included the Duce's birthplace as a site of peculiar sanctity. It was this event that drew public attention to the dimensions of "Mussolini's American Empire" and provoked the backlash over the next year.

The Pennsylvania founder of the OFDI was Giuseppe DiSilvestro, who founded the liberal Philadelphia newspaper *Voce del Popolo*, later renamed *La Libera Parola*.[47] Under the editorship of Giuseppe and his son Anthony, the *Parola* acted as the voice of the Sons of Italy and loyally supported the Mussolini government. Anthony DiSilvestro was an officer of the Pennsylvania grand lodge of the OFDI and in 1936 began his lengthy career as a Democratic state senator.[48] Pennsylvania figures within the OFDI at this point included Oreste Giglio of Williamsport, C. James Todaro, and, especially, Judge Eugenio V. Alessandroni.[49]

Alessandroni was the only rival to the DiSilvestro dominance over Italian Philadelphia, and significantly, the conflict between the two factions was fought out within the twin settings of the OFDI and Fascist politics. Alessandroni, "Mr. Sons of Italy," served as great venerable of the Pennsylvania order from 1923 to 1965. From 1927 until his death he also served as a judge of the Philadelphia Court of Common Pleas. With Giovanni DiSilvestro, Todaro, and others, Alessandroni was one of the group of powerful lawyers and public officials at the core of the Fascist cause in Philadelphia. This reinforces yet again the exceptional nature of the Italian rightists, as no public supporter of the Nazis, Klan, or Silver Shirts could have retained so visible a political office by the mid-1930s without at least encountering severe criticism and constant investigation.

Though not a Fascist Party member, Alessandroni was a fellow traveler, whose "fervent Italianism" earned him the rank of *Commendatore* from the Italian government in 1930. He attended a meeting of the Philadelphia *fascio* at least by 1927, and possibly earlier, and spoke at a number of explicitly Fascist venues, including the 1935 celebration of the Birthday of Rome. He traveled to Italy in 1928 and 1931 to organize the OFDI's pilgrimage to that land, on the former occasion traveling in the company of Giovanni DiSilvestro. In 1940 the anti-Fascist paper *Il Paese* denounced the pro-Fascist sympathies of Alessandroni and the OFDI, but to little avail. In 1943 Alessandroni was the leading Fascist supporter in the city, whose adherence to a patriotic wartime coalition was regarded as a major coup.[50] The judge retained his role as community leader long after the fall of Mussolini, urging his listeners to the last to be "always conscious and proud of the contributions of the centuries-old Italian heritage and civilization."[51]

The fraternal organizations promoted Fascist influence over

Italian American youth. In 1923 the Independent Order of Sons of Italy invited the Italian consul at Philadelphia to attend exercises at one of their schools, where he explained how "Italy had been reborn" due to the Duce.[52] Largely through the efforts of the fraternal orders, Fascist-sponsored schools and Doposcuola clubs were active throughout the state, often using parochial schools as venues. Propaganda endeavors were intense. The Fascist paper *Il Grido Della Stirpe* quoted a Pittsburgh student addressing a consul, "a man who represents our King and our *Duce*, who . . . wants us to learn the language which is spoken in the Fatherland." The consul was urged to tell the Duce "that there are many Italian children here who love him. . . . Tell him that we too are obedient to him like those children who live in Italy and that we wish to grow up worthy children for our dear Italy which he has made so powerful and so beautiful."[53]

From 1928, Fascist groups in Pittsburgh and elsewhere organized trips to Italy for emigrants and their children, events that had a powerful propaganda purpose. "Many children and young men of Italian descent . . . were sent to Italy, during that period, to the Marine and Mountain colonies for the *Balilla*, the Avanguardist, and the UFA (University Students) groups, during the summer vacation months."[54] The Balilla and Avanguardist groups were Fascist youth organizations, respectively, for boys aged eleven to fourteen years and for those between fourteen and seventeen, and they served as models for Germany's Hitler Youth.

As with German and native groups in the United States, war veterans' organizations were also significant to rightist movements. It is often difficult to tell whether the Italian Combattenti group in a particular community was established by the *fascio*, or vice versa.[55] In Philadelphia, typically, the *fascio* secretary was also president of the veterans' association. Italian veterans in North America were at an advantage because they had fought on the Allied side in the Great War, so they did not face the issue of divided loyalty that was so easily raised against former German or Austrian soldiers.

Fascist dominance extended to the media. Some Italian American papers were hostile to Fascism, especially those that reflected socialist or labor sentiment, and this group included Pittsburgh's *Lavoratore Italiano*. Philadelphia's weekly *Il Paese* offered exposés

about the leadership of the local Italian community. However, John
Diggins suggests that about 90 percent of Italian American newspapers nationwide supported Mussolini's regime, and this number included Philadelphia's influential *Il Popolo Italiano* and *La Libera Parola* as well as *La Stella di Pittsburgh*.[56] *Libera Parola* was consistent in praising Fascism and denouncing its enemies. Mussolini speeches were reported in fulsome terms and headlines such as "La Nazione Trasfigurata."[57] Anti-Fascist organizer Gaetano Salvemini was dismissed in 1927 as "Mercenario, Tradditore . . . una mostruosa morale, questo eterno nemico del proprio paese, questo rinnegatore del proprio sangue."[58] He had betrayed his native land and even dared to plot against "l'Uomo [*sic*] e contro il partito che hanno salvato la Patria."[59] In 1927 the paper reviewed plots against the regime as "quattro anni di lotte insidiosi, di tentate sedizioni di consumati tradimenti."[60] In 1929 the success of a Fascist plebiscite was greeted with the headline "Resurrezione!" and a ringing declaration of the total unity of the Fascist Party and the Italian nation.[61]

The ownership and political orientation of Philadelphia's Italian press was fundamentally restructured in the early 1930s to the consistent benefit of the Fascist cause. *L'Opinione*, originally founded by Charles Baldi, was acquired in 1933 by Generoso Pope, an intimate friend of the Italian regime.[62] *Il Popolo Italiano*, founded in 1935, gained some 16,000 daily subscribers throughout Pennsylvania. It was one of seven daily papers in North America that received "free wire service from Rome under the Fascist Ministry of Press and propaganda," in effect a Fascist press syndicate.[63] In 1936 the Sons of Italy founded a new official organ with the politically charged title *L'Ordine Nuovo*, New Order. Filippo Bocchini, an "ardent Fascist" published *La Voce Italiana*. Fascist and pro-Mussolini commentary pervaded the Italian-language radio programming available in major cities such as Philadelphia and Pittsburgh. Italian-made propaganda films were popular in Philadelphia and Reading.[64]

The Fascists had no fear of criticism from the church, at least after the 1929 Concordat resolved the decades-long struggle between the Vatican and the Italian state. We do not have for Philadelphia or Pittsburgh the kind of detailed analysis that permitted Salvemini to demonstrate that at least half the Italian parishes in

New York City were served by pro-Fascist clergy.[65] However, Fascist supporters were content to note that "all the priests in the zone of Pittsburgh PA were cooperating in every work of faith and patriotism." The local party branch was headed by a Carnegie priest, Father De Dominicis.[66]

Similar unanimity would almost certainly have been found in the sixteen Italian parishes of contemporary Philadelphia. In 1926 Philadelphia's Cardinal Dougherty was the honored guest at the inauguration of an Italian parochial school in Frankford. The meeting was attended by representatives of the local *fascio* and the FLNA, with speeches "very enthusiastically applauded, exalting religion and Fascist Italy."[67] Addresses were delivered by the cardinal himself, by the Italian vice-consul, and by Father Tonini, "who in a brilliant discourse, referred to the admirable work of the *Duce* and Fascist government, putting special emphasis on the wise work of Fascism in strengthening and revitalizing religious sentiment." In the 1930s the priest of the historic South Philadelphia parish of St. Mary Magdalene de Pazzi was legendary as "an ardent anti-communist," and in the war years the Italian clergy were vehemently opposed to the U.S. alliance with Russia. One declared that this pact made Roosevelt "the most diabolical president that we have ever had." The only Italian cleric in the city to denounce Fascism in vaguely comparable terms was the isolated figure of Pastor DiDomenica, minister of the tiny Italian Baptist congregation.[68] DiDomenica held positions that put him far outside the Italian political mainstream, including a virulent anti-Catholicism that led him to cooperate with Klansman Samuel Stouch.[69]

Most Catholic leaders of the time were sympathetic to Mussolini, including those who would in later years have harsh words for the Nazis and for anti-Semitism. In Cardinal Dougherty's case there were particular reasons for conciliating the Italian American community. He was suspicious of the whole system of national parishes, and his efforts at Americanizing immigrant Catholics led to widespread disaffection and to scandalous civil unrest in South Philadelphia in May 1933, in the "affair of Our Lady of Good Counsel."[70] The favor extended to local Fascists may have been an inexpensive means of showing friendship and sympathy. He worked closely with the Sons of Italy, and in 1933 the cardinal presided personally at the funeral of Elizabeth DiSilvestro.[71]

Fascist penetration of cultural life is illustrated by a 1933 banquet organized by the Sons of Italy for young Italian Americans recently graduated from Pennsylvania institutions of higher education.[72] Sponsorship by a respected fraternal society depoliticized the proceedings sufficiently to permit attendance by representatives of Pennsylvania universities as well as the mayor's office, the state judiciary, and a member of Governor Pinchot's cabinet. Speakers included Judge Alessandroni, the Italian ambassador to the United States, and the editor of the Italian newspaper *L'Opinione*. Each acted as a representative of Italy and Italian cultural life, and left unstated was the fact that each was a dedicated supporter of the Fascist movement.

A 1967 account of Italian American history in Pennsylvania notes with unusual frankness that "the great majority of our professional and business men and women, the prominent leaders of our fraternal orders and societies, the members of our clergy, high and low, Italians and non-Italians, professed openly their admiration for Mussolini, visited the consulates in the United States to obtain an introduction to any Fascist hyerarch [*sic*], in Rome or anywhere else in Italy, and hankered after the recognition of a *Cavaliere* or *Commendatore* decoration."[73] This solidarity is suggested by the broad cross-section of Pennsylvania businesses and individuals who chose to support pro-Fascist commemorative volumes such as Scilla di Glauco's *La Nuova Italia*.[74] Following a concert in 1936, *Ordine Nuovo* remarked succinctly, "La funzione non sarebbe completa se non venisse inviato un telegramma al creatore delle nuove fortune d'Italia ed al fondatore del Nuova Sacra Impero, S.E. Benito Mussolini."[75] Within the Italian American community, Fascism had become commonplace, unremarkable—a routine fact of the social landscape.

THE KHAKI SHIRTS

The successes of the Fascist movement made its leadership cautious about encouraging flagrant or violent public manifestations that might discredit the cause. This sensitivity was apparent in 1933, when Italian Americans were the central actors in the brief and farcical history of the Philadelphia-based movement known as the Khaki Shirts of America.[76] The aspiring duce of this movement was Art J. Smith, a self-described international soldier of fortune who has been dismissed as "a confidence man peddling shirts and boots to a handful of dimwitted followers."[77] Dimwitted perhaps, but scarcely a handful: this scathing judgment understates the short-lived popularity of the group and especially its appeal among Italian Americans, who constituted the majority of the membership. Smith apart, many of the known members of the group in Philadelphia bore an Italian name, and the appeal of the movement may have owed much to the foundations laid by the Fascisti. However, official Fascist institutions maintained a healthy distance from the Khaki Shirts and evaded any blame from the subsequent fiasco.

Art Smith formed his group in late 1932 from the Philadelphia remnants of the Bonus Army that had been driven out of Washington by the forces of Douglas MacArthur. His schemes also owed much to the example of Mussolini, and especially the March on Rome, which may account for the appeal to Italians in Philadelphia and New York. While not part of the official Fascist apparatus in North America, Smith called his movement the U.S. Fascists. He sought to expand his operations via the Fascist-dominated Italian political clubs, and followers used the familiar straight-arm salute as well as a variant of Mussolini's familiar black shirt.[78] Italian influence was also apparent in the threat to discipline recalcitrant union members with "a dose of castor oil."[79] Such a threat was particularly potent in the mainly Italian unions that the movement targeted for annexation, such as the Amalgamated Clothing Workers.[80] Conversely, the Khaki Shirts attracted the opposition of Italian anti-Fascist groups and leaders, including Carlo Tresca.[81] The chronology of the movement was significant, growing as it did in those months in early 1933 when Italian patriotic sentiment was stirred by twin atrocities, both of which seemed a direct assault on the local community: the DiSilvestro bombing in January and the archdiocesan encroachments on national parishes, which culminated in the May riots.

The height of Smith's influence came in June 1933 when 2,000 supporters penetrated a mass rally of unemployed veterans in Reyburn Plaza.[82] Shortly afterward 150 "Khaki Shirts and Fascists" engaged in a street fight with a like number of Communists in South Philadelphia, near Passyunk Square, a battle that resulted in the death of one of Smith's followers. Italian Americans predominated on both sides of the conflict. The funeral cortege was given added international credibility by the presence of a group of uniformed Nazis from a German ship in port.[83] Smith boasted about this time that he had 7 to 10 million men, "equipped with artillery, tanks, machine-guns and rifles."[84] In reality supporters carried clubs and gaspipe in readiness for street confrontations with Communist foes.

For all their braggadocio and hyperbole, the Khaki Shirts were indeed numerous, with between 1,000 and 2,000 members in Philadelphia alone, and audiences of a thousand were by no means uncommon at meetings. In June 1933 "General" Anthony Siani, commander of Shirt forces in South and West Philadelphia, told a thousand supporters of his plans to eliminate Communism in the city.[85] Smith claimed (fictitiously) a large police membership, and more seriously he sought to infiltrate existing veterans' groups to capitalize on pro-Bonus agitation.[86] A Khaki Shirt "invasion" threatened to capture the state Veterans of Foreign Wars convention.[87] The group had an imposing headquarters in Hunting Park as well as several subsidiary drill halls, and members appeared impressive with their hired horses and military-style uniforms. Legionnaires purchased helmets for $1.25 with plumes, 50 cents without; shirts cost $2.00. Members bore pseudo-military ranks, with an overrepresentation of majors, colonels, and generals; privates were scarce.

By the autumn Smith was said to be plotting to take over Philadelphia and seize the National Guard arsenal at Broad and Wharton Streets, where the Shirts would acquire the arms necessary for their own "March on Washington." After following orders to "shoot and kill all Communists," the Khaki Shirts would establish Roosevelt as dictator, "kick out every damn crook," and begin a massacre of Jews. The event was planned for the appropriately Italian date of Columbus Day, and several hundred followers actually did assemble at party headquarters and other buildings to await the order to march. This threat was taken sufficiently seriously to justify extensive surveillance, and at least three of the headquarters staff were infiltrators: one federal agent, one federal informant, and a reporter for the liberal *Philadelphia Record*.[88]

The Khaki Shirts were preempted by the Philadelphia police, some armed with machine guns. They stormed Smith's headquarters, arresting twenty-seven followers and seizing a sizable arms cache, including at least forty rifles. Meanwhile other officers were required to pacify the remaining militants who had begun to sack Khaki Shirt offices in protest at being misled. In the event, only a few dozen Khaki Shirts from Baltimore and Camden arrived in Washington to establish their new order. Smith, meanwhile, had decamped with $25,000 of the organization's funds.[89] In 1934 he was jailed following an incident in which a follower killed an anti-Fascist protester on Long Island.

Even after this catastrophe a few loyalists attempted to keep the Khaki Shirts in being as an official arm of the Italian Fascist movement, but they obtained a frosty reception from Giovanni DiSilvestro.[90] The organization was said to be "out of date" and nonfunctioning by 1938, but it retained a shadowy existence as the American Fascists and/or American Nationalists, until these in turn merged into the Christian Front.[91] Smith himself died in 1939, by which point he held a job as road boss under the WPA; "Many of his men found jobs there too."[92] After 1933 the militancy and adventurism that had attracted supporters to the Khaki Shirts would increasingly be channeled through the core Fascist movement.

ETHIOPIA

Fascist activism expanded and consolidated during the mid-1930s. Anti-Fascist militants such as Gaetano Salvemini saw this as a direct response to the failure of the McCormack-Dickstein Committee to investigate the group, which was "like a go signal."[93] However, the upsurge may also have reflected an anxiety not to be eclipsed by the sensational attention devoted to Nazi Germany and its American representatives. The Birthday of Fascism commemorations in March 1935 were on an unparalleled scale, and Blackshirt marches became more flamboyant.

From October 1935 Mussolini's intervention in Ethiopia served as a powerful catalyst for pro-Italian enthusiasm.[94] Fascist sympathizers naturally supported the invasion, and Judge Alessandroni's analysis was simple: "Mussolini needed land. He took it. He never concealed or camouflaged his design. And we can honor him for it."[95] Giovanni DiSilvestro was equally clear: "The primary motive of the war in Ethiopia was justice, and if all wars are for the same purpose, then God bless war. Mussolini has given su-

perior social justice to the world, work for the workers and peace
and prosperity. He will give Ethiopia civilization and colonization, the fruits of the genius of Rome."[96] The action was compared to the American Civil War, which had similarly been fought to liberate black slaves from a feudal tyranny.[97] It was also a Catholic and Christian action, opening up "un vasto campo per convertire milioni di Etiopi."[98] *Libera Parola* greeted the invasion with a large photograph of a steel-helmeted Duce and a headline appealing to the First World War spirit of Vittorio Veneto.[99]

The action won support among the hitherto less committed, who joined the mass rallies in Philadelphia and other cities in support of Mussolini's war effort, and a thousand Americans were recruited for service in the Italian war.[100] "The Italians of Philadelphia . . . responded with generosity to the appeals of the Sons of Italy, during the period of the vague and ineffectual sanctions imposed against Italy by the League of Nations." Throughout the state, women gave up their wedding rings and other gold items, receiving in exchange Italian-made steel rings acknowledging their sacrifice with the phrase "Oro alla Patria" and the date on which sanctions had been imposed. The new rings, inscribed with the date in the Fascist calendar, were consecrated by Italian priests in imposing public ceremonies.[101] Pro-Mussolini enthusiasm focused on U.S. attempts to maintain strict neutrality in the crisis, denounced as "vicious and unfair" by a delegation of the Italian American Union led by Judge Alessandroni.[102] Similar assertions were organized by other supporters of the Mussolini policies, such as the Philadelphia Society of the Friends of Italy, which raised funds for the war effort.[103]

In 1936 the victory of Italian forces was consolidated by the capture of Addis Ababa, and the Duce's proclamation of the rebirth of the Roman empire on May 9 gave the American Fascisti an addition to their already extensive ritual calendar, *nove Maggio*.[104] This incident was the highwater mark of pro-Fascist enthusiasm among Italian Americans. Philadelphia celebrated with "a torchlight parade and great rejoicing" organized by the Friends of Italy, who met at the familiar Fascist venue of the Dante Alighieri Hall.[105] Many declared their patriotism by singing the Fascist anthem "Giovinezza," which significantly was now accepted as a national rather than a party song.[106] A "monster victory procession"

TABLE 4.1. *European Events, 1933–1941*

Many of the political confrontations that occurred in Pennsylvania in these years were at least nominally a response to events in contemporary Europe and the Mediterranean area. This table lists, very selectively, some of the major occurrences that had a particular impact in the United States.

1933
January   Hitler gains power in Germany

1935
October   Italian invasion of Ethiopia

1936
March   Hitler occupies Rhineland
May   Italians secure rule over Ethiopia
July   Military revolt initiates civil war in Spain

1938
March   Germans occupy Austria; *Anschluss*
September/October   Munich crisis; Germans occupy Sudetenland
November   *Kristallnacht* attacks on Jews and Jewish property in
                                  Germany; Italy introduces anti-Semitic laws

1939
January   Spanish Nationalists occupy Barcelona
March   Germans conquer remnants of Czechoslovakia
March/April   Nationalist victory ends Spanish civil war
May   Germany allies with Italy
June   Italy extends anti-Jewish laws
August   German-Soviet nonaggression pact
September   Germans invade Poland; Britain and France declare
                                  war on Germany
November   U.S. Congress amends Neutrality Act to permit
                                  belligerents to purchase munitions on "cash and
                                  carry" basis

1940
May/June   Fall of France
June   Italy declares war on Allies
June–September   Battle of Britain
September   United States gives fifty destroyers to Great Britain
                                  in exchange for naval bases in Western Hemisphere

TABLE 4.1. *Continued*

107
*Italian
American
Fascism*

1941	
March	U.S. Congress passes Lease-Lend Bill
June	German invasion of USSR
December	United States at war with Axis powers
1943	
July–September	Fall of Mussolini; Italy surrenders

in South Philadelphia was sponsored by some 300 organizations and lodges in the hope that it could draw an attendance of some 50,000. However, this was prevented by Mayor Wilson, not from ideological qualms but out of well-substantiated fears that the demonstration would cause a racial confrontation with black residents, who had identified with the Ethiopian cause. Parade supporters such as Judge Alessandroni and Giovanni DiSilvestro complained that the city was prepared to permit demonstrations by "radical elements," pacifists, and Communists but not by "loyal and conservative citizens" like themselves. The identification of the pro-Mussolini cause as loyal and conservative was substantiated by the presence of community leaders who were also prominent in conventional government and party politics, such as Judges Eugenio Alessandroni and Joseph Tumolillo and Magistrate Charles Amodei.[107] Fascist supporters were probably correct in dismissing as an unrepresentative minority those anti-Fascist groups that denounced the victory commemoration.

Days before the elections that November Mussolini made a speech urging Italians to remember the international sanctions, a move taken as an appeal for Italian Americans to seek revenge on Roosevelt. The hint was ignored. Politically the Italian community in 1936 demonstrated unprecedented unity in supporting the causes of Mussolini overseas and Roosevelt at home. In Philadelphia the Italian vote went two-to-one for Roosevelt, a larger Democratic share than ever before, while the state legislature included by far the largest number of Italian representatives in its history, thirteen of fourteen of whom were Democratic. The Roosevelt revolution was boosted by Italian patriotism. From the mid-1920s the once loyally Republican Italians were thoroughly alienated by the anti-immigration stance of Republican senators Reed and Davis, and Democratic activists such as Tumolillo had exploited this ethnic hostility for partisan ends. Over the next decade both parties recognized the need to pay full respect to awakened national aspirations, with the Republicans struggling to compete with the Democrats. In 1938 even the Republicans offered South Philadelphia a solidly Italian slate, led by Judge Alessandroni's brother John.

Both Democratic and Fascist strength among Italian Pennsylvanians can be seen as different aspects of a related phenomenon. By the mid-1930s both *La Libera Parola* and *L'Opinione* became in effect organs of the Democratic cause in Philadelphia. In local radio broadcasts in the Italian language the slate of Democratic Party speakers was largely composed of community leaders with Fascist connections or histories: Filippo Bocchini, Anthony DiSilvestro, Michael A. Musmanno, and C. James Todaro. When in 1936 the Democrats attempted to found a fraternal federation to rival the Republican-dominated Sons of Italy, they chose both a name and a rhetoric geared to appeal instantly to Fascist sentiment: the new Dante League was intended to "secure for the Italian people the place in the sun that they justly deserve."[108]

INVESTIGATION

By 1936 a self-confident Fascist movement had expanded its paramilitary activities. Italians formed a counterpart to the Bund's uniformed branch in the Blackshirt Legion, which on one occasion mobilized 10,000 supporters at its Camp Dux in New Jersey. In 1937 Blackshirts and uniformed Bundists held a joint rally at Camp Nordland in the same state, a collaboration that contributed to public and congressional concern about paramilitary activities.[109] This persuaded congressional leaders to include the Fascists as part of a general investigation of totalitarian organizations. In 1938 anti-Fascist militant Girolamo Valenti told the Dies Committee that "American-Italian Black Shirt Legions, ten thousand strong, are marching in America with the same resounding tread as those of the goose-stepping detachments of German-American Bund storm-troopers."[110] Pittsburgh was one of several cities where "the

Black Shirts and the Nazi Bund have formed a tight coordinated little Rome-Berlin Axis of their own."[111]

Valenti emphasized the direct connections between the American Fascist movement and the organs of the Italian state: "Italian consular officials and secret Fascist agents are spreading Fascist propaganda throughout the ranks of some two hundred Italian American organizations in the United States. In addition, they are also expending every effort to penetrate *bona fide* Italian American fraternal societies with a view to gaining control of these organizations for the purpose of increasing the influence of Fascist dictatorship."[112] Claims about the role played by consuls would have surprised nobody who read the references in the party's press to diplomatic participation in the meetings of any *fascio*.[113] Active consuls included Eduardo Pervan in Philadelphia and *Cav.* Siroana in Pittsburgh.[114] Consuls coordinated fund raising in American cities and promoted statements of loyalty to the Mussolini regime, in which they were particularly successful with Philadelphia's Italian clothing manufacturers. Like the Germans, Italian consulates offered hospitality to American rightist and anti-Semitic groups.[115]

Mussolini's envoys attempted to suppress anti-Fascist activities among Italian Americans, and the Johnstown consul Angelo Iannelli was reported to be intimidating Italian dissidents in Cambria County.[116] Pressure was possible because so many immigrants had relatives in Italy who would be subject to official retaliation. Of Italian-born residents of Pennsylvania in 1930 only 62 percent were naturalized, leaving some 85,000 with their original citizenship. The fate of the remainder was a matter of concern to Italian officials, who discouraged further naturalizations.[117] However, the number seeking U.S. citizenship rose dramatically during the international crises of the late 1930s, as Italian Americans sought to avoid military service in Ethiopia or Spain. Through the consular network the Italian government attempted to levy taxation on Italian Americans resident in the United States, using, for example, the notorious "bachelor tax" imposed on unmarried men. The implied threat was that nonpayment would lead to reprisals against relatives in the homeland.[118]

Valenti's account raised concern about Fascist activities in North America, though the attention paid to the phenomenon was always

pallid in comparison with the notice given to the German presence. Together with activists such as Tresca and Salvemini, Valenti
coordinated anti-Fascist activities among Italian Americans, a task
that became somewhat easier after Mussolini passed his racial laws
in 1938. In 1939 several hundred anti-Fascists mobilized in Philadelphia to hear speeches by Valenti and other exiles and labor
spokesmen, and local organizing efforts bore fruit in the formation
of Salvemini's national Mazzini Society.[119] In comparison with the
German anti-Nazi movement, however, the Italian experience was
circumscribed in its base of support and its broader impact.

WAR

Fascist support in Italian American communities was reflected
in attitudes to foreign policy, especially after the Italian declaration of war on Britain and France in June 1940. *Il Popolo Italiano*
and other Italian papers complained of Roosevelt's friendship with
England and scoffed at his Italian henchmen such as Fiorello La
Guardia ("Lord Little Flower of the Guard"). Roosevelt's belligerent attitudes created unprecedented conflicts among his Italian
supporters, who demonstrated little enthusiasm at the prospect of
American involvement in war. In June 1940 a speech in which the
president attacked the Italian "stab in the back" against France was
regarded as a *calumnie*, and the text of the *insulto* was freely distributed by Willkie supporters in Pennsylvania. Equally unpopular
was the Alien Registration Act of 1940, which was portrayed as a
discriminatory law equivalent to the 1924 Immigration Act. Across
Pennsylvania these policies contributed to a rapid decline in the
Italian Democratic vote between 1940 and 1942. The slide was not
halted until the administration's generous treatment of the post-
Mussolini Italian governments in 1943, when Italy was treated not
as a defeated foe but as a new cobelligerent against Germany, and
de facto indemnity was granted to most former Fascists.[120]

This evidence of popular support for the Italian cause might
suggest that Italian Americans would have posed a serious danger
of subversive activity. In the event, there was no such dissidence
and indeed little public fear of general disloyalty by Italians. This
was largely explained by domestic political conditions. Italian communities were an integral component of the New Deal coalitions,
and the Democratic Party acted as the essential conduit of patron-

age and official jobs. The DiSilvestros and other *prominenti* found

no difficulty in combining this domestic loyalty with wholehearted
devotion to the Duce in overseas affairs, provided that no challenge
was posed to their power within their ethnic base, and no such
threat emerged. The Italians also differed from both the German
and the Irish experience in that popular anti-Semitism was weaker,
which removed a good deal of potential ethnic conflict. The Italians may well have taken warning from the harsh treatment meted
out to the Bund.

From mid-1940 community leaders made every effort to assert
their undivided American patriotism, whatever internal qualms
they may have had about international affairs. Following the Italian entry into war in 1940, OFDI leaders Judge Alessandroni and
Ernest Biagi declared, "We are as one with the President of the
United States in his endeavors for the defense of our country in
every possible way. The Order Sons of Italy, its members and families, stand side by side in the defense of liberty and democracy,
and for their perpetuation." Anthony DiSilvestro declared, "I am
an American. My leader is the President of the United States."[121]
This position was repeatedly reinforced over the next year, and
when the United States and Italy went to war in December 1941,
there was no public opposition within the Italian American community to a wholehearted pledge of patriotic commitment.

Some days after Pearl Harbor, Judge Alessandroni announced
that the resources of the Sons of Italy would be dedicated to secur-
ing an Allied victory.[122] The Sons would struggle "for this great
cause, for the triumph of the American flag, for our sacred ideals of
justice and freedom." State senator Anthony DiSilvestro believed
that the war should be pursued until the dictatorial menace of
Hitler and Mussolini had been destroyed. *Il Popolo Italiano* regret-
ted Mussolini's declaration of war on the United States and called
for the central goal of "THE DEFEAT OF THE AXIS." The enemy, it
declared, was not Italy but "the ruling group in our land of birth
that, influenced by a powerful neighbor, has been pushed into
war."[123] The Italian American political consensus shifted seamlessly toward the patriotic American cause so successfully that
1941 marked not the slightest hiccough in the social and political positions of the community's leaders. As late as 1950 it was
remarked, "The DiSilvestros and the Alessandronis have kept up

a running battle for the last twenty years in South Philadelphia. Philadelphia politics among the Italians can be partly viewed as a war of two personalities, Judge Alessandroni and State Senator DiSilvestro."[124] The two families were key players in the political life of Italian Pennsylvania into the 1960s.

In 1967 a historian of Italian Philadelphia rejected the "stupid, ridiculous and malicious" criticism, "libelous and venemous [*sic*] propaganda" from those who condemned Mussolini's American supporters, "some of the most worthy members of our community,"[125] and it is difficult to find any American Fascist supporter having suffered for his or her loyalty. Italian ultra-rightists provided a model of enduring success that other ethnic and political groups could only envy.

5 | Silver Shirts among the Brown
The Rise of Political Anti-Semitism

or all their apparent similarities, by the late 1920s the Klan and the Italian Fascists stood at the opposite ends of a political spectrum defined by religion and ethnicity. Over the next few years both movements were drawn into an emerging "front" of right-wing groups, united by a common opposition to Communism and the Left. This was partly a reaction to perceived leftist advances under the New Deal, but the growth of new movements was stimulated by a new concern with Jews and a militant anti-Semitism that owed much to Nazi influence. The closely related ideologies of anti-Semitism and anti-Communism fostered the development of a host of shirt organizations inspired by the models of Mussolini and Hitler, most notoriously the Silver Shirts founded by William Dudley Pelley. Other sects ostensibly existed to fight Communism but in reality drew little distinction between Communism and Judaism. These anti-Jewish political groups, such as the ACS of Philadelphia, laid the foundations for the network of far-Right and pro-Axis movements that flourished at the end of the decade.

ANTI-SEMITISM

Anti-Semitic practice and rhetoric had a long record in Pennsylvania, manifested, for example, in the exclusion of Jews from various clubs and hotels, which continued long after the Second World War. There had also been more violent manifestations, and in 1913 charges of ritual murder had surfaced in the Berks County community of Clayton.[1] In the 1920s anti-Jewish books and tracts circulated freely, including Henry Ford's newspaper the *Dearborn Independent*, which publicized the forged *Protocols of the Elders of Zion*.[2] However, political organizations did not develop. At least in Pennsylvania, Jews featured little in the rhetoric of the 1920s Ku Klux Klan. When in 1919 the Philadelphia *Public Ledger* serialized the *Protocols* as the "Red Bible," the manifesto of the "Red plot to smash [the] world in 1919," the paper deleted all references to Jews to make the text appear purely Bolshevik.[3]

Anti-Semitic parties developed only after the rise of Hitler, who inspired a host of American imitators, ranging from semiserious splinter groups to sizable activist movements. Between 1933 and 1941 at least 120 anti-Semitic groups were founded in the United States, and that figure excludes most of the ethnic fascist movements.[4] The growth of racist sects was accelerated by the refugee question and the fear that Nazi persecutions might result in a flood of Jewish exiles to a country recovering only slowly from the depression. This would reopen the immigration question that appeared to have been settled in 1924, arousing fears that traditional American values would be overwhelmed by an unwholesome alien presence. The scale of the threat was enhanced by exaggerated estimates of the number of Jews in the United States. Pelley believed there were already 12 million by 1937. James B. True apparently coined the term "refujews."[5]

These fears were not shaken by the hostility of the American public to Hitler and the Nazis. Despite all the publicity about persecutions, opinion polls in 1938 showed massive resistance to any softening of immigration restrictions, even when the question was phrased to emphasize child refugees.[6] Rightist groups capitalized on this sentiment, and in January 1939 the Pennsylvania Klan declared that 90 percent of the 880,000 foreigners applying for entrance to the United States were Jewish.[7] Handbills set the numbers of potential refugees alongside the figures for unemployed Gentile Americans, implying that the Jews were coming to steal the few remaining jobs. America should not become "the world's almshouse." Specific rumors alleged that Jewish businesses and department stores had dismissed Gentile employees in order to make room for German Jewish refugees, an explosive issue in the depression era. In 1939 General Moseley noted, "The other day in Philadelphia, I heard a lot of feeling expressed due to the number of Jews who were infiltrated throughout the entire locality. From two different sources I learned that Sears Roebuck and Co. had discharged two hundred gentiles, replacing them by an equal number of Jews. I have the feeling we should take care of our own first."[8]

JEWS IN PENNSYLVANIA

The growth of militant anti-Semitism in the 1930s had a peculiar relevance for Pennsylvania, which contained some large and visible Jewish communities.[9] A long-standing Jewish presence in Philadelphia had been massively augmented by immigration between about 1880 and 1920. By 1940 there were an estimated 300,000 Jews in the Philadelphia metropolitan area, perhaps 15 percent of the city's population. In 1940 Philadelphia supported five Jewish periodicals, and an estimated 35,000 homes subscribed to Yiddish papers. Jews were originally concentrated in areas of the historic city, especially the southern wards, but in the 1920s better-off families began to move to newer areas, where they encountered hostility and prejudice. Pittsburgh's Jewish community grew from 2,500 in 1880 to 60,000 in 1920, and the 1920s and 1930s were marked by a migration from the Hill district ghetto to more salubrious sections such as the East End and Squirrel Hill.[10]

Though he was anything but typical, Albert M. Greenfield, a Russian-born immigrant who developed a Philadelphia financial empire based on retailing, banking, and real estate, epitomized the changing fortunes of Pennsylvania's Jews.[11] He dominated the City Stores conglomerate, which controlled the well-known Lit Brothers department stores. A supporter of the Republican machine in the 1920s, his defection to the Democrats did much to reestablish that party as a force in city and state politics, and he supported Stern's *Philadelphia Record*, the other great bastion of New Deal Pennsylvania. He was also a major philanthropist. His one great failure occurred in 1930 when other tycoons reneged on their promises to support his Bankers Trust Company, causing a ruinous failure that inflicted immense social damage on the city.

As a Jew, a financier, and a Democrat, Greenfield represented everything that was sinister and undesirable to the political Right, all the more so given his alliance with a Jewish-run liberal paper. The Bankers Trust affair permitted the disasters of the depression to be laid directly at his door, though in reality the collapse owed much to the hostility of the business establishment to this parvenu, who failed to receive the favors readily extended to established figures. Throughout the decade Greenfield was the target of anti-Semitic attacks, which occasionally entered state and city politics.[12] In 1935 mayoral candidate Davis Wilson denounced his rival John B. Kelly as the tool of Jewish interests represented by Stern and Greenfield. He charged that Democratic leaders Kelly and McCloskey, despite their Irish origins, were in the pockets of Greenfield's Bankers' Security concern, forcing Greenfield to deny that he was seeking control of the Democrat machine.[13] Allegiances in this contest were complicated, and Wilson was actively supported by Annenberg's *Inquirer*; but the allegations linking "Jewish money power" to New Deal Democrats were ominous. In 1938 Stern and Greenfield were part of the Democratic faction said to be seeking "domination and control" over the whole state.[14] In the elections of that year Republicans listed Greenfield and Stern alongside John L. Lewis, Senator Guffey, and David Lawrence as the arch-villains of the Democratic leadership.[15]

In 1937 Governor Earle chose Greenfield to direct the state's commemoration of the 150th anniversary of the U.S. Constitution. The choice was denounced by Charles B. Helms, secretary of the POS of A, which represented some 60,000 Pennsylvanians.[16] Helms complained that Greenfield was not native born and was "known purely for his commercial and political enterprise," charges that led to a vigorous public controversy. Though not explicitly anti-Semitic as a body, the POS of A was one of many organizations in these years to demand stringent immigration restrictions, a platform that in practice would most directly affect potential Jewish refugees.[17]

Attacks on Jews also focused on figures far less reputable than Greenfield. When an anti-Semitic pamphleteer in 1938 claimed that Jewish bootleggers had ruined the noble experiment of Prohibition, the statement had rather more substance than most of the allegations contained in such material.[18] By the 1930s organized crime in Philadelphia had for decades contained a powerful Jewish element, with notorious figures such as Max Hoff, Nathan Schaeffer, and Nig Rosen (alias Harry Stromberg).[19] Between 1937 and 1939 the city's media reported the results of a grand jury investigating civic corruption, in which Rosen and Schaeffer figured as the alleged puppet masters controlling the mayor, the police department, and the "politico-gambler-police tie-up" that ran Philadelphia.[20] Jewish organized criminals were also leading figures in the activities of other cities, including Pittsburgh, Reading, Chester, and Scranton. Syndicates were multiethnic in character, with Irish, Italian, and Polish components, but the preponderance of Jewish names in news reports tended to associate organized crime with this particular ethnic group more than others.[21]

CONGRESSMAN McFADDEN

One Pennsylvania figure emerged as a national anti-Semitic leader in his own right. In 1933 Louis McFadden attracted widespread publicity for his speeches on the threat from the Jewish financial conspiracy, not because his views were particularly novel or cogently argued, but because they were presented on the floor of the U.S. House of Representatives. This gave his utterances a visibility denied to thousands of less prestigious agitators.

First elected to Congress in 1914, McFadden represented the Fifteenth District in rural northeastern Pennsylvania and was president of the Pennsylvania Bankers' Association.[22] He chaired the powerful House Committee on Banking and Currency from 1920 to 1931. A deadly enemy of liberal Republicans, he twice defeated attempts by Gifford Pinchot's wife, Cornelia, to usurp his seat.[23] From 1930 he campaigned against the financial policies of the Hoover administration, charging the Federal Reserve System with improper collusion with other international banks and chiefly the Bank of International Settlements. In his view these contacts with international finance and the world "Money Trust" amounted to a treasonable conspiracy to destroy constitutional government in the United States and turn power over to "the international bankers of New York City" and the Bank of England.[24] He opposed any gesture toward internationalism or membership in world organizations and in 1931 attacked the administration's attempt to forgive war debts and reparations. In 1932 he was expelled by the Republican Party but retained his seat on an independent Democratic and Republican ticket.[25]

McFadden was not at this stage openly anti-Semitic, never mentioning the word "Jewish" in a public forum. He emphasized that "most of the international bankers are of German origin"[26] and was as much anti-British as anti-Jewish.[27] However, his rhetoric had many points of contact with the common denunciations of "international Jewish finance" and world conspiracies. The bankers "who came here from Europe" had manipulated world politics, sponsored the Russian revolution and the ensuing reign of terror, and brought Trotsky to stir up Red revolution in New York City.[28] Applied to Jews, these charges would become mainstays of the anti-Semitic mythology propounded by Father Coughlin and other demagogues. McFadden was personally close to Coughlin, whom he inspired to deliver a controversial 1931 radio speech asserting that the "illegitimate" Treaty of Versailles was the root of the world depression.[29]

As he had already (1932) called for the impeachment of Hoover as a dangerous internationalist, it is not surprising that McFadden was deeply hostile to the Roosevelt administration.[30] On May 29, 1933, McFadden made a House speech alleging a Jewish conspiracy in terms that went far beyond the conventional anti-Semitism of the day. Roosevelt's desertion of the gold standard meant that "in the United States today, the Gentiles have slips of paper while the Jews have the gold and lawful money."[31] The Democratic administration "had given the gold and lawful money of the country to the international money Jews of whom Franklin D. Roosevelt is the familiar. . . . This country has fallen into the hands of the international money changers." Invoking the shades of Concord bridge, he pledged that modern invaders of American rights would meet with similar violent resistance.[32] Announcing that "the provisions of this repudiation bill were foretold by a writer in the *Dearborn Independent* some years ago," McFadden proceeded to read into the congressional record sections of *The Protocols of the Elders of Zion*, arguing that this document provided the blueprint for subverting the currency.[33]

Over the next year McFadden abandoned restraints about identifying the "international bankers" who had erected their "dictatorship" in the United States,[34] and he used radio broadcasts as well as his Congressional platform to spread his anti-Jewish message. America was controlled by the machinations of the Jewish banking houses—the Warburgs, the Schiffs, the Rothschilds, and Kuhn Loeb and Co.—and their "Gentile fronts and sycophants."[35] Jewish bankers orchestrated mass Jewish immigration into the United States, they spread lies about anti-Semitic atrocities in Europe, and they had destroyed Russia.[36] The Soviet regime was a Jewish administration.[37] In June 1933 he denied that Hitler was persecuting German Jews and claimed the only real victims were some 200,000 Communist "Galician Jews," whom the world conspiracy sought to import into the United States. This would be done through agents such as Labor Secretary Frances Perkins, "an old hand with the international Jewish bankers. If she were not, she would not be here in a Jewish-controlled administration."[38] In 1934 he attacked a proposed immigration of Jewish refugees into the United States and denounced gullible Christians who permitted themselves to be manipulated by Jewish masters.[39]

For McFadden the Zionists were active through fronts such as the Brains Trust and the English Fabian Society, led by "Israelites" carrying out their "world plan," "the Jewish plan of a world state."[40] "The superstate is a Jewish creation,"[41] and the League of Nations was a stage toward implementing this. World Zionism was allied to occultism and "Masonic illuminism" in a "Judeo-Masonic program."[42] Having conquered England, its next target was the United States, through such emissaries as Bernard Baruch, Samuel Untermyer, and Felix Frankfurter.[43] These conspirators had drafted the New Deal and the NIRA decades before these schemes were finally implemented by their puppet Roosevelt in 1933, and these programs were now run by Jewish lawyers and administrators.[44] Communism was an alternate face of the Zionist plot within the United States.

For the anti-Semitic Right, McFadden played a role in the 1930s little inferior to that of Henry Ford in earlier years. His speeches were reprinted in the Silver Shirt newspaper *Liberation*, and in pamphlet form the May 1933 philippic enjoyed long popularity on the literature stalls of the pro-Nazi sects.[45] As late as 1970 McFad-

den's speeches were reprinted as a warning against "foreign influences of alien conspiracies carried out through fetid and subterra-
nean corridors of power, the work of the government that dares not
speak its name." [46] In 1936 the racist newspaper *American Gentile*
blamed a Jewish conspiracy for the death of a man who has been
described as "the patron saint of latter day fascists." [47]

DONNING THE SHIRTS

In Pennsylvania the first organized group to combine the shirt
mystique with political anti-Semitism was the Khaki Shirts, which
enjoyed a meteoric career during 1933 and which confirmed public
perceptions about the corrupt and thuggish quality of the "Nightgown Riders." [48] This was an inauspicious beginning to a lengthy
vogue for shirt movements, the most important of which was
the Silver Legion of America. [49] The Silver Shirts would remain
throughout the decade the most significant of the purely domestic
organizations on the anti-Semitic Right. [50]

The legion was founded by William Dudley Pelley, who in his
youth explored most of the available fringe religions, including
British Israelitism, Atlantis theories, and pyramidology. [51] By the
late 1920s Pelley was a leading figure in what was even then termed
the "southern California cult racket," with its ideas on theoso-
phy, spiritualism, and the concept of the Ascended Masters, all of
which Pelley integrated into his later political theories. [52] Following
an alleged near-death experience in 1928, he repeatedly tried to in-
form the world of the great truths he had learned during his "seven
minutes in eternity" and subsequent messages received from the
"Great Souls" via the "Psychic Radio." [53] Pelley, like Christ, was
presented as a leader of the cosmic forces of light. [54]

The rise of Hitler focused Pelley's attention on the Jews as the
source of most evils and problems in the world, and he offered
a solution based on the formation of a Christian Commonwealth.
Pelley found a new inspiration for his life when Hitler took office
as German chancellor, and Pelley created his Silver Legion with
its militaristic structure of national commander, field marshal, and
general staff. Divisions would respectively address public enlightenment, patriotic publicity, crime erasement, industrial rehabilita-
tion, and public morals and mercy. (The "enlightenment" function

was presumably translated directly from the title of Goebbels's office of *Aufklärung*). The legion had its SS Ranger Service, complete with Officer Training School, whose alumni were taught to quell a hostile crowd, apprehend racketeers, and combat syndicalist agitators.[55] The legion, in summary, was "picking up the leavings of the Klan, adding a dash of populism and Huey Longism, drawing on the German Nazis for technique and slogans, and working it all up into what Mr. Pelley calls the Christ-Democracy."[56]

Pelley became the nation's best-known figure on the paramilitary far Right, and he may well have been the inspiration for Sinclair Lewis's imaginary American dictator Buzz Windrip. In 1934 Pelley made one of the lasting contributions to that cause when he published an invented document known as the Pinckney prophecy, allegedly an extract from the diary of Founding Father Charles Pinckney. This reported a lost speech attributed to Benjamin Franklin during the Constitutional Convention, arguing that "Jews are a menace to this country if permitted entrance, and ought to be excluded."[57] Historians showed that the story was apocryphal, contained ludicrous anachronisms, and not only distorted Franklin's views but actually reversed his generous liberalism. However, the speech was a familiar mainstay of propaganda for over a decade and was quoted in Nazi papers in Germany itself. Through the decade Pelley's ragtag legion continued to circulate its views through books such as *No More Hunger*, *The World Hoax*, and of course, *The Protocols*. Together with his friend McFadden, Pelley largely shaped the anti-Semitic agenda of the 1930s, as the two were the (usually unacknowledged) source for countless diatribes and pamphlets.

The Silver Shirts enjoyed much success and may have had up to 25,000 members nationwide at its height in 1933–34.[58] They were most active in the West and Midwest and were strong in Cleveland and in the Youngstown steel districts.[59] They cooperated with the various Little Steel employers, including those in western Pennsylvania. The Silver Shirt presence in this area accounts for the otherwise odd remark that in 1937 a new extreme Right coalition in Cleveland supported the causes of "anti-union, strikebreaking sentiment . . . anti-semitism, Jim-Crowism, anti-Catholicism, *and at least some astrology.*"[60]

In 1934 an application by the Silver Legion to incorporate in Pennsylvania was challenged by a powerful coalition of religious, labor, fraternal, and patriotic groups, including the American Legion, and the request was denied by Richard Beamish, Gifford Pinchot's liberal secretary of the commonwealth. This solid coalition may have reflected popular disgust not merely with overseas fascist movements but with the state's recent encounter with the Khaki Shirts. However, the lack of formal Silver Legion organization conceals a great deal of activity within the state from the movement's earliest days. Some of its earliest activists were from Pennsylvania, especially the Philadelphia area. This included the legion's national treasurer, Harry F. Sieber of Wynnewood, who in 1934 was one of the movement's original five incorporators.[61]

Another Philadelphia militant was Paul Von Lilienfeld-Toal, an exiled Estonian aristocrat with White Russian connections.[62] He had known Pelley since 1931 and ran the "letter service" disseminating publicity for the national office of the Silver Shirts. In 1934 he took a position with the North German Lloyd shipping line in Philadelphia, an appointment that brought him to the notice of the McCormack-Dickstein committee.[63] He was "the German correspondent and adjutant of William Dudley Pelley," and he wrote of Pelley in 1933 as "our Beloved Chief."[64] With his employer R. T. Kessemeier, he was a leading figure in the Association of the Friends of the New Germany (FNG), precursor to the German American Bund. Both men shared an interest in the occult and theosophical aspect of the Silver Legion and the "revelations" that Pelley received from the Ascended Masters.

Von Lilienfeld-Toal espoused extreme anti-Semitic opinions.[65] He circulated tracts warning of alien conspiracies against the American people, one of which warned that Jewish domination of the American food processing industries would permit the contamination of the food supply with fatal germs, "leaving the conquest of America easier for certain oriental interests who will play with the Soviet regime."[66] The United States should emulate Germany, which "has been awakened under the leadership of Adolf Hitler, and has freed herself from the Semitic yoke."[67] His aspiration was that the Silver Shirts and the FNG would collaborate "to emasculate Communism and its mighty ally, the International Jewish Capitalist, who is financing this Communism."[68] By mid-1933 Von Lilienfeld-Toal had brought Kessemeier into touch with Pelley, to whom Kessemeier wrote about the "simply perfect" conditions he had observed during his visit to Nazi Germany.[69] Pelley and Kessemeier met on a number of occasions during 1933, at least once in Philadelphia, and one goal was to give the Silver Shirt leader entrée into German American fund-raising circles. Pelley was brought into contact with German-based groups such as the Fichte-Bund and the propaganda agency Weltdienst.[70] Over the next decade congressional investigators and antifascist journalists would often remark on the very close relationship that existed between the Silver Legion and the German organizations, both the FNG and the Bund.

Collaboration between the FNG and the Silver Shirts about this time was suggested by the sensational case of Louis McFadden. His views were often pro-German in addition to anti-Semitic, and he was close to the contemporary German far Right in his belief that Germany in the First World War had fallen victim not to battlefield defeat but to a "stab in the back." In 1930 he claimed that Germany in 1918 had been "an unconquered enemy, giving up his arms in reliance upon the good faith of an armistice agreement . . . [and] afterwards tricked into the power of his adversary," who "compels him to accept the burden of a colossal war tribute."[71] He further attacked "the tangled web of deception in the treaty of Versailles."[72]

McFadden's polemic attracted the attention of muckraking journalist John L. Spivak, who obtained a gold mine of incriminating documents from his colleague Frank Prince, an investigator of anti-Semitic activities.[73] These materials demonstrated close links between McFadden and a number of "patriotic" and anti-Semitic groups. The most important was the Order of 76, an intelligence network founded by Royal Scott Gulden with the aim of exposing treasonous activities by Jews and Communists.[74] The congressman used his franking privileges to mail propaganda from the order and also addressed the group.[75] Gulden's project was supported by Nazi activist Colonel Edwin Emerson, possibly with the assistance of the German consul-general in New York City.[76] Emerson was connected with both the Friends of Germany and the FNG.

McFadden was further linked to the Silver Legion, into which Gulden's followers subsequently merged.[77] Spivak produced telegrams and correspondence between McFadden and Pelley. In addition McFadden had been in contact with California Silver Shirt leader Henry D. Allen of Pasadena and possibly with Art Smith of the Khaki Shirts.[78]

Apart from the congressman's political ties, Spivak was able to show that McFadden had repeatedly engaged in financial impropriety.[79] In the 1920s, for example, McFadden had sought permission to sell what he claimed to be $1.3 million worth of stock in a company called the Federated Radio Corporation. Following an investigation, he was forced to reduce the estimated value of the shares to a mere $60,000. In another case McFadden was shown to have taken a $25,000 kickback in a "fraudulent conspiracy" involving stocks. The dedicated foe of insidious economic manipulators appeared himself to be a rapacious shark. This material formed the basis for an exposé of the "Jewbaiter and Crook," originally published in the *New Masses*.[80] Forty thousand copies of the story were distributed to constituents, contributing to McFadden's defeat in the 1934 elections.

Much of the subsequent history of the Silver Shirt movement in Pennsylvania has to be reconstructed from chance references, but these are quite abundant. Many concern the legion's "field marshal," T. Roy Zachary, who earned notoriety in May 1938 when he announced to a joint Bund–Silver Shirt meeting in Chicago that if no one else was prepared to assassinate President Roosevelt, then he would undertake the assignment.[81] In late 1939 Pelley's growing legal problems left Zachary as virtual head of the movement.[82] He was a regular speaker in Pennsylvania, where he appeared on the platforms of the Silver Shirts and of other like-minded organizations, such as the Philadelphia ACS.[83] In 1939 he attended General Moseley's anti-Roosevelt speech in Philadelphia.[84]

The Silver Shirts had contacts in western Pennsylvania, including Victor Hoye of New Castle, a financial supporter of the movement.[85] "An organizer or officer of the Silver Shirts" was the curious Charles Bruce Swift of Pittsburgh, who had wide and somewhat mysterious connections with the American Legion and perhaps the naval intelligence community.[86] Swift's choice of

Zachary and George Deatherage as invited speakers suggests a strong local current of organized anti-Semitism and pro-Nazi sentiment. As early as 1935 Pelley himself had addressed the Pittsburgh "Bund" (presumably the FNG) and declared that "the Silver Shirts were completely in sympathy with the aims of the Bund." In late 1938 the Dies Committee heard that "the Silver Shirts in Pittsburgh are cooperating with the Bund."[87] The following year "Bunders and Silver Shirts" dominated Pittsburgh's Christian Front organization.[88]

THE ACS

The case of Charles B. Swift suggests how the emerging shirt groups built on the earlier organizational efforts of older rightist societies that had been active for several years. The nature of their political ideology is often hard to determine, in that some of the most extensive accounts of the leadership derive from congressional inquiries following the outbreak of war. By this time most activists had good grounds to fear investigation and possible prosecution for sedition or pro-Axis propaganda and thus presented themselves as aggressive superpatriots rather than anti-Semitic agitators. However, enough earlier evidence exists to contradict this image.

The best-known leader in Philadelphia was Bessie R. Burchett, who held a doctorate from the University of Pennsylvania in classical literature and mythology and who taught at South Philadelphia High School for Girls, which had a high concentration of immigrant and especially Jewish children.[89] In 1935 she denounced Jewish-Communist infiltration in the teaching profession and the National Education Association and the sympathy she observed there for collectivist, socialist, and internationalist opinions.[90] Philadelphia teachers were propagandizing for "anti–child labor legislation, birth control, and other Communistic doctrines."[91] This perception led her to initiate a local Red Scare within the public school system.[92] Among the Communist and subversive writers that she protested were such respectable figures as Charles A. Beard, G. D. H. Cole, and Henry N. Brailsford, but the major grievance was the popular series of history textbooks by Harold Rugg, viewed on the Right as socialistic and unpatriotic.[93]

To counter the threat, Burchett emphasized the use of the pledge of allegiance and daily Bible reading in Philadelphia classrooms and demanded that loyalty oaths be imposed on all teachers.[94]

Burchett regarded the CIO as an overt arm of international revolution: "When 'sit-down' strikes began here in America, I knew what they meant, for I had read . . . an enthusiastic account of how in Russia, by the very same tactics, the workers took over one factory after another."[95] Communism meant far more than the puny party that went by that name. It was "a vast secret society whose members are not known but who are working for the establishment of Communism," and in this sense, "the New Deal policy is an international policy, a Communist policy."[96] Communism meant internationalism, which threatened the liquidation of most or all of the white race, to the benefit of the "lesser breeds." For Burchett, "Democracy . . . is the RED way of pronouncing Communism."[97]

To prepare for a confrontation with armed subversion, she recruited students for paramilitary and ultrapatriotic organizations, with likely prospects offered the chance of training in weaponry at her farm in Bucks County, near the Bund's training and paramilitary establishment, Camp Deutschhorst. She herself always carried two pistols as a precaution against Communist attack. In 1937 her activities were publicized by the *Philadelphia Record*, and the ensuing controversy resulted both in an embargo on carrying weapons on school premises and in her transfer to West Philadelphia High School. This last measure may have been a blunder, as she was now placed in contact with the Catholic Coughlinite movement in that section of Philadelphia, an alliance that would bear fruit in later years.

Over the next five years Bessie Burchett provided the *Record* with abundant copy, often of a semihumorous tone. A typical 1938 headline was "Two-Gun Bessie Foils Lurking Reds Again."[98] Her positions became so extreme that her opponents included not only the expected Left and liberal groups but such customary bastions of anti-Communism as the American Legion and the POS of A.[99] Burchett herself might be viewed as a solitary crank, but her anti-Communism campaign attracted supporters alienated by the New Deal, the CIO, and the assault on Christian civilization by the Spanish republic. "A committee of strong patriots was formed to

investigate . . . seditious, un-American, Communistic or atheistic
teachings" in the schools, and it circularized the city's network of "patriotic" organizations.[100] By 1937 supporters coalesced into the ACS, formed by Burchett with the aid of Mr. and Mrs. David D. Good, and Republican political figure Kern Dodge.[101] The society's manifesto stood "For God and Country" and required members to swear that they were "native born citizens of the USA . . . [and] believe in God and the teachings of Jesus of Nazareth."[102] It exalted "the American Form of Government" and "the Constitution which has made ours the most prosperous nation on Earth."[103] The group met twice monthly in a hall at 1920 Spruce Street, drawing an audience of seventy-five.[104] The ACS sponsored speeches by leading rightists, including Samuel Stouch. Another guest was Elizabeth Dilling, author of the exposé work *Red Network*, which Burchett had quoted so freely in her own writings.[105]

PROFESSIONAL PATRIOTS

The ACS included "proper Philadelphians" from the traditional elite, who were mainly Episcopalian or Quaker.[106] This was a significant departure from the normal stereotype of Coughlinite support as "almost entirely a low status public."[107] ACS leaders represented a common strand in the local extreme Right, the sort of upper-crust ultrapatriots characterized by a contemporary pamphleteer as "Dress Shirts."[108] They had been active in patriotic and "fraternary" societies as well as the rightist pressure groups that had been formed during or shortly after the First World War with the goal of rooting out Communism and syndicalism, and whose activities became identified with anti-Semitism.[109] Many such groups were affiliated with John B. Trevor's American Coalition of Patriotic Societies, "an organization to coordinate the efforts of patriotic, civic and fraternal societies to keep America American." The hundred or so member organizations were often innocuous in their own right, but Trevor's refusal to exclude openly anti-Jewish and vigilante movements led to the larger coalition being condemned as a fascist movement in the late 1930s.[110] The American Coalition became the "largest organized group restricting itself solely to the circulation of anti-foreign-born propaganda," and Trevor retained his rightist connections into the 1950s.[111]

Patriotic groups were not necessarily anti-Semitic or extremist, but they did contain such elements. Among the organizations most active in rightist crusading in these years were the Daughters of the American Revolution (DAR); the Military Order of the Loyal Legion; the POS of A; and the Daughters of Colonial Wars. The annual state conventions of the DAR rarely lacked a speaker who would warn of Red subversion in apocalyptic terms, while the national organization sponsored radio broadcasts in which Louis McFadden condemned the perils of internationalism.[112] Throughout the 1930s one of the consistent themes in DAR rhetoric concerned Bessie Burchett's cherished issue of infiltration in the schools, with a focus on the same enemies, above all Harold Rugg. In 1934 the Philadelphia convention warned that "under the guise of idealism and liberalism," "many cults seek to reach the youth in colleges, schools and elsewhere through clubs, forums and societies. . . . These organizations are then used for spreading un-American doctrines which make strong appeal to the unthinking."[113] In 1935 and 1941 the DAR supported proposed legislation that would require loyalty oaths for Pennsylvania teachers.[114] The society campaigned to purge Red textbooks from the schools, focusing on the titles and authors singled out by Burchett.[115] The National Defense Committees of the DAR played an activist role comparable to that of the Americanism Commissions of the American Legion.[116]

The impeccable social credentials of Bessie Burchett's allies are illustrated by Philip Meredith Allen, who wrote the foreword to her *Education for Destruction* and who later chaired the ACS. Allen's social affiliations and memberships read like a catalog of the most prestigious activities available to a Philadelphian of his class. He boasted membership in the Sons of the Revolution; the Descendants of the Signers of the Declaration of Independence; the Descendants of the Continental Congress; Houston Post, number 3, American Legion; the Magna Charta Society; the Genealogical Society of Pennsylvania; the Historical Society of Pennsylvania; the Germantown and Chestnut Hill Historical Society; the Governor's War Library and Museum; and the Center Square Fire Company. He was also a Freemason, in Mitchell Lodge number 296, F. and A.M. (thirty-second degree).[117]

Allen was a member of a range of ultrapatriotic organizations affecting an absolute loyalty to what they defined as traditional American values. This included the Military Order of the Loyal Legion, a group founded in 1865 and restricted to military officers who served in the Civil War, or their eldest male descendants. Allen belonged to both the Pennsylvania commandery and the Commandery in Chief, and it was in his capacity as chair of the state Americanization Commission that he investigated and corroborated Burchett's allegations of Red subversion in the schools. He was also a member of the elite Union League, which required its members to swear that they had never cast a ballot for any political candidate other than a regular Republican. Allen defined himself primarily as a Republican rather than as a follower of any shirt group, but his views drew him toward the most extreme of the new fascist movements.

Other anti-Communist militants of wealthy origins included Herbert Lawson Smith, who boasted of pure descent from English settlers who had crossed the Atlantic in the 1660s and who graduated from Republicanism toward Nazi organizations.[118] Letitia Whitney Good (Mrs. David Good) was a Daughter of the American Revolution and a Colonial Dame and from 1938 to 1942 served as president of the Dames of the Loyal Legion. Through these connections she became close to Trevor's American Coalition.[119] A "dear friend" of Bessie Burchett, she tried to induce her pupils to swear that they were being subjected to Communist propaganda in their schools.[120] Like Allen and Smith, Mrs. Good began a career of two decades in the anti-Semitic fringe politics of Philadelphia.[121]

Alongside the proper Philadelphians were a core of Catholic activists such as Joseph A. Gallagher and the Blisard family, whose political concerns focused on the Spanish conflict and who found their mentor in Father Coughlin. These were usually independent businessmen. Gallagher was in real estate, Thomas Blisard Sr. was a printer, and his son Thomas was a dealer in marine supplies. They were active in both the ACS and the Committee for the Defense of Constitutional Rights (CDCR) and in a number of front groups, such as the Aryan American Citizenship Organization.[122]

Together the groups sought to expose and destroy Communism in all its guises, including the New Deal and the infiltrated Christian churches. The worst offenders in this regard were the Quakers —"the Little Red Quaker Meeting"[123]—though Bessie Burchett viewed her own Episcopalian denomination as the "Church of the Soviet" as much as the "Church of England."[124] Great Britain also occupied a senior role in ACS demonology, with British conspiracies often scarcely distinguishable from those of the Communists.[125] In 1941, of all years, Burchett described England as "the greatest of all aggressors."[126]

However, the "Jewish Question" occupied a primary place in the movement's rhetoric. Bessie Burchett and the other ACS leaders denied charges of anti-Semitism, and she herself argued that "good Jews" might care to join her in the fight against Communism.[127] This defense seems thin in light of the movement's aggressive, frankly homicidal rhetoric. Already in November 1938 Burchett warned that all American Jews must either be expelled or exterminated.[128] In October 1939 Burchett and some allies attended a Quaker-sponsored gathering at the Race Street Forum, at which the Nationalist cause in Spain was denounced by Rabbi William H. Fineshriber, who had played a leading role in organizing anti-Nazi protests over the previous year.[129] At this gathering Fineshriber allegedly blamed Christians in general and Catholics in particular for crippling progress and democracy. Burchett asked, "Do you realize there are four million Jews in the United States? . . . Now, isn't that a coincidence. There are just four million lampposts." She further explained that although her estimate of Jewish numbers might seem high, the remaining million lampposts would serve for hanging the Quakers.[130]

Attacks on Communists and New Dealers merged seamlessly into anti-Jewish threats with an ease that is only explicable if Burchett and the others regarded Jew and Communist as synonymous. One of her pamphlets proclaimed, "Let us have Christian schools with Christian teachers for Christian children. . . . Communism is Jewish. . . . The Jew Deal has ruined our industries. . . . Who has the job you ought to have? A Jew who wants war?"[131] A characteristic Burchett tirade declared, "The president is a traitor. We must do all we can to break down the president, and have the people know what kind of man he really is, and then proceed to impeach him. If Hitler does come here, he should drop a bomb on the right place in New York. You all know where I mean." This description was elucidated to refer to "a skyscraper full" of Jews.[132]

Similar sentiments, though usually expressed with a little more discretion, were shared by all the leaders of the anti-Communist network. In July 1939 Donald Shea of the National Gentile League listed Philip M. Allen as one of Philadelphia's leaders in the struggle against the Jewish conspiracy.[133] When summoned before the Dies Committee in 1942, Allen asked, "Can anyone in this committee doubt that Communism is as much a racial move as Fascism or Nazism?"[134] He asserted the truth of the *Protocols*, or at least "would not say" that the Jewish religion did *not* include that document as an article of faith.[135] On the Palestine question and the contemporary Arab revolt, Thomas Blisard Jr. remarked, "I think the Arabs are swell. I think the Arabs have done a good job over there on the Jews who have tried to take the country away from them."[136] Joseph Gallagher believed that "the Christians alone should hold office and own land and vote."[137] An ACS meeting in 1938 featured a speaker who attacked "Jewish control of the US," which included " 'President Rosenfeld,' John L. Lewis, head of the CIO, and 'the white slave and dope rings.' "[138] When Gallagher-Blisard ally William Rigney spoke in West Philadelphia in 1939, "every other sentence . . . had something in it about 'down with the Jews.' He said the Jews were to blame for conditions in Germany, that was why Hitler drove them out, and that we'll have to drive them out of this country."[139]

Members of this network were well connected with anti-Semitic writers and pro-Axis propagandists and organizers across the country, including Colonel Sanctuary, Peter Stahrenberg, Robert Edmondson, and especially James B. True, who was often mentioned as a close associate and a visitor to Philadelphia. Edmondson spoke to anti-Communist gatherings in Philadelphia and Allentown on the evils of "Adulterating Americanism—Unassimilated Immigration."[140] The group was well acquainted with George Deatherage, who is best known in contemporary accounts in the context of his activities in the South. Philip Allen's summary was "I know him. Fine fellow."[141]

While the ACS eschewed formal affiliation with national organizations, it worked closely with the Silver Shirts, and Burchett
and Gallagher sponsored appearances by Roy Zachary and other
speakers from the movement.[142] In 1938 Zachary's Philadelphia
speech echoed McFadden's views when he condemned the "behind the scenes manipulations of the Jewish people to gain control
of the United States. He said that all the policies of the New Deal
were planned and outlined long before Roosevelt was elected by
a Jewish Congress in Geneva, Switzerland."[143] In 1942 the Dies
Committee was investigating whether the son of Herbert L. Smith
was the organizer of a Silver Legion unit among the students at
the University of Pennsylvania.[144] This impressive network of contacts was inherited by the Christian Front movement that emerged
in Philadelphia during 1939, when it was remarked that "Nazi
Bundists and fascist Silver Shirt leaders have also been frequent
speakers at these [Front] meetings."[145]

ANTI-JEWISH PROPAGANDA

From the mid-1930s, anti-Semitic propaganda proliferated and
was so widely produced and circulated that only rarely can we
link leaflets or tracts to any particular group, still less to an individual. Material was produced by a variety of sources, including
Front members themselves (Thomas Blisard Sr. was a printer by
profession), but also the Bund and the Silver Legion.[146] As the
war threat grew, the anti-Semitic groups even made use of Communist Party stickers and flyers that stressed isolationist themes,
warning, for instance, "The Yanks Are NOT Coming." By 1939
the FBI described Philadelphia as "a fount of pro-Nazi and anti-
semitic propaganda" and identified a Bund-linked printing house
as the source of much of this.[147]

The ACS and other ad hoc groups placed leaflets "on coun-
ters in stores, on seats in trolley cars, and any other place where
they might come to the attention of the public."[148] Bessie Burchett
sponsored the wide distribution of materials through the school
system, so that by 1939 "a most unbelievable lot" of anti-Semitic
literature had circulated in the schools and on college campuses
in the Philadelphia area.[149] The Bund scattered bundles of leaflets
from the tops of tall buildings, while its affiliate, the Deutscher
Konsumverband (DKV) posted anti-Semitic stickers on the win-

dows of Jewish-owned stores.[150] The Christian Front expanded this leafleting operation in 1939, reaching a spectacular climax that Christmas when the city was bombarded with anti-Semitic leaflets dropped from an aircraft.[151]

Pamphlets and handbills generally followed the themes publicized by McFadden and Pelley. Jews were an alien and exploitative race. Their aggressive intentions were amply spelled out in their own scriptures and secret doctrines, including the *Protocols*, but also the Talmud, which was the reputed source of a corpus of remarks that insulted and dehumanized non-Jews. This pseudo-Talmud was reputed to say that "all property of other nations belongs to the Jewish nation," that Gentiles were beasts and that a Jew could treat a non-Jewish woman "as he treats a piece of meat," and that the sexual exploitation of any Gentile girl over the age of three years was morally and religiously justified. Nor was the blood libel extinct. Ritual murder allegations were popular in the early part of the decade and were used to explain the Lindbergh kidnapping of 1932.[152]

Jews controlled Communism, with its military center in the Soviet Union and its far-flung empire of subversives and saboteurs. It is rarely profitable to attempt to distinguish between "Jewish" and "Communist" in rightist rhetoric, as the two were usually identical: Communism was the armed political manifestation of the Jewish race and religion. The equation seemed plausible in cities like Philadelphia, where the Communist Party did indeed draw its members disproportionately from the Jewish population. In Pittsburgh the *Sun-Telegraph* printed without comment the original names of local Communist CIO leaders, leaving readers to draw the obvious ethnic conclusion, that the Left was under Jewish control.[153] Communism was not Jewish, but many of its Pennsylvania supporters genuinely were.

A typical handbill of the late 1930s made no distinction between the two phenomena, concluding, "*Communism is Jewish! Out with Jews!* Let White people run this country as they did before the Jewish invasion. Wake up! Wake up! . . . Get in touch with your nearest Anti-Communist organization."[154] Jews and Communists had thoroughly penetrated the New Deal administration and the CIO, and pamphlets offered lists of Roosevelt appointees and associates with conspicuously Jewish names, with Felix Frankfurter usually high on the list. Jews were said to exercise a secret control over American politics and business, in the interests of the clandestine Jewish elite that exercised hegemony throughout the world ("the central Kehillas or Kahala"). These arcane plots extended to the organization of pogroms against Jews themselves, according to a leaflet circulated by the Gallagher-Burchett group in Philadelphia in 1939. Racial migrations were caused by "a 'pogrom' or a sudden 'persecution' of Jews, [which] also is planned carefully by the migration committee of the powerful central Kehilla. Hitler and Mussolini put forth their edicts of expulsion of Jews upon the advice and with the consent of Zionist Jewish leaders." Even anti-Semitism was a tactical device of "organized international Jewry."[155]

The Jewish onslaught required defensive measures, including commercial boycotts: "Don't strike the Jew; Don't be rude to the Jew; and Don't BUY from the Jew." Jewish-owned shops were placarded with signs reading, "Buy here and help Communism" or "Help Zionism send all Jews to Palestine."[156] Bystanders were urged to sign a pledge to "Buy Christian," to "Live Christian, Vote Christian, and Trade Christian."[157] This campaign exploited Christmas, viewed as a central Christian holiday that had been stolen by Jewish merchants and businessmen for their own sordid profits. Philip Allen, an advertising executive by profession, designed a campaign with verses of his own composition. One began, "Down the chimney Santa comes, Buying gifts from Rosenblum."[158] In December 1939 the Christian Front ordered the printing of 100,000 leaflets and handbills on the theme of "Buy Christian for Christmas."[159]

These tirades were personally directed at Jewish businessmen and storekeepers. In 1938, postcards addressed "Dear Shopper" purportedly invited customers to patronize Lit Brothers department store, where Albert Greenfield would explain why "his store is the only place to purchase your Christmas gifts in honor of the birthday of Our Lord Jesus Christ."[160] Greenfield received some of this material, which included hate letters at the time of *Kristallnacht* warning, "This is what has caused the Jews' plight in Germany. . . . You may be a shrewd (crooked) Jew but you certainly open yourself for condemnation. Within five years, America will turn the Jews out. 'Believe it or not.'" Another flyer argued

that Jews participated in bootlegging, gambling, fencing, and pornography. They were active as "chiselers, price cutters and sweat
shops [*sic*]."[161]

CONCLUSION

Extreme anti-Semitism did not in its own right constitute fascism, nor did militant anti-Communism or a militant belief in the
supremacy of white Protestants. In the late 1930s, however, these
diverse strands became united in a powerful ideological synthesis
that identified the New Deal administration as a component of a
Jewish-dominated conspiracy and further proposed that the solution to this danger could only be found in a determined political
movement on the lines pioneered in Italy and, increasingly, Germany. Activists on the extreme Right came to perceive a linkage
between domestic and international crises, in each of which could
be observed the same cast of heroes and villains. If Jewish Communism represented the ultimate danger to the race and to civilization as a whole, then Hitler's Germany was the primary bastion
against this menace. Nativist, racist, and reactionary politics were
increasingly defined by attitudes toward the "New Germany" and
toward the American-based groups that spoke for that cause.

6 | Germany Calling
The Bund

he Nazi seizure of power in Germany provided an attractive model for some who saw strong government as a bulwark against communism, while the rise of Hitler permitted some Americans of German descent to feel that their homeland was being restored to its proper dignity in the world.[1] Pro-German activism was a patriotic reaction to the fervor of left-wing and anti-Nazi groups, which called for boycotts and sanctions against the Hitler regime. Agitation seemed only to prove the truth of Nazi assertions of an international conspiracy against the German people.

The German government had both pragmatic and ideological reasons for cultivating supporters in North America. Mobilizing German Americans reinforced Nazi claims to speak for the whole German world, while the creation of a pressure group in the United States could be of inestimable value in future diplomatic or military confrontations. Germans also noted Italian successes in organizing their overseas compatriots to give the impression of Fascism as a world movement. Fascist hegemony over the Italian American community was at its zenith between about 1933 and 1936. However, the German regime would fluctuate in its willingness to see explicitly Nazi tactics and symbolism employed in the

United States, for fear of creating an unfavorable reaction. Pro-
German organizations thus had to tread a delicate path in balancing expressions of *Deutschtum* and Americanism.

By the 1920s there were in the United States numerous German groups with a strongly right-wing and nationalist character. After 1933 these organizations provided a fertile recruiting ground for new associations dedicated to promoting the ideals and interests of the Nazi government. The Teutonia Association of 1924 was succeeded by a series of groups variously intended for German citizens and for American citizens of German origin. In 1933 the Association of the Friends of the New Germany was founded at a convention in Chicago, under the leadership of Heinz Spanknoebel, and organized according to the Nazi structure of Gaus and Gauleiters, Orts and Ortsgruppen.[2]

The group's title caused concern that "Friends of the New Germany" "sounds too German and makes the people shy and keeps them back from joining."[3] In 1936 a national convention changed the name to the German American Bund, the Amerikadeutscher Volksbund, under *Bundesleiter* Fritz Julius Kuhn. Kuhn transformed the group into an aggressively Nazi organization pledged to personal loyalty to himself and closely connected to the Auslands-Organization of the German National Socialist Workers' Party, or NSDAP.[4] The reformed Bund imitated the German Nazis to the extent of providing the leader with a personal honor guard in the uniformed Ordnungs-Dienst (OD).[5] The Bund survived officially until 1942, when many of its leaders were arrested for espionage or sedition. During its brief existence the Bund was the group most often presented both as the public face of fascism in the United States and the official representative of Hitlerism.

GERMAN PENNSYLVANIA

Pennsylvania would inevitably play a major role in the new German American movements. Pennsylvania had had a vigorous German element virtually since the foundation of the colony.[6] Germantown represented the first German settlement in North America, and the arrival of the first settlers under Franz Daniel Pastorius in 1683 was commemorated each year as German Day, which remained a national celebration until the First World War. In 1933 some 15,000 people marched in Germantown to commemorate the 250th anniversary of the settlement, a celebration greeted by telegrams from Hitler and President Hindenburg.[7] In Germany Nazi scholars lauded the Pennsylvania Dutch as models of true Aryanism, ironically in view of their pacifist traditions.[8] They should be "held up to other German Americans as examples of how *Deutschtum* could be preserved in an alien environment."[9]

Pennsylvania remained a favored destination for German migrants in the nineteenth and early twentieth centuries. In 1930 111,000 Pennsylvanians had been born in Germany and 50,000 more in Austria.[10] In the cities alone, over 100,000 foreign-born people reported German as their mother tongue, and that takes no account of the sizable German-speaking communities long native to the state.[11] In 1930 Philadelphia alone had 38,000 German-born residents and 94,000 more with one or both German parents. There were 53,000 foreign-born German speakers in Philadelphia, 19,000 in Pittsburgh, 3,900 in Allentown, 3,500 in Erie, 2,500 in Scranton, and 1,800 in Altoona and Reading. In 1930 at least a quarter of the German-born residents of Pennsylvania were noncitizens, probably 20,000 of whom had not taken out the "first papers" required to begin the naturalization process. There were well-defined German areas in the cities—in Philadelphia, for example, around the junction of 6th Street and Erie Avenue in North Philadelphia. Pittsburgh's counterpart was in the 24th Ward on the north side.

There was a rich tradition of social and cultural organizations as well as political movements and newspapers of all ideological shades.[12] By the 1930s Pittsburgh produced the old, established *Sonntagsbote* and the *Volksblatt und Freiheits-Freund*; Altoona had the *Deutscher Volksführer*; and Erie boasted the *Deutsche Zeitung*. Philadelphia had four German papers, including the *Gazette-Democrat*, the *Herold*, the Socialist *Tageblatt/Sonntagsblatt*, and the Catholic *Nord-Amerika*. In 1899 an assortment of local German societies had joined to form the Zentralverein, the Central Union of German American societies in Pennsylvania, and in 1901 a meeting at Philadelphia created a National German American Alliance, which at its height claimed 2 million members.[13]

During the First World War these German associations had campaigned against the Anglo-French cause, opposing loans and denouncing the sinister agitation of Allied agents trying to lead the United States into war.[14] At this critical moment the president of the National Alliance was Sigmund von Bosse, a minister representing the Philadelphia General Conference of the Lutheran church and who would be a leading figure in later Bund activism.[15] After the U.S. entry into war, an anti-German panic produced countless rumors about sedition and espionage within Pennsylvania.[16] However, there were some authentic incidents of sabotage and widespread evidence of pro-German sentiment.[17]

In the aftermath of war many German American groups were dissolved, while those that remained found it difficult to resume their earlier activism and generally kept a lower public profile in Pennsylvania as elsewhere.[18] In 1933 the commemoration of the Germantown settlement was marked by a controversy over the failure to display the swastika flag, a perceived insult that caused the German ambassador to cancel his participation.[19] From 1919 the Steuben Society worked to promote a more positive image of Germany and the Germans.[20]

PRO-NAZI MOVEMENTS IN PENNSYLVANIA

Pan-German political sentiments revived following Hitler's seizure of power, less initially out of positive ideological support for the Nazi cause than from opposition to its critics. In 1933 Jewish and left-wing groups organized a series of mass protests, including mass demonstrations in Philadelphia and Pittsburgh that spring, and there was an effective boycott movement against German goods.[21] German American reaction was conditioned by memories of the war hysteria of 1917–18. Later Bund leader Gerhard Wilhelm Kunze recalled that as a schoolboy at that time, "I received enough beatings to remind me of that for the rest of my life."[22] The primary need in 1933 was to discredit the propaganda that depicted Germany as an aggressive monster.

The FNG formed a Philadelphia branch in early 1933, and the group soon had about 220 active members. The city became important in the organization of the FNG, which held its national convention there in 1935.[23] Another subsidiary was formed to fight the boycott and to promote the loyalty of German American citizens to businesses in their own community. This was the DAWA, Deutschamerikanischer Wirtschaftsausschuss, or German American Economic Alliance. In 1937 this reorganized as the DKV, the German American Business League.[24] The new groups drew their support from already existing German cultural societies. In 1934 the local leaders of the FNG were Carl Gartner and Hermann Leudtke, whose earlier activities had been in, respectively, a German bakers' association and a musical club, the Liedertafel.[25] Other members derived from German Masonic groups, *Freimaurer*, although they were required to renounce membership on joining the FNG.[26]

In May 1934 the leadership of the Philadelphia FNG was summoned before the congressional McCormack-Dickstein Committee. Carl Gartner and his associates were subjected to hostile questioning seeking to show the foreign and conspiratorial nature of their movement. Philadelphia members were indeed in close contact with New York Nazi activists such as Heinz Spanknoebel, and the group had Nazi trappings: meetings concluded with the German party anthem, the "Horst Wessel Lied," and prospective members had to swear that they were of Aryan descent, free of either Jewish or colored ancestry. On the other hand, the FNG was not as unequivocally Nazi as comparable movements would become at the end of the decade, and Gartner denied that his group should be described as Nazi at all.[27] While Hitler's name was celebrated with Nazi salutes, equal respect was paid to Hindenburg and President Roosevelt, whose names were each greeted with three loyal cheers. On Jewish issues Gartner's views were (in the context) quite moderate. While Jews were excluded from joining the FNG, Gartner suggested that they could join the DAWA. He rebutted charges of anti-Semitism by reporting that his own sister living in Germany was a convert to Judaism. Obviously he did not suspect what was likely to happen to her under the Nazi regime. In Pittsburgh there was consternation about this time when a member attempted to bring a Jewish friend to an FNG gathering.

Anxious to prove that pro-Nazi groups were tied in to broader conspiracies, the congressional investigators had more success in the case of R. T. Kessemeier, the Philadelphia-based manager for the two main German steamship lines, the Hamburg-American and the North German Lloyd Line.[28] Throughout the decade the German shipping lines were often accused of espionage and the importation of contraband or propaganda into the United States, while the companies operated in close collaboration with German consular authorities. Congressional attention focused on Kessemeier, who was in contact with fascist groups and leaders across North America, as an outspoken supporter of the Hitler regime. Kessemeier's politics were illustrated by a postcard that he sent from Germany in 1933, remarking, "Germany also politically is simply perfect. It's paradise on earth, everything perfect. Heil Hitler!"[29] He worked to promote the image of the new German government in the United States and offered free shipping to Germany for selected influential individuals.[30] Strongly Nazi views were also evident among Kessemeier's closest political confidants in the Philadelphia area, such as his deputy Paul Von Lilienfeld-Toal. Investigations of the two men demonstrated intimate links between the German American groups and native fascists, especially the Silver Shirts.

The shipping lines provided free passage to Germany for individuals or groups who were thought likely to promote Nazi policies in the United States, with academics as a main target group. The McCormack-Dickstein Committee published a list of Pennsylvania college professors of German descent who were to be offered such favors, including scholars from the University of Pennsylvania, Swarthmore College, Lehigh University, LaSalle College, and others. The University of Pennsylvania was felt to be especially vulnerable to these temptations, in view of the activism there by domestic extremist groups such as the Order of 76, the Paul Reveres, and the Silver Shirts. This ultra-Right presence led to recurrent disputes over academic freedom, and Governor Pinchot intervened to prevent the University of Pennsylvania from dismissing an alleged Nazi propagandist from its faculty.[31]

GERHARD WILHELM KUNZE

While the FNG might be dismissed as a sentimental drinking club, the Bund was more ostentatious in its adoption of Nazi ideology and regalia. Again, Philadelphia played a critical role in the new movement. The first leader was Camden-born G. Wilhelm Kunze, a former chauffeur-mechanic who joined the FNG in 1933.[32] He went on to serve as national public relations director for the movement, and became deputy führer.[33] Following Kuhn's conviction on charges of forgery and embezzlement in December 1939, Kunze became national leader, in part because the Bund needed a U.S. citizen in this sensitive position.[34] Theodore Martin then succeeded him as head of the Philadelphia Bund.[35]

Kunze's speeches at national Bund gatherings earned him a reputation as "the Goebbels of the Bund," an orator far superior to Kuhn, with his opera buffo quality. Kunze was a frank Nazi who believed in "the elimination of international Jewry" and a policy to maintain "a White man's United States."[36] One of his 1939 speeches opened memorably with a salutation to "*Mein Bundesführer*, OD-men who help us secure our right to peaceable assembly and free speech, Bund members, our boys and girls, fellow White Americans, and other non-parasitic guests." Central to his thought was the "racial question," "the profound, ineradicable racial differences between the Aryan, in other words, White Gentile races on the one hand, and the Asiatic, African and other non-Aryan races on the other." Culture was founded on race, so that "international" or "interracial" culture was a contradiction in terms. "These United States also are the product of a particular Racial Group, the ARYAN." Jews, in contrast, were "the small, ever-homeless minority which alone has anything to gain by tearing nations asunder and by pitting them against themselves and each other"; they constituted the menace of "atheistic, Asiatic, Jewish-Marxism." The United States could only be saved by "Race-Legislation" to ensure that those who rule, judge, and educate the American people "MAY ONLY BE WHITE MEN."[37]

Kunze loathed the Roosevelt administration. He contrasted FDR with Hitler, "the greatest talker and thinker that Europe has ever produced,"[38] "the greatest man since the time of Christ."[39] In August 1939 he described the "Bund's program to rid America of President Rosenfeld, his New Deal and the nation's Jewish democracy. . . . By learning a few lessons from the smart nations abroad, we could make a paradise out of this country in a few years."[40] Like most of the Bund leaders, he retained close links with Nazi Germany. In 1937 he was among those presiding over the Stuttgart Congress of Germans Abroad.[41]

MEMBERSHIP

Bund membership is difficult to assess. Nationwide, Fritz Kuhn had on occasion claimed 100,000 members, but by 1939 this had been whittled down to a somewhat more plausible 20,000.[42] Herzstein suggests a lower figure of 6,500 activists, "encouraged by fifteen to twenty thousand sympathizers."[43] These were dispersed through every state except Louisiana, but support was concentrated in certain regions and cities, of which Philadelphia was one of the most vital. The original Bund society there had 200 members; 138 were aliens, mostly German citizens.[44] This branch alone would certainly have claimed a minimum of several hundred members at its height in 1938, and the figure for the whole state might have reached 2,000 to 3,000. By late 1939 anti-Nazi militant A. Raymond Raff had compiled a list of 400 known members in and around Philadelphia, including both present and former adherents.[45] In addition to the Bund proper, there were associated groups such as the DKV, the veterans' Frontkämpferschaft, the women's Frauenschaft, and the youth members of the Deutsche Jungenschaft und Mädchenschaft.

The FBI suggested that the official Bund records concealed a dark figure of perhaps ten supporters for each full member.[46] In 1940 the agency estimated that the Bund had influenced perhaps 8,000 in the greater Philadelphia area alone.[47] While German Americans predominated, a substantial share of the membership nationwide was drawn from non-German groups, mainly Irish, with some White Russians and a handful of other nationalities.[48]

LOCAL SUPPORT

Within Philadelphia the geography of Bund support and activity resembled that of the Klan a decade previously, with an obvious center around 6th Street and Erie Avenue. The DKV had its headquarters at 3644 North Broad Street, and the Bund proper operated from 3718 North 5th Street, which also contained the editorial offices of the party's paper, the *Philadelphia Deutscher Weckruf und Beobachter*.[49] The bookstore at this address sold a panoply of German publications, including *Das Schwarze Korps* and Julius Streicher's *Der Stürmer*, as well as domestic fascist papers such as the *American Gentile*. The Bund had its two most popular meeting places in this area. The Turngemeinde Hall stood at Broad Street and Columbia Avenue, while the Liedertafel Sangebund Hall at 3647 North 6th Street was a social center of German Philadelphia, with its facilities for music and chess and a meeting hall that became a Bund drill room. Other key Bund territories included Germantown, where there was also a Christian Front branch by 1939.[50]

Pittsburgh was a major Bund center throughout the decade. The group there originated in order "to counteract Communism and take counter-measures against boycotts on German goods." There were over a hundred active members by early 1939, with thirty OD-men, and it recruited within the existing German cultural societies and news media. The group was led by Allen Goeppel, an engineer.[51] By 1938 Pittsburgh had its own distinct boys' unit and operated a German school that attracted fifty youngsters. However, it never fulfilled plans to build a separate camp for military drill and training. The group's activities were epitomized by the member who reported that "we drank beer and sang songs, and the officers made speeches about the Nazi accomplishments in Germany." [52]

Bund branches were also located in Lancaster and Sellersville, and by 1938 there were recruiting efforts in other German centers, including Erie, Allentown, and Norristown.[53] There was a strong presence in the Reading area, under the leadership of Paul Kullman and Henry Seegers.[54] By 1938 this city may actually have had more Bund members than Philadelphia, and Kuhn claimed that 15,000 supporters had turned out for one Reading rally.[55] A hundred OD were regularly seen on "Nazi feast days." [56] Like Philadelphia, Reading had its Frauenschaft, and its Deutsche Jungen- und Mädchenschaft. In 1938 Kuhn announced that the Reading Bund was planning its own training camp in Berks County, modeled on Philadelphia's Camp Deutschhorst.[57] Stiff opposition from patriotic and labor groups ensured that the proposal never came to fruition, although the local branch had its own shooting range.[58] In 1939 Kuhn's arrest on theft charges occurred near Reading, raising suspicions that he may have been seeking refuge in that area.[59]

The Bund's strength in this region was attributed to the foothold obtained in the company unions at the Wyomissing Berkshire Mills complex following the traumatic recent strikes and the consequent support from the local employers.[60] By 1938 the Bund was "the largest and most powerful secret organization in the community," and it took over the Chestnut Street headquarters of the traditional German society, the Liederkranz.[61] However, the Reading

Bund succeeded where its Philadelphia counterpart failed abjectly, in maintaining the secrecy of its membership and even the location of its real headquarters.

GERMAN AND AMERICAN?

The Bund sought to re-create in Pennsylvania the atmosphere of German Nazism, with drills and rallies in which uniformed *OD-Männer* were conspicuous in their paramilitary uniforms.[62] The swastika was prominently displayed at these gatherings. In June 1938, for instance, the Turngemeinde Hall in North Philadelphia was the setting for a gathering of some 1,500 Germans and Austrians, some in old military uniforms, who celebrated the *Anschluss* by singing "Deutschland über Alles" and the "Horst Wessel." "Assorted Teutonic uniforms stood out among the civilian clothes and colorful Teutonic peasant costumes. There were twenty *Ordnungsdienst*, or organization policemen, in blue pants and overseas caps, grey shirts and black military belts, and dozens of boys in the Hitler Youth uniform. Also present were twelve members of German World War veterans organizations in Philadelphia in uniform. Several wore the drab garb of the *Stahlhelm*." Sigmund von Bosse spoke, and "virtually all hands shot up in the Nazi salute, and three heils boomed through the hall at the end." Books on sale included *Mein Kampf* and the works of Julius Streicher.[63]

The centerpiece of state Bund activities was Camp Deutschhorst at Sellersville, in Bucks County, where in 1934 the organization took over a home for wayward girls. This was the setting for important national gatherings, including the 1935 meeting at which Kuhn established his position as a national leader.[64] It was also used for training exercises for the city's youth branch, modeled on the Hitler Youth.[65] Forty boys and twenty-five girls found places at the youth encampment, where there was also a rifle range.[66] The camp was administered by Norbert Biele, a veteran of the FNG and an associate of Kessemeier. He was also prominent in Kuhn's national OD. Title was held by John Diekman, who in 1939 was listed by the Justice Department as a German agent.[67] Theodore Martin served as vice-president of the Deutschhorst Country Club.[68]

The national Bund also sponsored paramilitary camps such as Nordland and Siegfried, which aimed to re-create "the spirit of German National Socialism."[69] Carlson suggests abundant Pennsylvania representation at Camp Siegfried meetings in Long Island.[70] By 1938 the movement was restraining overt Nazi enthusiasm. At Camp Deutschhorst a "Philadelphia storm trooper" boasted of how the Bund had deceived the investigating journalists of the *Philadelphia Record* by replacing the customary swastikas and Nazi regalia with purely American symbols.[71] When Bund leaders were arrested on the outbreak of war, their homes were reported to contain copious Nazi regalia, including portraits of Hitler in clandestine shrines dedicated to the führer.[72] One Philadelphia activist was said to be such a Hitler devotee that he was motivated "to grow an identical moustache and imitate his every word and gesture."[73]

In all its activities, the Bund encountered the recurrent and perhaps insoluble ideological dilemma illustrated by its "German American" title. The fundamental beliefs and values of Nazi Germany differed from those of the United States at many points, and it was likely that the two nations would once again find themselves at least in diplomatic conflict, if not actual warfare. It was difficult to maintain a dual loyalty. However, the double face occasionally offered a valuable propaganda opportunity when Bund activities could be combined with traditional American rhetoric, with the goal of attracting political sympathizers of non-German origin. Kunze himself was adept at exploiting the German American character of his organization, proclaiming himself "racially a German and politically an American."[74] A typical Kunze address asserted that the Bund's controversial uniforms were of American rather than foreign inspiration: "They are American uniforms. The swastika is not foreign but one hundred percent American. The Indians always used it. And our salute is the symbol of free men everywhere. . . . The only purpose of the Bund is to make better Americans of those of German blood."[75]

The movement aspired to be a focus for "Americanist" activism by other rightist groups, including respectable conservatives attracted by the Bund's isolationism and fervent anti-Communism. At the same time the Bund leadership was promoting a broad fascist political front beyond the German American community. Kunze aimed to forge alliances with other like-minded groups, including the Ku Klux Klan, the Christian Front, and the ACS. In March 1939 he wrote of his efforts "to develop stronger bonds between the Bund, the Silver Legion and the numerous other patriotic organizations subscribing to our basic racial and social convictions, with the ultimate object of helping to bring about a desperately needed American national movement of all the one hundred million Aryans."[76]

WASHINGTON'S BIRTHDAY

Coalition-building activity was most in evidence on the American patriotic holidays conspicuously favored by the Bund as a means of proving their loyalty. Possibly the movement was emulating the Communist Party's effort to coopt Americanism by devices such as their "Lincoln-Lenin" memorial gatherings.[77] In February 1939 a Washington's Birthday commemoration allowed the Bund its greatest national triumph when over 20,000 supporters attended a mass rally in Madison Square Garden.[78] In Philadelphia a related celebration on February 17 became the source of controversy when the Nazi-influenced veterans' organization, the Kyffhäuserbund (KB), held a Washington's Birthday festivity at the Quartette Hall on Germantown Avenue. The *Philadelphia Record* enumerated the groups present, focusing on the serving or former U.S. military officers, who attended in uniform: "A colonel; a major general, retired; a colonel in the reserve; a major in the medical reserve; . . . six National Guardsmen; four Naval Reserve officers; fifteen troopers of the *Deutsche Frontkämpferschaft*; twenty Italian veterans of the world war; twenty members of the *Kyffhäuserbund*; members of the Federation of Italian World War veterans."[79] The swastika was displayed alongside the U.S. flag, and the "Horst Wessel" was sung. Guests included the city's German consul, Arno P. Mowitz.

Also present were far-Right militants such as Bessie Burchett and Joseph Gallagher, who gave Nazi salutes.[80] Though Burchett affected to condemn the ethnic-based rightist groups as un-American, she was a faithful ally of the Bund, received substantial packages of pamphlets and propaganda materials directly from Germany, and addressed Bund rallies at the Liedertafel Hall. She admitted acquaintance with Kunze and Karl Schumacher and heard Fritz Kuhn speak in New York City.[81] Burchett was one of several ACS leaders to gravitate toward the Bund. By 1941 Herbert L. Smith was described as a member of this organization, in addition to the Coughlinite Social Justice Union, the ACS, and the CDCR.[82] In 1938 Thomas Blisard Jr. felt sufficiently sympathetic to the German cause to send a telegram to Hitler to apologize for anti-Nazi remarks made by American politicians.[83]

These allies might give the impression that only convinced rightist agitators supported the Bund, but there was also a contingent of respectable politicians and civic leaders. Congressman Fritz Gartner inevitably held a place of honor at the Washington's Birthday festivities. So did several other state and city officials, including Edwin A. Lee, state representative from the 22nd Ward in Germantown, and municipal judge Eugene C. Bonniwell, a former gubernatorial candidate for the Democratic Party in 1918 and 1926.[84] Bonniwell, a prominent Catholic, was a distinguished member of numerous patriotic groups and a leader in the local Sons of the Revolution. Lee, Bonniwell, and the rest were denounced by the Left as Nazi sympathizers, but their mere presence gave a cachet of respectability to the occasion, as did that of retired major general Robert H. Brookfield, a distinguished veteran of both the Spanish-American War and the First World War.[85]

Brookfield illustrates the difficulties of assessing the motives of such non-German fellow travelers. He disagreed with the Bund on significant issues, and a friend stated that he had assisted a Jewish couple to flee Germany. According to his own account the meetings in question were purely patriotic: "Washington and his German instructor of troops, General von Steuben, were praised. . . . The speaker drew parallels in the lives of Goethe and Washington. There was no mention of Nazism but an attack on Communism. Afterward there were German bands and dancing. I had a good time."[86] The invitation came not from the Bund but from the veterans' societies, the KB and the Stahlhelm. His account of a sentimental gathering of old soldiers appears convincing, if naive, but other reports suggested a different picture. Brookfield attended a total of three Bund-sponsored events, and it is dubious that on each separate occasion he was equally startled by the massed Hitler salutes. The FBI also claimed to have photographic evidence of Brookfield himself giving such a "German greeting." Brookfield was a teacher in Central Philadelphia High School, and it might be that through this educational setting he encountered the rightist activism of Bessie Burchett.[87]

Brookfield represents a strand of conservative opinion that, while not actively pro-Nazi, was drawn to the aggressive anti-Communism of the Bund and found there no contradiction to an ideology of Americanism. In September 1939 he was prepared to advocate the suppression of the Bund, but only because of the current Nazi entente with Communism. This suggests the breadth of the movement's potential appeal to conservatives outside the German community strictly defined. Some months later the FBI was examining the "number of prominent Philadelphians" who had received the bibulous hospitality of Camp Deutschhorst.[88]

THE BUND AND THE GERMAN SOCIETIES

The Bund created a Nazi-influenced coalition within the German American community, raising troubling questions about the relationship between German national or cultural loyalties and devotion to the particular ideology of the Nazi party. This was a pressing issue in Pennsylvania, where so many residents could claim at least some German inheritance.[89] By no means all German Americans were enthusiastic about the new Germany, but the Bund aggressively expanded its influence over the network of the state's German associations and cultural societies, which were coordinated in the Zentralbund. Represented were groups as diverse as the Frankford Schulverein, the West Philadelphia Männerchor, the Tioga Liedertafel, the Philadelphia Quartette Club, Haus der Deutschtums, the von Mackensen Drill Corps, the Cannstatter Volksfest-Verein, and the Austrian-American Society of Philadelphia.[90] The blue-ribbon German Society, founded in 1764, included members from such wealthy Philadelphia families as the Drexels and the Wanamakers.[91] There were also Bund subsidiaries such as the DKV.[92] In Philadelphia alone the total membership of German societies stood at 52,000 in 1939.[93] At least until 1938, Bund and pro-Nazi militants had little difficulty in making their presence felt in most of these groups, or in renting their halls for political meetings. The Quartette Club, for example, which hosted the Washington's Birthday meeting, also provided a venue for openly Nazi speakers like Colin Ross.[94] Nor were there serious qualms about Bund use of such community landmarks as the Liedertafel Sangebund Hall or the Turngemeinde Hall.

German veterans' organizations were particularly prestigious and were promising sources of support. The rightist Stahlhelm was represented in Pennsylvania, as were the German War Veterans, but there were many other specific bodies, including Austro-Hungarian units. Philadelphia even had its unit of former Württemberg Grenadiers. The Bund concentrated its energies on Karl Schumacher's Kyffhäuserbund, the Kyffhäuser Kameradschaft von Hindenburg.[95] Based in North Philadelphia, this became a potent national organization.[96] In 1937 the group also incorporated in Pittsburgh.[97] The KB was valuable because it permitted pro-Nazi activities that would have been condemned if they had openly derived from the Bund of Kuhn and Kunze. The case of General Brookfield shows how a patriotic conservative could justify participating in KB-sponsored activities, as a gesture of reconciliation toward a gallant former enemy.

Kunze also attracted the support of respectable community figures such as Lutheran clergyman Kurt E. Molzahn, who provided a useful counterweight to the group's sometimes unsavory image. Another valuable acquisition was Sigmund von Bosse, of Roxborough, by this time an open Nazi sympathizer who spoke at New York Bund meetings. At the Madison Square rally in 1939 he denounced the "internationalist serpents of intrigue" and asserted that "if Washington were alive today, he would be friend of Adolf Hitler, just as he was of Frederick the Great."[98] In January 1939 von Bosse succeeded as *Staatspräsident* of the Pennsylvania Zentralbund. The presence of established community figures was useful for the Bund in letting it appear as a mainstream and respectable group, despite the flood of bad publicity about its Hitlerite connections and the personal scandals surrounding Fritz Kuhn.

The success of this mainstream strategy is suggested by the election to Congress of Fritz Gartner. A former attorney for the Bund paper, the *Philadelphia Weckruf*, he served in the state house of representatives in 1933–34. His congressional campaign was organized and managed by another pro-Bund paper, the *Herold*. Gartner was an avid joiner of fraternal groups, and his memberships included the Masons, the Shrine, the Moose, the Elks, the Artisans, and the Eagles, in addition to the American Legion.[99] He was also national president of the German American Federation of the United States and subsequently president of the Philadelphia Alliance of German Societies, which by 1938 were closely affiliated to the Bund. Dinnerstein describes Gartner simply as a Bund supporter, though Gartner himself responded to such charges with libel suits.[100] He "has spoken to Bund meetings in his district with Fritz Kuhn on the platform and when heiled with Nazi salutes, raised his arm likewise in response."[101] As a congressman, however, he could be neither ignored nor excluded from political life, especially when his constituency was likely to be one of the rare Republican strongholds in the metropolitan area.

The Bund itself tried to present itself as a willing ally of mainstream conservatism. In 1938 the DKV requested all Philadelphia Bund supporters to vote the straight Republican ticket, to help "destroy Communism and bring to a success the hope for government by and for Aryans." "We are assured that if elected our organization will bear the friendship of Judge James and the Republican Party."[102] About this time the Republican administration of Philadelphia approached Fritz Kuhn to urge him to hold the 1939 convention of the DKV in the city, suggesting the relatively "normal" manner in which this Bund front was still viewed.[103]

The dilemmas caused by the Bund's position in German American cultural life were illustrated in October 1939, when the Zentralbund held its customary German Day celebration at Philadelphia's Metropolitan Opera House.[104] The issue for community leaders was how best to separate the commemoration of Germany and the German people from the political exaltation of Hitlerism, as swastikas and Bund uniforms had been much in evidence in the celebrations of each of the three previous years. In response to earlier controversy, conspicuous Nazi symbolism was muted on this occasion, while the German consul in New York tactfully withdrew his sponsorship of the meeting. Even so, the event was chaired by Sigmund von Bosse, and it was a major coup for the extremists when they secured U.S. Senator James J. Davis as chief speaker.[105] Despite the absence of Nazi emblems, Davis's calls for peace in the current European conflict were greeted with "Heils" and Hitler salutes.[106] A similar welcome was extended to two U.S. congressmen in attendance, Representatives James P. McGranery and, of course, Fritz Gartner.

PROPAGANDA

Between 1936 and 1939 the Pennsylvania Bund possessed a political influence far beyond that suggested by its numbers. Philadelphia especially was crucial to the propaganda activities of the national Bund. It was one of only three cities outside New York to publish its own local version of the party newspaper, the *Deutscher Weckruf und Beobachter*.[107] Many of the Bund's newspapers and pamphlets were printed in the Philadelphia area by the firm William B. Graf and sons (formerly Graf and Brueninger), who also produced the weekly *Philadelphia Herold* from their shop at 1631 Germantown Avenue.[108] Until 1938 the *Philadelphia Weckruf* included a swastika on its masthead, and even after this was removed, it retained its slogan, "For a single Germanism in America and at home." The paper advertised itself as *Das Kampfblatt Gross-Philadelphias für ein starkes, freies und zielbewüsstes Amerikadeutschtum*. The *Weckruf* was supported by advertising revenue from small German American businesses in the Philadelphia area, suggesting the extent to which it and its sponsors were seen as an accepted component of community life.[109]

The Graf firm was a vital asset for the Bund, though the management subsequently minimized its ideological commitment to the propaganda enterprise. Around the time of American entry into war, for instance, the firm announced that it was solely a business enterprise that happily accepted customers of any nationality, creed, or political outlook. "That is their sole business, in which politics, religion, -isms etc have had no part. . . . We disclaim any connection with the organization which has placed the printing order with us." According to this account, Graf printed the *Weckruf* because several years previously they happened to have placed the lowest bid on a commercial venture.[110] Graf had a stormy relationship with the Bund and its publishing subsidiary, A. V. Publishing Co., which had accumulated a $5,800 debt by June 1940, $7,000 by late 1941, by which point the account was turned over to a collection agency.[111] Graf was nervous about the stigma acquired from the Bund link: "It is absolutely impossible for us to continue under those conditions, since with the publicity we are receiving at the present time, regarding us printing the *Weckruf*, we are loosing [*sic*] considerable business."[112] The following year the firm complained miserably of the "contumely, humiliation" it had received as part of the ongoing fifth column campaign.[113]

But Graf can hardly be viewed as an exploited and politically naive victim, since the long continuation of the unpaid debts meant

that in practice the printing firm was subsidizing the Bund. This
clearly indicated "where Mr. Graf's sympathies lay" (though in fairness, the depression was not a time for any small business to be too scrupulous about demanding prompt payment from a customer).[114] Moreover, the *Herold* that it published long before the formation of the Bund was an unabashed friend of the "New Germany" and from 1933 was offering a regular diet of praise for the Nazi regime, and condemnation of its enemies.[115] The paper supported the Bund and carried advertisements for associated groups such as the KB.[116] Like other German papers in the state, such as the *Pittsburgh Sonntagsbote*, the war news that the *Herold* presented from the European front was a digest of official statements from the German government, citing confident claims about German victories and "the year of Axis victory."[117] Following the outbreak of war and the suppression of the Bund, the FBI undertook a detailed scrutiny of pro-Nazi activities alleged against the *Herold*, which included accepting advertising from firms linked to the German government and from travel agencies offering to assist stranded German patriots wishing to return to fight for the fatherland.[118]

The Graf link raised many opportunities for the dissemination of Bund material. In March 1938 the *Philadelphia Inquirer* exposed an attempt by the German government and American sympathizers to create a Nazi and anti-Semitic newspaper network in major cities across the United States. Coordinated from the Austrian Embassy in Washington, D.C., the scheme involved sponsoring German American journalists to establish a newspaper chain in which they would serve as editors. The chain would use the facilities of Bund-affiliated print shops, the best known of which were located in Philadelphia. The plan collapsed when a majority of those invited to participate walked out from what they saw as a subversive undertaking.[119]

Though not directly affiliated with the Bund, the German propaganda cause had another powerful media friend in Ralph Beaver Strassburger, who owned the established *Norristown Times-Herald* in suburban Montgomery County.[120] Strassburger came from an old Pennsylvania German house and was active in the Sons of the Revolution, but his own views were apparently pro-Nazi.[121] The *Times-Herald* was conspicuous for its paeans to German military successes, boasting on the fall of France that the country's new rulers were far superior to the old, to "her own rascally lewd leaders—the warmongers who have sapped and stolen her warmth and vigor—and bring back her pristine graciousness and loveliness under a true government of her own people."[122] Strassburger invested in German industrial concerns and was well acquainted with German diplomats in North America. In 1940 his Norristown Press cooperated with Hans Thomsen and the German embassy in publishing and disseminating nationwide *The German White Paper*, propaganda material intended to prove Roosevelt's belligerent intentions, with the aim of discrediting him in the forthcoming elections.[123] As a bonus for local consumption, the materials were embarrassing for U.S. ambassador William C. Bullitt, the friend and political mentor of former governor Earle.[124] This was "probably the most successful single piece of Nazi propaganda so far as this country was concerned" and led isolationists like Hamilton Fish to propose Roosevelt's impeachment.[125]

Within Pennsylvania the intensity of pro-Nazi propaganda was the subject of an influential series of exposés published in the *Philadelphia Record* in January 1938 that were timed to coincide with Fritz Kuhn's visit to Philadelphia.[126] Forms of propaganda included short-wave radio broadcasts from Berlin, schedules for which were published in the *Herold* and corresponding papers in other cities. The Bund distributed anti-Semitic leaflets and stickers in "German and Negro sections of the city" from 1937 onward.[127] The stickers generally urged citizens to boycott Jewish stores and businesses. In the fall of 1937 Jewish homes and businesses around 5th Street and Wyoming Avenue were "plastered" while the occupants were attending Yom Kippur services. Nazi supporters were accused of infiltrating pro-German comments in otherwise innocuous material, and in 1938 an official of Philadelphia radio station WPEN was dismissed for inserting pro-Nazi commentary in German-language programming. The man involved later undertook propaganda broadcasts from Berlin to the United States.[128]

THE BERLIN CONNECTION

Propaganda endeavors were organized through a network of agencies in both Germany and the United States, coordinated through the German Embassy in Washington. The propaganda attaché reported that he had been in sporadic contact with Pas-

tor Molzahn, who "had done everything in his power to win over
the people in his congregation for the Third Reich." Molzahn received schoolbooks and other materials from Carl Gunther Orgell,
American representative of the Volksbund fur das Deutschtum im
Ausland, or League for Germandom Abroad.[129] By 1939 these activities had received a major fillip from the vigorous new chargé
d'affaires, Hans Thomsen.

Within Pennsylvania the Bund disseminated films and propaganda materials locally, often serving as a conduit for official productions of the German government's propaganda machinery, for
books and pamphlets from Berlin's Propaganda Ministry or Terra-
mare Press. In 1938 the Berlin Deutsches Auslands-Institut listed
among those most useful distributing propaganda in the United
States two familiar names from the Philadelphia Bund, R. T.
Kessemeier and Pastor Molzahn.[130] By the spring of 1940 *The Hour*
was reporting a "fascist boom in Philadelphia."[131] "The distribution of anti-semitic literature, the holding of Nazi and anticommunist meetings, the radio and newspaper publicity given Hitler propaganda films—all bear witness to the fact that a drive is taking
place to rejuvenate the fascist movement in this city." Every weekend German films were shown at the Moose Hall, often productions of the Universum Film Aktiengesellschaft (UFA). These
were advertised through the two local papers, the *Herold* and the
Weckruf. For students and intellectuals the virtues of German
"high" culture were disseminated through bodies such as the Carl
Schurz Foundation and DAAD, both of which worked with the
German-based Amerika Institut.[132] Apart from the natural German constituency, it was remarked in 1941 that Irish anti-Semites
in Philadelphia "have been keeping in close touch with and receiving assignments from the German Library of Information" in
New York City.[133]

German consuls were visible at gatherings of the Bund and affiliated societies, giving the meetings a sense of official approval. In
April 1940 the new Philadelphia consul Erich Windels attended a
Hitler birthday celebration and "Fatherland Memorial Meeting" at
the Philadelphia Rifle Club in Olney, a popular venue for German
American social events.[134] "The hall was decorated with American and Nazi flags hung side by side. A picture of Hitler graced
the stage, and under it hung a banner with the slogan *Ein Volk—*

Ein Reich—Ein Führer. The Star Spangled Banner and the *Horst Wessel* were played. . . . Greeting the audience with a Nazi salute, [Windels] burst into an ecstatic eulogy of *Der Führer.* . . . A UFA newsreel with scenes from Nazi Germany was shown and received with much applause." Windels worked closely with Schumacher of the KB.[135]

The role of German officials and consuls in Bund activities raised the question of whether the group was an authentic society or an agent of a potentially hostile foreign regime. Diplomats, moreover, had legal immunity from investigation and prosecution. A key figure for the Pittsburgh Bund was local consul William F. Knoepfel, whose career as representative for the North German Lloyd steamship line was felt to offer splendid opportunities for espionage and propaganda.[136] Between 1933 and 1940 the German official presence in Philadelphia expanded from a "small business formerly conducted by an acting consul" to "a full-fledged ex-minister and envoy as its consul, with staff."[137] After the outbreak of war the consulate combined its activities with those of Kessemeier's Hamburg-American line and FORTRA, an agency to transmit American supplies and food packages to relatives in Germany.[138]

As with the Italians, it was alleged that German diplomatic representatives were putting pressure on Pennsylvania residents with relatives in Germany to subdue potential critics and perhaps to recruit potential agents or saboteurs.[139] In 1939 "Nazi agents" were said to be collecting addresses of German families in Pennsylvania so that they could receive "floods" of Nazi propaganda literature mailed directly from Germany. The most active agent was a non-German and a reserve army officer, presumably a member of the ACS or the CDCR.[140]

DIPLOMACY AND ESPIONAGE

The Bund's enemies pointed to these diplomatic and propaganda connections to argue that the Bund was little more than an arm of German intelligence.[141] Generally the German government discouraged recruitment of active Bund members as their affiliations made them too blatant to be useful, and Consul Windels spurned direct contacts with would-be agents.[142] In the case of Philadelphia, however, allegations of espionage had more than a kernel of truth, in that Wilhelm Kunze was indeed an agent, who contacted German and Japanese allies through a ring based in Mexico. A key partner was Philadelphia pastor Molzahn, who graduated from being an agent of Günther Orgell to running his own discrete ring as "the chief V-man the Abwehr had in the Philadelphia region, one of the most energetic and productive agents in the United States."[143]

In 1938 Kunze linked up with a "rambunctious Ukrainian underground"[144] headed by Prince Anastase Vonsiatsky.[145] He was also linked to Japanese intelligence. For Kunze the Ukrainian connection offered wonderful potential for domestic sabotage and intelligence gathering, especially since its penchant for violence was easily explained by its ostensible hatred for Soviet and Communist causes.[146] In December 1940 the group hatched the "Chicago Plan" for massive sabotage of American munitions plants and defense installations, and some of these acts may have been undertaken over the next few months.[147]

However, Vonsiatsky proved unreliable in that he was sufficiently unwise to confide in Alexei Pelypenko, a Ukrainian priest of apparently solid fascist credentials who was in fact acting as an FBI informant. The federal government was thus able to trace the German connections of the group headed by Kunze, Molzahn, and Vonsiatsky.[148] In the summer of 1941 Pelypenko was also told that Father Coughlin was directly involved in these plots.[149] The group gathered "a wealth of information on the US Army and Navy on both the Atlantic and Pacific coasts, which the conspirators gave to Molzahn and which he had conveyed to Hans Thomsen in Washington."[150]

THE BUND IN CRISIS

Despite its extensive political network and influential connections, the Philadelphia Bund appeared to collapse precipitously in late 1939. Apart from the recent Kuhn scandals, this reflected ideological disputes following the Nazi-Soviet pact in August, and a hundred members were said to have left the city's branch about this time.[151] In the fall of 1939 a Bund meeting held in conditions of great secrecy was attended only by fourteen or fifteen members.[152] A leading item on the agenda was discussing the resignation papers of seventy-two members.[153] By October Theodore Martin had resigned as Philadelphia party boss, and in December the local Bund was said to have been dissolved altogether.[154]

The Bund was the victim of its own success, as its enormous publicity had also attracted to it much of the obloquy excited by Nazi activities in Europe. Growing hostility restricted the Bund's capacity to operate publicly. Already in January 1938, when seventy-five "uniformed, swastika-banded storm troopers marched" to hear Fritz Kuhn speak in the Liedertafel Sangebund Hall, the speech was followed by rioting between pickets and OD-men.[155] The following month the hall was destroyed by a large bomb that made North 6th Street look "more like Prague or Vienna than North Philadelphia."[156] Analyzing the decline of the organization a year later, Theodore Martin singled out this event as the death blow.[157]

Shortly afterward protesters stormed a Bund meeting at the Turngemeinde Hall, causing a riot that left fifty people injured. In September another explosion destroyed the home of a physician working for the German consulate, who was also a director of the German Society of Pennsylvania.[158] In December the Turngemeinde officially sought to change its name to the Philadelphia Turners, to avert further Nazi associations, and the governing board elected an anti-Nazi majority.[159] However, this did not prevent a revival of picketing and mass protests at any cultural gathering believed to have the slightest pro-Nazi component.[160] The Graf printing firm was targeted for a "crude bomb at the door of our shop." Assassination threats and hate mail were endemic.[161]

As the international situation deteriorated from mid-1938 onward, every major crisis had local repercussions in the form of demonstrations against diplomatic or commercial targets. In September 1938 the Sudeten crisis was marked by protesters at the German consulate at 1420 Walnut Street bearing placards with slogans such as "Save Czech Babies from German Bombs" and the perennially popular "Hitler ist nicht Deutschland; Deutschland ist nicht Hitler."[162] In April 1939 2,000 Philadelphians rallied in support of the Czech nation on the eve of its absorption into greater Germany.[163] Protests reached a crescendo in the Winter of 1938–39 following the pogroms of *Kristallnacht*.[164] Fascist and Nazi sympathizers encountered persecution or physical violence.

Leaders of anti-Semitic sects such as the ACS and the CDCR often complained of assaults and sabotage by political opponents, including beatings and the destruction of mail or checks.[165] Some Bund members lost their jobs when their activities became known. In Pittsburgh a proposal to have Kunze address a meeting stirred violent opposition from Bund members themselves. His "very appearance . . . would cause a breach among Pittsburgh Germans and probably will cause a riot against the Bund by Americans."[166]

In addition the Bund was being harassed by state and local governments. From the fall of 1938 the organization was seen as a sufficient threat to merit the close scrutiny of the House Un-American Activities Committee, while Kuhn faced a searching interrogation in August 1939 and again that October.[167] Published accounts of the group at this time emphasize the close parallels with German Nazism, the role of German diplomats and intelligence agencies, the indoctrination of youth, and the concealment of the organization's true goals. In reaction local restrictions were imposed on activities, liquor licenses were rescinded, and the public wearing of uniforms was prohibited.[168] The Pennsylvania Liquor Control Board cited Camp Deutschhorst for violating its license by disreputable activities.[169] In 1940 Kunze and some associates were arrested for violating New Jersey's ban on uniforms at an Independence Day rally at Camp Nordland. The same state prosecuted him under an innovative statute against inciting racial hatred.[170]

The Bund also encountered lively opposition within the German American community from older groups such as the Steuben Society and from a number of key activists, notably A. Raymond Raff, "rip-snorting antagonist of intolerance, especially in its Hitlerian form," who held a politically powerful office as collector of the Port of Philadelphia. A sharp speech against the Hitler regime in 1936 led to Raff being denounced to the U.S. customs commissioner for offending a foreign government. Following an investigation by the Customs Service and the FBI, he was congratulated on his courageous stand and thereafter operated with at least the acquiescence of the federal government.[171] Raff's agitation contributed to the launching of a federal investigation of local Bund activities in the spring of 1939, an effort that he was able to assist enormously by supplying the agency with a detailed 500-page report on Bund activities in the Philadelphia area. His endeavors were so damaging that Bund members from the Reading area were said to have plotted his assassination.[172]

Raff coordinated a series of anti-Nazi meetings, and in 1938 representatives of over twenty German organizations met in Philadelphia to protest the "militarism and racial hatred" of the Hitler regime. These bodies combined to form the Deutsch Amerikanischer Kultur Verband, the German American League for Culture, in order to combat Nazi influence (*Verband* was to distinguish it from *Bund*).[173] Raff was the organization's president, and the *Philadelphia Record* noted that "Raff and the German American League for Culture are interchangeable."[174] Within a year the Philadelphia branch alone claimed the allegiance of 20 of the 100 German societies. League affiliates had a total membership of 11,000, though activists numbered around 500, comparable to the strength of the Bund itself.[175] League activities ensured that the great majority of German societies were increasingly distanced from Bund sympathies. Most prohibited swastikas or Nazi regalia, which by 1939 were confined to a handful of overt Bund sympathizers. In 1938 Raff personally tore down the swastika flag, "that damned dirty rag," at the prestigious Charity Ball of the German Society.[176] In 1940 the Carl Schurz Foundation condemned Hitler's "totalitarian government" for its suppression of traditional German culture and ended its program of awards for research in Germany.[177]

Hostility to Hitlerism reached a new height with the German attack on Poland in 1939 and the perceived likelihood of imminent American entry into war. It was disastrously inopportune for Fritz Kuhn to give a speech at Camp Deutschhorst on September 3 in which he declared that "Hitler can lick the world" and denounced the machinations of "Rosenfeld." By this stage it was an open secret that FBI and state police were present under cover at Bund meetings, and the remarks were widely quoted in the press.[178] A mob stormed the camp shortly afterward, and over the following weeks random attacks became so frequent that the sound of fire sirens automatically inspired the question "Is it the camp?" Innocent travelers in the vicinity were greeted with stones and shouts of "spies." Meanwhile, surveillance and picketing were maintained

by the local American Legion.[179] Over the next year financial problems and tax delinquency added to the camp's woes.[180]

Though accurate surveys are lacking, anecdotal evidence in the
press suggested broad opposition to Nazi policies in the established
German community of Philadelphia.[181] While there were some
activists within the German societies who thought Hitler "absolutely justified in waging war to solidify the German Empire,"
there were at least as many who denounced Hitler and the blind
obedience that was leading his country to disaster.[182] Among those
publicly rejecting aggression were the leaders of the Cannstatter
Volksfest-Verein, the German Society of Pennsylvania, the Turners, and of course the League for Culture. Within a few months
Raymond Raff could tell his league that the Nazis had been "prac-
tically driven out of Philadelphia." By the spring of 1939, similarly,
"There is no Bund activity in Pittsburgh. . . . The members have
stopped paying dues. There is no meeting room. The only tan-
gible thing that remains is a broken movie projector with which
the Bund intended to show propaganda movies."[183]

CONTINUITY?

If in fact the Bund had ceased to exist in a major center like
Philadelphia in the fall of 1939, it would be difficult to imagine
a more inopportune piece of timing. A cornucopia of new political opportunities was becoming available in terms of the issues of
war and neutrality, and the potential for growth was demonstrated
by the success of the new Christian Front in recruiting members
in just these months. In reality the Bund's demise was more cos-
metic than real, and activities did continue through a number of
front organizations. The KB became the alter ego of the supposedly collapsed Bund.[184] In fact, the "extinction" of the Bund can
be seen as a continuation of a deliberate trend that had begun at
least as early as mid-1938, whereby the group systematically di-
luted Nazi symbolism. Bund materials can be reliably dated by the
growing discretion about the use of the swastika, the Hitler salute,
and the slogan "Heil Hitler." Prior to mid-1938 all were used enthusiastically, for example, in handbills for the *Philadelphia Weckruf*. Over the next year a determined policy swept away the Nazi
symbolism so that the customary "Heil Hitler" in correspondence

was replaced first by *mit deutschem grüss*, a seemingly harmless and patriotic phrase, but which for cognoscenti signified the straight-arm salute. By 1939 even this generally became "Free America!," with the recipient left to conclude from what or whom the nation was supposed to be freed.[185] In 1937 Kunze's correspondence used a frank "Heil Hitler!" or *mit deutschem Heil grüss*; by 1939 "Free America" was standard, and obligatory.[186] Sigmund von Bosse's mailings to Zentralbund members were signed with the anodyne compromise *mit deutsch-amerikanischem grüss*.

The same process affected the KB, which in late 1938 used as emblem a shield that combined the swastika with the Kyffhäuser monument symbolizing the unity and rebirth of Wilhelmine Germany. Within a year, only the monument remained, an apparent claim to the assertion of non-Nazi patriotism. The Philadelphia group replaced the *Hakenkreuz* with the letters "USA."[187] However, the organization was led by Schumacher as *Bundesführer*, a title more blatant than Kuhn or Kunze would have dared assume. Schumacher's correspondence and charitable appeals were signed *mit deutschem grüss* throughout 1940, when the Bund itself had become more cautious. Once war broke out in Europe, the KB acquired a new lease on life with the Kyffhäuser-Hilfswerk, raising money to be sent to Germany, ostensibly for the relief of German prisoners of war in Canada. As a "nonpolitical" group, the KB operated among Pennsylvania's German churches and cultural societies with a freedom the Bund had not enjoyed since before the days of Raymond Raff, and the charitable Hilfswerk had a statewide network that included Reading, Erie, and Wilkes-Barre.[188] Funds raised were channeled through the Hamburg-America steamship line.[189]

The *Herold* now encouraged enthusiasts to divert their attention to the KB and some of the cultural societies of the Zentralbund.[190] Through such organizations, propaganda and antiwar activities may actually have increased during early 1940, though not necessarily under the Bund label. As so often, Philadelphia served as the "laboratory" for organizational developments elsewhere.[191] The Bund was perhaps following the strategy pioneered by the Italian Fascist movement in America. In 1929 Fascist supporters had deflected charges of foreign domination by dissolving the large FLNA organization but had maintained cohesion through a network of ostensibly decentralized cultural, fraternal, and veterans' groups.

The disintegration of the Bund can be seen as a stratagem designed to meet the circumstances of the fall of 1939, in that antiwar propaganda would be less effective coming from a group allied to one of the foreign combatants, rather than from an ostensibly patriotic American group like the Christian Front or a broad coalition like America First. Once Germany was involved in the European war, the Bund looked subversive rather than isolationist. Newspapers regularly carried derisive cartoons of swastika-clad Bund members speaking in stage-German accents and opposing measures to strengthen national defense. In the *Philadelphia Inquirer* in 1940 a ludicrous Bund figure reacts to Uncle Sam's Selective Service Act with the words "Dot's Un-American, dictatorial—und besides, I don't like it!" The caption asks, "Sez Who?"[192] The existence of the Bund was a propaganda boon for the interventionists, with opinion polls showing that a substantial majority of Americans regarded American Nazism as a serious threat.[193] Removing German American activism from the public spotlight was a matter of urgent necessity.

The tactical nature of the Bund's eclipse is suggested by Theodore Martin's reaction to an invitation in 1941 that he should join a new "American Christian League," led by the Moylan brothers and other Christian Front associates. He wrote, "I do not think it advisable for any organization to include even former members of the much maligned German American Bund. . . . Secondly, I deem it best for any citizen of German birth to take his place on the sidelines just now and like it." He did offer to publicize the new group among friends "who I know to be Gentile and trustworthy."[194] German propaganda kits sent to sympathetic Americans listed other groups that they might care to support in lieu of the Bund, such as the ACS.[195]

The surviving Bund leadership sought new roles. Norbert Biele became one of the *Rückwanderer* who returned to Germany at the outbreak of the European war. So did most key figures in the Pittsburgh leadership, including Anton Fuchs, Allen Goeppel, and OD leader Willi Wenisch, as well as Henry Seegers of Reading.[196] Fuchs, one of Kuhn's closest henchmen, would later serve in Rommel's *Afrika Korps*.[197] Wilhelm Kunze himself sought in 1941 to renounce his American citizenship and to seek German papers, but he unfortunately found himself in the United States when the war started and was imprisoned for espionage.[198] He remained formally in charge of the national organization until December 1941.

The remnants of the national Bund organization voted to disband some days before the Pearl Harbor attack, but the Bund as a structure had long since outlived its usefulness.[199] However, groups influenced or infiltrated by German Nazism continued to operate in Pennsylvania up to the outbreak of war, albeit lacking the trappings of Hitlerite emblems and uniforms. In substance, there was a clear ideological continuity from the movement of Kunze and Biele to successors who adopted the rhetoric of Christian and Catholic militancy.

7 | The Franco Way
The Coughlin Movement

In 1940 the arrest of Christian Front activists in New York City attracted media attention to the most plausible candidate to date for the much-discussed American fifth column.[1] Pro-Roosevelt newspapers presented cartoons that portrayed the Front as a very serious threat, using terms as grave as "civil war." The *Pittsburgh Press* depicted Father Coughlin and Martin Dies both nervously pretending to ignore a dangerous-looking terrorist armed with a rifle. The caption read, "Anybody Know Anything About This?"[2] Though early fears were dispelled and the alleged seditionists acquitted, the Front and associated groups were crucial to extreme Right organization for several years afterward. Within Pennsylvania the movement attracted supporters in numbers at least comparable to those achieved by the Bund at its height and for a few months in 1939 caused real fears of social unrest in the streets of Philadelphia and Pittsburgh.

The sudden appearance and rapid development of the Front is best explained in terms of the close parallels that existed between this group and the ethnically based ultra-Right movements respectively drawn from German and Italian Americans. Like them, the Christian Front succeeded, albeit briefly, because it built successfully on older and widely accepted ideologies. As Italian Fascists and German Nazis relied on visceral patriotism for the country of origin, so the Christian Front was founded on traditions of Irish nationalism, anti-British feeling, and absolute Catholic loyalty. All three movements similarly developed deep community roots in their respective neighborhoods and sections of certain cities: the Bund in German North Philadelphia, the Fascists in Italian South Philadelphia, and the Christian Front in Irish West Philadelphia and Kensington. All received a massive initial boost from the perceived excesses of their opponents, whose campaigns had the unintentional effect of awakening and mobilizing latent loyalties. While it is a gross oversimplification to see the Coughlinite movements as simply "Irish fascism," there were definite analogies between the components of the Christian Front and the better-known groups that directly modeled themselves on European examples.[3]

ORIGINS

The terminology of a "Christian Front" had been popular for several years before the establishment of the specific group, and its connotations were originally of the Left. It derived from progressive Catholics anxious to devise socially aware alternatives to both Marxism and laissez-faire capitalism and thus to implement the social teachings of papal encyclicals such as the 1931 *Quadragesima Anno*.[4] In Pennsylvania this Catholic tradition was represented by activist priests such as Charles Owen Rice, who supported strikers and radical protesters, or James R. Cox, who in early 1932 led thousands of unemployed workers from Pittsburgh to Washington, D.C. Similar ideas motivated Pittsburgh-based CIO leader Philip Murray, the standard-bearer of Catholic social thought in the labor movement.[5] In this context "Catholic" or "Christian" activism could easily be harnessed to the New Deal cause and support of organized labor. The best-known contemporary "fronts" were the European Popular Front coalitions that allied Socialist and Communist parties. From 1935 a radical lay Catholic journal titled *Christian Front*, inspired by the *Catholic Worker* movement, was published at Pennsylvania's Villanova University.[6]

One visible exponent of the Catholic social tradition was Father Charles E. Coughlin of Royal Oak, Michigan, who from 1931 onward earned celebrity for his radio broadcasts supporting economic reform.[7] His National Union for Social Justice claimed 4 million members nationwide at its height, and in 1936 the organization attempted to support an independent presidential campaign, through the Union Party.[8] Thereafter the Coughlinites swung increasingly against Roosevelt and indeed against political democracy as such, largely under the influence of European events. For American Catholics of the mid-1930s the Spanish Civil War represented a Manichaean struggle, with the forces of Christianity and civilization pitched against those of Communism and tyranny, and the American failure to help the Nationalists was a source of bitterness.[9] Coughlin's followers adopted the battle cry "Long live Christ the King," which aligned them with the far-Right Catholic Action movements of several European and Latin American nations.

In the spring of 1938 Coughlin's paper *Social Justice* began calling for the establishment of a paramilitary "Christian Front" in the United States to combat Communism.[10] Each "platoon" would comprise twenty-five men and in turn formed part of larger "riflemen's groups," which would ultimately (he hoped) join a national army some 5 million strong. This was what Coughlin termed "the Franco Way."[11] In New York City the first Christian Front units were formed in semiclandestine conditions during that summer. They gained public visibility in late 1938, when Coughlin's broadcasts and newspapers demonstrated a sharp turn to anti-Semitism and the far Right.[12]

While initially condemning Nazi persecutions of Jews, Coughlin declared that such violence was in reality directed against a Communism that was equally menacing to Germany and the United States, and he produced evidence purporting to prove that Jews had directed the Russian revolutionary cause since its inception. As McFadden had shown, the Bolshevik movement was financed by Jewish bankers on Wall Street, so that Communism and Zionism were effectively identical.[13] Radio stations became reluctant to present his material, and some refused his business altogether. From December 1938 offending stations in New York City and elsewhere found themselves subject to mass picketing by Christian Front supporters, sometimes thousands strong.

This controversy occurred just when the American media were reporting the Nazi assaults on German Jews and their property that November, on *Kristallnacht*, and American radio stations had no wish to carry material that could incite violence and persecution in this country. For Front supporters, however, the vandalism and random assaults carried out by German storm troopers offered a model that they attempted to emulate, especially in New York City. Over the next year Front members undertook many acts of casual violence against Jews, including street beatings, tire slashings, and incidents of arson and vandalism against Jewish homes and synagogues.[14] At its height in mid-1939 the Christian Front organization in New York City may have had some 12,000 members. The group acquired a paramilitary tinge, with members training in the use of firearms through sporting clubs and gun clubs, under the supervision of police officers and national guardsmen. Critics alleged that weapons were being stolen or smuggled from army facilities such as Fort Dix.[15]

THE COUGHLIN MOVEMENT IN PENNSYLVANIA

New York City would be the main Christian Front center, but by late 1939 there were powerful Front units in most major cities, including Chicago, Baltimore, Cleveland, and Boston.[16] Pennsylvania played a crucial role in the national movement, and there was a long-standing Coughlinite presence in the state.[17] In 1935 Philadelphia radio station WCAU held an unofficial "plebiscite" on the radio priest when it requested listeners to choose whether a slot would be given to Coughlin or the Philharmonic concerts. Coughlin won with 187,000 votes to 12,000.[18] He was on good terms with Governor Pinchot and especially with Gifford's brother Amos Pinchot, who continued to contribute to *Social Justice* during its most vociferously anti–New Deal phase.[19] Amos Pinchot was a former Progressive active in the Bull Moose Party, but he was also a leading isolationist whose convictions would ally him with the political Right.[20]

Coughlin's Royal Oak Party picked up a paltry 67,000 Pennsylvania votes during the 1936 presidential campaign, but even at this stage some nuclei of support were visible, especially in Catholic neighborhoods, both Irish and Italian. The party won some 18,000 votes in Philadelphia, 2 percent of the vote for the whole county, with concentrations in the 22nd, 38th, and 43rd Wards, to the north and northwest of center city; the 34th in West Philadelphia; and the 40th to the southwest.[21] Each ward gave Coughlin's cause a thousand or so votes. Neighboring Delaware and Montgomery

Counties turned out respectable totals, with 3,700 votes combined. In Pittsburgh Allegheny County produced over 16,000 votes, with the best turnout in the wards across the river to the south and west of center city. Together the 19th and 20th Wards gave Coughlin's ticket some 1,400 votes, or more than 5 percent of the whole. There was a definite focus among Catholics in the northwest of the state, where 6,000 votes in Erie County gave the Royal Oak 9 percent of the poll and came close to making it a plausible third party.[22]

The 1936 election was a debacle, and the National Union for Social Justice was dissolved shortly afterward; but over the next two years the Coughlin movement continued to exist in the form of the Social Justice clubs. These existed both to distribute the magazine *Social Justice* and to discuss the "sixteen principles" of Coughlin's theory. The structures were innocuous in themselves, but they provided the potential basis for more sinister political organization. By late 1939 the Philadelphia clubs comprised twenty or twenty-five units each of twelve to fifteen individuals, suggesting 300 to 400 activists in the whole city. However, these figures should be taken as a minimum, since they stem from movement leader David Scannell, who was anxious to minimize Coughlin support in the aftermath of the New York sedition charges.[23]

THE RADIO CONTROVERSY

The fall of 1938 marked a decisive transformation in the nature of the Coughlin movement, because of the anti-Nazi clamor that followed *Kristallnacht*.[24] There were anti-Nazi demonstrations and protests against anti-Semitism in Philadelphia and Pittsburgh, and the boycott movement received a major fillip. In one characteristic gathering in West Philadelphia, 2,500 protesters marched in a torchlight rally in the 24th Ward, with its large Jewish population and lively Communist activity. Hitler was burned in effigy and hundreds of stores closed in sympathy.[25] Other demonstrations occurred on the college campuses of Bryn Mawr, Swarthmore, and the University of Pennsylvania, and the picketing at the German consulate on Walnut Street became so frequent as to constitute a regular fixture of city life. In Pittsburgh Protestant and Catholic clergy joined Jewish groups in supporting pickets and boycotts, orchestrated through the League for the Protection of Minority Rights.[26] Hostility to Nazism was reflected in violent attacks on

American groups believed to epitomize similar ideologies, such as the "Nazified Silver Shirt Legion" whose meeting was routed in Sharon on November 17. Speaker Roy Zachary was forced to flee a meeting hall through a rear exit. As "a wave of indignation against Nazi terrorism of Jews in Germany swept the community," the house of a local Silver Legion supporter was also attacked.[27]

Though outbursts were often spontaneous, leftist and "broad front" groups played a role in arranging meetings, often organizations close to the Communist Party, including most visibly the American League for Peace and Democracy, the American Students Union, and the Citizens' Anti-Nazi Committee.[28] For the Right the role of Communist and front groups in the anti-Nazi campaign merely confirmed charges about the connections between Jews and radicals and the gullibility of the Christians and liberals who supported them. Jewish leaders themselves were sensitive to accusations that the anti-Nazi reaction was confined to any one race or religion, and they discouraged protests that lacked at least token support from Christian denominations. Broad ecumenical support was thus sought and easily achieved.[29] Gatherings were addressed by Protestant and Catholic speakers, and placards emphasized the broad nature of Nazi persecutions. A typical poster urged bystanders, "Raise your Voice against Persecution of Jews and Catholics." Brotherhood and tolerance were major themes in the pulpits of all mainstream Protestant churches, and the Philadelphia Federation of Churches denounced Nazi atrocities.[30] "Tolerance" meetings sponsored by religious, labor, or civic groups became a well-established tradition, incorporating speakers from a variety of Jewish and Christian groups.

In this atmosphere of near-universal condemnation it is easy to understand the sensitivity of Pennsylvania radio stations about broadcasting Coughlin's messages, at least without demanding prior screening of his scripts. Philadelphia's WDAS was one of several local stations to suspend his programs in late November, leaving citizens no opportunity to hear the priest except on an inconvenient station from Atlantic City. On the other hand, Coughlin had scarcely been silenced, and his defenders exaggerated the censorship to which he had been subjected. Well into 1940 there were still half a dozen Pennsylvania stations that continued

to broadcast Coughlin's increasingly virulent diatribes, including
WJAS in Pittsburgh as well as stations in Harrisburg, Reading,
Erie, and Wilkes-Barre, and by this stage WTEL in Philadelphia
itself.[31]

The issue of Coughlin broadcasts provided an organizational
focus for his followers. The immediate cause was to pressure
WDAS to reverse its decision, but this specific protest soon provided a vehicle for other demands. In December 1938 a thousand
Coughlin supporters, organized by the Social Justice clubs and
the Loyal Score Club of East Germantown, picketed the station's
studio at 1209–11 Chestnut Street.[32] Demonstrators sold copies
of *Social Justice*. This marked the start of a long tradition: 5,000
protesters were there on December 11, perhaps 2,000 on December 18, and a steady 1,000 or so for most Sundays through January and February 1939. The protests continued every Sunday for
over a year.[33] The "Social Justice Workers" arranged mass protest
meetings, one of which drew 2,000 supporters to Harmer Hall at
Shackamaxon Street and Girard Avenue, in the Irish northeastern section of the city.[34] In February 1939 2,000 more attended a
meeting in the city center.[35] The numbers are impressive, especially as the scale of the demonstrations was confirmed by the liberal and pro-Jewish *Philadelphia Record*, which had a vested interest in understating sympathy for Coughlin.[36] Protesters attacked
not only WDAS and its advertisers but also tried to prevent Irish
and Catholic groups from using bands who had appeared on the
station.[37]

Initially demonstrators concentrated their ire on WDAS and the
free speech issue, a plausible cause in which they received wide
support. Philadelphia's city treasurer decried "censorship," and
even the regional director of the CIO declared that the suppression of Coughlin was "a dangerous precedent . . . the first step
towards fascism." [38] Other and broader themes soon emerged in
pro-Coughlin rhetoric, which portrayed the conflict as part of a
confrontation with Communism. Already in December 1938 protesters' placards proclaimed that "WDAS is Red" and "WDAS
Supports Communism," while others invited supporters to "Join
the Christian Front," to oppose the "perverted minority" that
tried to silence Coughlin.[39] In January the pickets selected as their

theme the fight to keep Felix Frankfurter from being appointed to the U.S. Supreme Court.[40] WDAS became for the Right a physical symbol quite as potent as that of the German consulate for leftist or Jewish groups.

During 1939 the protests acquired a more explicitly anti-Jewish tone, stressing that freedom of speech was being denied to a "*Christian* leader."[41] It was galling when another Philadelphia station to reject Coughlin was WJMJ, which chiefly served an Irish Catholic constituency (the call sign was reputed to stand for "Jesus, Mary, and Joseph"). Station owner Patrick Stanton refused to yield in the face of a torrent of abusive mail that followed familiar Front themes declaring, "Boycott Jews! Buy Gentile!"[42]

DEFENDING CONSTITUTIONAL RIGHTS

Coughlin's supporters formed the CDCR.[43] The leadership included Thomas Blisard Jr., whose father, Thomas Sr., was an organizer for the Pilgrims' Club and the West Philadelphia Social Justice Club. Both men were strongly rightist, and Thomas Sr. was quoted as remarking, "It is too bad [Roosevelt] didn't go down in history the day that assassin's bullet missed him." Several members of the Blisard family, who were based at 5215 Chester Avenue, emerged as activists over the following months. Also prominent was Joseph A. Gallagher, chair of the ACS and a member of mainstream Catholic groups such as the Knights of Columbus and the Holy Name Society.[44] The committee's vice-president was J. T. Howshall.[45]

In West Philadelphia especially, the CDCR became the leading force in anti-Semitic agitation and allied so closely with the patricians of the ACS that the two groups became effectively indistinguishable. In February 1939 the CDCR sponsored a mass meeting at Town Hall at which Coughlin ally Father Brophy (from Long Island City) spoke alongside Bessie Burchett, who was by this point "one of the most ardent and vociferous Coughlinites in the Quaker City."[46] The two groups provided the nucleus for the new Christian Front, with a shared commitment to the Coughlinite cause and the Franco Way. *Equality* asserted that both organizations swore "fanatical loyalty to Father Coughlin" and used *Social Justice* and the Brooklyn *Tablet* as primary texts.[47] By early 1939, ACS propaganda was declaring, "The fascists whom the Reds talk about are all liberty-loving American Christian Patriots. Only a united Christian Front can save America."[48]

As with Coughlin himself, Spain proved to be a defining issue for the Philadelphia groups. In 1938 Thomas Blisard Jr. was on probation following a conflict at a leftist rally, while Gallagher was arrested for incitement to riot against supporters of the Spanish Republic.[49] Gallagher circulated Christian Front leaflets portraying Jews of the Young Men's Hebrew Association drilling with rifles, and he warned of an imminent Jewish-Communist putsch on the lines pioneered in Spain.[50] Bessie Burchett wrote of "the Communists (later called loyalists)."[51] In the view of Burchett or Gallagher, the majority of self-proclaimed Christians not only failed to see the Communist threat but were actively collaborating with the enemy through subversive "tolerance" and boycott campaigns. Sympathy for Jews was indistinguishable from providing aid and comfort for Communist subversion, and the city's mainstream Protestant pastors were condemned out of their own mouths.

In early 1939 Coughlin followers were blamed for the appearance of anti-Semitic stickers on synagogues and Jewish-owned stores in West Philadelphia and Kensington and an attack in which the windows of a black church were broken.[52] "Street fights were not uncommon. Synagogue windows were smashed, and members of Jewish men's clubs beaten."[53] A detective from the police radical squad declared, "At meetings of this crowd, speakers have been brought in from the German-American Bund. They have distributed this literature, set neighbor against neighbor and at times actually terrorized sections of West Philadelphia. They have thrown bricks through windows and uttered statements amounting to threats."[54] It was a common tactic for a claque of speakers to attend a "Communist" meeting and disrupt the proceedings by heckling or outright intimidation. Joseph Gallagher was accused of leading "a flying wedge of anti-semitic hecklers" that regularly disrupted West Philadelphia meetings they perceived as Communist, a category that included any anti-Hitler protest.[55] Even the singing of "God Bless America" was regarded as a provocation to violence, given its Jewish authorship. Gallagher himself attempted to provoke confrontation at these meetings by wearing a swastika armband.[56] In February 1939 alone Coughlinites disrupted two "tolerance" meetings at the West Philadelphia Jewish Community

Center, one an ecumenical gathering of Protestant, Catholic, and Jewish clergy.[57] Protestant religious services were also disturbed, to the horror of mainstream clergy.[58]

On March 14, 1939, simmering local conflicts suddenly entered the wider consciousness of the city when some thirty Coughlinites attended a meeting of the Committee for Racial and Religious Tolerance at the West Philadelphia YMCA, at 52nd and Sansom, which was being addressed by prominent political and religious leaders.[59] This committee was a distinguished manifestation of the ecumenical spirit that had grown up since November, with a glittering list of sponsors that included Protestant clergy such as Daniel A. Poling and Leroy S. Ewing, Quaker Rufus M. Jones, Rabbi C. Davis Matt, and Catholic congressman Francis J. Myers. At the meeting in question the Coughlin supporters heckled speakers, proclaimed that "Hitler is right," and posted their leaflets on the walls.[60] The police, who had been previously alerted to the likelihood of violence, intervened and arrested several rightists. Tellingly for the anti-Semitic militants, the police unit involved was the radical squad, under the leadership of a Jewish detective, Jacob Gomborow. Further disruption occurred at City Hall when several members of the Blisard family arrived to demand that their kin be freed from police custody. Thirteen Coughlinites were eventually placed under arrest, including Joseph Gallagher, Joseph Rigney, and the brothers Frank and John Blisard.[61] Most of the militants came from West Philadelphia, chiefly between 52nd and 60th Streets. The ensuing committal proceedings produced a further melee in the courtroom. A Jewish magistrate recused himself from the case for fear of arousing charges of prejudice; but his Irish Catholic successor accused the Coughlinites of attempting to spread "European" conditions in Philadelphia, and attorneys engaged in scuffles after charges of Nazism were hurled.

The episode at the YMCA was not untypical or unusually violent for West Philadelphia in these months; but this was the first incident to be widely reported, and it gave local news media an opportunity both to discuss the upsurge of anti-Semitic violence in the city and to describe the extremist network. As the YMCA attack was reported on the same front pages that were currently announcing Hitler's capture of Prague, this juxtaposition encouraged the grimmest interpretations of the event and the "tolerance raiders." The *New York Times* spoke of "terrorists" belonging to a "Nazi Group" in Philadelphia. The *Philadelphia Record* concurred that this was "a local Nazi organization with headquarters near 52nd and Warren Streets" and described Joseph Gallagher as "a local leader of the German Bund."[62] Even the conservative *Inquirer* attacked the "Nazi effort to incite riot here" and used the affair as the basis for an editorial arguing that "It's Time to Disband the Bund."[63] An adjacent cartoon portrayed the "German-American (?) Bund" (*sic*) receiving "Nazi Gold" from "Hitler's World Conquest Headquarters." Meanwhile city and federal agencies intensified surveillance of anti-Semitic activities in the city and explored possible ties to Nazi organizations.[64]

Rightists redoubled their efforts to combat "Communism," and an April meeting of the Women's International League for Peace and Freedom at the same YMCA was canceled after threats that the building would be bombed.[65] Several speakers to a rally of the American League for Peace and Democracy described West Philadelphia as one of the most virulent centers of anti-Semitic and antidemocratic agitation in the entire country. Those fighting for democracy in this area were "right in the trenches."[66] In May "Nazi hoodlums and thugs" provoked a riot at 57th and Beaumont, as part of "a deliberate campaign of Nazi elements to terrify racial groups living in that neighborhood." Labor's Non-Partisan League appealed to the mayor for urgent police action to control the area, while the Philadelphia Peace Council organized a rally at Bessie Burchett's West Philadelphia High School.[67] In June Protestant clergymen held a meeting at the Academy of Music to promote racial and religious tolerance. As so often before, the gathering was attacked by the "well known bands of Nazi hoodlums who are ranging the city," some of whom sought to prevent the academy ever again being made available to these "Communists."[68]

During these months the rightist societies made propaganda use of the YMCA incident and the related disorder, attributing great significance to the role of Jewish police officers in the arrests. The Blisard family circulated leaflets to "American Gentiles," alleging that this was part of a systematic "Racial, anti-Gentile, Red frame-up," in which "nine young Christians were kidnapped by a gang of Jew detectives. . . . Is this the Jew-Communist Reign of terror? . . . Shall a handful of disreputable Jew thugs rule over the gentiles of

Philadelphia? If you're interested in law, order and justice, in saving your city and country from the horde of atheistic, Asiatic Jews, you may send a donation to the defense fund." [69] The atrocity was all the greater given the timing of the arrests, the "Jewish persecution of innocent Christians," so close to St. Patrick's Day. The "Tolerance Riot" became a cause célèbre for the national Right, and the defense fund was supported by New York Christian Front leaders John Cassidy and William Bishop. [70]

The critique of the police had a surprising resonance for conservative Republicans, who had been engaged in a bitter struggle with maverick Republican mayor Davis Wilson. Wilson had made unrestrained use of the police machinery against his rivals, targeting gambling and vice operations in wards dominated by recalcitrant party chiefs and using the detective force to wiretap and disrupt enemies from the regular Republican Party machine. Charges of a Wilson "Gestapo" were already familiar to conservative leaders Jay Cooke and Thaddeus M. Daly, president of the city's Civil Service Commission, and Daly and Wilson were at odds over the former's alleged preference for fellow Catholics. [71] This recent history may explain Daly's rallying to the extremists. He addressed an ACS rally, promising an investigation of leftist bias in the police and city government. [72] Though not sanctioning anti-Semitic violence, Daly's presence maintained the legitimacy of the "anticommunist" movement as part of the conservative spectrum.

CREATING THE CHRISTIAN FRONT

Before the summer of 1939 the media saw the violent activities of the Philadelphia Right as the work of local groups such as the CDCR and the ACS, but at that point there occurs a significant change of terminology. Not only were subsequent actions by these groups associated with the "Christian Front," but commentators retroactively attributed to the group earlier outbreaks such as the YMCA riot, which was contextualized together with similar attacks in other East Coast centers. [73] The Philadelphia situation well illustrates Irwin's 1940 remark that "outside New York, what is known as the Christian Front is wholly a membership setup, perhaps affiliated with or screened by state Social Justice clubs and superpatriotic bodies." [74] The Front drew its strength from the older groups, which faded from the limelight over the next two

years. However, the new organization was significantly more than
a mere name of convenience under which the Burchett-Gallagher network could expand its operations, and the scale of activities increased dramatically. Where the ACS could draw eighty or a hundred members to a meeting, the new Front attracted thousands. The publicity given by Coughlin was a valuable weapon in recruiting new and more committed members.

By mid-1939 Coughlin's Philadelphia followers had begun a new stage of organizational development. In July Coughlin circumvented the radio ban by means of a telephone link from his Detroit headquarters, from which he addressed his Philadelphia devotees. *Social Justice* claimed that "more than 8,500 crusaders" had "jammed two Philadelphia halls to hear the voice of Father Coughlin," and local papers suggested only a slightly smaller turnout. The crowd filled the Metropolitan Opera House, and 2,000 more loyalists filled an overflow meeting at the Broadwood Hotel, where they were addressed by New York Front leader John Cassidy.[75] The priest denounced Reds who were hoping "to make of Philadelphia another Barcelona," especially the labor leaders who were "Judas Iscariots," betraying "Christianity and Americanism."[76] He urged his followers to concentrate on the labor front: "Join the labor unions. And when you get in them, clean them out. Yes, clean them out! Throw out the Communist Red leaders."

Reporting on recent successes by activists in New York and elsewhere, he "urged Philadelphians to emulate their Christianity and Americanism."[77] This patriotism would be manifested by the creation of a local Christian Front, and organizers from New York City were on hand to explain how this could be achieved. "Sketching the formation and growth of the Christian Front, . . . [John Cassidy], head of the organization, pointed out that units of the organization are now in formation in several cities of the eastern seaboard."[78] As Coughlin declared, "The fight will be one between the so-called Popular Front and the Christian Front, and it will be a battle for survival."[79]

The emerging Christian Front in Philadelphia was influenced by the experience of New York City, and organizational activities were undertaken by Catholic priests from the Brooklyn diocese, including Edward Lodge Curran and Edward Brophy. It was Brophy who assured a Philadelphia audience that they should not be disturbed if accused of being anti-Semitic: "Maybe you are!"[80] New Yorkers like Cassidy and Bishop urged local followers to train and arm under the guise of sporting or rifle clubs.[81] Addressing the West Philadelphia Coughlinites and ACS, Bishop announced that "we have the guns and soon we will call on Philadelphia to join our ranks."[82] "A considerable number of volunteers" were invited to practice with rifles "at a private rifle range in southwest Philadelphia," and Bishop had also organized rifle practice in Hazleton.[83] In August Bishop addressed a further meeting at the Knights of Columbus Hall at 38th and Market, in West Philadelphia. He proposed that some 10,000 rifles could be purchased at $5 each, while Thomas Blisard Jr. offered his services as instructor. However, Bishop stressed that rifles alone would not be adequate for the coming struggle, and thought should be given to procuring machine guns.[84]

In November the CDCR drew about a thousand followers to a mass meeting at the Metropolitan Opera House. By this stage the meetings had as their goal recruitment into the Christian Front, and Joseph Gallagher served as a major distributor of Front literature, in quantities running into the tens of thousands.[85] The organization was "said to number several Pennsylvania National Guardsmen among its members and to be headed by a Philadelphia real estate man," unquestionably Gallagher.[86] Also powerful behind the scenes was "a prominent Philadelphia professional man, a key cabinet member of a former city administration," which alludes to Kern Dodge.[87]

The Front's initial messages were isolationist and anticommunist, portraying the Front as "a defense mechanism against Red activities and as a protector of Christianity and Americanism," but virulent anti-Semitism soon came to the fore.[88] Though the Front was not the only group distributing anti-Semitic leaflets and other propaganda, it was the most active body from 1939 until the outbreak of war. In addition to pamphlets, Philadelphia activists sold *Social Justice*, and the city also produced its own anti-Jewish newspaper, the *Equalizer*, published by Leo and Charles Moylan of the American Christian League.[89]

Philadelphia was "not far behind New York" in Front activity.[90] Together with Boston the city supported the largest and most militant centers of the movement, and the Philadelphia Front was

under intense scrutiny throughout the second half of the year.[91]
The movement had influence elsewhere in the state. In Pittsburgh in early 1939 a "Christian Front" was founded, which on occasion attracted 200 members to its meetings. Venues were readily found because of the pro-Front sympathies of the Irish American businessman who managed both the Fort Pitt and William Penn Hotels, two of the city's most popular locations for meetings.[92] The city soon became "another Front stronghold," where Jewish shops were defaced with "ugly and obscene signs" and "several Jewish shopkeepers have been beaten." A Communist "college" in Oakland was sacked by forty young militants.[93] The local Front mobilized opposition to the showing of the film *Confessions of a Nazi Spy*, which depicted a German-sponsored movement clearly modeled on the Bund.[94] As in other cities, Pittsburgh Fronters used this issue to underline their hostility to the whole cinema industry, which was seen as a Jewish monopoly devoted to undermining Christian morality and to provoking unnecessary wars.[95] The movie theater involved was subsequently vandalized.

However, anti-Semitism and street violence caused tension with more traditionally patriotic members. The "Americanist" wing in Pittsburgh claimed that the group had lost its noble aims. Originally, "we did a good work in stressing the dangers of Communism and in attempting to prevent the lifting of the arms embargo. This latter cause was part of our anti-war principles." "Bunders and Silver Shirts" dominated, however, expelling moderate leaders and trying to make the group "anti-semitic, anti-government and anti-everything else." This led to difficulties in obtaining venues for meetings. Also, politicians attempted to "gain control for vote purposes," an interesting comment that suggests that the Front might have had a community influence well beyond that of the membership alone. The Christian Front organization in Pittsburgh fell apart by the end of the year.[96]

THE IRISH COMPONENT

In 1940 a hostile account of the Christian Front nationwide remarked, "Dominant are the young toughs and the elderly bigots, Irish Catholics and Nazi sympathizers."[97] Each of these components can be identified in Philadelphia or Pittsburgh, where the "elderly bigots" could well refer to the ACS circle of Bessie Burchett, Herbert L. Smith, Thomas Blisard Sr., and Philip M. Allen, all in their sixties about this time. However, the most obvious fact about the Coughlin movement in Pennsylvania was the predominant role played by Irish Catholics.

Much of the Christian Front's appeal was based on Irish nationalism and anti-British sentiment, at a time when the United States might be on the verge of war in the interests of Britain and her empire. The IRA was a romantic icon in such circles, in which the group's current bombing campaign on the British mainland was praised as a model for direct action in the United States. When anti-British terrorism was criticized, one Pittsburgh Front supporter responded, "How dare you take up for the English and defend their actions in Ireland? My father was born and raised there, he can tell you about the Black and Tans the English let loose in Ireland—and you think that's good!"[98]

Since before the First World War, Irish revolutionary sentiment had often been expressed in pro-German sympathies, or at least a willingness to engage in a tactical alliance with England's primary foe.[99] In 1915 German intelligence had listed Philadelphia Irish American Joseph McGarrity as one of three "absolutely reliable and discreet" agents in North America.[100] At least since 1914 McGarrity had made Philadelphia the leading American center of support for armed Irish nationalism, and his Clann na Gael had raised money and arms for use in Ireland.[101] The *Philadelphia Record* noted in 1938 that "he spent a fortune in the Irish cause."[102] Both Eamonn De Valera and Roger Casement were guests at McGarrity's West Philadelphia home, and he played a key role in saving De Valera's life after the Easter Rising. Some of the submachine guns he shipped to the IRA remained in use into the 1970s, in terrorist attacks still officially claimed in the name of Joe McGarrity decades after his death in 1940. "For the IRA the most important man in the *Clann* had become Joe McGarrity."[103] He dominated a network of Irish nationalist clubs in Pennsylvania and published the anti-British *Irish Press*.[104] Philadelphia was home to former IRA guerrillas such as Luke Dillon, and the city had its own organization of IRA veterans.[105]

McGarrity's Philadelphia circle shaped the policies of revolutionary Republican movements in Ireland itself, especially the militant tendency that plotted a terrorist campaign on British soil.

This plan was devised by McGarrity and Sean Russell, who, with German sponsorship, implemented the campaign in early 1939. At the same time the two men prepared to undertake anti-British terrorism in North America, possibly including an attempt on the British royal family.[106] When Russell was imprisoned in the United States, one of the Irish American leaders demanding his immediate release was Philadelphia congressman James P. McGranery, who gave bail for Russell. Higham portrays McGranery as a close ally of the Irish Republican movement and a deadly enemy of British interests.[107] His constituency in the Second District contained a large section of Irish West Philadelphia.[108]

Both McGarrity and Russell retained their German ties until the end. McGarrity visited Germany while returning from a 1939 trip to Ireland, while in 1940 Russell died mysteriously aboard a U-boat while en route to carry out a mission for German intelligence in Ireland.[109] The long German association with Irish nationalism may explain why in 1939 both the IRA and the New York Christian Front were said to be working closely with German agents.[110]

While Joseph McGarrity was an extremist, anti-British views enjoyed wide currency among Pennsylvania's Irish Americans, and activism reached new heights during 1939. In January a thousand sympathizers gathered at the Irish American Club on North Broad Street, under the auspices of Clann na Gael and the IRA veterans' organization, for the purpose of demanding American intervention to create a united Ireland. The meeting was addressed by the New York-based brother of Terence MacSwiney, one of the martyrs of the independence struggle.[111] The following month the same groups sponsored a mass rally chaired by Congressmen McGranery and Francis J. Myers and attended by 5,000 Irish Americans. In addition to customary demands for Irish unification, the group also stressed the Coughlinite and isolationist demand for the immediate repayment of outstanding debts from the First World War and protested against any future English alliances.[112] The gathering was addressed by isolationist Senator Robert R. Reynolds of North Carolina, who was denounced by antifascist investigators as not merely anti-British but an ally of pro-Nazi and anti-Semitic leaders like George Deatherage and Gerald Winrod. He was a leader in the fight to exclude Jewish refugees from the United States.[113] Reynolds's presence at such a gathering suggests the difficulty of distinguishing between the Coughlin movement and the Irish nationalist campaign in these years.

In early 1940 another IRA-sponsored gathering in Philadelphia called for a German victory over Britain, which "would mean dismemberment of the British Empire and the release of Ireland from the robber octopus which murdered, exiled and plundered our people for generations." A similar gathering in Pittsburgh heard the familiar slogan "England's distress is Ireland's opportunity" and warned of the imminent likelihood of a British attempt to seize bases in neutral Ireland.[114]

This Irish emphasis is reflected by the geography of support for the Coughlin movement in Philadelphia, where Front branches appeared in Mount Airy and East Germantown in the 22nd Ward as well as in the Chesters and in Camden, New Jersey.[115] The most violent activism and propaganda occurred in West Philadelphia and Kensington, both Irish working-class communities nervous about losing ethnic identity at the hands of newcomers seeking employment in local industries. Kensington had been notorious for mob violence over the previous century, and there had been savage labor conflicts in 1910, 1934, and 1937. This Irish neighborhood stood adjacent to traditional Jewish areas, and this contact provided abundant opportunities for neighborhood rivalry and conflict.[116] The core of Jewish settlement in this northeastern section was Port Richmond, popularly termed "Jerusalem" since the mid-nineteenth century and subsequently the base from which Jewish migrants had expanded along Allegheny Avenue and Richmond Street. West Philadelphia was another Irish community with a lengthy record of hostility to ethnic incursions, especially in the 34th and 44th Wards, and in 1918 it had been the scene of antiblack rioting.[117] In 1937 the West Philadelphia Interracial Forum was formed to soothe tensions between black and Catholic residents.[118]

OTHER GROUPS

The Front was open to ethnic and religious groups besides Irish Catholics. By late 1939 it was attractive to Germans after the discrediting of the Bund and the increasing unpopularity of overt pro-Nazi sentiment. This alliance was facilitated by the long-standing overlap between German and Irish communities in the major cities, and Joseph Gallagher had frequently attended Bund rallies.[119] He praised the great Bund gathering in Madison Square Garden as "the first really American meeting I've been to in a long time."[120] More innocently, Irish American groups felt no compunction in using German venues like the Turngemeinde Hall for such crucial events as St. Patrick's Day celebrations.[121] Pennsylvania had a strong German Catholic presence, and already in 1934 about 40 percent of the Philadelphia membership of the FNG was said to be of Catholic origin.

The Front had its Italian component. In New York City over half of all Catholic clergy serving predominantly Italian parishes demonstrated sympathy for the Fascist cause and thus cooperated with the emerging Front. There is no such direct evidence for Philadelphia, but the strength of Italian American Fascism in the city has been noted. The Front and associated groups such as the ACS certainly made use of Italian Fascist-linked premises such as the Dante Alighieri Hall.[122] In April 1940 a meeting here was offered three models for the course of rightist activism in the area: "It took Hitler eleven years to do it; Mussolini did it in four; Franco in three." One of the Coughlinite militants accused in the YMCA riot in 1939 bore the Italian name of Alphonso Pedlico.

THE FRONT'S BLACK ALLIES

In early 1939 the Philadelphia CDCR held a meeting at which the speakers included Bessie Burchett, Father Brophy, and a black teacher named Edward Bruce. Bruce agreed to appear under the mistaken impression that the committee was a liberal group that would support his belief in racial equality, and when he began to speak on this theme, he was silenced by the angry crowd.[123] What is surprising is not that his audience found his sentiments uncongenial, but that such a body found nothing inherently inappropriate in the presence of an African American speaker. This indicates one of the curious aspects of Christian Front support, namely the tactical alliance that the group formed with black anti-Semites. Later the same year, when the Christian Front wished to print leaflets for its Christmas campaign without having to encounter difficulties from Jewish-owned or union shops, the solution was provided by a black-owned establishment in Manayunk. The owner was neither unique nor eccentric, as Philadelphia's African American community included some visible anti-Semitic activists, who denounced

Jewish businessmen.[124] One such leader was Octavia Brown, a perennial candidate for electoral office in North Philadelphia and an ally of the local Civic League.

The Front may again have been following the precedent set by the Bund, which in Philadelphia had disseminated anti-Jewish literature in "German and Negro Areas" in 1937.[125] The following year the Bund circularized African American media figures and community leaders in an attempt to foment hostility toward Jews. In Pittsburgh the Bundists erred by sending materials to Robert Vann, editor of the distinguished *Pittsburgh Courier* and a prominent New Deal Democrat who had condemned nativist attacks on Albert Greenfield. He reported the overture to the investigators of the House Committee on Un-American Activities, who treated it as a serious attempt "to create an uprising among the Negroes in the Pittsburgh area. They were creating a wave of anti-semitism among the Negroes."[126] The "Free America" leaflets sent to Vann focused on Arab opposition to Zionist settlements in Palestine, presumably in an attempt to capitalize on pro-Muslim sentiment among African Americans.

Black Muslim sects in America were numerous and diverse, and at least some were ferociously anti-Jewish. Philadelphia was the home of Eugene Brown, who under the name Sufi Hamid became notorious as "the Harlem Hitler" until his death in 1938.[127] Pro-Axis sentiment focused on a number of sects and splinter religious movements which taught that the interests of the white and colored races were in conflict and that an apocalyptic war between the two was either imminent or already in progress. In this view the Japanese were represented as the militant arm of the colored world, whose victories would promote the liberation of black Americans. The best-known exponent of this view was New York's Robert Jordan, of the Ethiopian Pacific movement, who was active in the America First movement. In both Philadelphia and Pittsburgh, Muslim and Garveyite groups were investigated for antigovernment and pro-Japanese agitation well after Pearl Harbor. There was a little evidence of direct Japanese agitation, orchestrated through the Pacific Movement of the Eastern World, which developed chapters in both cities. Black pro-Axis sentiment was a source of major concern to federal authorities after the outbreak of war, when the Philadelphia field office of the FBI reported that "many Negroes have expressed pleasure over Japanese victories in the Pacific and in the Far East."[128]

Only sparse materials are available on the black anti-Semitism of this period, partly because major urban newspapers were directed chiefly at a white readership that was presumed to have little interest in black affairs. This produced a cyclical effect, in that the newspapers did not cultivate networks of black informants, journalists, or commentators and thus did not provide fair or adequate coverage of black affairs, which in turn enhanced the alienation of black readers from those papers. Well-established black newspapers such as the *Philadelphia Tribune* and the *Pittsburgh Courier* saw little profit in unnecessarily publicizing matters detrimental to their community. In consequence black anti-Semitic groups were not known to the white papers, except as a mildly ridiculous curiosity, while black papers had no wish to draw attention to this embarrassing novelty. The few sources available for studying this movement almost certainly conceal its real contemporary appeal in some cities.

Following customary prejudices about black passivity and ignorance, contemporary writers assumed that profascist sympathies must have been the work of external agitators or foreign agents. While these forces may have been at work, anti-Semitism was neither a new nor an alien development in black urban communities, where Jews were stereotyped as exploitative landlords and grasping merchants.[129] In the black press such hostility often gave a skeptical tone to coverage of anti-Semitic atrocities overseas. In 1934 the *Philadelphia Tribune* criticized Nazi treatment of Jews but also remarked that "perhaps most of what is told about Jewish treatment in Germany is propaganda since the Jews control to a great extent the international press."[130] Black papers were reluctant to join the denunciation of racist persecution in other lands by a media that had yet to acknowledge injustices at home. After all, "the plight of the Jews in Germany is not one bit worse than the plight of the Negro in America." Tension was exacerbated by the prospect of a renewed wave of Jewish immigrants, who might take jobs and opportunities that might otherwise promote black advancement. As late as 1943 the *Pittsburgh Courier* wrote of "the dangerous and disastrous spread of anti-semitism among Negroes."[131]

Denunciations of Jewish persecutions in Europe had far less effect in mobilizing blacks against fascism than the Italian invasion of Ethiopia, which galvanized urban communities and in Philadelphia led to confrontations between African and Italian Americans.[132] It was this action rather than anti-Jewish violence that led to calls for boycotts against the supporters of aggression, and the targets were Italian rather than German. Though the National Association for the Advancement of Colored People and other black groups did denounce Nazi atrocities, it is uncertain how fully they were representing the general views of the wider community.[133] The Christian Front would never gain a significant black following, but what is remarkable is that they had any contacts at all in these areas. This odd alliance suggests both the breadth of anti-Semitism and its potential to forge coalitions that would otherwise have been difficult or even inconceivable.

THE CATHOLIC RESPONSE

The ostensibly religious origins and activities of the Christian Front attracted both attention and opposition from a broader range of groups than had been common for earlier rightist movements such as the Bund. The wave of violence in mid-1939 was regarded as sufficiently serious to merit the creation of a special investigative commission by the Philadelphia Council of Churches. A state legislator introduced a bill to prohibit the circulation of material likely to incite violence on the basis of race, color, or religion.[134] The panic also contributed to a revival of Protestant nativism, as a defense against what was viewed as Catholic aggression and criminality.[135]

The fate of the Christian Front in a particular city depended above all on the attitude of the local Catholic clergy and hierarchy.[136] The firm opposition of Chicago's Cardinal Mundelein slowed the movement's growth in that city; but other dioceses such as Brooklyn were more ambiguous, and anti-Jewish clergy were active in cities like Boston.[137] Apart from anti-Semitism, veiled or overt, Catholics were reluctant to criticize the behavior of a priest or to join what might become a widespread public attack on church institutions. The national Jesuit paper *America* warned, "The attack on Father Coughlin has become, in reality, an attack on Catholicism."[138]

Some Pennsylvania clergy favored the Coughlin cause. One Spanish priest from Philadelphia addressed a Front rally in New York City, claiming that General Franco was fighting a Christian crusade in Spain and that Hitler and Mussolini were unfairly criticized in the American media: "Only the enemies of Christ are opposing Franco, Hitler and Mussolini in Spain."[139] Monsignor Edward Hawks of St. Joan of Arc Church in northeast Philadelphia was another Franco advocate, who spoke regularly on Red atrocities in Spain and lauded the Nationalist zones that he had visited. He declared in 1938 that "Franco's armies are good to the people, and Franco is especially kind towards the children."[140] He addressed CDCR meetings alongside such firebrands as Father Brophy, Thomas Blisard Jr., and Bessie Burchett.[141] Another priest ran the Catholic Information League of Philadelphia, which specialized in lurid accounts of Masonic atrocities, arguing further that "the supreme command is mainly in the hands of Jews"; proof of this assertion could be found in the *Protocols of the Elders of Zion*.[142] In early 1939, as Coughlin's "Christian" campaign for "Social Justice" was reaching its height, the Knights of Columbus were engaged in a "Crusade for Christian Justice," with the designated goal of combating Red subversion. Though the intent was innocent, both the timing and the terminology gave the unfortunate impression of abetting the rightist movement.[143]

Some Catholic leaders portrayed opposition to Coughlin and the Front as anti-Catholic or mobilized by Jews. Reporting on the refusal by several stations to carry Coughlin's broadcasts, the Altoona-Johnstown diocesan paper headlined, "Jews Back Radio Drive against Coughlin."[144] Bishop Boyle of Pittsburgh was initially receptive to claims that Jews might be mobilizing propaganda against the "priest of the Little Flower," though he generally detested both Coughlin and the Nazi persecutions.[145] There were also Catholic intellectuals who believed that "fascism, in a much greater degree than our modern idea of democracy, approaches the true Christian idea of the state" and was far preferable to Communism.[146] This was the view of Joseph R. Barr, who in 1940 was elected to the Pennsylvania state senate as a Democrat.

On the other hand, many Catholics were violently opposed to Coughlinism, especially its anti-Semitic tendencies. Father John A. Ryan denounced Coughlin in the pages of *Commonweal*, an act that earned him the hatred of Philadelphia Christian Fronters as "the reddest of the red."[147] The Catholic journal *Christian Front* wrote, "No one can hate Jews and love Jesus."[148] Embarrassed by the connotations of its name, in 1939 the periodical changed its title to *Christian Social Action*, disavowing the "nefarious activities" of "certain subversive and undemocratic groups."[149] In Pittsburgh Coughlin was denounced by radical priests such as Charles Owen Rice and James R. Cox, who depicted anti-Jewish activities as part of a spectrum that also included anti-Catholic agitation. To the horror of local Coughlinites, Cox was prepared to address "Tolerance" meetings organized by the League for the Protection of Minority Rights, even when the venue was a synagogue.[150]

In the summer of 1939 Rice declared in a radio broadcast that anti-Semitism constituted a mortal sin for Catholics, and Cox gave a strong anti-Coughlin speech at Dormont, in Pittsburgh. Cox argued that prejudice was indivisible: "If Father Coughlin is right, then the Ku Klux Klan is right, and if the Ku Klux Klan is right about the Jews, it is also right about the Catholics and colored people, and Father Coughlin thereby condemns himself and all that he represents. . . . The Jews today, the Catholics tomorrow, and the Negro always." The resulting spectacle was absurd: "A Catholic priest become a storm trooper! A Coughlin become a Hitler hatchet man!"[151] Coughlin responded to this attack by producing what he claimed was proof that Cox was in the pay of Jews, but he acknowledged that the controversy had cost him support.[152] The Dormont speech was published under the incendiary title *Hitler's Hatchet Man*. Stemming as it did from another priest, the attack permitted Coughlin opponents to present their arguments without appearing anti-Catholic. It was reprinted in Pittsburgh's *American Jewish Outlook*, in pamphlet form, and then in national antifascist periodicals such as *Equality* and *American Appeal*.

Father Cox was noted for his outspoken political views, but on the Coughlinites he was not far removed from the opinions of most diocesan authorities in Pennsylvania. His superior Bishop Boyle was closely allied with the local Democratic Party, and the *Pittsburgh Catholic* regularly condemned the "misled Catholics" who supported Coughlin. A similar situation prevailed in the Philadelphia archdiocese under Cardinal Dougherty, remarkably so given his long-standing record of sympathy toward Mussolini and his passionate opposition to the Republican cause in Spain. However, the archdiocese was consistent in its denunciations of Nazism and the German government and regularly condemned "racism." In the context of the time, "racism" usually meant anti-Semitism, but Dougherty actively campaigned to increase African American membership of the Catholic church.[153] On the Jewish issue the American hierarchy was following the example of Pope Pius XI, who by 1937–38 was a forthright critic of racial persecutions, but local factors may also have been at work. Dougherty was influenced by his personal friendship with Albert Greenfield, who advised the archdiocese in real estate matters and whose generous philanthropy extended to Catholic causes.[154]

Whatever the reasons, the Philadelphia archdiocese loathed Hitler as heartily as it favored Franco. In 1938 Dougherty was praised by Protestant and Jewish leaders for a pastoral letter aggressively asserting the virtues of the American democratic system. He declared that any Catholic "who discriminates on the basis of race, color or nationality is not loyal to the church, is a renegade to the faith and a scandal to fellow members of the Church."[155] In 1939 and 1940 the archdiocesan newspaper was aggressively anti-Axis and pro-Polish, and the accounts of Polish sufferings under the Nazis emphasized the anti-Catholic nature of the actions. In early 1940 the Vatican reported harrowing details of Nazi actions against the Polish people. The *Catholic Standard and Times* headlined, "Nazi Atrocities against Subjugated Poland. Barbarous destruction of whole population by dispossession, persecution, deportation, shooting and torturing, aim of conquerors. Document published in Rome reveals churches despoiled, clergy imprisoned and killed, laity deprived of religious rites." The cardinal requested all churches in his diocese to undertake special prayers on behalf of Poland and its people. In the context of contemporary thought, this attack established Nazism on a moral par with Bolshevism or Spanish republicanism, as an evil with which the Catholic church could never compromise. The bishop of Scranton juxtaposed the martyrdom of Poland with the sufferings recently inflicted on other Christian nations such as Mexico, Russia, and Spain. The Poles "have been the victims of a simultaneous assault of the un-Christian forces of pagan racism and atheistic Communism."[156]

This overseas context influenced attitudes toward domestic fascist and anti-Semitic groups. In January 1940 the *Catholic Stan-dard and Times* reacted to the arrests of Front leaders by expressing skepticism about the gravity of the alleged conspiracy. However, it editorialized that "it is a thousand pities that there is not a real Christian Front, based upon charity and truth and not under the least suspicion of hatred to any race, creed or color. . . . If there is not a real Christian Front then there will be caricature ones, that will injure the cause that they profess to aid."[157] No one ever accused Dougherty of being a liberal, but he was staunch in his antiracism.[158]

THE PLOTS

By the end of 1939 the Christian Front was widely viewed as an unsavory and violent organization that was at least as danger-ous as the Bund. The question of exactly how serious a threat this represented occupied national headlines in January 1940, when the FBI announced the arrests of seventeen New York City Front-ists accused of plotting a putsch.[159] Leaders included John Cassidy and William Bishop, both well known in Philadelphia, and a Pittsburgh-born activist named Macklin Boettger, one of several national guardsmen arrested.[160] The accused were mainly of Irish extraction, but there were also some Germans.

According to federal charges, the coup attempt would begin with an assault on Communist militants with the goal of pro-voking an armed reaction. Red insurrection would in turn inspire an armed reaction by police, national guard, and fascist paramili-taries, until the whole process culminated with General Van Horn Moseley seated in the White House.[161] The New York Front was said to be in direct contact with German government agencies and with IRA terrorists planning attacks on British targets in North America. The scale of connections elsewhere was controversial, but the FBI did investigate possible ties with the Front in Philadelphia. James B. True charged that the FBI had targeted Philadelphia for a purge on the lines of New York, deliberately choosing the former city as the scene of the most intense anti-Jewish boycott campaign over the previous year.[162] In the jittery atmosphere following the arrests, Pennsylvania newspapers gave headline coverage to thefts of explosives in the state, suggesting that these might be connected with Front activism.[163]

The reaction of ultra-rightists themselves was mixed, naturally enough, given the serious nature of the charges and the likelihood that further arrests were pending; this might portend the long-feared general crackdown on pro-Axis activity. *Bundesleiter* Kunze issued an immediate command to his followers ordering the severing of all official connections with the Christian Front, Christian Mobilizers, American Nationalist Party, and cognate groups.[164] Coughlin himself publicly repudiated extremism in the aftermath of the 1940 arrests and described the New York plotters as Communist agents. He declared that he was "neither the organizer nor the sponsor of the Christian Front."[165]

In Pennsylvania most leading Coughlinites initially disavowed conspiracy, including Thomas Blisard Jr., who had offered to train riflemen and who still boasted of his own "small arsenal" of weapons.[166] The claim was now that the Front no longer existed.[167] As public skepticism about the conspiracy grew, the Philadelphia CDCR formed a support group for the defendants, and Bessie Burchett declared that the New York Fronters "were anti-Communist, whatever faults they may have had."[168] The Blisards argued that the whole "plot" was a smear designed to destroy the Coughlinite movement and to assist Roosevelt's efforts to secure a third term in the White House.[169] This response echoed the concerns of civil rights activists, who denounced the sweeping nature of the prosecution.[170]

Like every extremist movement of these years, the scale and seriousness of the Christian Front was exaggerated by both its advocates and its enemies, and even more than with groups such as the Bund, it is difficult to achieve an objective assessment of the phenomenon. On the other hand, what made the Front peculiarly perilous was that it could be neither dismissed as the arm of a foreign power nor isolated as the expression of some alien ethnic group. In fact, its near immunity to serious analysis in the media was an enormous source of strength, in that to attack the Front or its inspiration was to inspire a reaction that might in turn enhance support for the movement among a large section of the urban community. Of all the activist groups, this had perhaps the greatest potential to become a genuine mass movement around which others could coalesce.

y 1939 the American far Right was a bewildering ferment of groups and ideological tendencies. Though movements were ethnically and ideologically heterogeneous, there were tentative signs of the Brown Front so often depicted in the jeremiads of the Left. Over the next two years the quest for political unity would be a dominant theme on the far Right, and there were some successes. However, this development could not occur in a political vacuum, and the fate of the ultra-Right was conditioned by the wider context, both domestic and international. Initially the threat of war offered rich opportunities, raising the hope that the Right could project its distinctive interpretation of the drift to war as a manifestation of Jewish political and economic domination. In reality the dream of a Christian Nationalist crusade was overwhelmed by growing popular hatred and fear of the Axis abroad and its supporters at home. The far Right was riven by the inevitable paradox of attempting to be hypernationalist and Americanist while at the same time espousing the cause of hostile foreign powers.[1]

At least in theory there were many reasons to see the boundaries between the different sects as insuperable. For example, both the Bund and the Italian Fascists were violently opposed to secret societies such as the Freemasons, who were a mainstay of the Klan. The Protestant Klan similarly had little reason to love the Catholic-dominated Christian Front, with its Irish leadership, and still less the Italian Blackshirts, both exponents of a virulent "inverted nativism" often targeted at traditional Protestant power. On a core issue like Spain, Klan members were generally delighted at accounts of a national rising intended to smash clerical power, seize church lands, and secularize education. While sections of the American Legion and the patriotic societies were attracted by the Bund's anti-Communism, these organizations loathed German militarism. The anomalous position of black anti-Semites in such a political context needs no further emphasis.

In practice, tactical collaboration between the various groups was always present, and there were repeated efforts to forge closer alliances, a "local Axis." Pittsburgh offers a typical observation. In August 1938 "Henry Ringler, an official of the Pittsburgh storm troops [the OD], stated . . . that the Italian Black Shirts of Pittsburgh are extremely cordial to the Bund; and that while they have not yet marched openly with them, they were expected to do so in the future. Ringler also stated that the Silver Shirts in Pittsburgh are cooperating with the Bund in that area."[2] There was a sizable overlap of membership between groups, especially the Bund and the Christian Front, and they shared speakers in a remarkably nonsectarian way. T. Roy Zachary was as likely to appear in a meeting of the Bund or the ACS as in a gathering of his own Silver Shirts. The groups shared propaganda and training facilities, so that the Bund's Camp Nordland was used by Italian Blackshirts and Ukrainian Brown Shirts as well as the Ku Klux Klan.[3] Arthur Derounian's masquerade as an Italian anti-Semite gave him instant entrée to all sorts of other groups: German, Russian, and Ukrainian Nazis, ultra-nativists and Klan, and isolationists.[4] In any other political context this hearty nonsectarianism would have been admirable.

Counteracting the centrifugal tendencies of the extremist fringe, a number of factors encouraged harmony, above all the shared anti-Semitism, which provided an all-encompassing social and political analysis.[5] By the late 1930s the groups were united by a common admiration for Nazi Germany, in much the same way that the successes of the Russian Bolsheviks had earlier cemented disparate leftist movements into common adherence to Communist doctrines. For the American far Right, Nazi Germany clearly worked as a society, and it superseded other models such as Mussolini's Italy. Nazi iconography and symbolism provided a common rhetorical language for domestic fascists, as indicated by the dissemination of the swastika emblem and the "Horst Wessel" among nativist, Catholic, and Slavic groups. German authorities cultivated loyalty with donations of funds and by generous distributions of propaganda packages. These offered nonsectarian pamphlets and papers from the anti-Semites of several nations in addition to official Berlin productions.

The interpenetration of ideas is suggested by the case of Klan grand dragon Samuel G. Stouch. He owned Nazi periodicals and pamphlets, including a German-printed volume of Hitler's speeches, as well as the works of domestic authors such as James B. True, Robert Edmondson, and Gerald P. Winrod. He subscribed to *Industrial Control Reports*, the *Edmondson Economic Service*, and the *Defender*. There were character sketches of the Nazi leadership and leaflets by the émigré Union of National Socialist Russians. Stouch read the Bund's *Deutscher Weckruf* and the newsletter *Facts in Review* published by Goebbels's Ministry of Propaganda. He assiduously collected the journals and propaganda sheets of all manner of fringe groups, including Ulster Protestants and Orangemen. Coughlin's *Social Justice* was notable by its absence, presumably because of its Catholic stance, but Stouch favored the creation of a "Christian Front" coalition. He appeared on ACS platforms and corresponded with Philip M. Allen and Bessie Burchett. He was close to Silver Shirt leader Harry Sieber. In mid-1938 Stouch applied to join the Bund.[6]

IN SEARCH OF A LEADER

The growth of common ideologies seemed to created a potential for a mass party or common front, and attempts to form a central command were apparent from mid-decade, usually involv-

ing the core triumvirate of Edmondson, True, and Deatherage.[7] In
1936 Asheville, North Carolina, was reportedly the setting for a
gathering of far-Right activists, including Pelley, Winrod, Colonel
Sanctuary, and the anti-Semitic "trinity."[8]

General George Van Horn Moseley was felt to be highly promising as a national leader on whom all could agree.[9] A veteran of the
Philippines and the First World War, Moseley had served alongside
Pershing and MacArthur, and he was a good friend of ex-president
Hoover. He first attracted attention for political activism in May
1938, while he still headed the Third Army, based in Atlanta.
During the public debate over the prospect of renewed mass immigration, the general asserted that future immigrants should be
sterilized as a means of protecting the American race. That October he again echoed the positions of the far Right when he warned
that the country was facing dictatorship. After taking retirement
in 1938, he was free to begin a speaking campaign for the purpose
of denouncing Jewish power and its effects on America in the New
Deal. As he was not known to be associated with any one of the
rightist sects, he was an attractive figure to present to a public con-
temptuous of individuals such as Fritz Kuhn, and he was courted
to deliver some major public speeches. These presentations were
influenced, if not actually written, by Deatherage.[10]

In March 1939 Moseley addressed Philadelphia's Women's National Defense Committee, meeting at the Bellevue Stratford
Hotel. The formal invitation was issued by the umbrella organization representing some seventy "patriotic" groups in the city, a
remarkable gesture in light of Moseley's well-known recent track
record of vituperative and controversial addresses.[11] The event took
place only a few days after the nationally publicized riot at the
West Philadelphia YMCA, while other speakers included Coughlin's intimate Father Curran. Though the content was likely to
be inflammatory, even seditious, sponsors included chapters of
such reputable groups as the Sons of the American Revolution,
the Colonial Dames, the Military Order of the Loyal Legion, the
Dames of the Loyal Legion, and the American Legion. Other
lesser-known "fraternary" groups represented the descendants of
the Continental Congress, the signers of the Declaration of Independence, the Mayflower Pilgrims, and the veterans of virtually every American military conflict. There were seven chapters

of the DAR alone: four from greater Philadelphia (Philadelphia, Germantown, Betsy Ross, Independence Hall) and three from suburban counties (Jephtha Abbott, Valley Forge, and Chester County). Though we do not know the exact process by which the sponsors decided to invite Moseley, we can identify several key individuals within these organizations who had demonstrated sympathy for extremist positions, including Mrs. David Good, Philip M. Allen, Judge Bonniwell, and Ralph B. Strassburger.[12]

About 1,500 people attended the speech, a group that included many Coughlinites and other extreme rightists. Moseley did not disappoint his audience in the vigor of his attack on Roosevelt and his foreign policy. He asserted that "the war now proposed is for the purpose of establishing Jewish hegemony throughout the world," and "it has the support of the man in the White House."[13] Facing the prospect of Jewish-Communist tyranny, desperate measures were needed. It was necessary to "[exterminate] from the life of this nation all traces of the New Deal, the principal backers of Communism," the "New Dealers, Brains Trusters, Communists, CIO's or what not."[14] The New Deal meant "the promotion of class hatred, exploitation of human misery, the promotion of communism, and the sob appeal." While he opposed foreign "-isms," he saw little wrong with Fascism and Nazism: "the finest type of Americanism can breed under their protection as they neutralize the efforts of the Communists."

Militant action could come from several directions. "If the administration went too far to the Left and asked our military establishment to execute orders which violated all American tradition, that Army would demur."[15] Suggestions of a coup or mutiny were reinforced by Moseley's specific recommendations for vigilante action:

> Your city fathers must have a definite plan for the protection of Philadelphia, with only Americans on guard at all critical points, such as your waterworks, your electric light plant, and in all those facilities which are necessary to enable your police and fire departments to function. . . . It is also the lawful duty of your city officials to be prepared at all times to protect your city and the citizens therein, regardless as to the opinion on law and order of the man sitting in the White House at the moment or

in your governor's chair. If the required number of police officers are not available, the plan should include the deputizing of
citizens to be called legally in an emergency. . . . Remember, it
is the first twenty minutes that count.

Moseley's reference to the governor's chair was intended to exploit hatred of the recently defeated George Earle. The general
was implying that a putsch or vigilante operation would be needed
to resist a leftist assault, which might stem either from Roosevelt
or a local satrap. Apart from conditions at the state level, Moseley
claimed that he was reacting to events in the city of Philadelphia,
where the fall of Mayor Wilson had created conditions in which
"the Mayor did not dare enter his office for fear of being served
with a warrant for murder. His secretary, who is a Jew, is thus in
command of the city and certainly this city has the jitters, and
rightly so."[16]

Moseley's remarks were cited on Berlin's World Service as the
words of "the well known American general."[17] Within the United
States Moseley was lionized on the Right as a convincing candidate for an American führer. In May he was the guest at a meeting of some fifty individuals at a house on Long Island, a meeting attended by representatives of many groups, including Fritz
Kuhn, Mrs. Good, and Wilhelm Kunze.[18] Critics were appalled by
his speech, coming so soon after fifth columns and putsches had
been prominently reported in news from Austria, Spain, and the
Sudetenland. There were calls for Moseley's court-martial, and
he faced a lengthy and unnerving interrogation before the Dies
Committee that May.[19] He was condemned by numerous patriotic
organizations, including the head of the American Legion in Pennsylvania, who was embarrassed by the role of some chapters in
sponsoring the presentation.[20]

Another potential unity figure was Father Coughlin, who attracted support from a number of groups. In the fall of 1939 an
antifascist activist in Pittsburgh warned of the danger of "Coughlin our next *Führer*, with Reynolds, Moseley, Deatherage etc. our
Goebbels and Goering."[21] However, Coughlin's Catholic following remained a stumbling block for nativists like the Klan, and by
1940 this had become the outstanding issue preventing a broader
coalition. The two sides were brought together by the irenic efforts

of Edward James Smythe of the Protestant War Veterans' Association. He had recently declared that the Catholic church was "a tricky proposition" and that "we, like Hitler, believe that the Roman church should be driven out of political life and out of state affairs." [22] However, Smythe joined Coughlinite protests and demonstrations, and it was through his efforts that in August 1940 the Bund and the Klan allied to promote a "monster anti-war pro-American mass meeting" at Camp Nordland, where 3,500 militants gathered under a flaming cross. The two groups held joint paramilitary exercises, and Stouch's Klan predecessor Arthur Bell was portrayed shaking hands with uniformed OD leaders. The Bund's vice-president declared, "The principles of the Bund and the principles of the Klan are the same." [23] There were also representatives of the mainly Catholic movements, the Christian Front and the Christian Mobilizers, who remained patient while Klan speakers lapsed into their familiar invective against "Romanism" and "dumb ring-kissers." [24]

ISOLATIONISM

By 1940 such promising gestures were taking place in a delicate political environment. In response to unflattering attention from Congress and the media, the Bund had been virtually forced underground, and the overt display of sympathy for foreign dictatorships had become controversial. While the Christian Front had some success in assuming the role of a purely domestic group, its violence created public fear and hostility and a law enforcement reaction that culminated in the January arrests. Left and liberal groups were now taking the fascist threat very seriously, and activist newsletters and magazines made investigations and exposés freely available to the mainstream press. Intense publicity made it more difficult for rightists to operate freely, at exactly the time that the foreign situation demanded their involvement.

However, new opportunities raised the prospect that the extremists might still be able to secure a mass audience for their views. The intervention issue was central to national politics from the fall of 1939, with the lifting of the arms embargo, subsequent debates over the supply of weapons to Britain, and the Lend-Lease debate of early 1941. [25] Isolationism was the perfect unity issue for the rightist groups themselves, a cause on which all sides could agree. All concurred that pressure for war stemmed from Jewish

influence, and thus antiwar sentiment could be mobilized in anti-
Semitic and anti-Communist directions. Philadelphia Bund leader
Sigmund von Bosse framed the war question quite simply: "The
main lineup is not democracy versus fascism, but fascism versus
Communism, and here our choice is clear."[26] The same themes
pervaded Moseley's speech at the Bellevue Stratford. Christian
Front leaflets in Philadelphia advised, "Keep America Out of War.
Rosenvelt [*sic*] and his Jewish supporters are trying to have Christians fight their battles."[27] In the fall of 1939 Christian Front units
in Pittsburgh were mobilizing telegrams and letters to oppose repeal of the Neutrality Act. The targets of the alleged Front conspiracy in New York City included those congressmen who voted
for repeal of the arms embargo.[28]

From this perspective, Lend-Lease was nothing short of
"treachery," leaving the United States "as helpless as Lenin could
have wished."[29] To quote Bessie Burchett, "The men who might
defend their homes against communists are being drafted, some
are being sent out of the country while locust hordes of aliens
are still coming in to take their jobs. . . . Is it not significant that
the men who have rushed England into this suicidal war are predominantly *not* of Anglo-Saxon stock? And that in our own Administration, the men who are pushing us relentlessly towards the
same bottomless abyss are not of English or traditional American
blood?"[30] This foreshadowed the ruin or extermination of "the
white race, white Christian civilization." The "Draft Bill" was
a "Dictator Bill."[31] Roosevelt was plotting to abdicate American
sovereignty to British imperial and financial suzerainty.[32] Russian
entry into the war in June 1941 made matters starker: "If we had
only kept clear of England's war, we should now be clear of England's evil ally."[33] All this was the consequence of ignoring "the
expert advice of our great Colonel Lindbergh."[34]

Moseley, Burchett, and von Bosse were normally beyond the
pale of acceptable political debate, but in this case their views were
echoing those of many mainstream Republicans and conservatives.
Conservatives, too, linked war fears to opposition to the New Deal
and charged that the Roosevelt administration would draw the
nation into overseas adventures to distract attention from internal
problems. In February 1940 when John M. Flynn made his presi-

dential address to the PMA, he argued that "every major move that the president has made during the last several weeks has been an obvious part of a palpable plan to divert public attention from the vital issues which face the people of this country."[35] He hoped that this was an issue on which the administration could be restrained, "for the American people unitedly have served notice that they are determined to keep out of the war in Europe." Otherwise, "the President would, consciously or unconsciously, drag us into war."[36]

Philadelphia congressman Gartner indicated the sentiment of his Republican constituency when he declared in September 1939 that his mail was running a hundred to one against any alteration in the Neutrality Act. At a mass neutrality meeting he declared that the administration was planning a repeat of the scenario that had proved so successful in 1917. American loans would be needed to maintain war production in the United States, "and then we'll have to go to war to save the people who owe us that money. . . . Not only American sympathies but American financial interests will become dedicated to an Allied victory."[37] Governor James urged that America's policy should "not only be one of isolation but also one of insulation." In October Senator Davis told the Philadelphia German Day commemoration, "In effect, we are urged to replace our present form of government with a centralized military government, in behalf of the age-old quarrels of the rival imperialisms of the Old World."[38] Other Republican politicians were equally concerned. In June 1939 two conservative Pennsylvania congressmen appeared on the executive board of Hamilton Fish's isolationist Citizens' National Keep America Out of War Committee. These were J. William Ditter, from Montgomery County, and Robert J. Corbett, from the Thirtieth District in the Pittsburgh area.[39] In June 1940 Philadelphia Baptist leader Daniel A. Poling wrote of the nation's crying need to stay out of war as the only means of preserving democracy.[40]

Initially the American Legion was another focus of antiwar sentiment. In 1940 the department convention resolved that "propaganda emanating from the warring nations will have a tendency to develop un-neutrality on our part. . . . Our post proposes that the Legion use its strength and influence to promote and encourage an aggressive counter education program."[41] Pittsburgh posts claimed an upsurge of support as a direct consequence of their neutrality campaign. Smaller veterans' groups expressed similar

views, and in June 1940 the state convention of the Order of the
Purple Heart declared opposition to loans or aid to Britain.[42] This
attitude probably changed over the next year, or at least the interventionists gained the upper hand; but veterans' groups were by
no means as united as the statements of the national organization
might suggest.[43]

Such opinions had a widespread potential appeal in an ethnically diverse state like Pennsylvania, where there were large communities with little reason to favor Roosevelt's foreign policy or his
obvious tilt toward the Allies. Apart from the Germans, Italians,
and Irish, Ukrainians and Lithuanians had a comparable hatred for
the Soviet regime that entered the war in 1941. This event caused
serious discontent among conservative Catholics who, though perhaps reconciled to aiding Britain, recoiled at American collaboration with the Communist regime.

AMERICA FIRST?

Antiwar sentiments were common in the Republican Party at
the national level, and it was at the 1940 party convention in Philadelphia that R. Douglas Stuart formed the idea of the America
First Committee, an umbrella organization to keep the United
States out of war.[44] This organization was much maligned at the
time as a cover for pro-Axis sentiment, but the overwhelming majority of members had no sympathy whatever for fascist causes.[45]
The movement as a whole addressed such fundamental issues as
the proper constitutional role of the presidency in matters of foreign policy as well as the ethnic basis of political power and the degree to which the nation had liberated itself from a European and
specifically British political orientation. As the *Weckruf*'s masthead periodically declared, "The USA is *not* a 'British' Nation."
Nor, in retrospect, is it acceptable simply to dismiss the authentic
fears about the potential carnage of war, which given technological
advances, seemed likely far to exceed the horrors of 1917–18. One
did not need to be a crypto-Nazi to oppose any but a defensive war
or to see Roosevelt's international policies as reckless buccaneering
cynically designed to provoke a war contrary to the overwhelming
weight of public opinion.

America First was officially established in September 1940 and was funded by sizable corporate donations. It ultimately claimed a membership approaching 800,000, including conservatives but also liberals, religious leaders, and pacifists.[46] Amos Pinchot was one of many former Progressives in the leadership.[47] The Philadelphia chapter of America First was under the highly "proper" chairmanship of attorney Isaac A. Pennypacker, nephew of the earlier governor Pennypacker and law partner of former senator George Wharton Pepper. He was also a leading member of Pennsylvania's Sons of the Revolution.[48] Another popular speaker in Philadelphia was former marine general Smedley K. Butler, who angrily rejected charges of any association with racist groups such as the Christian Front, and whose earlier revelations about rightist conspiracies had made him a folk hero on the Left.[49] Ex-senator David A. Reed was "prime mover" in the Pittsburgh group. Both Philadelphia and Pittsburgh produced thriving chapters, including members prominent in Republican Party politics, though Pittsburgh in particular attempted to broaden its Left-labor appeal.[50] Over the next year both cities played host to isolationist leaders, including Hamilton Fish, Philip LaFollette, Jacob Thorkelson, Charles Tobey, and Verne Marshall.[51] Senator Gerald P. Nye was actually addressing an America First rally in Pittsburgh on December 7th, 1941, when the news broke of the attack on Pearl Harbor.[52]

The political passions stirred by the isolationism issue are illustrated by the controversy that occurred in Philadelphia in May 1941, when Charles Lindbergh was billed to appear at an America First rally in Philadelphia, initially scheduled at the Academy of Music.[53] However, the academy refused to rent its auditorium because of the danger of attendance by Nazi and Coughlinite subversives, who had previously disrupted tolerance gatherings at this venue.[54] The academy had no wish to encourage a mob of "haters of England and lovers of Germany," especially at a time when the British cause was in such apparent danger. News headlines at this time were full of the Allied disaster in Crete and the sea battles that claimed the battleships *Hood* and *Bismarck*. The Christian Front disturbances of 1939 had left Philadelphia sensitive about the danger from "lovers of Germany," and advertising for the May rally was refused by radio stations KYW and WCAU and by the mass transit corporation.[55]

Lindbergh's speech was rescheduled at the Arena, where it proceeded with a distinguished body of speakers and platform guests that included Massachusetts senator David Walsh, novelist Kathleen Norris, and Lulu Wheeler, the wife of Senator Burton K. Wheeler.[56] The meeting attracted an audience of some 16,000, several thousand of whom listened outside in pouring rain.[57] This was in its own right impressive testimony to the degree of public involvement in the ongoing debate, but only the previous night a rival "Save Freedom Rally" in the city had drawn 12,000 to hear pro-Allied speakers such as Ambassador Bullitt and Fiorello La Guardia.[58] As there would presumably have been little overlap between the two crowds, that means that some 28,000 Philadelphians took the trouble to participate in the continuing national debate.

America First had great potential as long as it maintained its character as a mainstream pressure group, but it was discredited by the support it received from anti-Semitic extremists.[59] The extreme Right had to tread a rhetorical tightrope, exploiting isolationist sentiment to the full and employing it as an ideological vehicle, while at the same time refraining from any suggestion that their primary goals were pro-Axis and unpatriotic. They were rarely successful. The great Lindbergh rally at the Arena was at first sight a patriotic gathering of concerned Americans, but Lindbergh's call for "new leadership" in America was viewed as potentially seditious.[60] Moreover, "the hall was packed with members of native fascist, anti-semitic organizations," with reserved sections for leaders of the Christian Front, the Bund, and other German organizations.[61] The *Philadelphia Record* specifically remarked on the attendance of German American activists Sigmund von Bosse and William Schmidt, Ku Klux Klan leaders Frank Fite and his wife, and a gaggle of Coughlinite Irish priests. Also present was the head of the Hamburg-American line, generally regarded as an arm of German intelligence.[62] There were shouted slogans of "Impeach Roosevelt" and "Are we going to let the Jews run this country?"[63]

Reports of this extremist presence in the Philadelphia press damaged the antiwar cause. Even the *Philadelphia Inquirer*, no friend of Roosevelt, chose a suggestively Nazi-tinged word when it headlined that "16,000 *Hail* Lindbergh Here."[64] The *Philadelphia Record* published a cartoon titled "An Appreciative Audience," showing Lindbergh's speech being heard by a beaming trio of Hitler, Goering, and Goebbels.[65] Lindbergh was tainted with fascist sympathies long before his notorious anti-Jewish outburst in Des Moines that September.[66]

Similarly embarrassing were accounts of the penetration of local America First branches by outright fascists and anti-Semites, especially after Father Coughlin commended the movement. The committee of the Philadelphia chapter included Kern Dodge, the associate of the ACS, while Philip M. Allen wrote to Amos Pinchot expressing full support for the work of America First: "Everything you write that I've seen finds me in such enthusiastic agreement. . . . Keep up the splendid work!"[67] In West Philadelphia the America First organization was run by Mrs. Joseph Gallagher, an "active worker" in Coughlinite and other extremist groups.[68] Bessie Burchett joined her Mothers and Daughters of Philadelphia, and in October 1941 the group earned notoriety by singing the "Horst Wessel" at a meeting.[69] The Coughlinite Mothers of America picketed pro-Allied rallies, bearing placards declaring, "No Convoys–No AEF."[70] Another America First leader in Philadelphia was Edith Scott, who extended a membership invitation to the women of a local Nazi organization. Bertha Weber used Philadelphia's National Legion of Mothers as a vehicle to support America First's neutrality campaign, while at the same time forging close ties with the local Bund.[71] In Pittsburgh a "group of the less desirable Coughlinites" was prominent in the America First chapter until being expelled en masse in the fall of 1941.[72] The situation was reminiscent of Brooklyn, where the local chapter was "little more than the Christian Front by another name."[73] Philadelphia rally speaker Senator Walsh was a friend of Coughlin's intimate, Father Curran.[74]

During 1940 and 1941 the old activists of the ACS and the Christian Front focused their rhetoric on the isolationist cause.[75] In the summer of 1940 Thomas Blisard and the CDCR led a delegation to Washington to protest changes in the Neutrality Act.[76] In September 1941 some 300 attended a "Mothers' meeting" organized by Joseph Gallagher and Bessie Burchett at the Bellevue Stratford to protest Lend-Lease, a law "giving our armaments, clothes, food, money and our men to the British; and for what?" Britain itself was a parasite, unwilling to spare its own riches: "Why don't they give up more of their own wealth? But no, they want ours, and all for nothing." Bessie Burchett asserted that "Roosevelt is nothing but a Charlie McCarthy because he is

nothing but a stooge, even a stooge would know he is used as a stooge."[77]

In the same months Bund and ACS leader Herbert L. Smith was organizing protests against Bundles for Britain and picketing the British consulate. In a significant juxtaposition, he wrote in May that "the anti-war and anti-J[ewish] movement is getting stronger all the time."[78] By that summer *The Hour* listed Smith as one of the most active disseminators of German-produced propaganda in Philadelphia.[79] Smith and his colleagues were frequent visitors to the German and Italian consulates in Philadelphia, where they acquired large supplies of free literature. Even after American entry into war, Smith stubbornly continued to hold the Jews responsible for conflict: "Who are the warmongers? Lindbergh told you who they were. Father Coughlin told you who they were. Edmondson has told you."[80]

DISSENSION

The isolationist movement was made obsolete by the war, as by 1940 European events raised the prospect that the United States might soon have to encounter alone a Germany seeking world domination. Most Americans had by this stage decided that the Axis powers were to blame for the war.[81] In 1940 even a supporter of Irish Republicanism like Congressman McGranery spoke in the House about the possibly subversive ties of Hamilton Fish. McGranery voted for Lend-Lease the following March.[82] In May 1941 Philadelphia's Irish Democratic leader John Kelly was one of the organizers of the anti-Lindbergh Save Freedom Rally. American military involvement increased sharply during 1941, with growing naval cooperation with Great Britain, the rearmament campaign, and the introduction of peacetime conscription.[83] Vicariously at least, the United States was in all essentials a combatant power for most of 1941.

The ideological impact of war is suggested by the virtual collapse of the Ku Klux Klan in the aftermath of the Camp Nordland meeting. For some time there had been intense political debate in the old Klan groups in Pennsylvania, especially in the Rescue klavern, #311 in Wilkes-Barre. This was the scene of controversy between pro-Germans such as Paul Winter and the more moderate ultrapatriots such as Lewis W. Button.[84] With war imminent, Winter engaged in what increasingly appeared to be sedition: "In every speech he delivered he showed favoritism for Germany. We feel that our favorite is and should be the United States of America. He claims too that the United States is his first love, but he certainly does not show it. . . . [He] has boasted to at least two of our members that he belongs to a German organization whose headquarters are in Germany."[85] His activities horrified the "Americanist" faction of the Klan, as "his stand towards Nazi Germany was doing the Klan a great deal of harm," but he was not unique. The Nazi faction was also dominant in the Philadelphia klaverns, and Philip M. Allen of the ACS urged Samuel Stouch not to apologize for the Nordland meetings: "God knows we need them [the *Bund* and the Klan] these days."[86]

The Camp Nordland incident made the schism within the Klan irreparable, and Stouch was directly implicated as New Jersey fell within his three-state realm. Lewis Button led the Rescue klavern out of the Klan and denounced the "disgusting debacle from true Americanism. . . . Wrong rules the Klan, and waiting justice sleeps." In turn, Winter's pro-German clique expelled Button from the group; we still have the letters of both men, appealing to Stouch for support.[87] The *Fiery Cross* denounced the Nordland meeting for acts that had "shocked and horrified the nation" and urged that the whole affair be referred to the Dies Committee. It condemned Europe's dictators, not least for their suppression of the Masonic orders.[88]

The Klan had no option but to purge the leaders who had arranged the entente with the Bund, but it was too late to prevent remaining klaverns from falling apart across the region. In Stouch's New Jersey territories, Americanist Klansmen were in schism from "Hitler's Nazi henchmen."[89] In October 1940 it was presumably a patriotic Klan faction that burgled Stouch's Germantown home and appropriated the complete Klan archives dating back to the early 1920s, "several hundred pounds of material." They handed this embarrassing material over to the State Police, to help them build a full list of likely traitors and fifth columnists. In June 1941 the Pennsylvania State Police noted that the stolen Klan archives would be a useful source in case a "Legion of Death" became as active as the Black Legion had some years previously. By the end

of 1941 the Klan was unable to find a newspaper that would adver-
tise its meetings, even in a once-safe haven as loyal as Uniontown.[90]

THE MOTHERS' MOVEMENT

For some rightist groups the coming of war not only failed
to dampen their ardor, it actually opened a new range of propaganda opportunities. They exploited tensions resulting from the
war, notably hostility toward Jews who were supposedly failing to
participate fully in the struggle. The most influential of the continuing groups was the Mothers' Movement, a confederation of
local societies variously titled the Crusading Mothers of America;
United Mothers of Cleveland; the Mothers and Daughters of
Philadelphia; We, the Mothers; and We, the Mothers, Mobilize for
America. The movement claimed to represent the collective interests of American mothers whose sons were placed at risk in foreign wars.

This was an ironic reversal of the customary fascist use of the
rhetoric of motherhood, which exalted women's role in producing
children to serve the fatherland in war and peace. Conversely, on
this occasion leftist and liberal critics employed traditional anti-
feminist and antisuffragette rhetoric against rightist women, who
were derided as "the thundering herd," "frowsy, belligerent . . .
very poor and ignorant. . . . These poor women must have been
hirelings of someone." The Mothers were condemned for their
unfeminine aggression and were told condescendingly that their
authentic feminine role was at home, caring for their families. A
typical jibe suggested that if these were indeed the Mothers of
America, one trembled for the future of the race. Other critics
asked whether such old and unattractive women could indeed be
mothers.[91] On both sides the isolationist debate produced odd alliances and arguments.

Like local Communists, Philadelphia anti-Semitic movements
had long had a substantial female membership, and in 1939 it
was noted that the attendance at ACS meetings was often equally
divided between men and women.[92] In late 1939 Father Coughlin announced the creation of a National League of Mothers.
That November, the Mothers of America invaded the U.S. Capi-
tol at the time of the neutrality debates, blaming Jewish influence
for the perceived American drift to war.[93] In the fall of 1940 a

Mothers' March on Washington was planned to urge the impeachment of President Roosevelt.[94] Philadelphia's contingent was led by Catherine Veronica Brown of Darby, in Delaware County, who took the opportunity to visit the Japanese and German embassies to apologize for American provocations and to plead for peace.[95]

Though initial "Momist" claims were pacifist and isolationist, groups were opposed specifically to wars carried out against the Axis, and in their view the world's chief warmongers comprised the sinister alliance of Roosevelt, the British government, and the Jewish financial conspiracy.[96] National leaders included extreme rightists such as Robert Edmondson, Elizabeth Dilling, and Philadelphia's Mrs. David Good.[97] Local organizers had been active in the Christian Front and related groups, and Catherine V. Brown was one of many Catholics in the Mothers' leadership.

The campaign gained momentum on the outbreak of war with its appeal to women whose sons and husbands were absent in the armed forces. In 1945 the Mothers' movement in Philadelphia was said to be "fast turning the City of Brotherly Love into the City of Motherly Hate." The main group was led by Catherine V. Brown and Lillian Parks.[98] Beginning as the Crusading Mothers, this group soon adopted a number of aliases, including the Current Events Club and the National Blue Star Mothers of Pennsylvania, the latter title deliberately intended to cause confusion with reputable Blue Star Mother groups.[99] The Washington representative of the Philadelphia unit was Agnes Waters, a well-known Coughlinite and anti-Semitic lobbyist who successively campaigned against causes like Lend-Lease and the invasion of Normandy.[100] Catherine V. Brown herself was a close friend of Gerald L. K. Smith.[101] This was for her a "Jew war," "the Jew international bankers' war," started by "Jew Roosevelt" to destroy Christian civilization and set up a Communist World Government. The group circulated "vicious defeatist leaflets" parodying pro-Allied slogans like "Bundles for Britain."[102] One depicted a corpse and asked women, "Will this bundle be your son?"[103]

The National Blue Star and other Mothers groups tracked families whose members had become military casualties and then wrote the relatives to explain that these misfortunes were the result of schemes by Jewish or British interests, the "Jew bankers and Washington bureaucrats their sons and husbands died for."[104]

One example, sent in error to a Jewish mother, asked, "How long

are we going to permit our men to be slain to save the Jewish em-
pires all over the world? Did you know that certain Jews by the
hundreds are being trained to follow the armies and to be the ARMY
OF OCCUPATION, with all the prostrated nations under their control?"[105] The letter-writing campaign continued at least until the
German surrender in 1945.

Leaflets distributed on the streets were addressed to "Christian
Mothers." Citing the most recent total for U.S. casualties, they
asked, "Is this the price you are paying for Jewish revenge? . . .
Must we have another million Christian casualties just to make
Stalin the world dictator instead of Churchill or Roosevelt?"[106]
National Blue Star literature claimed that the war was fought
for Jewish interests and constituted a "Jew Holy War," in which
gullible Christians served as foot soldiers. Jews rarely served in
the armed forces, and the only Gentiles who received preferential
treatment were blacks, whose units had received special warning
of Axis assaults.[107] The situation clearly bore out the warnings of
the movement's greatest hero, Congressman McFadden, about the
conspiratorial Zionist elite.

A FIFTH COLUMN?

In May 1940 Roosevelt warned in a radio speech of "the
Trojan Horse. The Fifth Column that betrays a nation unprepared
for treachery. Spies, saboteurs and traitors."[108] Though antiwar
and pro-Axis propaganda undoubtedly continued through the war
years, it is not clear to what extent right-wing extremists were
either willing or able to make good on their vocal threats about
armed revolution or terrorism in the United States. Was there a
genuine fifth column?

The authorities took the danger seriously. In 1939, for example,
the king and queen of England visited Canada and the United
States. The royal couple were to travel from the Midwest to the
East Coast by train, and it was believed that the German government had mounted an assassination conspiracy, involving IRA
activists led by Sean Russell and Joseph McGarrity.[109] Though the
train was only intended to pass through Pennsylvania, the State
Police were conscientious about surveillance of the route, and the
preparations for this visit were far more intense than those for any

other celebrity for decades before or since. Though the mobilization of police and military personnel does not seem excessive in
retrospect, it was amazing by contemporary standards. As the royal
train made its way, the Pennsylvania State Police and the National
Guard mobilized over 1,000 officers. Every bridge and culvert was
placed under constant guard, with officers on the alert "for the
throwing of a bomb or hand grenade by someone standing in a
crowd or someone passing in an automobile[,] . . . for someone
sniping from a hillside with a rifle or someone in a crowd firing at
the trains[, or for someone] placing a charge of explosives on or
under any bridge or subway."[110]

If fascist groups were planning serious subversive activity, then
Pennsylvania was vulnerable as a critical center of the military
buildup in 1940–41 and of subsequent war production. At the
height of the war the Philadelphia Navy Yard alone would employ 70,000 workers. Fifty fighting ships were built there, and
over 1,000 more were repaired or serviced. For potential saboteurs,
Philadelphia also offered the Frankford Arsenal, the Quartermaster
Depot, and the Baldwin Locomotive Works. Elsewhere in the state
there were ordnance works near Williamsport and Meadville, the
navy supply depot at Mechanicsburg, the Letterkenny Ordnance
Depot, and the Sun Shipyards at Chester. By mid-1940 war production was in full swing in a dozen middle-sized Pennsylvania
cities, including York, Lancaster, and Pottstown.[111]

Would the munitions industries of the Delaware Valley be subjected to clandestine attacks of the sort believed to have disrupted
American production prior to the First World War, symbolized
by such incidents as the Kingsland and Black Tom explosions?[112]
These attacks were cited as likely precedents for German clandestine warfare in the future war.[113] In December 1939 the FBI
announced the strengthening of the Philadelphia office in order
to combat potential tampering with shipping along the Delaware
waterfront.[114] The new Pennsylvania Turnpike was seen as another
obvious target. In September 1939 a dynamite attack came close to
destroying a bridge in Bedford County. Charges of railroad sabotage and line tampering were numerous through 1940, and there
was an upsurge in patriotic vigilante societies seeking to prevent
such activities.[115]

Throughout the war, critics complained that anti-Semitic and antiwar leaflets were distributed freely in Philadelphia within sight of some of the nation's most sensitive defense installations, in a city with some 90,000 registered aliens.[116] Coincidentally or otherwise, Camp Deutschhorst was located close to the factory manufacturing gauges for the armed forces, and Bund rallies were said to have attracted workers from the navy yard and the Frankford Arsenal.[117] A Bundist said to be a member "of nearly every German club in Philadelphia" was employed at a factory making landing gears for bomber aircraft. Another man, an active official in the KB, worked for the aircraft department of a Philadelphia defense plant.[118]

Rumors about sabotage at military plants had been circulating for years, and in 1938 there was an abortive investigation of possible tampering with shell production at the Frankford Arsenal.[119] As war grew more likely, claims about fifth column activity became abundant, with some sources depicting as suspicious virtually every fire and explosion that could be linked, however tenuously, to the war effort. Sayers and Kahn report dozens of such incidents in Pennsylvania between 1940 and 1942.[120] In reality, all industrial facilities will have a quota of accidents, and not all acts of sabotage are politically motivated. However, some events appeared more suspicious than others, such as the three near-simultaneous explosions in munitions plants in New Jersey and Pennsylvania, a coincidence that, as Secretary of War Stimson remarked, "might suggest Teutonic efficiency."[121] In 1940 Philadelphia papers headlined a series of sabotage attempts at the Sun Shipyards in Chester.[122] In 1941 there were fires in the Philadelphia Navy Yard and the Frankford Arsenal.[123] The Philadelphia yard had been mentioned as a specific target of the Christian Front plotters arrested in January 1940.[124] While the FBI denied that sabotage played a role in any of the incidents, some modern writers have asserted that German rings were active, operating through either Ukrainian or Irish agents.[125]

The height of concern about sabotage activity came in June 1942 with the arrest of eight German agents landed by submarine in Florida and on Long Island. Most of the group had spent time in America and had been Bund members. They were assigned a number of critical military targets, which in Pennsylvania included a Philadelphia cryolite plant producing the materials essential for the manufacture of aluminum. Also listed was the horseshoe curve

near Altoona, the destruction of which would paralyze the production and transportation of coal and delay troop movements to
the East Coast. The scheme bore the appropriately Pennsylvania-
oriented name of Operation Pastorius.[126]

UKRAINIAN NETWORKS

Though the German Nazis and Italian Fascists were the best-
publicized among the various rightist movements, other ethnically
based organizations were available to enemy intelligence services.
Between 1940 and 1942 a number of Eastern European groups
attracted intense concern, American representatives of minority
nationalities such as the Lithuanians and the Croats, who had allied
with the Axis powers to secure their national aspirations.[127] Pittsburgh had a Croat nationalist community that welcomed the German overthrow of the Yugoslav state in 1941, and a leading activist
there was Ante Doshen, publisher of the rightist journal *American
Slav*.[128] White Russian émigrés were mobilized by the pro-Nazi
Prince Anastase Vonsiatsky.[129]

The most important group was the Ukrainians, who were well
represented in Pennsylvania.[130] In 1930 some 6,000 foreign-born
Pennsylvanians claimed Ukrainian as their mother tongue, with the
largest communities in Philadelphia (2,000), Pittsburgh (1,000),
and Scranton (700). There was also a thriving cultural network,
with several newspapers and magazines. Philadelphia was the center of the Ukrainian Catholic church in North America, and there
were some twenty-four Ukrainian parishes in and around Pittsburgh, both Catholic and Orthodox.[131]

Most Ukrainian expatriates were militantly anti-Communist.
During the 1930s, rightist sentiment had been exploited by new
groups closely affiliated with German Abwehr intelligence, for
whom they undertook terrorist attacks against Polish and Soviet
targets. These movements included the Organizace Ukrajinska Na-
cionalistov, headquartered in Rome, and the pro-Nazi Organization
for the Rebirth of the Ukraine (ODWU).[132] All were active in the
United States in the 1930s, where ODWU militants were involved
in kidnappings in New York City. Pennsylvania provided a critical
power base, and until 1938 the president of ODWU in the United
States was Gregory Herman, of Wilkes-Barre, an officer in the U.S.

army reserve.[133] As with the Germans and Italians, fascist groups

infiltrated and sought to annex established nationalist and cultural groups, especially the Ukrainian Nationalist Association. Another target was the Ukrainian Catholic church, which was influenced by a pro-ODWU priest named Monsignor Ivan Buchko, who declared that the organization represented "the flower of the Ukrainian nation." By 1940 some publications of the Ukrainian diocese of Philadelphia were expressing support for ODWU positions. After the German attack on the Soviet Union in 1941, the Philadelphia Ukrainian paper *America* called for the establishment of a pro-Nazi Ukrainian regime headed by one of the exile organizations.[134]

Ukrainians participated in the emerging Brown Front. In Chicago in 1938, "Ukrainians in greenish-brown shirts marched with white- and silver-shirted American Nazis at the Bund's German Day celebration."[135] A critical go-between was the White Russian leader Vonsiatsky, who was close to native American fascist leaders such as Pelley, Edmondson, and Henry Allen and was also linked to Wilhelm Kunze.[136] Vonsiatsky's contact to the Ukrainian fascists was Alexei Pelypenko, the covert FBI informant.[137] Also linking German and Ukrainian interests was Captain Leonid Klimenko, "a fascist Ukrainian emissary from the German war office" with extensive contacts in and around Pittsburgh.[138]

From at least 1934 the Ukrainian fascists actively organized for violent confrontation and sabotage in the United States. Initially this was undertaken under the guise of a Ukrainian aviation school in New York State. Pittsburgh was the movement's center of weapons training and also for espionage activity that included photographing industrial facilities throughout Pennsylvania. In early 1941 a U.S. army captain of Pennsylvania Ukrainian origins was court-martialed for betraying information to a foreign agent.[139] *The Hour* warned that Ukrainian fifth columnists were spreading across the country, targeting centers like "virtually the whole of Pittsburgh, with its mills, railroad yards and river barges."[140] In March 1941 Ukrainians were suspected of having sabotaged the Pennsylvania Railroad's Cleveland-to-Pittsburgh express train, which crashed near Ambridge in Beaver County, killing five people.[141] Railroad authorities were certain that tampering had been involved, but the political motive was less apparent. *The Hour* claimed that the real target had been another train that had passed the same spot some minutes earlier, carrying over forty members of a Soviet delegation.[142]

The Ukrainian networks offered a potential subversive threat comparable to that of the more conspicuous groups, though here, too, fascist influence was waning before the outbreak of war. Within the Ukrainian Catholic church, profascist activities were prohibited by Philadelphia's Bishop Constantine Bohachewsky, who reprimanded the pro-ODWU Buchko.[143] Buchko left the United States in late 1941.[144] In the fall of 1940 ODWU was condemned by the mass-membership Ukrainian fraternal associations such as the Workingman's Association of Scranton,[145] the National Mutual Aid Society of Pittsburgh, and Philadelphia's Provident Association, as well as the influential Scranton paper *Narodna Volya*.[146] By the end of the year the Scranton and Philadelphia fraternal groups were demanding the exclusion of fascist sympathizers from future Ukrainian American gatherings.[147] In 1941 the fascist Hetman organization abandoned its U.S. operations, and ODWU dissolved into several factions.[148]

THE SEDITION TRIALS

When war broke out, there were extensive raids on German and Italian offices, shops, and social clubs and signs of an incipient panic reminiscent of that in 1917. In the week following Pearl Harbor, perhaps 3,000 Germans and German agents were arrested and interned nationwide, and federal authorities in Philadelphia and Pittsburgh also seized Italian and Japanese aliens. Two hundred "potentially dangerous aliens" were interned at the nearby Detention Center in Gloucester, New Jersey.[149] The American Legion helped find and intern Bund sympathizers and maintain surveillance on suspected Nazis.[150] Camp Deutschhorst was a prime target for an FBI raid.[151] The atmosphere of the times is suggested by the letter of a German from Emmaus, Pennsylvania, to the *Philadelphia Weckruf*: "Kindly *do not* send the paper anymore, as this is a small town, and we have had enough trouble and more as always since we're up here."[152] To forestall a witch hunt, the German-American League of Culture orchestrated a patriotic demonstration in Philadelphia on December 12, pledging full support for the war effort. The main spokesman was Raymond Raff, whose impeccable anti-Nazi credentials gave credibility to patriotic declarations.[153] Even the *Herold* urged German Americans to unite "100 percent for America. At a time like this, there can only be one country for all — America."[154]

Law enforcement authorities arrested prominent rightists as real or potential spies and fifth columnists. Kunze fled to Mexico, hoping to be picked up by a German submarine. However, he was arrested and extradited in 1942 and served most of the following decade in a federal penitentiary.[155] The destruction of his ring also involved Vonsiatsky and Pastor Molzahn.[156] In late 1942 the FBI arrested several Silver Shirt leaders near New Galilee in Beaver County, including Pelley's daughter Adelaide Pearson as well as Victor Hoye and H. Victor Broenstrupp, who was under indictment for sedition.[157] Pennsylvania produced other smaller fry.[158] In 1943 Constance Drexel of Philadelphia was indicted for making pro-Axis radio broadcasts from Berlin, together with a list of fellow defendants that included Ezra Pound. Pittsburgh's pro-German propagandists included "Gertie from Berlin," who broadcast to American forces in Sicily.[159] Pro-Axis propaganda came under attack within the United States, and in April 1942 the federal authorities barred *Social Justice* from the mails, effectively killing the publication. The *Philadelphia Herold* was attacked at the same time.[160] In response to invasion fears, Roy Zachary and other Silver Shirt leaders were prohibited from residing near the Pacific Coast for the duration of the war.

Sensitivity to rightist plotting raised hopes among liberals and leftists that finally there would be a real purge of the far Right that would involve a clean sweep of powerful fascist sympathizers. In July 1941 a grand jury was convened in the District of Columbia under prosecutor William Power Maloney with the goal of examining foreign espionage and propaganda in the United States. This body called hundreds of witnesses and explored possible criminal violations as serious as sedition and espionage, as well as the failure to register as an agent of a foreign power and abuses of the congressional franking privilege. The jury indicted thirty or so rightists in January 1943, but at this point the removal of Maloney began a controversial series of events that entered the mythology of the Left. One view was that Maloney had been "kicked upstairs" for his excessive zeal in pursuing powerful traitors whose prosecution would be embarrassing.[161] A reconstituted grand jury pursued the investigation and indicted a somewhat different cast of characters, leading to a notorious sedition trial in 1944.[162]

The defendants included some well-known persons, including True, Edmondson, Pelley, and Deatherage as well as Lawrence Dennis, Elizabeth Dilling, Joe McWilliams, H. V. Broenstrupp, and Edward James Smythe, charged with a variety of infractions concerning the distribution of propaganda intended to undermine the morale of U.S. armed forces. Leftist critics of the prosecution produced a far longer list of those whom they believed should have been listed, and who had certainly been investigated as potential targets for prosecution. Most conspicuous among the absentees were Father Coughlin and his leading associates in New York, Boston, and Philadelphia, or indeed anyone from the Christian Front networks. Of the numerous Pennsylvania activists, the only one indicted was G. W. Kunze. Among groups cited as agents of German propaganda, the glaring omissions included a large majority of the isolationist clubs and leagues and most of the Mothers' movements that were becoming the leading force in antiwar agitation. Not only were no Italian Fascist groups or activists prosecuted, but the omission was scarcely mentioned by critics. Neither were Klansmen represented.

The administration was unwilling to explore possible subversive activities by organizations closer to the political mainstream. A singularly delicate issue was the group of twenty or so isolationist members of the U.S. Senate and House who had cooperated with German-sponsored propaganda and intelligence services, permitting mass mailings of pro-Axis literature to be distributed under their congressional frank.[163] The Left would have liked a roster of sedition defendants to include such political names as Hamilton Fish, Burton K. Wheeler, Robert Reynolds, Gerald Nye, Clare E. Hoffman, and (ideally) Charles Lindbergh. In the event, this hope was dashed.[164] Subsequent trials focused not on the most influential leaders of the prewar Right, but on a second tier of outspoken individuals.

While political fears influenced the selective nature of the prosecutions, federal authorities were nervous about the strength of their cases in such a seldom-tried area of law, and the 1940 Christian Front trial in New York City had been a disaster. The lesson

would thus be to focus on the strongest and most blatant cases,
but even here the sedition trials were unproductive. When the
trials finally got under way in 1944, the prosecution cases proved
unwieldy and confusing and were based on the difficult task of
attempting to prove lengthy chains of association and influence.
Defense lawyers were well prepared and portrayed the charges as
a gross attempt to muzzle free speech and discussion.[165] Meanwhile, ultraconservative politicians such as Clare Hoffman and
John Rankin were depicting the whole prosecution as a Red smear
directed by the White House and the CIO to renew the "fifth column" scare in time for the coming November elections. In this
view, prosecutor O. J. Rogge was a tool of a Communist conspiracy that also included fellow traveling puppets such as Walter
Winchell and John Roy Carlson.[166] The case was further complicated by a series of legal decisions during 1944 in which the U.S.
Supreme Court overturned unrelated convictions for sedition and
espionage, raising questions about the state of the law and the criteria necessary for successful conviction.[167] The affair was closed
by the untimely death of the judge, and a mistrial was declared. In
1946 the Justice Department dismissed Rogge, who had engaged
in what proved a quixotic campaign to reopen the trial and to include some of the elusive political figures.[168]

These anticlimactic events marked the end of the long-feared
threat of Nazi subversion within the United States. From the mid-
1940s, law enforcement attention turned, rather, to the alleged
threats from the Left, and investigations of the far Right declined
sharply. This shift of public attention gives the misleading sense
that the movements and opinions described here came to a sudden
end with the collapse of the organizational structure, but there was
some continuity. While Pearl Harbor marked a catastrophe for the
extreme Right, it did not terminate the history of those movements.

9 | After the War
The Extreme Right since 1945

After the Second World War it would be many years before the far Right again attracted as much attention as it had in the era of the Bund and the Christian Front. One might naturally assume that the war itself was the crucial turning point in this transition, and that the military encounter with fascism overseas had ruined the chances of any domestic movement. Public activities by extremist groups declined dramatically in wartime, naturally enough, given a patriotic rallying to the national cause as well as the conscription of thousands of young men who might otherwise have been attracted to the sects. Shared experiences in the armed services also accelerated the assimilation of diverse ethnic communities, a process well under way since the 1920s. An easing of religious conflicts was indicated by the popularity of postwar movements promoting interfaith understanding. In Philadelphia this trend was symbolized by the campaign in the late 1940s to erect a monument to the "four chaplains" of the USS *Dorchester*, the clergymen who gave their lifejackets to other men when the ship sank in 1943 and who perished together. The memorial at Temple University, with its altars and chapels for Catholics, Protestants, and Jews, was a stirring material symbol of a radical shift in the public mood.

Though there is much to this view, wartime circumstances do not in themselves provide a complete explanation of the decline of the Right. As the Mothers' movement indicates, at least some fascist activists remained active throughout the war and afterward, albeit on a reduced scale. However, we are also dealing with significantly different source materials and a sharp decline in the volume of media sources and official investigations concerning the far Right from about 1946. This was due to the massive political shift to the Right in these years and a perceived need to combat subversion from Communism and the Left. Over the next decade a charge of "fascism" had to be made with great care, as the term could invite the suspicion that the speaker was a leftist using a common epithet against political opponents. Though some groups, especially Jewish organizations, continued to investigate fascist and anti-Semitic activities, the attitude of much of the American media could now be epitomized as "no enemies on the Right."

219
The
Extreme
Right
since
1945

While the ultra-Right did survive in some form, it was severely attenuated, largely because so many of its policies had now entered the political mainstream. After 1946 fanatical anti-Communism became a sine qua non of participation in American public life, effectively removing this potent ideological weapon from the extremist arsenal. The far Right was now forced to rely on themes of anti-Semitism and racial hatred, which proved to have far less potential to create the kind of broad support that had been apparent in the 1930s.

THE NEW LOYALTY: McCARTHYISM IN PENNSYLVANIA

In the 1930s the far Right had argued that state and federal governments were covertly influenced by leftist, Communist, or CIO forces. After 1946, however, the inquisitorial hunt for Communist influences proved to all but a few deep-dyed anti-Semites that government was "sound." As in most states, the 1946 elections marked a triumph for right-wing Republicans in Pennsylvania. Edward Martin defeated Joe Guffey for U.S. senator, James Duff secured the governorship, and there were sweeping gains in the state legislature. Republican leader M. Harvey Taylor described the party's triumph simply as "a victory of Americanism over Communism."[1]

Measures that in the 1930s were advocated only by the most extreme Red-hunters and vigilantes now entered the practical legis-

220

The
Extreme
Right
since
1945

lative agenda, as Pennsylvania politicians in the decade after 1946 outdid themselves in the quest for ever more punitive and inquisitorial solutions to the Red menace. At the federal level the Supreme Court upheld internal security legislation so sweeping that, had it been applied a few years previously, it would have resulted in the successful prosecution of thousands of Axis sympathizers, rather than the handful who actually suffered. The key decision was the 1951 *Dennis* case, named, of course, for the Communist Eugene Dennis rather than the fascist Lawrence Dennis, who had emerged so relatively lightly from his own sedition trial.

Anti-Communism flourished in communities that had wholeheartedly joined the New Deal coalition, and the cause provided a common front on which old New Dealers and rightists could ally. Crucial to this change were the Roman Catholic church and the ethnic communities in which it was rooted.[2] In Pennsylvania more than most states, Democratic successes in the Roosevelt era had been predicated on the loyalty of ethnic minorities, which were predominantly Catholic or Jewish. While Catholicism never entirely lost its virulently anti-Communist tradition, this had been subsumed in the 1930s into social and economic issues of more immediate concern, such as promoting the sound development of organized labor. In overseas issues Catholic anti-Communism was complemented by a sturdy suspicion of Nazism. After 1945 the church focused sharply on the perceived Red peril and the threat of anti-Christian persecution, a menace personified by the idealized martyr figures of Archbishop Stepinac and Cardinal Mindszenty.[3] The Democratic Party and its natural allies now found themselves deeply committed to an apocalyptic war against Communism, "red fascism," a struggle that might any day be transformed into literal warfare of unprecedented savagery.[4] This Catholic emphasis became more marked following the emergence of Joseph McCarthy, whose ethnic and social bases of support resembled those of Father Coughlin. "Many felt the Senator was merely taking up where Father Coughlin had left off."[5]

The rightward shift in these years is suggested by the case of Pittsburgh, which between 1948 and 1951 experienced an anti-Communist purge as violent as that in perhaps any American city.[6] Pittsburgh maintained a lively radical tradition through the mid-1940s, and rank-and-file militancy during a power strike in 1946

came close to initiating a citywide general strike. However, the area 221
The
Extreme
Right
since
1945 offered a natural constituency for anti-Communism by virtue of the large populations with ties to Eastern Europe, including Poles, Ukrainians, Slovaks, Croats, and Hungarians. Also critical was the role of the Catholic church, particularly in the unions. The defeat of Communism in the labor movement was orchestrated by activist clergy such as Charles Owen Rice, who since the late 1930s had been calling for the CIO to be purged of Communists.[7] In the steel industry, leftist organizers were combated by long-standing CIO leaders such as the loyally Catholic Philip Murray. The anti-Red campaign in the unions was supported by Father Rice's friend Francis "Tad" Walter, U.S. representative from Easton, Pennsylvania, since 1933. The Communist threat led this long-serving Catholic Democrat to swing far to the Right. He drafted the xenophobic Walter-McCarran Immigration and Nationality Act and chaired the House Committee on Un-American Activities from 1954.[8]

The severity of the antiradical movement reflected the lack of criticism from major institutions, and the three Pittsburgh newspapers vied with each other in showing the most devoted support for anti-Communist informers and in denouncing the Left. The Pittsburgh purges were by no means the preserve of traditional Red-baiting groups of the far Right, the employers' groups, or the American Legion, but were favored by former New Deal supporters, including Father Rice, Mayor David Lawrence, and the *Pittsburgh Press*. Even the once-liberal Governor Earle, now a diplomat, became so fanatically anti-Soviet as to provoke international incidents.[9]

Another leading Democrat was Judge Michael Angelo Musmanno, the quondam admirer of Mussolini who had since developed impeccable prolabor credentials. In 1950, however, he emerged as one of the most active anti-Communist campaigners in the state.[10] As a judge Musmanno permitted extensive legal improprieties in his quest to convict suspected Communist militants, especially legendary party militant Steve Nelson, whom the judge termed an "Atom Spy." Musmanno drafted the legislation outlawing the Communist Party in Pennsylvania and participated in the struggle against Communist influence in the Westinghouse labor unions. His devoted support for McCarthy even survived

222

The
Extreme
Right
since
1945

the notorious army hearings of 1954.[11] Musmanno's Red hunt may have owed something to his electoral ambitions, but his writings in these years indicate a vitriolic hatred of Communism that is remarkable even by the standards of the time.[12] Communism, he wrote, must be pushed back to its "Asiatic frontiers"; the Communist Party headquarters in Pittsburgh was "the equivalent of an advance post of the Red Army," a "conspiratorial nest" planted by "Russian agents." When Musmanno and some detectives raided the buildings, on no known legal grounds, he observed with disgust its "Muscovite interior."[13]

Musmanno was active in the pressure group Americans Battling Communism, the leadership of which included prominent figures from Jewish and Polish ethnic organizations.[14] A strong Italian American presence included the former state attorney general Charles Margiotti. Americans Battling Communism was "closely allied" to Walter Alessandroni, Pennsylvania state commander of the American Legion.[15] Alessandroni's personal credentials were impressive, but as with Musmanno there were connections to a rightist past. Walter was the nephew of Judge Eugene Alessandroni, a key friend of Italian Fascists in prewar Pennsylvania, who after 1945 concentrated his political efforts on the anti-Soviet struggle.[16]

Pittsburgh was not unique in its anti-Red ardor. In Philadelphia, Communist Party membership reached its height in the mid-1940s, possibly 4,000 members in the metropolitan region, if the Young Communist League was taken into account.[17] However, the movement soon crumbled in the face of mass popular opposition. In December 1946 40,000 people demonstrated in Philadelphia against the persecution of the church in Yugoslavia and the imprisonment of Archbishop Stepinac. The gathering was organized by the Catholic War Veterans, a zealous arm of the anti-Communist movement, and it was vigorously publicized by the Catholic archdiocese, whose newspaper would rarely flag in its denunciations of Communism over the next decade.[18]

In 1947 Catholic War Veterans and American Legionnaires disrupted a meeting held to protest excesses of the House Committee on Un-American Activities. Mob violence was justified by the news media, and the York *Gazette and Daily* editorialized that "if it takes more rioting and some real skull-cracking to make Americans conform to the new loyalty, there'll be plenty of volunteers."[19]

Like the veterans, other Catholic groups such as the Knights of 223
The
Extreme
Right
since
1945
Columbus and the Holy Name Societies took the lead in anti-
Communist activism.[20] The patriotic upsurge was supported by
Catholic Democratic politicians who had earlier been noted for
their New Deal enthusiasm, such as U.S. senator Francis J. Myers.
As Truman's attorney general, former Philadelphia congressman
McGranery carried out the criminal penalties, deportations, and
denaturalizations imposed under the new anti-Red laws. Between
1953 and 1956 most of the Communist Party leaders in the Philadelphia area were arrested and prosecuted for sedition.[21]

In this context the writings of a once-derided figure like Bessie
Burchett seem almost routine. Most of her 1941 *Education for Destruction* would have occasioned little surprise a decade later, with
her by-now orthodox beliefs in the conspiratorial nature of Communism, the sinister infiltration of Communists into unions and
"pink" liberal pressure groups, and the evils of one-worldism, the
World Federation of Soviet States.[22] In 1953 the anti-Communist
purge focused on her ancient bugbear of the Philadelphia public school system. The ensuing "hurricane" claimed some forty
teachers, which seemed amply to confirm earlier claims about leftist infiltration.[23] By this point no Pennsylvania teacher would have
dared use the texts and materials that Burchett and DAR activists had denounced in the 1930s. In 1938 attending a meeting of a
group such as the American League for Peace and Democracy or
the Citizens' Anti-Nazi Committee exposed one to possible physical assault by Bund or Coughlinite militants; a decade or so later
the mere record of such attendance was enough to destroy one's
professional career.

Fear of Communism reached a new height with the Korean
War. Once again the American Legion emerged as the foremost
advocate of "militant opposition to Communism wherever it appears."[24] For both sides Communism was the central issue of the
1950 elections. Of course Republican gubernatorial candidate John
Fine attacked the "pink" connections of his Democratic oppo-
nent Richardson Dilworth, but more surprising was the extent
to which Pennsylvania Democrats used the "red fellow traveler"
smear against their Republican rivals. Francis Myers accused them
of "using Communist tactics and techniques" and found the Republicans weak on the defense of South Korea. Dilworth charged

224

The
Extreme
Right
since
1945

that corrupt political machines like Philadelphia's were breeding grounds of Communism.[25]

In 1951 the victorious Republican governor Fine announced that Pennsylvania was being placed on a war footing in expectation of imminent international hostilities.[26] That fall the legislature overwhelmingly voted to outlaw the Communist Party. The state adopted a criterion for dismissing supposedly subversive employees that was draconian even by the standards of the era, providing for removal of those where there was "reasonable doubt as to the loyalty of the person involved," rather than the customary need to prove subversive character.[27] The following year all state and local officials were required to take loyalty oaths.[28]

In 1954 Senator McCarthy chose a Catholic Day celebration in Johnstown to announce to a crowd of some 15,000 that "there are no tactics too rough to weed out the underground influence which threatens the very heart of the American republic."[29] The following year communities throughout Pennsylvania participated in the American Legion's educational May Day Takeovers of towns like Chambersburg, in which legionnaires posed as Communist troops, arresting civic officials, trampling civil liberties, destroying religion, and trying dissidents, all to give a "vivid lesson in the brutalities to which people behind the Iron Curtain were subjected every day."[30]

THE ANTI-SEMITIC RIGHT

With the political center of gravity having returned so far to the right, the old rightist sects might have found their work unnecessary. With Governor Fine, Judge Musmanno, and the Catholic War Veterans hard at work, what more could they possibly want? However, a core of activists continued to press for the anti-Communist crusade to be supplemented by a firmer line on the issues of race and anti-Semitism. Activity did therefore continue after 1945–46, with a new emphasis on the United Nations and the Dumbarton Oaks system as manifestations of Communism, one-worldism, and Jewish power. By the late 1940s the far Right concentrated its ire on international institutions that were allegedly subverting American institutions, major targets including UNESCO; the Atlantic Union; and the Genocide Treaty.[31]

Throughout the late 1940s and early 1950s Pennsylvania was

home for a number of anti-Semitic activists. Pittsburgh had the Salvation Tract Society and Maria Lohle's Defenders of George Washington Principles.[32] In 1948 Philadelphia rightists played host to Lawrence Dennis and other defendants from the wartime sedition trials, organized in the Justice for New Deal Victims Committee.[33] In 1951–52 attacks on Philadelphia synagogues were attributed to a Hitler Youth movement formed by German American students at Olney High School.[34]

In Philadelphia, Mothers' groups remained pivotal, above all the National Blue Star Mothers. The network was affiliated to W. Henry MacFarland Jr., Frankford-based leader of the Nationalist Action League, who published the *National Progress* and *Philadelphia Nationalist*, mimeographed racist sheets with a claimed 1947 circulation of some 400 or 500 each.[35] However, he had high aspirations and hoped that *National Progress* would become the leading "nationalist" newspaper in New York City.[36] His group urged a constitutional amendment "which would ban from further immigration all persons of Oriental, Negroid or Eurasian racial descent, and all others who are not of the Christian faith." In 1950 MacFarland mobilized various patriotic groups, including the POS of A, in a protest against an emergent world federalism movement, which was organizing nationwide meetings. He sought to prosecute libraries, schools, and other institutions that tolerated on their premises the advocates of "World Government Treason."

Both the Mothers and MacFarland's league were linked to the anti-Semitic preacher Gerald L. K. Smith, who aspired to fill the vacuum left by Coughlin and who established his own catena of Mothers' groups. Smith's network of institutions included the Committee of One Million, the America First Party, and the Christian Veterans of America, and he published the paper *The Cross and the Flag*.[37] He had close links with Pennsylvania activists. MacFarland and Smith toured the country on speaking tours;[38] while in Pittsburgh, Smith's speeches were sponsored by the Defenders of George Washington Principles.[39]

The Nationalist Action League was affiliated with a number of anti-Semitic groups and newspapers, including Gerald Winrod's *Defender* and Conde McGinley's news sheet, *Common Sense*. MacFarland and Brown were also the American distributors of anti-Semitic literature emanating from Sweden.[40] The clique revived

226

The
Extreme
Right
since
1945

old political alliances, as in 1945 when Catherine V. Brown spoke to a New York streetcorner gathering seeking to revive the Christian Front.[41] In 1946 the Pennsylvania Mothers affiliated with a national movement of Women for the United States of America, the leaders of which included veteran militants Bertha Weber and Maria Lohle.[42] In 1954 the remaining Mothers' groups and *Common Sense* were investigated by the House Un-American Activities Committee, which explored their ties to the (Nazi) National Renaissance Party, formed "to carry on the work of the Christian Front."[43]

MacFarland was central to the far-Right agitation of the time, and the House committee linked him to "three or four fascist movements."[44] Both the Nationalist Action League and the Committee for Nationalist Action were included on the attorney general's list of subversive organizations, at a time when only the most extreme rightist organizations qualified for this status. Another MacFarland group was the American Flag Committee, known for its denunciations of the United Nations and UNESCO. In August 1952 the nation's superpatriots and "hatemongers" promoted the presidential candidacy of General Douglas MacArthur in opposition to the dangerously liberal Eisenhower, the "Kikes' Ike." MacFarland addressed a national gathering of the organization in Chicago, and he was one of the leaders chosen at the formation of the New Constitution Party of the United States, which sought to draft MacArthur as president. Later that month the new party held another meeting in Philadelphia and declared its opposition to "international conspirators who derided and defied our constitution for more than a decade." Despite early hopes, the MacArthur movement garnered little electoral support.[45]

Political continuity from the 1930s is suggested by the experience of Mrs. David Good, one of the longest-serving Coughlinite stalwarts, who first emerged as an anti-Communist activist supporting Bessie Burchett's campaign against the Philadelphia school system in 1935–36. In 1939 Van Horn Moseley's appearance in Philadelphia was greeted with fulsome remarks from this "Philadelphia socialite," a leader of the patriotic "coalition" in the city.[46] Carlson links her to anti-Semitic propagandists such as Charles B. Hudson, publisher of *America in Danger* and a "trusted adviser" of Van Horn Moseley.[47] Hudson was another of the defendants in the federal sedition trial.[48] After the outbreak of war Mrs. Good herself was interviewed by the federal grand jury investigating subversive activities.[49] Like other Mothers, she remained active into the Eisenhower era, as vice president of the National Council for American Education. This group was founded by Allen Zoll, whose ultra-Right associations similarly dated back well into the 1930s. In 1938–39 he had mobilized Coughlinite picketing against a New York radio station.[50] In 1954 Mrs. Good appeared with John B. Trevor on the governing body of the Committee of Ten Million Americans, a McCarthyite pressure group with anti-Semitic tendencies.[51] Her associations were consistent and enduring.

227
The
Extreme
Right
since
1945

The rightist tradition that began with the ACS and similar groups can be traced into the 1960s, through the John Birch Society and kindred superpatriotic "God and Country" organizations.[52] Founded in 1958 the Birch movement's wealthy sponsors included members of the Pew family, those warhorses of militant anti-Communism.[53] Radical Right activism flourished following the victory of a Democratic president in 1960, in a reaction reminiscent of circumstances following the elections of 1932 and 1992. In 1962, as in 1934 or 1994, a national drift toward political liberalism was confronted by an upsurge of extreme rightist and paramilitary groups. Birchers were the chief political beneficiaries of this trend in the 1960s, while the movement spawned a well-armed paramilitary offshoot in the Minutemen. By the mid-1960s, liberals were explicitly comparing the wave of agitation to the days of "the Coughlinites, the America Firsters, the German-American Bund and other lunatic organizations."[54]

By 1967 the John Birch Society had "a pocket of strength in the communities clustered around Philadelphia" and an area of growth around Pittsburgh.[55] In both cases the movement's appeal was clearly concentrated in the white suburbs. As in the 1930s, extremism drew strength from respectable patriotic institutions. In 1959 the state convention of the Pennsylvania DAR chose as keynote speaker a representative of the fervently right-wing Christian Anti-Communism Crusade.[56]

While the Bircher organization officially repudiated anti-Semitic views, some of their associations attracted controversy. In 1965, for example, Robert Welch praised the prophetic warnings of the

228

The
Extreme
Right
since
1945

American Flag Committee about Communist infiltration of the black civil rights movement. That committee was one of several front groups run by W. Henry MacFarland Jr., who by this stage was affiliated with the Liberty Lobby.[57] Birchers and like-minded groups also offered an elaborate mythology about the misdeeds of international bankers throughout history, identifying precisely the firms, families, and individuals once named by Louis McFadden, though with ethnic associations now suppressed.[58]

WHITE SUPREMACY

From the 1940s, antiblack sentiment came to rival anti-Semitism as a motivating force on the extreme Right, with the Second World War marking the decisive shift in the nature of Pennsylvania's racial politics. Demand for labor inspired a renewed migration to the northern cities, and by the end of hostilities Philadelphia had an African American population of 300,000, some 15 percent of the whole. Tentative advances by blacks toward equal employment opportunities incited fears that white jobs would be lost once hostilities ceased. One focus of controversy was the Philadelphia Transit Company, which under pressure from federal authorities agreed to hire a number of black motormen. In August 1944 a wildcat strike by thousands of white workers, mainly Irish Catholics, brought the city to a halt. Racial tensions ran high and were incited further by the propaganda of "the Ku Klux Klan and other anti-Negro groups."[59] Blue Star Mothers leader Agnes Waters expressed her pleasure "that the people of Philadelphia had guts enough to riot at the PTC hiring Jews and Niggers. I wish we had held out longer." Governor Martin received letters urging the introduction of formal racial segregation in Philadelphia.[60]

Pennsylvania's nonwhite population continued to grow in the postwar boom years. Between 1940 and 1970 the black population of Philadelphia grew from 13.1 to 33.6 percent of the total, and this racial division superseded earlier neighborhood rivalries.[61] One beneficiary of these changes was the Ku Klux Klan, which had been all but destroyed in the 1940s by "filing of tax liens by federal authorities, revocation of KKK charters by state legislatures, *quo warranto* proceedings, court decisions and criminal prosecutions."[62] The movement revived in a very different form in the next decade. Originating once more in the South, the reborn Klan developed strength from opposition to desegregation and spread rapidly north as racial tensions increased in that area. Racist organizations gained impetus from the urban race riots of 1964–68 and the threat of urban terrorism. In Philadelphia the rioting along Columbia Avenue in 1964 polarized racial attitudes for years afterward.[63]

229
The
Extreme
Right
since
1945

Though the reaction to the liberalism of the Great Society was quite as extreme as that to the earlier New Deal, white resentment did not produce a mass social movement. While Klan membership nationwide reached a peak of 55,000 in 1967, this figure dropped dramatically in the face of vigorous law enforcement activity. All Klan sects combined could muster only 13,000 members in 1981 and 6,000 by the end of the decade. The movement has been prone to schism, giving rise to countless evanescent factions.

The movement's ideology also changed. Anti-Catholicism virtually ceased to be a major component of the public platform of Klan organizations, to be largely replaced by the pressing black-white issue, which today gives northern Klans a much more "southern" image. Post-1950s Klans have often drawn closer to the anti-Semitic views that once characterized other sections of the far Right, and anti-Semitism provides the ideological cement to explain the disparate challenges posed by world Communism, black civil rights, and the liberal social policies of successive U.S. governments. In Pennsylvania the merger of the Klan into a broad ultra-Right front is symbolized by the record of Grand Dragon Roy Frankhouser of Reading, who in the 1960s became an organizer for the Minutemen.[64] He was also associated with the National States' Rights Party and with the American neo-Nazi movement founded by George Lincoln Rockwell. The Klan and the anti-Semitic National Alliance also had a small unit in Kensington, in northeast Philadelphia, which overlapped with a number of anti-Semitic sects.[65] Kensington by the 1960s offered fertile ground for agitation, as a declining working-class community anxious to defend its role as the stereotypical "Whitetown, USA." [66]

In the 1970s tactical alliances on the far Right were consecrated by the growth of the Christian Identity movement, which explained that white northern Europeans were the authentic heirs of the biblical promises and covenants by virtue of their descent from the lost tribes of Israel. Jews, however, were false claimants

230

The
Extreme
Right
since
1945

to "Hebraic" status and were of the devil. Modern Identity groups often use "Aryan" terminology and pose at least a notional claim to church status. Such groups usually employ Nazi regalia and symbolism and often use some or all of the Nazi ritual calendar, especially the commemoration of Hitler's birthday on April 20.[67]

Pennsylvania includes representatives of all ideological shades of the contemporary extreme Right, including "Aryan" and Christian Identity groups, neo-Nazis, White Aryan Resistance, Posse Comitatus, survivalists, and Klansmen. By the mid-1990s several rural northern counties had "militias," not necessarily racist in ideology but deeply suspicious of federal authority and often with loose connections to established extremist groups.[68] Overall numbers are difficult to assess. In 1994 the Pennsylvania Human Relations Commission published a list of fifty-two white supremacist groups said to be active in the state, including seventeen factions or subdivisions of the Ku Klux Klan and eighteen groups of allegedly Nazi "skinheads."[69] The value of the list is uncertain, as it reflects reporting by local police and private agencies, who adopt very different criteria before identifying a group, still less defining it as "active." In some cases Klan and white supremacist groups clearly are present and quite well organized. In other cases, though, the report of activity is based on a few handbills or slogans. If "active" implies an organized and ideologically motivated group with more than a handful of members, then the Human Relations list should probably be reduced by 70 or 80 percent. At the same time, the account omits nonwhite hate groups, which is ironic in that anti-Semitic tracts like the *Protocols* are today found in black nationalist and separatist bookstores in the major cities, which serve a far larger clientele than their white racist counterparts.

There are areas of genuine white supremacist activity, for example, in the counties of York, Berks, Bucks, Northampton, and Huntingdon, and contemporary rightists demonstrate many of the characteristics of their 1930s predecessors. In the Klan especially, modern groups reproduce faithfully the ideological schisms of 1940 over the nature of their "Americanism" and are divided between overt Nazis and patriotic ultraconservatives. Klan activists in contemporary Pennsylvania ostensibly concern themselves with such mainstream issues as opposition to abortion, drugs, and pornography. However, the commitment to community projects has done nothing to diminish the hostility of the movement's numerous foes.[70]

231
The
Extreme
Right
since
1945

Also familiar is the Klan's tendency to establish itself as the militant focus of public resentments against groups perceived as alien, criminal, or threatening, which in the contemporary world tends to mean blacks rather than Jews or Catholics. In the rural midstate county of Huntingdon, Klan exploitation of local black-white tensions in the 1970s and 1980s produced strenuous activism by the Thomas Abbott klavern as well as other sects and rightist groups.[71] In 1994 two Blair County men faced federal charges concerning an alleged attempt to blow up the Raystown Lake dam in pursuit of extremist political goals. Elsewhere, sporadic racial conflicts since the mid-1980s have resulted in a series of Klan marches and rallies, which have given the movement disproportionate publicity.[72] As in the 1920s the Klan employs the violent reaction to its appearance to generate sympathy and to cast its opponents as irresponsible aggressors.[73]

Changes of attitude and phraseology shape public perceptions of the racist movements. While the Klan and cognate groups have been the subject of intense concern and press coverage, the numerical size of modern demonstrations is tiny. The shirts or Christian Fronters could at their height turn out thousands of supporters, as against the few dozen sympathizers available at any given point to the Klan, or the even smaller cliques available to the Nationalist Action League or similar factions. While the earlier movements could plausibly claim a degree of sympathy in the bystanders in a particular area, only a heavy police presence safeguards modern racists from angry crowds. Qualitative and quantitative differences are disguised by modern sensitivity about public expressions of racist or extremist views. Newspapers or television broadcasts today pay attention to activities that would have drawn no notice in the earlier era, while the scale of media newsgathering and reporting has increased massively.

The change is suggested by the hate crime statistics reported by government agencies, which seem to depict an increasingly intolerant society. In 1991 Pennsylvania agencies reported 300 acts of this sort, over 400 by 1993. Media report newly released figures with cautionary words about an "epidemic of hate" and rising racism.[74] The contrary case can also be made, that only a society in which such actions are no longer acceptable is willing or able to collect such data, which often involve verbal or symbolic insults rather than violence. If reports of sporadic racial or religious violence had been collected in 1924 or 1939, they would presumably have exceeded the modern figure by a factor of thousands. Far from being a natural social commonplace, "white supremacy" is now the label of a fringe movement generally stereotyped as deviant and cultlike. Despite apparent signs of continuity, the American racist Right finds itself in an utterly different world, where adherents have acquired the status of political lepers. There is a grim irony in the inevitable metaphor, that they have been consigned to a political ghetto from which escape seems impossible.

THE RELIGIOUS RIGHT

Changed perceptions of issues such as race and religion do not mean that the ultra-Right tradition is dead, and continuity with older traditions can be illustrated from several potent political movements of the mid-1990s, including the Christian Coalition and the broader religious Right, and the 1996 presidential campaign of Pat Buchanan. Key political themes of these years included such long-familiar topics as immigration, internationalism, and a far-reaching perception that governments are seeking to modify or corrupt traditional values or social structures. The perceived subversion of public education retains a central role in conservative rhetoric.

Other ideas survive in forms that are transmuted, if recognizable. Much of the bizarre mythology that once characterized nativist perceptions of the misdeeds of Catholics, Masons, or Jews now survives in the anti-Satanic literature, with its copious unsubstantiated tales of clandestine sexual exploitation and child murder. Continuity is reinforced by the alleged involvement of Masons in diabolist cults and sacrifices.[75] This new demonology is purveyed through networks of fundamentalist churches, religious bookstores, and televangelists, which collectively have become crucial vehicles for the propaganda of the modern Right. These institutions are also major sources for a pervasive conspiracy theory that implicates both international finance and U.S. governments, but in a nexus that is diabolical rather than Zionist. While public schools are attacked for their insidious indoctrination of children, the culprits are identified as crypto-occultist New Agers rather than Jewish Communists. Though the media are viewed as just as anti-Christian as they were in Coughlin's day, this is thought to be motivated not by Jewish interests but by Left-liberal secularism. However, the resulting picture of a sinister New World Order differs little from the nightmares of generations of conspiracy mongers. In the fundamentalist vision, the rationalist, secular, and anti-Christian dystopia epitomized by the term "New World Order" is barely distinguishable from the nightmare vision of the *Protocols of the Elders of Zion*.

This continuity is suggested by Pat Robertson's best-selling analysis titled *The New World Order* (1991). Robertson is a major political figure who mounted a serious presidential bid in 1988 and subsequently became the inspiration of the Christian Coalition movement that dominates Republican Party politics in many states. His tract depicts recent world crises as signs of manipulation by sinister clandestine forces, by international financiers linked to New Age religion, and ultimately by secret societies such as the Freemasons and the Bavarian Illuminati: "A single thread runs from the White House to the State Department to the Council on Foreign Relations to the Trilateral Commission to secret societies to extreme New Agers. There must be a new world order." In order to substantiate claims of machinations by bankers such as "the Schiffs, the Warburgs, the Kahns, the Rockefellers, the Morgans," Robertson cites as one source a book by anti-Semitic propagandist George Sylvester Viereck. Though Robertson was genuinely surprised by charges of anti-Semitism, his use of such tainted sources resulted in a public controversy in 1994–95.[76]

The explicitly religious emphasis epitomizes perhaps the most important shift in the rightist tradition in the last half-century, the movement toward explicitly religious justifications for belief and action. For all the Christian pretensions of the earlier groups, issues of religion and personal morality never played a role remotely comparable to what they play today. The far Right of the 1990s is often defined by matters that would have seemed peripheral to serious politics in 1940, such as concerns about abortion and homosexuality, and the issues arising from new concepts of women's rights.[77] In contemporary Pennsylvania the antiabortion movement is by far the most powerful and best-organized sector

234
*The
Extreme
Right
since
1945*

of the political Right, with a direct-action fringe that ventures into acts of illegality and terrorism.[78]

This ideological realignment has led to a historic alliance between the once diametrically opposed forces of the Roman Catholic church and evangelical Protestantism, a de facto Christian Front with a numerical base far larger than anything that might have been hoped for in the era of Coughlin or Stouch. However, "Christian" in the modern context no longer has the same implications of racial solidarity and anti-Jewish confrontation. While evangelical and fundamentalist Christian sentiment has grown sharply in recent decades, most groups express strong sympathy for Zionist aspirations and even incorporate them into their apocalyptic worldview. In contemporary conspiracy mythology Jews are seldom mentioned except as tragic victims of secularist and one-world plots, which are directly blamed for the Holocaust.[79]

The equivalence of "Christian" and "Gentile" has been a sensitive issue. In the 1970s the need to avoid this equation led to an evangelical political movement naming itself the Moral Majority rather than anything explicitly Christian, while the values of the religious Right are usually defined by the irenic term "Judaeo-Christian." Recently the matter of anti-Semitism has been regarded as sufficiently dormant to permit the unabashed use of terms such as "Christian Conservative" and "Christian Coalition," though in 1995 even this latter body was forced to deny that its ultimate aspiration was a "Christian nation."

Issues of gender, morality, and religion have revolutionized the older partisan divisions of Left and Right and largely supplanted the rhetoric of class politics. Older controversies have accordingly fallen in importance or have been excluded from the arena of acceptable political discourse, at least as an overt agenda. Race has been the most dramatic casualty of this change, for all that ethnic conflict may underlie current controversies over issues such as crime, welfare, and immigration. The contemporary religious Right is neither racist nor anti-Semitic, nor is it in any sense totalitarian. Its economic views are strictly laissez-faire, and conservative social policies today are diametrically opposed to the scientific racism and eugenic thought that was so widespread between the world wars and that provided the traditional pillars of fascist or

Nazi ideology. Many charges can be laid against religious conservatives, whose policies have been condemned by critics as authoritarian, nativist, misogynist, or obscurantist. Except as an empty epithet, however, the views cannot be characterized as "fascist." As a serious political movement, American fascism is now extinct.

10 | Conclusion

or a few years fascist and ultra-Right movements enjoyed a vogue in Pennsylvania. This chapter considers the nature of the attraction exercised by extremist groups on a wide variety of Pennsylvanians, and the reasons why this popularity declined so sharply. Explanations must address the shifting character of the ideas that were regarded as acceptable within mainstream discourse and the capacity of the ultras to exploit these political and racial commonplaces for their own goals. Though we cannot here consider how typical was the history of Pennsylvania in these matters, some general issues and problems can be suggested. The main conclusion is that a great deal still remains to be known about the ultra-Right in these years, and that gaps can only be filled by local and regional studies.

A STUDY IN FAILURE?

By any reasonable standard the story of the extreme Right in the earlier era is one of ignominious failure, culminating in virtual collapse in 1941–42. This later history affects our historical perspective on earlier events, so that in retrospect it is tempting to dismiss the whole experience of the far Right in the 1930s as basically irrelevant. Smith epitomizes the common view of Coughlin, Kuhn,

and Pelley as "waste products of the Great Depression."[1] Though
a few politicians were close to the extremist sects, no one ever won
election on the explicit ticket of a Pennsylvania fascist group, not
even to the state senate or a city council, and guilt by association
terminated the political careers of Louis McFadden and probably
Fritz Gartner. The best that could be hoped was that, as in the
case of Judge Alessandroni, the extremist label would not detract
from an otherwise solid community position.

By 1941 the main importance of the rightists was chiefly negative and even counterproductive, in providing a weapon for the
Roosevelt administration and its media allies to discredit the isolationists. Anti-Semitic violence in American streets reinforced the
role of European events in promoting Jewish-Christian dialogue
and the tolerance movement, a sensitivity suggested by the new
preference for Judaeo-Christian terminology in advocating religious values. In the aftermath of the Christian Front, Christian
Mobilizers, and Pelley's Christ Democracy, the far Right tainted
"Christian" politics for a generation.[2]

On the other hand, the far-Right tradition should not be dismissed too lightly, if only because so many of its basic assumptions
became political orthodoxy after 1946. With the crucial exception
of anti-Semitism, most of the platform planks of the ACS and
its ilk were firmly rooted in the mainstream by 1950. In addition,
the ultra-rightists contributed indirectly and unwillingly to later
developments, in that the fifth column scare of 1939–40 contributed to shaping perceptions of the likely Communist menace a
decade later. When Governor Fine's administration clamped down
on potential Red plotting in 1951, it was taking precisely the actions that had so urgently been demanded against the alleged Nazi
agents a decade earlier. The Brown Scare left a legacy for the later
Red Scare, not least in legitimizing and glamorizing the role of the
defector and infiltrator.[3] In institutional terms the FBI that led the
internal security purge of the Truman years was the body trained
and socially licensed by the politically popular hunt for Nazi spies
and seditionists.

The unpalatable extremism of one generation may yet become
the commonplaces of the next. In this context it is useful to consider the outpouring of academic work on the far Right during the
early and mid-1960s by a generation of liberal scholars appalled

by the Bircher upsurge and the 1964 Goldwater campaign.[4] Ultra-conservatism was denigrated by association with the most hysterical nativist movements of bygone years and discussed as a form of social-psychological pathology. This condescending literature reads oddly three decades later, following the Reagan-Bush era, the virtual extinction of Communism, the precipitous decline of liberal Christian churches, and the creation of a social orthodoxy that canonizes many, though not all, of the old conservative nostrums.

The long-term failure of the 1930s' sects leaves open the question of whether they were ever a serious political threat or if they were always a political illusion exploited by their enemies. Paradoxically, the best testimony to the potential political impact of the fascist Right may be found in the circumstances of its failure. The extreme Right lost its credibility because for all its boldness, the Roosevelt administration never undertook two ventures that were central to the debates of the time. The United States never agreed to the mass admission of European political refugees, which in the context of the time meant an immigration of several hundred thousand Jews, and it did not become involved in the European war until after experiencing a direct military assault from the Axis. Avoiding these critical decisions permitted the government to isolate and ghettoize the Right.

Though speculation about alternative realities is always perilous, the experience of Pennsylvania suggests that had either of these radical courses been taken, say in 1939, the impact would have been to galvanize the far Right, to create the potential for political disorder in major cities, and perhaps to stimulate mass resistance or sabotage, which could have been channeled into explicitly fascist directions. In Philadelphia or Pittsburgh, fascist activists were not numerous; but they had developed a network of organizations and propaganda facilities, and they were well ensconced in legitimate cultural, fraternal, and religious groups. In the language of counterinsurgency theory, they were close to achieving the degree of "insulation" that is the prerequisite for undertaking a successful campaign of subversion or terrorism.[5] One factor preventing this was the absence of a political detonator like the resumption of mass immigration, which could have turned the sects into mass parties. For all his political skills, Roosevelt knew that the extreme Right existed because it focused real public fears and concerns, which could only be soothed gradually.

This is relevant to the controversial issue of the administration's failure to help European Jewry and, as we now know, to save many lives that were in fact lost. For some this has been the darkest stain on Roosevelt's record.[6] However, the government's options were constrained by concern about a destructive popular backlash, and in the light of contemporary political realities, these fears were not unreasonable. That the importance of the far Right was negative does not mean that it was negligible. It can be argued that for whatever reason, at least two of its crucial goals were realized, in that the great Jewish migration never occurred and that a massive anti-Communist purge did indeed sweep away the once impressive network of leftist organizations, institutions, and social and cultural fronts. The near-disappearance of the far Right following 1946 may have reflected not its irrelevance but the near-totality of its success.

THE APPEAL OF THE FAR RIGHT

Leftists, liberals, and antifascist groups all believed, or affected to believe, that the extreme Right was a deadly political menace, with at least the chance to grow into the sort of mass movement that had become notorious in so many European nations. Many charges in this debate were spurious ("a million fifth columnists"), but the issue of potential growth is less obvious. Might different government policies have sparked a widespread rallying to the extreme Right? In order to assess the possible social reaction, we must understand the appeal of the rightist groups and the nature of their various constituencies. What is striking about this analysis is the relatively conventional and socially approved motives that inspired such support, and the degree to which the groups drew on familiar ideologies. This suggests that given the proper circumstances, contemporary fears of dramatic expansion by the extreme Right were by no means ludicrous.

The diversity of the groups indicates the difficulty of making straightforward statements about the reasons for sympathy or recruitment. No one reason or group of reasons drew a farmer or railroad worker to become a Klansman, a Philadelphia socialite or teacher to support the Coughlin movement, a chauffeur to join the

240
Conclusion

Bund, a Ukrainian miner to work for ODWU, or a judge to favor Italian Fascism. However, some common themes do emerge. For all the European trappings of the movements, most fall into the long history of nativist, xenophobic, and countersubversive traditions in American history. Scholars have often discussed the appeal of such movements: factors include a fear of rapid social change, especially when that threatens a loss of relative social status or prestige, and a reaction to far-reaching transformations of social and economic relationships that are poorly understood and for which culprits must be sought. However confused, the reactions are commonplace.[7]

Malevolent forces are personalized, if only because the mind finds it easier to comprehend evil acts inflicted by a rational intelligence rather than the misfortunes visited by an impersonal Providence, or the disasters inflicted by climate or erosion, economic cycles, or the disruption of commerce. Social calamities must of necessity be the work of highly placed enemies, who manipulate society through covert agents, organized into cabals whose very existence flouts democratic principles. These groups alter the course of events in their own interest, through criminal acts that include sabotage and assassination. At different times these conspirators have been identified as the Illuminati, Masons, Jesuits and Catholic Cardinals, slaveholders, Jews, Communists, and Satanists.[8]

Whatever their identity or their ultimate goals, malefactors have as a primary goal the destruction of distinctively American social and political patterns and the subjection of the American people to foreign ways of life and thought. American constitutional liberties, the American farmer, free labor, the thriving middle class, the institution of the family—all stand in the way of these nefarious conspirators and are imperiled by them. Mutatis mutandis, this conspiratorial perspective unites numerous political movements in American history, including bizarre fringe groups, but on occasion becomes central to mainstream political discourse.[9] At times, as in the late 1930s, American political conflict acquires the character of a duel between rival conspiracies. While the ultra-Right was untangling the sinister links between "President Rosenfelt," his Jewish masters, and the Moscow-backed CIO, New Dealers were extracting profit from their attack on "Tory plots," the Liberty League, and the machinations of Berlin and Tokyo.

Some of the far-Right movements fit well into the general nativ-

ist scheme, with the economic catastrophe of the time providing
the context of inexplicable social strain and conflict. In the ACS
the initial impetus was less a positive impulse to create some ideal
future state on fascist lines than an authentic horror at the contemporary world, and a genuine fear that worse was about to happen if urgent remedial action were not taken. This dark vision had
several facets, which in retrospect appear mutually contradictory.
Some militants were appalled by the dehumanizing indignities of
depression-era society. When asked to explain his radical Right
views, patrician Herbert L. Smith focused on issues of poverty
and degradation. Even in Philadelphia, he said, "I have seen a man
go to slop buckets and take food out of them."[10] Instead of urging
social reform as a solution to such conditions, the group saw leftist political campaigns as a cynical endeavor to subject the whole
society to a tyranny that would extend mass impoverishment and
ultimately lead to a general catastrophe for the white race. The depression and the labor conflicts it produced were dual aspects of
one conspiratorial endeavor to subvert and crush American society,
and the culprits were readily identified in the unholy nexus of
Jewish finance, the New Deal, and the crypto-Communist labor
movement.

The model that best epitomized the conservative nightmare was
the Spanish war, which as understood in the United States proved
how social reform masked a Red revolution designed to sweep away
all property and religion, and which could only be stopped at the
cost of a million lives. While some viewed the war as a struggle of
classes and ideologies, most Americans applied to it the interpretations of ethnic and religious conflict to which they were so well
accustomed. Joseph Gallagher asserted, "There was over a million
Christians over there who had been slaughtered and the Jews engi-
neered that, in my humble opinion, that Spanish revolution."[11]

While this populist reaction is best remembered for its anti-
Semitic expression, the ACS did engage in other activities that
from a modern perspective seem understandable and even praise-
worthy. The organization presented itself as a populist representative of local communities threatened by paternalistic government
and was approached for assistance by residents' groups. The ACS
organized opposition to a redevelopment scheme in Southwark
that would result in the replacement of older housing by "the

flimsy rabbit warrens of the Housing Project" and the destruction of "a real community."[12] Bessie Burchett "compared these victims of New Deal oppression with refugees from Germany: they were just as badly off, threatened with loss of homes and livelihood; they were just as terrified."[13] This campaign attracted little contemporary attention because it failed to provide the scandalous copy sought by the press, but it reveals much about the ideological assumptions of the far Right—about values such as the defense of community, about the fearful distrust of expansive government and of social engineering, and about the dread of submergence into a faceless, bureaucratic beehive. These ideas are also seen in the group's emphasis on education and the correct upbringing of youth. Communists threatened to indoctrinate the young with their twisted alien values, an enterprise that demanded vigilance and rigorous countermeasures by those committed to traditional values.

Jews fitted this broader picture as ideal representatives of unacceptable modernity; as examples of all that was commercial, antinational, and deracinated; and moreover as the group with the power and the will to impose these insidious values through the media and the schools.[14] War threats drew together the various fears: the loss of national sovereignty to Jewish and foreign puppet-masters, the regimentation imposed by New Deal bureaucrats, and accelerated social and economic changes that could complete the destruction of traditional society wrought since 1932. Though ostensibly defending the traditions and continuity of American society, the analysis of the ACS led it to advocate radical solutions that if implemented would have transformed all social and political relationships. The group thus offers a classic example of what Hofstadter termed "pseudo-conservative" dissent.[15]

REVOLUTIONARY NOSTALGIA

The experience of the ACS could also be applied to other sects, especially the Silver Shirts and the followers of anti-Semitic demagogues such as Gerald L. K. Smith, James True, and Robert Edmondson. To some extent it is also true of the ethnic fascist movements, to whom the label of "nativist" cannot be applied.[16] However, here, too, the radical and socially revolutionary rhetoric of the far Right veiled, usually thinly, a deep hatred and fear of

social change and a wistful nostalgia for an imagined past. The New
Germany that attracted the adulation of the Bund and its fellow *Conclusion*
travelers was conceived as a reiteration of the idealized Wilhelmine
Germany, with Hindenburg its personification as much as Hitler.
For the Italians the past evoked by Mussolini's regime was at the
same time the nation forged by the Risorgimento, and the shade
of the Roman Empire. For both Germans and Italians, imagined
nations of bygone days had been challenged or destroyed by the
soulless radical forces that attempted to crush traditional glory and
against which ultranationalist movements had launched their social
revolutions.[17] As with the Klan, these movements were above all
intended to prevent a repetition of the "Red dawn" of 1919.

In both cases, too, conditions in the home country were uncan-
nily echoed and reinforced by the American experience. The com-
munal pride and solidarity of immigrant groups was immeasurably
strengthened by the awareness of continuing ties to the homeland,
but between 1917 and 1924 these links were tested to the breaking
point by international conflict, the upsurge of American xenopho-
bia, and the near-collapse of both German and Italian society into
Red revolution. This crisis produced a generation far more sensitive and defensively proud of its ethnic identity and links to the
home country, more aware of being Italian or German rather than
merely migrants from Palermo or Munich, Bavaria or Sicily. Patriotic sensibility was enhanced by the presence of so many veterans
from the various armed forces, whose organizations provided a
critical nucleus for authoritarian nationalism. Support for the new
movements did not imply a rejection of Americanism but a deter-
mination that assimilation would be achieved on honorable terms,
without forsaking ethnic pride or tradition. As Kunze asserted
(with whatever personal reservations), "The only purpose of the
Bund is to make better Americans of those of German blood."

A new ethnic solidarity was ironically crowned by the respective antifascist campaigns that were perceived as a direct assault on
the nations and nationalities that adopted the new fascist creeds,
rather than the ideologies themselves. In the face of these assaults
the only appropriate responses were either an apologetic commu-
nal self-abnegation or an angry reassertion of the virtues of the
reborn homeland. Within the United States, ethnic communities
additionally shared the fears of Bessie Burchett and her like about

the revolutionary intentions of the social and labor reformers, an analysis to which they brought their distinctive European traditions and conspiracy theories. For the ethnic fascists as much as their domestic counterparts, extremist positions were a panicked response to perceived threats of social catastrophe, what we might term a case of revolutionary nostalgia.

IN SEARCH OF EXTREMISM

All societies have some individuals who are alarmed by the decline of social structures they knew and felt they understood, who deplore the progress of modernity, and who see liberal or radical political change as a lethal menace. Some also see government itself as a pernicious inciter or ally of subversion. Only in some eras, however, are these concerns translated into activism as extreme, violent, and racially oriented as that of the 1930s. This may have reflected the profound nature of the social crisis. In these years more than almost any, a plausible case could be made that there was much to be panicked about. Additionally, though, the extremist reaction must be placed in the context of the "normal" spectrum or bell curve of political belief and action.

In many of its positions, even some that sound most startling in retrospect, the extreme Right between the wars was not that drastically removed from the accepted political consensus. One did not have to seek far within the Republican Party to find a firm conviction of the reality of Communist subversion in the United States, both in the labor movement and within liberal political parties. The Red-baiting of the LaFollette movement in 1924 perfectly prefigured the more extensive attacks on the New Dealers in the next decade, and the depth of anti-Roosevelt feeling within the regular Republican party has been described above.[18] Despite the overwhelming Democratic electoral victories in the Roosevelt years, his Republican presidential opponents never received less than 40 percent of the national ballot, suggesting the breadth of suspicion of the New Deal at its height, and the number of enemies grew steadily from 1937 onward. Anti-Communist fears have been cited to explain the collaboration of otherwise respectable conservatives with the anti-Semitic or paramilitary Right: of the Republican politicians who sympathized with the ACS, of the proper Phila-

delphians who attended Bund rallies, and of the Liberty League
magnates who funded violent sects.

What was true of conservative political organizations was amplified in the religious context, and the social orthodoxy of the Roman Catholic church included much that would be compatible with extremist or fascist thought. The noblest endeavors of numerous American prelates and clergy could not eliminate an anti-Semitic current that found expression in church-approved publications, while all but the most liberal clerics were deeply imbued with anti-Communist and anti-Masonic notions that were customarily associated with a sharply polarized worldview. In economic terms, too, much of the Catholic radicalism and anticapitalist rhetoric of the era derived from theories that exalted the small property owner against the faceless international banker, an image that was all too easily transformed into anti-Jewish polemic. The social action campaigns of Fathers Rice or Cox were explicitly intended to ameliorate the conditions of the poor in order to stave off Communist temptations. In international terms the anti-Communist and pro-Franco stance of the Catholic press in the mid-1930s included virtually nothing that could offend a devotee of the ACS or the Lictor Federation, at least until the Jewish issue became central around 1938. While the Catholic church of the 1930s was emphatically not crypto-fascist, it is easy to see how the genuine extremists could present themselves as standing on a somewhat different area of the same political spectrum.

The "extremists" were not as extreme as they sometimes appear in terms of the degree to which they challenged or rejected social orthodoxies. This was clearly true of the Ku Klux Klan. In 1921 H. L. Mencken wrote tellingly, "If the Klan is against the Jews, so are half of the good hotels of the Republic and three quarters of the good clubs. If the Klan is against the foreign-born or the hyphenated citizen, so is the National Institute of Arts and Letters. If the Klan is against the Negro, so are all the states south of the Mason-Dixon line. . . . If the Klan lynches a Moor for raping someone's daughter, so would you or I." The Klan was "as absolutely American as chewing gum, crooked District Attorneys, and chautauquas."[19]

In its racial theories, too, many commonplaces of the ultra-Right were part of the ideological currency. Wilhelm Kunze's aspiration of "a White man's United States" would have been unexceptionable in the political rhetoric of many states and of some mainstream circles in all parts of the country.[20] Ideas of Nordicism, Anglo-Saxonism, and white supremacy were at their height in the 1920s and retained public adherents into the war years and afterward. To take positions that today seem quite outré, in Pennsylvania at least the most systematic expositions of eugenic views, biological determinism, and scientific racism came neither from the Bund nor the Coughlinites, but from sober administrators who served both Republican and Democratic regimes and who would have termed themselves liberals and New Dealers. Between about 1905 and 1940 Pennsylvania was a national center of eugenic thought.[21] At the Elwyn home for the feebleminded, in Delaware County, medical experts wrote extensively on eugenic theories and advocated segregation and sterilization for the mentally and morally deficient, policies that won admirers worldwide.[22]

In the criminal justice system the liberal Pinchot administrations patronized a group of progressive- and eugenic-minded penal theorists. In 1937 the Democratic Earle regime passed a draconian "defective delinquent" law to permit the indefinite incarceration of the troubled individuals believed to commit a large proportion of serious crime. The measure was denounced by Republicans and other conservatives who felt that crank biomedical theories were being used to replace traditional concepts of individual responsibility.[23] Based on research into the intelligence level of inmates, these same penal reformers purported to demonstrate a correlation between race and social performance, with northern Europeans at the apex of a hierarchy that proceeded downward through Mediterranean and Slavic types and thence to African Americans.[24] Criminological and medical theories portrayed society as the prey of the hereditary defective, of inferior racial types whose humane control and removal was a noble political goal. Such "liberal" ideas became the working orthodoxy of the state's justice and mental health apparatus in the interwar years.

The far Right did not introduce racial theories into political debate, and the ease with which rightists resorted to the language of extermination and paramilitary action was to some extent an echo of more general commonplaces of the era. Direct mass action

and physical confrontation had by the mid-1930s become a grimly
familiar element of social and industrial life. This is not to assert that "the other side started it," especially given the decades-long record of brutality against strikers and protesters by police, public and private. Nor is it intended to excuse the rightist rhetoric, still less the real violence which was its direct consequence, but it is essential to understand the context that gave rise to the whole world of militant fronts and vigilantism, street combat, and rifle training.[25] For the rightists, their actions were justified and necessary because they were purely defensive. Revolution was not only imminent; it actually had begun in Russia and Spain and under the guise of CIO unionism was now in progress in the United States. In any other time the forces of government could have been relied on to quell the revolutionary threat, but Johnstown and a hundred other conflicts showed that neither federal nor state administrations were sound. If the social contract had been abandoned, citizens wishing to defend life and property were to rely on their own resources. However bizarre the perspective seems in retrospect, the groups of the extreme Right usually viewed themselves as loyal and conservative, pledged not to aggression but to the defense of themselves and the political order.

EXPLOITING THE FAMILIAR

The rightist organizations that won public support did so by portraying themselves as the authentic if unpopular voice of some urgent popular need or sentiment, ideally one that was not being met by a conventional party. Their success depended on the degree to which their particular ideology or approach could be presented in terms of an already familiar system of belief. Propagandists or recruiters could therefore take for granted that a potential audience would be familiar with certain basic assumptions, some evocative concepts, and code words, which would not require elucidation. For the Klan leader of the 1920s, for example, a few phrases—about the Inquisition, babies buried under convents, or a papal nuncio seated in the White House—contained a rich rhetorical message appealing to ancient fears and a whole cultural tradition of anti-Catholicism. Other groups could with equal profit build on other established stereotypes and nightmares appropriate to a particular audience, about Moscow gold, international bankers, the bayonets of the CIO, the German defeat by a stab in the back, and so on.

The commonest such shorthand involved "Americanism"—"Real Americanism"—a shorthand for patriotism, free enterprise capitalism, and opposition to all forms of leftist subversion or propaganda as "alien" ideologies, whether Communist, Socialist, or syndicalist. One of the conservative triumphs of the 1930s was the annexation of the terms "Americanism" and "Un-American" as part of the vocabulary of the Right, a victory that unintentionally redounded to the advantage of the ultras. If Americanism and anti-Communism were accepted as core political values, then all that remained for the far Right was to show that their particular doctrine or interpretation was a natural and logical extrapolation of those ideas. If it could be stipulated that Communism was alien, conspiratorial, and dangerous, all that remained was to prove that it was, in addition, Jewish. As scientific orthodoxy infallibly showed the seriousness of the threat of racial degeneracy and the necessity for remedial action, the ultra-Right needed only to indicate exactly which groups posed the gravest threat to the American racial community. By 1940 the forces arrayed against American participation in war included not only a substantial portion of the Republican Party but also a large part of the Left and elements of the anti-fascist press.[26] Opposing war was not extreme, but only a little further along the spectrum were those who specifically opposed it as a Jewish war.

Nativists, Bundists, Fascists, and Coughlinites all shared at least some themes that had adherents in the mainstream society. These ideas were accepted to a far higher degree within the particular communities within which individuals lived and in which they experienced the great majority of their social interactions. For an Italian American, loyal support of Mussolini was an idea that would not have been regarded as bizarre or unacceptable in political conversations at any social level up to and including the national political or media elite. It was normal and sometimes obligatory within the particular ethnic subculture, where the virtues of Fascist Italy were rehearsed in the majority of newspapers and radio programs, in the pulpits, and on the platforms of fraternal or veterans' organizations. The deviants in this setting were perhaps, rather, the anti-Fascists, whose political institutions were margin-

alized by the mid-1930s. Nor was the Italian experience unique.
For a brief spell in the mid-1920s, there were many industrial and suburban communities where the Ku Klux Klan exercised a like hegemony over public opinion, and there were always sections or subcultures where the Bund had a similar hold.

The Coughlinites offer a notable example of the degree to which the extremists built on themes rooted within a particular subculture, both ethnic nationalism and Catholic social thought. In Irish Catholic neighborhoods of Philadelphia or Pittsburgh there was nothing new about virulent anti-British sentiment, about populist and corporatist economic doctrine, or even about sporadic conflicts with Jews. Moreover, the communities in which these ideas flourished believed in the likelihood or inevitability of unjust persecution, which meant that outside criticism was almost certain to be counterproductive. Attacks on Father Coughlin were guaranteed to reinforce support and solidarity for the target of criticism and to draw to his aid others who might hitherto have been lukewarm or hostile. At least until late 1938 the Coughlinite message was the subcultural orthodoxy purveyed through sermons, religious newspapers, and ethnic magazines. It was available on the radio stations serving the broader community, while the priest himself was seen to consort with powerful political leaders. Obviously there could be nothing deviant or sinister about his message, giving credence to charges that later attempts to remove him from the air were the product of a Jewish-Communist clique. As in the case of the Italian Fascists, the question is less why so many supported Coughlin long after he had ventured into extremism, but how others subject to the same influences might have come to challenge or disavow him. The degree to which Coughlinism was seen as a reflection of community values is suggested by the scale and rapidity of the backlash against the radio stations, in New York, Philadelphia, and elsewhere.

Once elements of a community were convinced by the extremist analysis, contemporary political circumstances made it probable that a resulting movement would assimilate itself to the organizational and rhetorical style made famous by the contemporary mass media. The rapidity with which shirt movements spread from 1933 onward was a tribute to the astonishing successes enjoyed by the European movements publicized in the newspapers and newsreels, and a desire to emulate them. The emphasis on unquestioned leadership made the fascist style immensely appealing to countless political entrepreneurs, who borrowed the half-understood leftist terminology of fronts, cells, and social revolution.

Accounts of modern extremist movements have to resort to quite sophisticated sociological and psychological explanations of the means by which healthy individuals can accept such a bizarre worldview as that of the neo-Nazis, skinheads, or white supremacists. As when dealing with a fringe religious cult, observers must analyze how subjects become increasingly severed from conventional ideologies, perhaps through a pattern of differential association, and thus tend increasingly to accept the deviant attitudes of the group or subculture.[27] While this might be a valid approach today, it would be of limited value in dealing with the Bundists or Christian Fronters, precisely because their assumptions were by no means deviant or exceptional. They were extreme chiefly in their normality.

The nature of the extremist appeal before 1941 is relevant to the sharp decline of that attraction in subsequent years. While there are points of resemblance between the modern history of the extreme Right and the developments of the depression era, the differences are enormous. Changing sensibilities mean that the extreme Right is no longer, as in the 1920s or 1930s, a somewhat magnified and activist representative of quite conventional attitudes and beliefs. In the earlier period anti-Catholic and anti-Semitic groups were presenting views that could acceptably be expressed in polite society, and these movements were not ostracized from the social mainstream. This is indicated by the affiliation of both clergy and elected officials to pro-Fascist or Nazi organizations, or the willingness of public school districts to accept Klan donations of Bibles or American flags. Public officials appeared on the platforms of such groups; police were often reluctant to appear too severe toward them. Even Gifford Pinchot did not publicly spurn Klan endorsement, whatever his private reservations. In the aftermath of the Jewish Holocaust and the black civil rights movement, the issues of race and anti-Semitism have driven the views of the extreme Right off the spectrum of what is considered acceptable political belief. Any sympathy or association with such a group is almost certain to destroy the career of a public official. While an individual might

still espouse a consistently fascist or Nazi worldview, the chance
that this will gain any broad influence is currently negligible.

251
Conclusion

EXTENDING THE STUDY

Though a study of Pennsylvania provides no support for extravagant charges about fascist plots and subversion, it does suggest the significance of the far-Right groups as an integral part of the respective communities, rather than an eccentric outgrowth. These political currents were scarcely lunatic, and many of their ideas were not fringe. From this viewpoint it is curious that recent historians have paid so little attention to the far Right in comparison with the abundant coverage lavished on leftist, socialist, and syndicalist movements, including some that in their day authentically were confined to the far fringes of political or labor history. The agendas of the ultra-Right were at least as likely to enter the mainstream political consciousness as those of the Left, even if their origins and connotations were not fully acknowledged.

The example of Pennsylvania confirms the value of local and regional studies of the extreme Right in this period, but it also indicates the difficulty of accurate generalization beyond the level of the state or even the city. Even within a state, extremist movements tended to be strongly local and regional in character. The ACS remained a Philadelphia phenomenon, while Silver Shirts enjoyed their chief impact in the west of the state. While the various groups generally cooperated, there were times and places in which coalition-building endeavors were sabotaged by ideological issues, frequently the religious schism between Protestants and Catholics. There are also real mysteries, in which particular communities act contrary to the patterns that elsewhere appear near-universal. As an illustration, the city of Erie had all the characteristics that elsewhere produced a substantial ultra-Right presence, including large Italian and German populations, a hefty Coughlin vote in 1936, and proximity to Silver Shirt strongholds in Ohio. In fact, the city is scarcely mentioned in any contemporary accounts of the far Right and had neither a Bund chapter nor a Christian Front presence.

Some obvious characteristics of Pennsylvania society and politics make it unlikely that findings there could be reproduced in other regions of the country. In a sense the state is simply too rich in its diversity, with a greater range of activist groups than one would probably find in a smaller or more homogeneous area. Catholics were unusually well represented, with all that implied for the success of the Coughlin movement. Conversely there is little evidence of much of the "old Protestant Right," of the anti-Semitic fundamentalists who had their chief impact in the Midwest and West.[28] Of this group, only Gerald L. K. Smith constituted much of a presence in Pennsylvania, and that chiefly after 1945. Even his contacts in the state tended to be Catholic.

There are other issues. The state at this time had no Hispanic presence, and we find no echoes here of the relationship between domestic fascists and Mexican rightist movements, a connection that might be expected to emerge in the Southwest. Oddly, the only Pennsylvania rightists with any demonstrated interest in Latin affairs were the Klan, who lavishly praised the anticlerical policies of the revolutionary Mexican government. In addition, there were no significant Asian minorities in Pennsylvania, very little Japanese diplomatic or cultural presence, and no Japanese consulate to excite fears about espionage and conspiracy. Only a handful of Chinese were available to support antifascist and anti-Japanese protests.

Regional factors also played a role, so that the isolationist movement and the America First Committee were far stronger in the Midwest and areas under the metropolitan influence of Chicago than in either the east or west coast. Again, we would expect the Pennsylvania experience to be very different from that of the South, not least because of the far deeper roots of the Klan and antiblack traditions in southern states, while anti-Catholicism might well have immunized parts of the Bible Belt from the Coughlin appeal. As Hofstadter writes, "Up to the time of Huey Long's assassination, the South had its own native and more appealing messiah."[29] However, the experience of George Deatherage suggests that regional political subcultures were not hermetically sealed.

We would naturally expect different findings in other regions, with their particular ethnic makeup and geographical orientations, so that extremist politics in the late 1930s would be very different in Philadelphia or Reading from what we would expect in Atlanta, Chicago, or Los Angeles, to say nothing of medium-sized communities. However, the Pennsylvania cities were far from unique in the vigor of their Fascist and far-Right activism, and we readily find other centers with a network of militant groups. Obvious examples include Detroit, the home area of Father Coughlin, with its huge German American presence, its ferocious industrial vigilantism, and its national role in the manufacture and distribution of anti-Semitic propaganda. Los Angeles was another city with its own edition of the *Deutscher Weckruf*, its Blackshirt *squadristi*, and a potent Silver Shirt tradition.[30] The survival of abundant Silver Shirt material from the Pacific Northwest indicates a vibrant far-Right network in this region.[31] The opportunities for profitable case studies seem abundant.

The Pennsylvania movements suggest certain directions for subsequent explorations. One lesson is that in this political area, parties and organizations do not provide particularly useful units for analysis. Organizations themselves were usually short lived and were prone to frequent changes of name that were deliberately intended to confuse. There was also much overlap of membership, so that a study of the Bund, for example, in a particular region or city would miss a great deal of the story, unless a researcher were willing to explore the myriad associated clubs and fronts. Over the space of seven or eight years the Friends of the New Germany became the Bund, which largely transferred its operations to a network of cultural, fraternal, and veterans' organizations. However, a core of individuals survived these changes, figures such as Norbert Biele and Wilhelm Kunze. The Ku Klux Klan was exceptional in maintaining essentially the same tradition and organizational identity over a two-decade period, and this is deceptive given the eclipse of the movement in most of the state during the mid-1930s.

The Philadelphia Coughlinites demonstrate how political trends and movements outlasted specific organizations. In the late 1930s we can identify a current of political thought that can be termed "Coughlinism," which included components of isolationism, violent opposition to the New Deal, and a pervasive anti-Semitism. The Coughlinite movement was associated with a core of diverse individuals who were successively involved in a series of groups and causes, some tenuously linked to national organizations. The ACS and CDCR developed as local ad hoc groups and merged into the new Christian Front during 1939. Over the next decade the same people appeared as leading figures on the pro-Axis wing of America First and were involved in the different groups of the Mothers' movement, which combined anti-Semitism with radical opposition to the war. After the silencing of Coughlin, they transferred their allegiance to the still more peripheral cause of Gerald L. K. Smith. Through a bewildering array of names and fronts, the movement can be traced from about 1936 into the Eisenhower era.

None of these organizations can be studied meaningfully except in the context of the broader tradition and of the careers of specific militants such as Joseph Gallagher and Bessie Burchett, who created the ephemeral groups and parties. These individuals were often strikingly durable. Paul Winter was a mainstay of the far Right for two decades; W. Henry MacFarland and Catherine V. Brown, for over a decade. The individual political career of Mrs. David Good spanned at least twenty years, from 1935 to 1954, although none of the specific parties with which she was connected lasted nearly as long.

In terms of source materials, too, Pennsylvania epitomizes the problems likely to be encountered in any local study of the extreme Right in this era. Both the media and official investigations inevitably tended to emphasize the German and Nazi component at the expense of other ethnic groups — Ukrainians and Italians in Pennsylvania, or whatever other communities might have been present in another region. It is difficult to imagine newspapers or radio stations of any city being bolder than the *Philadelphia Record* in publicly confronting or denouncing the Catholic rightist organizations.[32] As in Pennsylvania, the local history of Coughlinite movements is likely to prove intractable, and so, especially, are their wider ramifications in the network of Catholic organizations.

Admitting all these difficulties, all the issues of distortion, exaggeration, and mendacity in the sources, it is still desirable to pursue such local studies in a wide variety of states and cities. Not only can they illuminate the political, ethnic, and social history of those areas during a critical era, but local experiences are essen-

tial for understanding the interplay between foreign and domestic
policies in these deeply dangerous years. The depression era still offers rich opportunities for pursuing the history of those nativist and racist movements that have so frequently shaped, and mis-shaped, American history.

Notes

CHAPTER ONE

1. Michael Sayers, "A Challenge to America," *The Hour* 41 (April 20, 1940): 5. All references to *The Hour* are from the reprinted edition, Robert Sobel, ed., *The Hour* (Westport, Conn.: Greenwood, 1970).

2. Neil R. McMillen, "Pro-Nazi Sentiment in the United States, March 1933–March 1934," *Southern Quarterly*, October 1963, 48–70.

3. U.S. House of Representatives, Special Committee on Un-American Activities (the McCormack-Dickstein Committee), *Investigation of Nazi Propaganda Activities and Investigation of Certain Other Propaganda Activities, 1934–35*, 73d Cong., 2d sess., and 74th Cong., 1st sess. (Washington, D.C.: Government Printing Office, 1935).

4. Travis Hoke, *Shirts!* (New York: ACLU, 1934); Edward Dahlberg, *Nightgown Riders of America* (New York: Commission Investigating Fascist Activities, 1934); *Fascism* (New York: ACLU, 1934); Norman Thomas, *After the New Deal, What?* (New York: Macmillan, 1936). John L. Spivak's series appeared in *New Masses* in October–November 1934 and as *Anti-Semitism Exposed: Plotting America's Pogroms* (New York: *New Masses*, 1934). See also Charles A. Beard, *Exposing the Anti-Semitic Forgery about Franklin* (New York: League for Labor Palestine, 1935); Ludwig Lore, "Nazi Politics in America," *Nation*, November 29, 1933, 615–17; Harold Loeb and Selden Rodman, "American Fascism in Embryo," *New Republic*, December 27, 1933, 185–86; Samuel McCoy, "Hitlerism Invades America," *Today*, April 7, 1934, 26–28; George E. Sokalsky, "America Drifts towards Fascism," *American Mercury* 32 (July 1934); J. B. Matthews and R. E. Shallcross, "Must America Go Fascist?," *Harpers*, June 1934.

5. Raymond Swing, *Forerunners of American Fascism* (New York: Messner, 1935).

6. Sinclair Lewis, *It Can't Happen Here* (New York: New American Library, 1970).

7. Stefan Heym, *Nazis in USA* (New York: American Committee for Anti-Nazi Literature, 1938); Leon G. Turrou, *The Nazi Spy Conspiracy in America* (1939; reprint, Freeport, N.Y.: Books for Libraries, 1972); John L. Spivak, *Secret Armies: The New Technique of Nazi Warfare* (New York: Modern Age Books, 1939); Harold Lavine, *Fifth Column in America* (New York: Doubleday, Doran, 1940); George Britt, *The Fifth Column Is Here* (New York: Wilfred Funk, 1940); Donald S. Strong, *Organized Anti-Semitism in America: The Rise of Group Prejudice during the Decade 1930–1940* (Washington, D.C.: American Council on Public Affairs, 1941); *To Bigotry No*

*Sanction: A Documented Analysis of Anti-Semitic Propaganda, Prepared by
the Philadelphia Anti-Defamation Council and the American Jewish Committee*
(New York: Industrial Press, 1941); Struthers Burt, "Why Hate the Jews?,"
Forum and Century 101, no. 6 (June 1939): 291–95; "Fascism in America,"
Life, March 6, 1939, 57–63; Victor Riesel, "800 US Organizations Work to
Build a Fascist America," *Reading Labor Advocate*, January 27, 1939; Riesel,
"Two Pro-Fascist US Senators Aid Nationwide Vigilante Drive," *Reading
Labor Advocate*, February 10, 1939; Riesel, "New York Bund Meeting Spurs
Fascist Action in US, Canada, Mexico," *Reading Labor Advocate*, March 3,
1939.

8. Among the leading antifascist writers of these years were George
Seldes, John L. Spivak, and Albert E. Kahn. See, for example, Seldes, *You
Can't Do That* (New York: Da Capo, 1972); Spivak, *Secret Armies*; Spivak,
Honorable Spy (New York: Modern Age Books, 1939); Spivak, *Pattern for
American Fascism* (New York: New Century, 1947); Spivak, *A Man in His
Time* (New York: Horizon, 1967); Kahn, *High Treason: The Plot against the
People* (New York: Lear, 1950).

9. Louis De Jong, *The German Fifth Column in the Second World War*,
trans. C. M. Geyl (Chicago: University of Chicago Press, 1956).

10. John Roy Carlson, *Under Cover* (New York: World Publishing, 1943),
9; Carlson, *The Plotters* (New York: Dutton, 1946). The 1943 publication of
Under Cover inspired renewed interest in the fifth column threat: see George
Seldes, *Facts and Fascism* (New York: In Fact, 1943), 80–121; Allen Chase,
Falange: The Axis Secret Army in the Americas (New York: Putnam's, 1943);
Lewis Browne, *See What I Mean?* (New York: Random House, 1943); *"Under
Cover" Uncovered: Carlson, alias George Pagnanelli, and His Backers Exposed*
(New York: *National Republic*, 1943).

11. Michael Sayers and Albert E. Kahn, *Sabotage: The Secret War against
America* (New York: Harper, 1942), 151.

12. Britt, *Fifth Column Is Here*, 2.

13. O. John Rogge, *The Official German Report* (New York: Yoseloff, 1961),
418.

14. Sayers and Kahn, *Sabotage*, 18–21.

15. Robert E. Herzstein, *Roosevelt and Hitler* (New York: Wiley, 1994),
274, 369–70; Neal Gabler, *Winchell: Gossip, Power, and the Culture of Celebrity* (New York: Knopf, 1994); "Ickes Hits Lindy and Father Coughlin as
Nazi Tools," *Philadelphia Record*, November 21, 1940. Charges against the
internal fifth column were reinforced by allegations of Nazi plotting in Latin
America, which became such a major feature of the media by mid-1940.
See, for example, John W. White, "Documents Show Nazis Plan to Absorb
South America: US Warship in Uruguay," *Philadelphia Record*, June 19,
1940; Chase, *Falange*.

16. Herzstein, *Roosevelt and Hitler*, 328.

17. Alan A. Block and Marcia J. Block, "Fascism, Organized Crime, and Public Policy: An Inquiry Based on the Assassination of Carlo Tresca," in *Research in Law, Deviance, and Social Control: A Research Annual*, vol. 4, ed. Steven Spitzer and Rita J. Simon (Greenwich, Conn.: JAI, 1982), 53–84.

18. For the Bund, see Sander A. Diamond, *The Nazi Movement in the United States, 1927–1941* (Ithaca, N.Y.: Cornell University Press, 1974); Susan Canedy, *America's Nazis: A Democratic Dilemma* (New York: Margraf, 1991); Leland V. Bell, *In Hitler's Shadow: The Anatomy of American Naziism* (Port Washington, N.Y.: Kennikat Press, 1973). For Coughlin, Michael Kazin, *The Populist Persuasion: An American History* (New York: Basic Books, 1995); Alan Brinkley, *Voices of Protest: Huey Long, Father Coughlin, and the Great Depression* (New York: Knopf, 1982); Sheldon Marcus, *Father Coughlin: The Tumultuous Life of the Priest of the Little Flower* (Boston: Little Brown, 1973); Geoffrey S. Smith, *To Save a Nation: American Counter-Subversives, the New Deal, and the Coming of World War II* (New York: Basic Books, 1973); David H. Bennett, *Demagogues in the Depression: American Radicals and the Union Party, 1932–1936* (New Brunswick, N.J.: Rutgers University Press, 1969); Charles J. Tull, *Father Coughlin and the New Deal* (Syracuse, N.Y.: Syracuse University Press, 1965); Seymour M. Lipset, "Three Decades of the Radical Right: Coughlinites, McCarthyites, and Birchers," in *The New American Right*, rev. ed., ed. Daniel Bell (New York: Anchor, 1964). Compare Glen Jeansonne, *Gerald L. K. Smith: Minister of Hate* (New Haven: Yale University Press, 1988).

19. Kazin, *Populist Persuasion*; Michael Barkun, *Religion and the Racist Right* (Chapel Hill: University of North Carolina Press, 1994); Leonard Dinnerstein, *Anti-Semitism in America* (New York: Oxford University Press, 1994); David H. Bennett, *The Party of Fear*, 2d ed. (New York: Vintage, 1995); Leo P. Ribuffo, *The Old Christian Right: The Protestant Far Right from the Great Depression to the Cold War* (Philadelphia: Temple University Press, 1983); Michael W. Miles, *The Odyssey of the American Right* (New York: Oxford University Press, 1980); Seymour M. Lipset and Earl Raab, *The Politics of Unreason: Right Wing Extremism in America, 1790–1970*, 2d ed. (Chicago: University of Chicago Press, 1978).

20. Smith, *To Save a Nation*; Charles Higham, *American Swastika* (New York: Doubleday, 1985).

21. Herzstein, *Roosevelt and Hitler*.

22. John McIntyre Werly, "The Millenarian Right: William Dudley Pelley and the Silver Legion of America" (Ph.D. diss., Syracuse University, 1972); Donnell Byerly Portzline, "William Dudley Pelley and the Silver Shirt Legion of America" (Ed.D. diss., Ball State University, 1966); Edward C. McCarthy, "The Christian Front Movement in New York City, 1938–1940" (master's essay, Columbia University, 1965); Morris Schonbach, "Native Fascism during the 1930s and 1940s" (Ph.D. diss., UCLA, 1958); Victor C. Fer-

kiss, "The Political and Economic Philosophy of American Fascism" (Ph.D. diss., University of Chicago, 1954).

23. John P. Diggins, *Mussolini and Fascism: The View from America* (Princeton: Princeton University Press, 1972); David F. Schmitz, *The United States and Fascist Italy, 1922–1940* (Chapel Hill: University of North Carolina Press, 1988).

24. See Chapter 3, below, for the recent literature on the Ku Klux Klan.

25. Glen Jeansonne, *Women of the Far Right: The Mothers' Movement and World War II* (Chicago: University of Chicago Press, 1996). See also Chapter 9, below.

26. Though see Martha Glaser, "The German American Bund in New Jersey," *New Jersey History* 92, no. 1 (1974): 33–49; Philip Jenkins, "The Ku Klux Klan in Pennsylvania, 1920–1940," *Western Pennsylvania Historical Magazine* 69 (1986): 121–38; Eckard V. Toy Jr., "Silver Shirts in the Northwest: Politics, Prophecies, and Personalities," *Pacific Northwest Quarterly* 80 (1989): 139–46; Martin Robin, *Shades of Right: Nativist and Fascist Politics in Canada, 1920–1940* (Toronto: University of Toronto Press, 1992).

27. McCarthy, "Christian Front Movement"; Gaetano Salvemini, *Italian Fascist Activities in the United States* (New York: Center for Migration Studies, 1977).

28. Carlson, *Under Cover*.

29. Strong, *Organized Anti-Semitism*.

30. U.S. House of Representatives, Special Committee on Un-American Activities (the Dies Committee), *Investigation of Un-American Propaganda Activities in the United States: Hearings before a Special Committee on Un-American Activities*, 75th Cong., 3d sess., and 76th Cong., 1st sess., on H. Res. 282 (Washington, D.C.: Government Printing Office, 1938–41), 5:3554, 3559 (May 1939).

31. "Protestant Action League Formed to Teach Democracy," *Philadelphia Record*, May 15, 1939.

32. "Police Aid Sought against Nazi Thugs," *Philadelphia Record*, May 28, 1939; "West Philadelphia Called a Stronghold of Fascism," *Philadelphia Record*, March 24, 1939.

33. Gordon Sager, "Swastika over Philadelphia," *Equality*, August 1939, 3–8; "Fascist Boom in Philadelphia," *The Hour* 45 (May 18, 1940): 3–4.

34. Paul Lyons, *Philadelphia Communists, 1936–1956* (Philadelphia: Temple University Press, 1982), 51–56.

35. "4000 Listen to Earl Browder Attack US Aid to Finland," *Philadelphia Record*, February 10, 1940.

36. Dennis J. Clark, "Irish-Jewish Relations in Philadelphia," in *Jewish Life in Philadelphia, 1830–1940*, ed. Murray Friedman (Philadelphia: Institute for the Study of Human Issues, 1983), 253–75.

37. Records of the German American Bund, RG 131, National Archives, College Park, Md.

38. U.S. House of Representatives (McCormack-Dickstein Committee), *Investigation of Nazi Propaganda Activities.*

39. U.S. House of Representatives (Dies Committee), *Investigation of Un-American Propaganda Activities in the United States*; William Gellermann, *Martin Dies* (1944; reprint, New York: Da Capo, 1972); August R. Ogden, *The Dies Committee: A Study of the Special House Committee for the Investigation of Un-American Activities, 1938–1944* (Washington, D.C.: Catholic University of America Press, 1945); Walter Goodman, *The Committee: The Extraordinary Career of the House Committee on Un-American Activities* (New York: Farrar, Straus and Giroux, 1968). Libel dangers were significant. Even the impeccable sources of journalist John L. Spivak were not sufficient to prevent him from being arrested for criminal libel charges after he accused a number of rightist militants of Nazi sympathies. See "Author, Foe of Coughlin, Arrested on Libel Charge," *Pittsburgh Press*, March 26, 1940; "Propagandist Writer for Reds Jailed on Second Libel Charge," *Pittsburgh Post-Gazette*, April 1, 1940.

40. Salvemini, *Italian Fascist Activities*, 194; Hugo V. Maiale, "The Italian Vote in Philadelphia between 1928 and 1946" (Ph.D. diss., University of Pennsylvania, 1950).

41. Salvemini, *Italian Fascist Activities*, xxxi.

42. *Father Coughlin—His Facts and Arguments* (New York: American Jewish Congress, 1939).

43. George Seldes, *Lords of the Press* (New York: Blue Ribbon, 1941), 34–35; compare Seldes, *The Catholic Crisis* (New York: Messner, 1939); Paul Blanshard, *American Freedom and Catholic Power* (Boston: Beacon, 1949), 195–98. For the church and the media in these years, see Frank Walsh, *Sin and Censorship: The Catholic Church and the Motion Picture Industry* (New Haven: Yale University Press, 1996).

44. Bennett, *Demagogues in the Depression*, 281–82.

45. Henry R. Hoke, *It's a Secret* (New York: Reynal and Hitchcock, 1946), 120–45.

46. U.S. House of Representatives, Special Committee on Un-American Activities, *Investigation of Un-American Propaganda Activities in the United States: Executive Hearings*, 77th Cong., 1942, vol. 6 (Washington, D.C.: Government Printing Office, 1942), 2517–2655.

47. Herzstein, *Roosevelt and Hitler*; Smith, *To Save a Nation*, 132–35, 172–73.

48. National Labor Relations Board, Division of Economic Research, *Collective Bargaining in the Newspaper Industry* (Washington, D.C.: Government Printing Office, 1939).

49. Paul B. Beers, *Pennsylvania Politics Today and Yesterday: The Tolerable Accommodation* (University Park, Pa.: Penn State Press, 1980), 115.

50. J. David Stern, *Memoirs of a Maverick Publisher* (New York: Simon and Schuster, 1962); Seldes, *Lords of the Press*. For the bitter relations between Annenberg and the Stern/Greenfield alliance, see the polemics in the Albert M. Greenfield Papers in the Historical Society of Pennsylvania, Philadelphia; also see many articles in the pro-Greenfield *Jewish World* of Philadelphia, 1938–1940.

51. Seldes, *Lords of the Press*, 156; for Greenfield, see Chapter 5, below.

52. "The Pot and the Kettle," *Philadelphia Record*, February 16, 1935.

53. "US District Attorney Asks Court to Stop Publication of Record's Nazi Spy Articles," *Philadelphia Record*, June 23, 1938.

54. Seldes, *Lords of the Press*, 166–70.

55. Smith, *To Save a Nation*, esp. 66.

56. George Seldes, *One Thousand Americans* (New York: Boni and Gaer, 1947), 197.

57. Smith, *To Save a Nation*, 67; see Chapter 2, below.

58. Editorial, *Philadelphia Record*, November 3, 1938.

59. "McClure Ring Hit as Fascist Threat," *Philadelphia Record*, October 31, 1938; Beers, *Pennsylvania Politics Today and Yesterday*, 136–40.

60. Benjamin Stolberg, *The Story of the CIO* (New York: Viking, 1938), 93.

61. For rightist charges of "fascism," see U.S. Congress, *Investigation of Un-American Activities in the United States: Gerald L. K. Smith* (Washington, D.C.: Government Printing Office, 1946), 19; Louis T. McFadden, *Collective Speeches of Congressman Louis T. McFadden* (Hawthorne, Calif.: Omni, 1970), 503; "Daly Pledges Free Speech before Meeting of 'Antis,' " *Philadelphia Record*, March 17, 1939. Antiunion activists used the epithet against New Deal administrations; see U.S. Senate Subcommittee on S. Res. 266 (LaFollette Committee), *Violation of Free Speech and Rights of Labor*, parts 19–20, *Employer Associations and Citizens Committees*, 75th Cong., 2d sess. (Washington, D.C.: Government Printing Office, 1938), 7331.

62. Editorial, *Philadelphia Herold*, December 6, 1941.

63. Ze'ev Sternhell, *The Birth of Fascist Ideology*, trans. David Maisel (Princeton: Princeton University Press, 1994); Martin Blinkhorn, ed., *Fascists and Conservatives: The Radical Right and the Establishment in Twentieth Century Europe* (London: Unwin Hyman, 1990); Detlef Muhlberger, ed., *The Social Basis of European Fascist Movements* (London: Croom Helm, 1987); Walter Laqueur, ed., *Fascism: A Reader's Guide* (London: Pelican, 1979); Robin, *Shades of Right*; Lita-Rose Betcherman, *The Swastika and the Maple Leaf* (Toronto: Fitzhenry and Whiteside, 1978); Francis L. Carsten, *The Rise of Fascism* (London: Methuen, 1967); Hans Rogger and Eugen Weber, eds., *The European Right* (London: Weidenfeld and Nicholson, 1965).

64. Herzstein, *Roosevelt and Hitler*, 150–63: note the plural.

65. Strong, *Organized Anti-Semitism*, 2–4.

66. Bennett, *Party of Fear*, 244.

67. Smith, *To Save a Nation*, 66–76.

68. Christians is quoted in Carlson, *Under Cover*, 149–50; Juan J. Linz, "Comparative Study of Fascism," in Laqueur, *Fascism*, 25; Ze'ev Sternhell, "Fascist Ideology," in Laqueur, *Fascism*, 325–406; Sternhell, *Birth of Fascist Ideology*.

69. Thomas H. Coode and John D. Petrarulo, "The Odyssey of Pittsburgh's Father Cox," *Western Pennsylvania Historical Magazine* 55 (1972): 217–38; "VFW Fear Clash with Khaki Shirts," *Philadelphia Record*, June 17, 1933.

70. Lawrence Dennis, *The Coming American Fascism* (New York: Harper, 1936). The White Shirts of George W. Christians were "American Fascists": Carlson, *Under Cover*, 149.

71. Robert Benewick, *The Fascist Movement in Britain*, rev. ed. (London: Allen Lane, 1972).

72. U.S. House of Representatives, *Investigation of Un-American Propaganda Activities in the United States: Executive Hearings*, 1942, 6:2653; Annette Thackwell Johnson, "Christ or Coughlin?," *Equality*, August 1939, 9.

73. Werly, "Millenarian Right."

74. Portzline, "William Dudley Pelley," 142–43.

75. For the diversity of fascisms, see Laqueur, *Fascism*; Rogger and Weber, *European Right*; Carsten, *Rise of Fascism*. A similar diversity is equally evident among contemporary European groups: Luciano Cheles, Ronnie Ferguson, and Michalina Vaughan, eds., *The Far Right in Western and Eastern Europe*, 2d rev. ed. (London: Longman, 1995). For mystical trends in fascism, see Nicholas Goodrick-Clarke, *The Occult Roots of Nazism* (Wellingborough, England: Aquarian, 1985).

76. Bessie Rebecca Burchett, *Education for Destruction* (Philadelphia: Privately printed, 1941), 9, 117.

77. "Democracy Will Not Work, Bessie Burchett Asserts," *Philadelphia Record*, August 15, 1938.

78. Burchett, *Education for Destruction*, 169.

79. Sager, "Swastika over Philadelphia," 3; U.S. House of Representatives (Dies Committee), *Investigation of Un-American Propaganda Activities in the United States*, 3:2356–57.

80. U.S. House of Representatives, *Investigation of Un-American Propaganda Activities in the United States: Executive Hearings*, 1942, 6:2564–66.

81. Burchett, *Education for Destruction*, 118–19.

1. Jordan A. Schwarz, *The New Dealers* (New York: Vintage, 1994); Kenneth S. Davis, *FDR: Into the Storm, 1937–1940* (New York: Random House, 1993); Robert S. McElvaine, *The Great Depression: America, 1929–1941*, new ed. (New York: Times Books, 1993).

2. This account draws on Michael P. Weber, *Don't Call Me Boss* (Pittsburgh: University of Pittsburgh Press, 1988); Russell F. Weigley *Philadelphia: A Three Hundred Year History* (New York: Norton, 1982); Paul B. Beers, *Pennsylvania Politics Today and Yesterday: The Tolerable Accommodation* (University Park, Pa.: Penn State Press, 1980); and Philip S. Klein and Ari Hoogenboom, *A History of Pennsylvania*, 2d ed. (University Park, Pa.: Penn State Press, 1980).

3. Klein and Hoogenboom, *History of Pennsylvania*, 455.

4. John Gunther, *Inside USA*, rev. ed. (New York: Harper, 1951), 654–61.

5. J. Roffe Wike, *The Pennsylvania Manufacturers' Association* (Philadelphia: University of Pennsylvania Press, 1960), 209–51.

6. Ann Hawkes Hutton, *The Pennsylvanian: Joseph R. Grundy* (Philadelphia: Dorrance, 1962).

7. Amos Pinchot, *History of the Progressive Party, 1912–1916* (New York: New York University Press, 1958).

8. Beers, *Pennsylvania Politics Today and Yesterday*, 96–97.

9. Richard Calvin Keller, "Pennsylvania's Little New Deal" (Ph.D. diss., Columbia University, 1960), 79–88.

10. "Score Injured as Police and Radicals Clash," *Philadelphia Inquirer*, May 1, 1932; Fredric M. Miller, Morris J. Vogel, and Allen F. Davis, *Philadelphia Stories* (Philadelphia: Temple University Press, 1988), 90.

11. Mauritz A. Hallgren, "Mass Misery in Philadelphia," *Nation* 134 (1932): 275–77; Weigley et al., *Philadelphia*, 611.

12. George Wolfskill, *The Revolt of the Conservatives: A History of the American Liberty League, 1934–1940* (Boston: Houghton Mifflin, 1962).

13. Keller, "Pennsylvania's Little New Deal," 80.

14. Klein and Hoogenboom, *History of Pennsylvania*; Thomas H. Coode and John F. Bauman, *People, Poverty, and Politics: Pennsylvanians during the Great Depression* (Lewisburg, Pa.: Bucknell University Press, 1981), 224–53.

15. Keller, "Pennsylvania's Little New Deal," 214–17; Joseph F. Guffey, *Seventy Years on the Red Fire-Wagon* (Privately printed, 1952).

16. Quoted in William Pencak, *For God and Country: The American Legion, 1919–1941* (Boston: Northeastern University Press, 1989), 255; Terry Radtke, *The History of the Pennsylvania American Legion* (Mechanicsburg, Pa.: Stackpole, 1993), 46.

17. Bruce M. Stave, *The New Deal and the Last Hurrah: Pittsburgh Ma-*

chine Politics (Pittsburgh: University of Pittsburgh Press, 1970); Weber, *Don't Call Me Boss.*

18. Klein and Hoogenboom, *History of Pennsylvania*, 465; Hugo V. Maiale, "The Italian Vote in Philadelphia between 1928 and 1946" (Ph.D. diss., University of Pennsylvania, 1950).

19. John P. Rossi, "The Kelly-Wilson Mayoralty Election of 1935," *Pennsylvania Magazine of History and Biography* 107 (1983): 171–94.

20. Weigley et al., *Philadelphia*, 616–30.

21. Grand Jury Investigations of Vice, Crime, and Law Enforcement, RG 30, Pennsylvania State Archives, Harrisburg, Pa.; Marquis W. Childs and John C. Turner, "The Real Philadelphia Story," *Forum and Century* 103, no. 6 (June 1940): 289–94.

22. For Philadelphia politics, see S. A. Paolantonio, *Frank Rizzo: The Last Big Man in Big City America* (Philadelphia: Camino, 1994); cf. Weigley et al., *Philadelphia*.

23. All electoral figures are derived from the biennial *Pennsylvania Manual.*

24. Weigley et al., *Philadelphia*, 613; Coode and Bauman, *People, Poverty, and Politics*; Priscilla F. Clement, "The WPA in Pennsylvania," *Pennsylvania Magazine of History and Biography* 95 (1971): 244–60.

25. Keller, "Pennsylvania's Little New Deal."

26. Beers, *Pennsylvania Politics Today and Yesterday*, 134.

27. Ronald L. Filippelli, ed., *Labor Conflict in the United States: An Encyclopedia* (New York: Garland, 1990); Carl I. Meyerhuber Jr., *Less Than Forever: The Rise and Decline of Union Solidarity in Western Pennsylvania, 1914–1948* (Selinsgrove, Pa.: Susquehanna University Press, 1987).

28. Louis Adamic, *Dynamite!: The Story of Class Violence in America* (New York: Viking, 1935); J. P. Shalloo, *Private Police* (Philadelphia: American Academy of Political and Social Sciences, 1933).

29. George Seldes, *One Thousand Americans* (New York: Boni and Gaer, 1947), 185.

30. Albert E. Kahn, *High Treason: The Plot against the People* (New York: Lear, 1950), 137; compare Ken Fones-Wolf, "Philadelphia General Strike of 1910," in Filippelli, *Labor Conflict.*

31. Philip Conti, *The Pennsylvania State Police* (Harrisburg, Pa.: Stackpole, 1977); Katherine Mayo, *Justice to All: The Story of the Pennsylvania State Police*, 2d ed. (New York: Putnam's, 1917). The State Police varied in its exact designation and from 1937 to 1943 was known as the Pennsylvania Motor Police.

32. Klein and Hoogenboom, *History of Pennsylvania*, 433; compare the fictional account in John Dos Passos, *The Big Money* (New York: New American Library, 1979), 154–57. For union attacks on the State Police as the

brutal "Cossacks," see the extensive papers in State Police Archives, RG 30, Pennsylvania State Archives; Conti, *Pennsylvania State Police*.

33. George Seldes, *You Can't Do That* (New York: Da Capo, 1972), 15.

34. Quoted in Seldes, *You Can't Do That*, 82. For Pennsylvania strikes in these years, see Pennsylvania State Police, Bureau of Crime and Traffic Law Enforcement, Special Duty 1914–1964, "Strike Reports," RG 30, Pennsylvania State Archives.

35. Miller et al., *Philadelphia Stories*.

36. "5000 Workers Overwhelm 100 Police and Seize Control of Hosiery Mill," *Philadelphia Record*, May 7, 1937; "Apex Sit-Downers Ordered Ousted by US Circuit Court," *Philadelphia Record*, June 22, 1937; "Apex Heads Accuse Police of Laxity in Strike Rioting," *Philadelphia Record*, June 2, 1937.

37. "PRT Ready to Abandon Old Company Union in Face of CIO Campaign," *Philadelphia Record*, June 6, 1937.

38. Keller, "Pennsylvania's Little New Deal," 215–17.

39. U.S. Senate Subcommittee on S. Res. 266 (LaFollette Committee), *Violation of Free Speech and Rights of Labor*, parts 19–20, *Employer Associations and Citizens Committees*, 75th Cong., 2d sess. (Washington, D.C.: Government Printing Office, 1938), 8222, 8316.

40. Klein and Hoogenboom, *History of Pennsylvania*, 462.

41. "Earle Calls Off Miners' March," *Philadelphia Record*, June 20, 1937; Peter Gottlieb, "Steel Strike of 1937," in Filippelli, *Labor Conflict*, 508; Howard T. Curtis Papers, SWOC Collection, Steel Workers Archives, Historical Collections and Labor Archives, University Park, Pa.; Pennsylvania State Police, "Strike Reports," Johnstown Strike, June–July 1937.

42. Wike, *Pennsylvania Manufacturers' Association*.

43. Seldes, *One Thousand Americans*, 61.

44. Gunther, *Inside USA*, 657.

45. Beers, *Pennsylvania Politics Today and Yesterday*, 192.

46. Gunther, *Inside USA*, 657; J. Howard Pew, *Faith and Freedom* (Grove City, Pa.: Grove City College, 1975).

47. Keller, "Pennsylvania's Little New Deal," 214–15, 350.

48. "The Gang's All Here," *Philadelphia Record*, October 22, 1938.

49. Thomas F. Armstrong, "The Public Educational Programs of Selected Lay Organizations in Pennsylvania" (Ed.D. diss., Temple University, 1947), 184–85, 340.

50. Keller, "Pennsylvania's Little New Deal," 225.

51. Ibid., 226.

52. Ibid., 226–28, 348–49.

53. Ibid., 348.

54. "Cooke Sees Nazism If New Deal Stays," *Philadelphia Inquirer*, September 14, 1940.

55. Klein and Hoogenboom, *History of Pennsylvania*, 472.

56. "Score Injured as Police and Radicals Clash," *Philadelphia Inquirer*, May 1, 1932; "25 Denounced and Jailed as Riot Plotters," *Philadelphia Inquirer*, May 2, 1932.

57. "Dodge Hits Back, Criticizes Courts," *Philadelphia Inquirer*, January 31, 1933; Harold J. Wiegand, "Dodge to Remain: Aloofness Policy of Mayor Scorned," *Philadelphia Inquirer*, February 11, 1933; Wiegand, "Mayor Rebuffs Call for Action in Police Crisis," *Philadelphia Inquirer*, February 14, 1933.

58. "Dodge Asks Mayor Real Reasons for Firing of Simmler," *Philadelphia Inquirer*, July 20, 1936.

59. "Dodge Says Communism Is Taught in High School," *Philadelphia Record*, February 18, 1939.

60. Gordon Sager, "Swastika over Philadelphia," *Equality*, August 1939, 6.

61. "Ex-City Official Accused in Christian Front Probe," *Philadelphia Record*, January 17, 1940.

62. "Walter S. Steele," *The Facts* (Anti-Defamation League) 2, no. 9 (September 1947): 21; *Social Justice*, February 12, 1940; James B. True, "Read between the Lines," *Industrial Control Reports*, June 17, 1939, no. 270.

63. Wike, *Pennsylvania Manufacturers' Association*, 100.

64. Keller, "Pennsylvania's Little New Deal," 122, 137.

65. Klein and Hoogenboom, *History of Pennsylvania*, 459, 470.

66. Keller, "Pennsylvania's Little New Deal," 347.

67. Wike, *Pennsylvania Manufacturers' Association*, 166.

68. Ibid., 102 (1944).

69. Ibid., 239 (1948).

70. Ibid., 166.

71. Ibid., 97.

72. Ibid., 99.

73. Gottlieb, "Steel Strike of 1937," 505. For older antistrike movements, see, for example, Fones-Wolf, "Philadelphia General Strike of 1910."

74. Abraham Bernard Magil and Henry Stevens, *The Peril of Fascism: The Crisis of American Democracy* (New York: International, 1938), 224–26; Benjamin Stolberg, *The Story of the CIO* (New York: Viking, 1938), 108–13. For the Johnstown citizens' committees, see the Curtis Papers, for example, box 3. The Clinton Golden Papers in this collection concern industrial spies and vigilantes in the same disputes.

75. Senate Subcommittee on S. Res. 255, *Violation of Free Speech and Rights of Labor*, parts 19–20, 8282.

76. Ibid., 7331.

77. Ibid., 8282.

78. Ibid., 7305; Robert E. Herzstein, *Roosevelt and Hitler* (New York: Wiley, 1994), 154; Donald S. Strong, *Organized Anti-Semitism in America:*

The Rise of Group Prejudice during the Decade 1930–1940 (Washington, D.C.: American Council on Public Affairs, 1941).

79. Senate Subcommittee on S. Res. 255, *Violation of Free Speech and Rights of Labor*, parts 19–20, 7298–99.

80. Ibid., 7294.

81. Ibid., 8282; Henry R. Hoke, *It's a Secret* (New York: Reynal and Hitchcock, 1946).

82. Curtis Papers, box 3, file 30.

83. "Pro- and Anti-Union Literature and Publications," handbill of citizens' committee, and "The American Plan of Labor," leaflet, Berkshire Knitting Mills Collection, Historical Collections and Labor Archives, University Park, Pa.; Henry G. Stetler, *The Socialist Movement in Reading, PA, 1896–1936* (Storrs: [University of Connecticut], 1943), 76–86. The strike occurred not in Reading proper but in Wyomissing, a separate incorporated borough in the vicinity.

84. Pencak, *For God and Country*; Radtke, *History of the Pennsylvania American Legion*.

85. Armstrong, "Public Educational Programs," 31.

86. Pencak, *For God and Country*, 82.

87. See Radtke, *History of the Pennsylvania American Legion*, 58, for the African American presence.

88. Pencak, *For God and Country*, 248–49.

89. "Bund Picks a Crown Prince," *Philadelphia Record*, October 27, 1939.

90. Radtke, *History of the Pennsylvania American Legion*, 53.

91. Ibid., 24.

92. Pencak, *For God and Country*, 269; Andrew Eric Dinniman, "Academic Freedom at West Chester: The Controversy of 1927" (Ph.D. diss., Pennsylvania State University, 1978).

93. Radtke, *History of the Pennsylvania American Legion*, 35–36.

94. Pencak, *For God and Country*, 155; Stetler, *Socialist Movement in Reading*.

95. Norman Hapgood, ed., *Professional Patriots* (New York: Albert and Charles Boni, 1927), 58–59.

96. Pencak, *For God and Country*, 165.

97. Armstrong, "Public Educational Programs," 43.

98. A. J. Foglietta, "State Legion Urged to Fight Nazi Bunds—Purge Own Ranks," *Philadelphia Record*, August 19, 1938.

99. "Legion Chief Denies Earle Was Jeered at State Parley," *Philadelphia Record*, August 20, 1938.

100. "Legion Calls on Nation to Deport 8,000,000 Aliens," *Philadelphia Record*, April 2, 1939.

101. Radtke, *History of the Pennsylvania American Legion*, 48–49, argues that the rightist and strikebreaking activities of the legion were much exag-

gerated. For allegations of legion involvement in national conspiracies, see
Jules Archer, *The Plot to Seize the White House* (New York: Hawthorn, 1973);
George Seldes, *Facts and Fascism* (New York: In Fact, 1943), 80–121. See
Pencak, *For God and Country*.

102. Justin Gray and Victor H. Bernstein, *The Inside Story of the Legion*
(New York: Boni and Gaer, 1948), 138; compare Pencak, *For God and Country*, 221–34.

103. Pencak, *For God and Country*, 224–26, 315–16; Gray and Bernstein,
Inside Story, 58.

104. Gray and Bernstein, *Inside Story*, 142–43; Seldes, *You Can't Do
That*, 111.

105. Seldes, *You Can't Do That*, 111.

106. Pencak, *For God and Country*, 315–17.

107. Gray and Bernstein, *Inside Story*, 143–44; Radtke, *History of the
Pennsylvania American Legion*, 48–50.

108. Senate Subcommittee on S. Res. 255, *Violation of Free Speech and
Rights of Labor*, parts 19–20, 8240; Gray and Bernstein, *Inside Story*, 147.

109. Radtke, *History of the Pennsylvania American Legion*, 49.

110. Amy Schechter, "Fascism in Pennsylvania," *Nation*, June 19, 1935.

111. Gervase N. Love, "Hershey Sit-Ins Ejected in Riot," *Philadelphia
Record*, April 8, 1937; Jesse Laventhol, "CIO Pickets Not Molested: Will
Carry On," *Philadelphia Record*, April 9, 1937; Donald Kennedy, "Hershey,
PA, Chocolate Workers Strike of 1937," in Filippelli, *Labor Conflict*, 234–36;
Pennsylvania State Police, "Strike Reports," Hershey Strike, April 1937.

112. Radtke, *History of the Pennsylvania American Legion*, 49–50.

113. Senate Subcommittee on S. Res. 255, *Violation of Free Speech and
Rights of Labor*, parts 19–20, 7286.

114. Berkshire Knitting Mills, Historical Collections and Labor Archives:
see, for instance, "Employees Association"; NLRB Hearing Transcripts,
1938–1940; Donald Kennedy, "Berkshire Knitting Mills Strike of 1936–37,"
in Filippelli, *Labor Conflict*, 40–42.

115. Stefan Heym, *Nazis in USA* (New York: American Committee for
Anti-Nazi Literature, 1938), 24–25.

116. Senate Subcommittee on S. Res. 255, *Violation of Free Speech and
Rights of Labor*, parts 19–20, 7327.

117. "Anti-Union Power of Nazis Bared in Berkshire Strike: Tight Grip
Held on Reading," *Philadelphia Record*, January 6, 1938; Heym, *Nazis in
USA*, 22–25.

118. "Anti-Union Power of Nazis Bared in Berkshire Strike"; Heym,
Nazis in USA, 22.

119. Hanns Gramm, *The Oberlaender Trust, 1931–1953* (Philadelphia: Carl
Schurz Foundation, 1956).

120. Gramm, *Oberlaender Trust*, 64.

121. "Anti-Union Power of Nazis Bared in Berkshire Strike."

122. See Chapter 4, below. Gaetano Salvemini, *Italian Fascist Activities in the United States* (New York: Center for Migration Studies, 1977). For the idea of class collaboration, see Adrian Lyttelton, ed., *Italian Fascisms* (New York: Harper Torchbooks, 1975).

123. Coode and Bauman, *People, Poverty, and Politics*, 144.

124. Magil and Stevens, *Peril of Fascism*, 203–4.

125. U.S. House of Representatives, Special Committee on Un-American Activities (the Dies Committee), *Investigation of Un-American Propaganda Activities in the United States: Hearings before a Special Committee on Un-American Activities*, 75th Cong., 3d sess., and 76th Cong., 1st sess., on H. Res. 282 (Washington, D.C.: Government Printing Office, 1938–41), 2:1226–27.

126. American League against War and Fascism, *Facts and Figures on War and Fascism*, August 1, 1937.

127. U.S. House of Representatives (Dies Committee), *Investigation of Un-American Propaganda Activities in the United States*, 3:2237–44 (November 1938).

128. Ibid., 2238. "Silver Shirts Traced Here," *Pittsburgh Press*, November 15, 1938.

129. U.S. House of Representatives (Dies Committee), *Investigation of Un-American Propaganda Activities in the United States*, 3:2239–41.

130. Ibid., 2241.

131. "Front Group Disbanded as Interest Lags," *Pittsburgh Press*, January 15, 1940.

132. Wolfskill, *Revolt of the Conservatives*, 59.

133. Hapgood, *Professional Patriots*, 170–72; see Strong, *Organized Anti-Semitism*, for parallel bodies of these years, such as the American Vigilant Intelligence Federation.

134. Seldes, *One Thousand Americans*, 183, 212–13.

135. Seldes, *You Can't Do That*, 170.

136. Gunther, *Inside USA*, 658.

137. Kahn, *High Treason*, 210–11.

138. Quoted in Seldes, *You Can't Do That*, 105–6.

139. "Rev. Coughlin Spoke in Comradely Terms of Christian Front Leader," *Pittsburgh Press*, January 17, 1940.

CHAPTER THREE

1. There is a lively literature on Klan activities during the 1920s, though far less is available on the afterlife of the Klan in the 1930s. See, for example, Shawn Lay, *Hooded Knights on the Niagara* (New York: New York University Press, 1995); Nancy MacLean, *Behind the Mask of Chivalry: The Making*

of the Second Ku Klux Klan (New York: Oxford University Press, 1994);
Kenneth T. Jackson, *The Ku Klux Klan in the City* (Chicago: Elephant,
1992); Lay, *The Invisible Empire in the West* (Urbana: University of Illinois
Press, 1992); Richard K. Tucker, *The Dragon and the Cross: The Rise and Fall
of the Ku Klux Klan in Middle America* (Hamden, Conn.: Archon, 1991);
Leonard J. Moore, *Citizen Klansmen: The Ku Klux Klan in Indiana, 1921–
1928* (Chapel Hill: University of North Carolina Press, 1991); Kathleen M.
Blee, *Women of the Klan: Racism and Gender in the 1920s* (Berkeley: University of California Press, 1991); William D. Jenkins, *Steel Valley Klan*
(Kent, Ohio: Kent State University Press, 1990); Larry Gerlach, *Blazing
Crosses in Zion: The Ku Klux Klan in Utah* (Logan: Utah State University,
1982); Robert Alan Goldberg, *Hooded Empire: The Ku Klux Klan in Colorado*
(Urbana: University of Illinois Press, 1981); Seymour M. Lipset and Earl
Raab, *The Politics of Unreason: Right Wing Extremism in America, 1790–1970*,
2d ed. (Chicago: University of Chicago Press, 1978), 110–49; David Mark
Chalmers, *Hooded Americanism* (Garden City: Doubleday, 1965).

2. Michael Feldberg, *The Philadelphia Riots of 1844* (Westport, Conn.:
Greenwood, 1975); John Higham, *Strangers in the Land: Patterns of American Nativism, 1860–1925* (New Brunswick, N.J.: Rutgers University Press,
1955).

3. John Bodnar, *Immigration and Industrialization: Ethnicity in an American Mill Town* (Pittsburgh: University of Pittsburgh Press, 1977).

4. Richard A. Varbero, "Philadelphia's South Italians in the 1920s," in *The
Peoples of Philadelphia*, ed. Allen F. Davis and Mark H. Haller (Philadelphia:
Temple University Press, 1973), 255–76.

5. Pennsylvania newspapers are listed in the biennial *Pennsylvania
Manual*.

6. Hugo V. Maiale, "The Italian Vote in Philadelphia between 1928 and
1946" (Ph.D. diss., University of Pennsylvania, 1950), 82.

7. Peter Gottlieb, *Making Their Own Way: Southern Blacks' Migration to
Pittsburgh* (Urbana: University of Illinois Press, 1987); Miriam Ershkowitz
and Joseph Zikmund, eds., *Black Politics in Philadelphia* (New York: Basic
Books, 1973), 13; Charles Pete T. Banner-Haley, *To Do Good and to Do Well:
Middle Class Blacks and the Depression in Philadelphia, 1929–1941* (New York:
Garland, 1993).

8. John Bodnar, Roger Simon, and Michael P. Weber, *Lives of Their Own:
Blacks, Italians, and Poles in Pittsburgh, 1900–1960* (Urbana: University of
Illinois Press, 1982), 30; Joe T. Darden, *Afro-Americans in Pittsburgh* (Lexington, Mass.: Lexington Books, 1973).

9. Irwin M. Marcus, "The Johnstown Steel Strike of 1919," *Pennsylvania
History* 63, no. 1 (1996): 96–118; Dennis C. Dickerson, *Out of the Crucible:
Black Steelworkers in Western Pennsylvania, 1875–1980* (Albany: State University of New York Press, 1986); Carl I. Meyerhuber Jr., "The Bituminous

Coal Strike of 1927," in *Labor Conflict in the United States: An Encyclopedia*, ed. Ronald L. Filippelli (New York: Garland, 1990), 50–54; Meyerhuber, *Less Than Forever: The Rise and Decline of Union Solidarity in Western Pennsylvania, 1914–1948* (Selinsgrove, Pa.: Susquehanna University Press, 1987); Richard B. Sherman, "Johnstown vs. the Negro: Southern Migrants and the Exodus of 1923," *Pennsylvania History* 30, no. 4 (1963): 454–64.

10. Emerson H. Loucks, *The Ku Klux Klan in Pennsylvania: A Study in Nativism* (Harrisburg, Pa.: Telegraph Press, 1936). The Klan archives for Pennsylvania, New Jersey, and Delaware are in the Pennsylvania State Archives, Harrisburg, Pa., in the State Police Archives, RG 30. This collection contains five boxes of correspondence from 1922 to 1940 and three boxes of general material from the same period. This collection is hereafter cited as Klan Archives, PSA.

11. Philip Jenkins, "The Ku Klux Klan in Pennsylvania, 1920–1940," *Western Pennsylvania Historical Magazine* 69 (1986): 121–38.

12. Chalmers, *Hooded Americanism*, 236–42.

13. "10,000 Gather at Klan Rally in Huntingdon," *North American* (Philadelphia), July 5, 1924.

14. Paul M. Winter, *What Price Tolerance?* (Hewlett, N.Y.: All-American Book, Lecture, and Research Bureau, 1928), 36–42.

15. It subsequently emerged that the fatal shots were probably fired by a black resident protesting the Klan celebration. See "Two Policemen Shot Trying to Disperse Ku Klux Gathering," *North American*, July 4, 1924; "Shoot to Kill Klan Members, Order to Lower Merion Cops," *North American*, July 5, 1924; "Lower Merion Police Order War on Klan," *Philadelphia Inquirer*, July 5, 1924. For the Haverford incident, see "Policeman Dying Shot in Klan Raid," *Evening Public Ledger* (Philadelphia), July 5, 1924; "Ku Klux Gunmen," *Evening Public Ledger*, July 7, 1924; "Three Held for Killing in Lower Merion," *North American*, September 15, 1924; Mark Butler and Carole Fleck, "Sixty Years Ago, Shootings Caused a Furor," *Philadelphia Inquirer*, July 5, 1984. I am grateful to Victoria Donohue for her generosity in providing me with materials on this case.

16. Klavalier Enlistment Forms, Klan Archives, PSA.

17. "Main Line Klan Victim Is Dead," *North American*, September 15, 1924; "Shoot to Kill Any Klansman," *Philadelphia Record*, July 5, 1924. For lynchings in Pennsylvania, see Dennis B. Downey and Raymond B. Hyser, *No Crooked Death: Coatesville, PA, and the Lynching of Zachariah Walker* (Urbana: University of Illinois Press, 1991).

18. Winter, *What Price Tolerance?*, 90–99.

19. Scrapbooks, Archives of the Archdiocese of Philadelphia, Philadelphia, Pa.; "New Jersey Towns Hear Neva Miller, Ex-Nun, Lecture," *Catholic Standard and Times*, May 23, 1925; "Camden Newspaper Supports Claim of Faker as Ex-Nun," *Catholic Standard and Times*, June 20, 1925; Philip

Jenkins, *Pedophiles and Priests: Anatomy of a Social Crisis* (New York: Oxford University Press, 1996).

20. Winter, *What Price Tolerance?*

21. Ibid., 71.

22. Ibid., 1–2.

23. Ibid., vii.

24. Ibid., 19.

25. Ibid., 200–233.

26. Ibid., 5.

27. Ibid., 116–19.

28. Ibid., 13. William D. Jenkins (*Steel Valley Klan*, 88–93, 160) emphasizes the role of the pietist Protestant churches in the Klan movement in eastern Ohio and stresses the element of religious (rather than merely ethnic) nativism in its appeal.

29. Winter, *What Price Tolerance?*, 33.

30. Klan Archives, PSA.

31. Winter, *What Price Tolerance?*, 110–12.

32. Ibid., 56.

33. Ibid., 54–55.

34. "3500 Orangemen in Parade to Mark Battle of the Boyne," *Philadelphia Record*, July 13, 1939.

35. Winter, *What Price Tolerance?*, 54–56.

36. Klan Archives, PSA.

37. Moore, *Citizen Klansmen*, 5, 9, 11, 45. Both Moore and William D. Jenkins (*Steel Valley Klan*) stress that the Klan in power did not attempt to impose discriminatory laws on Catholic or black residents, leading them to suggest that Klan supporters must have been motivated by issues other than racial and religious fears. Goldberg, *Hooded Empire*, confirms the wide distribution of the Klan presence in large, middling, and small communities in Colorado.

38. Loucks, *Ku Klux Klan in Pennsylvania*, 27; Klan Archives, PSA.

39. Loucks, *Ku Klux Klan in Pennsylvania*, 57.

40. Porter Versfelt III, "Behind the White Mask: The Ku Klux Klan in Pennsylvania," television script of a program broadcast on WPSX-TV, State College, Pa., 1993.

41. Compare the impact of disputes and riots concerning foreign-born workers in William D. Jenkins, *Steel Valley Klan*, 20–22, 74–75.

42. Peter Gottlieb, "Steel Strike of 1919," in Filippelli, *Labor Conflict*, 498–502.

43. Versfelt, "Behind the White Mask." For the prominent role of German Americans in the Ku Klux Klan in states bordering Pennsylvania, see William D. Jenkins, *Steel Valley Klan*; Lay, *Hooded Knights on the Niagara*.

44. Klavalier Enlistment Forms, Klan Archives, PSA.

45. Loucks, *Ku Klux Klan in Pennsylvania*.

46. Ibid., 108.

47. John O'Hara, *Appointment in Samarra* (New York: Modern Library, 1994), 94–97.

48. Loucks, *Ku Klux Klan in Pennsylvania*, 110–11.

49. "Good News for the Country," *Catholic Observer* (Pittsburgh), December 11, 1930; L. Richmond to Samuel Stouch, March 16, 1936, Klan Archives, PSA.

50. Banner-Haley, *To Do Good and to Do Well*, 46; see Chapter 6, below.

51. Khaki Shirt headquarters stood at 4430 N. Broad St.

52. John P. Rossi, "The Kelly-Wilson Mayoralty Election of 1935," *Pennsylvania Magazine of History and Biography* 107 (1983): 171–94.

53. Joseph F. Guffey, *Seventy Years on the Red Fire-Wagon* (Privately printed, 1952), 103; Ickes is quoted in Kenneth J. Heineman, "A Catholic New Deal: Religion and Labor in 1930s Pittsburgh," *Pennsylvania Magazine of History and Biography* 118 (1994): 370. The handbill "Romanized Democratic Party" is from Klan Archives, PSA. The first Catholic governor of Pennsylvania was David Lawrence, elected in 1958.

54. "Ku Klux Klan Is Being Reorganized on Big Scale," *The Register* (Altoona-Johnstown diocesan paper), February 26, 1939.

55. "Cardinal Dougherty Presides at Co-Cathedral Dedication," *Atlanta Journal*, January 18, 1939; newscuttings in scrapbooks, 1939, Archives of the Archdiocese of Philadelphia.

56. Michael Sayers and Albert E. Kahn, *Sabotage: The Secret War against America* (New York: Harper, 1942), 50–51; for Colescott, see U.S. House of Representatives, Special Committee on Un-American Activities, *Investigation of Un-American Propaganda Activities in the United States: Executive Hearings*, 77th Cong., 1942, vol. 6 (Washington, D.C.: Government Printing Office, 1942), 2909–49.

57. "The Klan Again," editorial in *Catholic Standard and Times* (Philadelphia), March 1, 1940.

58. "Klan Comeback Attempt Runs Foul of Law," *The Register*, May 26, 1940.

59. Klan Archives, box 5, 1939–1940, PSA; "Revival of Ku Klux Klan Extends to Eastern States," *The Hour* 22 (December 2, 1939): 3; "Klan's Imperial Wizard to Tour East," *The Hour* 29 (January 27, 1940): 2; "Klan Holds Secret Konvention in Philadelphia," *The Hour* 30 (February 3, 1940): 3; "KKK Increases Activity in Pennsylvania," *The Hour* 78 (January 4, 1941): 1. All references to *The Hour* are from the reprinted edition, Robert Sobel, ed., *The Hour* (Westport, Conn.: Greenwood, 1970).

60. "Klan Again."

61. "KKK Increases Activity in Pennsylvania."

62. Ibid.

63. "Klan Holds Secret Konvention in Philadelphia."

64. Rossi, "Kelly-Wilson Mayoralty Election."

65. "Protestant Action League Formed to Teach Democracy," *Philadelphia Record*, May 15, 1939; *League for Protestant Action* (pamphlet, Philadelphia, 1939) and extensive pamphlet literature of the league in Klan Archives, PSA.

66. "New Anti-Catholic Society Established," *The Register*, June 25, 1939. In 1949 Poling's *Baptist Herald* again attracted Catholic anger for publishing anti-Catholic materials: "Ex-Priest Tells His Dismal Story," *The Register*, March 20, 1949. For Poling's cool relationship with the local Catholic hierarchy, see Daniel Alfred Poling, *Mine Eyes Have Seen* (New York: McGraw-Hill, 1959), 251–62.

67. "3500 Orangemen in Parade to Mark Battle of the Boyne"; "5000 Orangemen Celebrate Here in Gala Parade," *Philadelphia Record*, July 13, 1940.

68. Klan Archives, PSA.

69. Ibid.

70. Philip Jenkins, "Klan in Pennsylvania."

71. Annette Thackwell Johnson, "The Christian Front in Pittsburgh," *Equality*, November 1939, 30–31.

72. See Chapter 7, below.

73. For example, the cartoon captioned "Back Again" in *The Register*, May 19, 1940.

74. "KKK Increases Activity in Pennsylvania."

75. Loucks, *Ku Klux Klan in Pennsylvania*, 116.

76. Davidson to Stouch, March 4, 1939, General Correspondence 1939, Klan Archives, PSA (emphasis added).

77. Winter, *What Price Tolerance?*, 112.

78. Donald S. Strong, *Organized Anti-Semitism in America: The Rise of Group Prejudice during the Decade 1930–1940* (Washington, D.C.: American Council on Public Affairs, 1941), 53; for the White Shirts, see John Roy Carlson, *Under Cover* (New York: World Publishing, 1943), 149–50.

79. Strong, *Organized Anti-Semitism*, 52; for Von Lilienfeld-Toal, see Chapter 5, below. Klan Archives, PSA (General Correspondence, 1939), includes Sieber's application forms for Klan membership and correspondence with Stouch about the establishment of new klaverns in Delaware. See, for example, letter of Sieber to Stouch, March 7, 1939, and Stouch to Sieber, April 11, June 28, 1939.

80. Loucks, *Ku Klux Klan in Pennsylvania*, 169–75; Jackson, *Ku Klux Klan in the City*.

81. Winter, *What Price Tolerance?*, 90, 241–53; compare John P. Diggins, *Mussolini and Fascism: The View from America* (Princeton: Princeton University Press, 1972), 207, for Klan hostility to the Italian American Fascists.

82. Winter, *What Price Tolerance?*, 241.

83. Ibid., 270.

84. Ibid., 8.

85. Ibid., 241.

86. Ibid., 259.

87. Ibid., 184–86.

88. Ibid., 270–78.

89. Strong, *Organized Anti-Semitism*, 141.

90. Carlson, *Under Cover*, 417. Carlson was apparently not aware of Winter's Klan background.

91. Ibid., 419–26.

92. Ibid., 420–22.

93. Ibid., 417.

94. Ibid., 425.

95. Harold Lavine, *Fifth Column in America* (New York: Doubleday, Doran, 1940), 74–78; Strong, *Organized Anti-Semitism*, 124–28, 152–57.

96. O. John Rogge, *The Official German Report* (New York: Yoseloff, 1961), 209.

97. Lavine, *Fifth Column in America*, 79–82; Carlson, *Under Cover*, 146; Strong, *Organized Anti-Semitism*, 79–82; "The Defendants in the Washington Sedition Trial," *The Facts* (Anti-Defamation League) 3, no. 1 (January 1948).

98. Carlson, *Under Cover*, 146.

CHAPTER FOUR

1. David F. Schmitz, *The United States and Fascist Italy, 1922–1940* (Chapel Hill: University of North Carolina Press, 1988); Gaetano Salvemini, *Italian Fascist Activities in the United States* (New York: Center for Migration Studies, 1977); Philip Cannistraro, "Fascism and Italian-Americans," in *Perspectives on Italian Immigration and Ethnicity: Proceedings of the Symposium Held at Casa Italiana, Columbia University, May 1976*, ed. Silvano M. Tomasi (New York: Center for Migration Studies, 1977); John P. Diggins, *Mussolini and Fascism: The View from America* (Princeton: Princeton University Press, 1972); Morris Schonbach, "Native Fascism during the 1930s and 1940s" (Ph.D. diss., UCLA, 1958); Frances Keene, ed., *Neither Liberty nor Bread: The Meaning and Tragedy of Fascism* (New York: Harper and Bros., 1940). Compare Luigi Bruti Liberati, *Il Canada, L'Italia e Il Fascismo, 1919–1945* (Rome: Bonacci, 1984); Gianfranco Cresciani, *Fascists, Anti-Fascists, and Italians in Australia, 1922–1945* (Canberra: Australian National University Press, 1980).

2. Diggins, *Mussolini and Fascism*, 81.

3. Paul M. Winter, *What Price Tolerance?* (Hewlett, N.Y.: All-American Book, Lecture, and Research Bureau, 1928), 241.

4. Marcus Duffield, "Mussolini's American Empire: The Fascist Invasion of the United States," *Harper's Magazine*, November 1929, 661–72.

5. Schonbach, "Native Fascism," 70–118.

6. U.S. House of Representatives, Special Committee on Un-American Activities (the Dies Committee), *Investigation of Un-American Propaganda Activities in the United States: Hearings before a Special Committee on Un-American Activities*, 75th Cong., 3d sess., and 76th Cong., 1st sess., on H. Res. 282 (Washington, D.C.: Government Printing Office, 1938–41), 2:1181–1201 (October 1938).

7. Salvemini, *Italian Fascist Activities*, 71.

8. Diggins, *Mussolini and Fascism*, 24–27; Robert E. Herzstein, *Roosevelt and Hitler* (New York: Wiley, 1994), 151–52; Schmitz, *United States and Fascist Italy*.

9. William Pencak, *For God and Country: The American Legion, 1919–1941* (Boston: Northeastern University Press, 1989), 21.

10. Richard Calvin Keller, "Pennsylvania's Little New Deal" (Ph.D. diss., Columbia University, 1960), 122.

11. George Seldes, *You Can't Do That* (New York: Da Capo, 1972), 190.

12. *La Libera Parola*, August 24, 1929.

13. Richard A. Varbero, "Philadelphia's South Italians in the 1920s," in *The Peoples of Philadelphia*, ed. Allen F. Davis and Mark H. Haller (Philadelphia: Temple University Press, 1973), 255–76; S. A. Paolantonio, *Frank Rizzo: The Last Big Man in Big City America* (Philadelphia: Camino, 1994), 16–34; Hugo V. Maiale, "The Italian Vote in Philadelphia between 1928 and 1946" (Ph.D. diss., University of Pennsylvania, 1950).

14. John Bodnar, Roger Simon, and Michael P. Weber, *Lives of Their Own: Blacks, Italians, and Poles in Pittsburgh, 1900–1960* (Urbana: University of Illinois Press 1982), 207–36.

15. Ernest A. Biagi, *The Italians of Philadelphia* (New York: Hearthstone, 1967); Maiale, "Italian Vote in Philadelphia," 116–17.

16. Biagi, *Italians of Philadelphia*, 125.

17. David Caute, *The Great Fear* (New York: Simon and Schuster, 1978), 218.

18. Michael A. Musmanno, *Across the Street from the Courthouse* (Philadelphia: Dorrance, 1954), 349; Musmanno, *Verdict!: The Adventures of the Young Lawyer in the Brown Suit* (Garden City: Doubleday, 1958).

19. See Chapter 9, below.

20. Salvemini, *Italian Fascist Activities*, 11, 119.

21. Ibid., 177.

22. "DiSilvestro Hints Anarchist Bombing," *Philadelphia Inquirer*, February 7, 1933.

23. Salvemini, *Italian Fascist Activities*, 11–13, and see below.

24. "Hunt Terrorists in Bomb Death of Mrs. DiSilvestro," *Philadelphia Inquirer*, January 29, 1933; "Offer $15,000 for Capture of Bombers," *Philadelphia Inquirer*, January 30, 1933; "DiSilvestro Hints Anarchist Bombing," *Philadelphia Inquirer*, February 7, 1933.

25. Salvemini, *Italian Fascist Activities*, 12–15.

26. Duffield, "Mussolini's American Empire," 664.

27. Biagi, *Italians of Philadelphia*, 27, 162–64; "Italians Fete Departing Consul, Greet Successor," *Pittsburgh Post-Gazette*, August 27, 1928; "Four Hundred Women Here Receive Steel Rings from Duce," *Pittsburgh Post-Gazette*, June 15, 1936.

28. John P. Diggins, "The Italian-American Anti-Fascist Opposition," *Journal of Modern History* 54 (1967): 579–98; Alan A. Block and Marcia J. Block, "Fascism, Organized Crime, and Public Policy: An Inquiry Based on the Assassination of Carlo Tresca," in *Research in Law, Deviance, and Social Control: A Research Annual*, vol. 4, ed. Steven Spitzer and Rita J. Simon (Greenwich, Conn.: JAI, 1982), 53–84.

29. Diggins, *Mussolini and Fascism*, 133.

30. Ibid., 123.

31. "Hunt Terrorists in Bomb Death of Mrs. DiSilvestro."

32. See *La Libera Parola*, February 4–11, 1933; "Bare Plot to Kill DiSilvestro by Shot at Office," *Philadelphia Inquirer*, February 16, 1933.

33. "Hunt Terrorists in Bomb Death of Mrs. DiSilvestro"; "Bombing Ring of Nationwide Extent Sought," *Philadelphia Inquirer*, February 1, 1933; "DiSilvestro Asked for $30,000 for Bomb Clue," *Philadelphia Inquirer*, February 2, 1933.

34. "Offer $15,000 for Capture of Bombers."

35. Ibid.; "DiSilvestro Asked for $30,000 for Bomb Clue."

36. Salvemini, *Italian Fascist Activities*, 13–14.

37. "DiSilvestro Hints Anarchist Bombing."

38. "Hunt Terrorists in Bomb Death of Mrs. DiSilvestro."

39. "Offer $15,000 for Capture of Bombers."

40. Ibid.; "Bombing Ring of Nationwide Extent Sought."

41. "Dopo L'Orrende Crimine," *La Libera Parola*, February 11, 1933; "Bombing Ring of Nationwide Extent Sought."

42. Salvemini, *Italian Fascist Activities*, 9.

43. Biagi, *Italians of Philadelphia*, 155, 230–38.

44. "Italians, Germans, Vow US Loyalty," *Philadelphia Inquirer*, December 12, 1941; Biagi, *Italians of Philadelphia*, 213.

45. Salvemini, *Italian Fascist Activities*, 123.

46. Schonbach, "Native Fascism," 84.

47. Paul Winter denounced DiSilvestro as an enemy of Americanism; see *What Price Tolerance?*, 242–43.

48. Biagi, *Italians of Philadelphia*, 181–83.

49. Salvemini, *Italian Fascist Activities*, 95, 99.

50. Luigi Antonini, "Who Are the Italian Anti-Fascists?," *New Leader*, December 4, 1943, 4; Maiale, "Italian Vote in Philadelphia," 97.

51. Biagi, *Italians of Philadelphia*, 152–56.

52. Salvemini, *Italian Fascist Activities*, 105.

53. Duffield, "Mussolini's American Empire," 666.

54. U.S. House of Representatives (Dies Committee), *Investigation of Un-American Propaganda Activities in the United States*, 2:1192–94 (October 1938); Biagi, *Italians of Philadelphia*, 123.

55. Salvemini, *Italian Fascist Activities*, 119.

56. Diggins, *Mussolini and Fascism*, 83.

57. "La Nazione Trasfigurata," *La Libera Parola*, June 25, 1927.

58. "Mercenary, traitor . . . a moral monster, this eternal enemy of his own country, this renegade against his own blood."

59. *La Libera Parola*, January 15, 1927.

60. "La Fine di un Equivoco," *La Libera Parola*, October 8, 1927.

61. "Resurrezione!," *La Libera Parola*, March 30, 1929; "Mentalita Umanitaria e Mentalita Affaristica," *La Libera Parola*, December 24, 1932.

62. For the Italian press in Pennsylvania, see Maiale, "Italian Vote in Philadelphia," 112–21; Gaetano Salvemini, "Mussolini's Empire in the United States," in Keene, *Neither Liberty nor Bread*, 336–55.

63. U.S. House of Representatives (Dies Committee), *Investigation of Un-American Propaganda Activities in the United States*, 2:1194; "German, Italian, Papers Continue," *Philadelphia Inquirer*, December 12, 1941.

64. "Reading PA: *Terra Madre*," *La Libera Parola*, December 24, 1932.

65. Salvemini, *Italian Fascist Activities*, 157.

66. Ibid., 146; "Italians Fete Departing Consul, Greet Successor."

67. Salvemini, *Italian Fascist Activities*, 147; Biagi, *Italians of Philadelphia*; "S.E. Il Cardinale Dougherty Visita L'Orfanotropio Dante Alighieri," *Libera Parola*, December 10, 1927.

68. Maiale, "Italian Vote in Philadelphia," 124; "DiSilvestro Hints at Anarchist Bombing."

69. DiDomenica to Stouch, August 10, 1940, Klan archives for Pennsylvania, New Jersey, and Delaware, in State Police Archives, RG 30, Pennsylvania State Archives, Harrisburg, Pa.; Angelo DiDomenica, *Is Washington in the Grip of the Roman Church?* (pamphlet, Philadelphia, 1938).

70. James F. Connally, ed., *The History of the Archdiocese of Philadelphia* (Philadelphia: Archdiocese of Philadelphia, 1976); Varbero, "Philadelphia's South Italians in the 1920s," 264–72.

71. "Bombing Ring of Nationwide Extent Sought."

72. "In Onore Della Giuventu Studiosa," *La Libera Parola*, February 11, 1933; "Italy's New Envoy Reviles Bombers," *Philadelphia Inquirer*, February 8, 1933.

73. Biagi, *Italians of Philadelphia*, 123.

74. Ibid., 127–29; Scilla de Glauco, *La Nuova Italia: The New Italy* (New York: Nikolas Press, 1939).

75. "The function would not have been complete without a telegram being sent to the creator of Italy's new fortune, and the founder of the New Holy Empire, His Excellency, Benito Mussolini" ("Memorabile Triunfo di Giovedi Sera alla Convention Hall," *Ordine Nuovo*, May 24, 1936).

76. Biagi, *Italians of Philadelphia*, 124.

77. David H. Bennett, *The Party of Fear*, 2d ed. (New York: Vintage, 1995), 244.

78. John Beffel, "Murder and the Khaki Shirts," *Nation*, November 29, 1933, 620; John M. McCullough, "Khaki Shirt Plot to Loot Armory Foiled," *Philadelphia Inquirer*, October 12, 1933.

79. "Khaki Shirts Held Menace to Unions," *Philadelphia Record*, June 13, 1933.

80. "5 Held in Battle of Khaki Shirts," *Philadelphia Record*, June 19, 1933.

81. "Nine Anti-Fascists Released as Judge Denounces Police," *Philadelphia Record*, June 29, 1933.

82. "Khaki Shirts Try to Steal Spotlight at Vet Meeting," *Philadelphia Record*, June 12, 1933; "Art Smith, Would-Be Dictator, Dies on WPA," *Philadelphia Record*, May 2, 1939.

83. "Reds Battle Khaki Shirts in Street Riot," *Philadelphia Record*, June 18, 1933; "5 Held in Battle of Khaki Shirts."

84. Beffel, "Murder and the Khaki Shirts."

85. "5 Held in Battle of Khaki Shirts."

86. "30 Khaki Shirt Generals Flee Bonus Army Privates," *Philadelphia Record*, June 18, 1933.

87. "Khaki Shirt Boast Stirs City to Check Policemen in Body," *Philadelphia Record*, June 16, 1933; "VFW Fear Clash with Khaki Shirts," *Philadelphia Record*, June 17, 1933; "Khaki Shirt Attack on VFW Parade Fails to Develop," *Philadelphia Record*, June 18, 1933.

88. Herzstein, *Roosevelt and Hitler*, 153; Emmanuel A. Piller, *Time Bomb* (New York: Arco, 1945), 19; McCullough, "Khaki Shirt Plot to Loot Armory Foiled"; "Art Smith, Would-Be Dictator, Dies on WPA."

89. McCullough, "Khaki Shirt Plot to Loot Armory Foiled"; Herman A. Lowe, "Smith in Flight as Raiders Smash Khaki Shirt Racket," *Philadelphia Inquirer*, October 13, 1933; David G. Wittels, "General Art Smith's Gone, Also Khaki Shirts Treasury," *Philadelphia Record*, October 13, 1933; "Installment Men from Khaki Shirts Take Last Relics," *Philadelphia Record*, October 15, 1933; "Khaki Shirts Routed," *Altoona Tribune*, October 13, 1933.

90. "Khaki Shirts Seek Link with Fascists," *Philadelphia Inquirer*, October 14, 1933.

91. Theodore Irwin, "Inside the Christian Front," *Forum and Century* 103, no. 3 (March 1940): 102–8; U.S. House of Representatives (Dies Committee), *Investigation of Un-American Propaganda Activities in the United States*, 3:2384.

92. "Art Smith, Would-Be Dictator, Dies on WPA."

93. Salvemini, *Italian Fascist Activities*,

94. John Norman, "Pro-Fascist Activities in Western Pennsylvania during the Ethiopian War," *Western Pennsylvania Historical Magazine* 25 (1942): 143–48.

95. "Philadelphia Judge Admires Mussolini," *The Hour* 56 (August 3, 1940): 2 (from the reprinted edition, Robert Sobel, ed., *The Hour* [Westport, Conn.: Greenwood, 1970]).

96. "Italian-Americans Here Hail Victory," *Philadelphia Inquirer*, May 11, 1936.

97. "Four Hundred Women Here Receive Steel Rings from Duce."

98. "Cattolicismo in Etiopia," *Ordine Nuovo*, June 27, 1936.

99. "Italia di Vittorio Veneto, In Piedi," *La Libera Parola*, October 5, 1935.

100. Diggins, *Mussolini and Fascism*, 302; Norman, "Pro-Fascist Activities in Western Pennsylvania."

101. Biagi, *Italians of Philadelphia*, 123–24; "Four Hundred Women Here Receive Steel Rings from Duce"; "Oro alla Patria," *Ordine Nuovo*, May 24, 1936.

102. Salvemini, *Italian Fascist Activities*, 216.

103. "Philadelphia Friends of Italy Protest to Roosevelt," *Philadelphia Inquirer*, October 9, 1935; "Victory Is Hailed by Italians Here," *Philadelphia Inquirer*, May 6, 1936.

104. Salvemini, *Italian Fascist Activities*, esp. 191.

105. "Victory Is Hailed by Italians Here."

106. "Italians Threaten to Parade Despite Order by Wilson," *Philadelphia Inquirer*, May 9, 1936; "Italian-Americans Here Hail Victory."

107. "Italians Threaten to Parade Despite Order by Wilson"; "Italians Abandon Victory Parade," *Philadelphia Inquirer*, May 10, 1936; "Italian-Americans Here Hail Victory."

108. Maiale, "Italian Vote in Philadelphia," 81–101, 115–30.

109. U.S. House of Representatives (Dies Committee), *Investigation of Un-American Propaganda Activities in the United States*, 2:1210; Diggins, *Mussolini and Fascism*, 105, 343; Mary Testa, "Anti-Semitism among Italian Americans," *Equality*, July 1939, 27–29; Severin Winterscheidt, *2 Jahrbuch des Amerikadeutscher Volksbundes auf das Jahr 1938: Kampfendes Deutschtum* (Philadelphia: Graf und Sohne, 1938).

110. U.S. House of Representatives (Dies Committee), *Investigation of*

Un-American Propaganda Activities in the United States, 2:1182; William Y. Elliott, *Why Tolerate Mussolini's Agents?* (Washington, D.C.: American Council on Public Affairs, 1940).

111. George Britt, *The Fifth Column Is Here* (New York: Wilfred Funk, 1940), 63.

112. U.S. House of Representatives (Dies Committee), *Investigation of Un-American Propaganda Activities in the United States,* 2:1182.

113. For Pittsburgh, see Salvemini, *Italian Fascist Activities,* 21.

114. "Consul Here Named as Propagandist Recalled by Italy," *Philadelphia Record,* October 18, 1938; U.S. House of Representatives (Dies Committee), *Investigation of Un-American Propaganda Activities in the United States,* 2:1183–85; "US Is Probing Italian Consuls, Hull Announces," *Philadelphia Record,* June 16, 1940.

115. U.S. House of Representatives (Dies Committee), *Investigation of Un-American Propaganda Activities in the United States,* 2:1198; U.S. House of Representatives, Special Committee on Un-American Activities, *Investigation of Un-American Propaganda Activities in the United States: Executive Hearings,* 77th Cong., 1942, vol. 6 (Washington, D.C.: Government Printing Office, 1942), 2539.

116. U.S. House of Representatives (Dies Committee), *Investigation of Un-American Propaganda Activities in the United States,* 2:1183–84.

117. Schonbach, "Native Fascism," 80.

118. "Naturalizations Here Jump as Fascists Sound War Cry," *Philadelphia Record,* February 27, 1938; Duffield, "Mussolini's American Empire," 670.

119. Salvemini, *Italian Fascist Activities,* xxxiv–xxxvi; "Italian Group Here Assails Duce's Fake Anti-Semitism," *Philadelphia Record,* February 4, 1939; Britt, *Fifth Column Is Here,* 18.

120. Maiale, "Italian Vote in Philadelphia," 94–101. The FBI investigated charges that Italian taxi drivers had encouraged black Philadelphians to resist the war, on the grounds that this was a "white man's war caused by the Jews" (Robert A. Hill, ed., *The FBI's RACON: Racial Conditions in the United States during World War II* [Boston: Northeastern University Press, 1995], 215).

121. Eugenio Alessandroni, "Our Duty in the Present War," *Ordine Nuovo,* June 15, 1940; "Sons of Italy Are As One with Roosevelt," letter in "Mailbag," *Philadelphia Record,* June 15, 1940; "200,000 Italians Here Calm over War—Leaders Pledge Loyalty to United States," *Philadelphia Record,* June 11, 1940; "Sons of Italy Back Defense Program," *Philadelphia Record,* June 13, 1940.

122. "Italians, Germans, Vow US Loyalty."

123. "German, Italian, Papers Continue."

124. Maiale, "Italian Vote in Philadelphia," 148; Stefano Luconi, "Machine Politics and the Consolidation of the Roosevelt Majority: The Case of Italian Americans in Pittsburgh and Philadelphia," *Journal of American Ethnic History* 15, no. 2 (1966).

125. Biagi, *Italians of Philadelphia*, 129.

CHAPTER FIVE

1. Leonard Dinnerstein, *Anti-Semitism in America* (New York: Oxford University Press, 1994); Frederic Cople Jaher, *A Scapegoat in the New Wilderness: The Origins and Rise of Anti-Semitism in America* (Cambridge, Mass.: Harvard University Press, 1994); David A. Gerber, ed., *Anti-Semitism in American History* (Urbana: University of Illinois Press, 1986); Abraham G. Duker, "Twentieth Century Blood Libels in the United States," in *Rabbi Joseph H. Lookstein Memorial Volume*, ed. Leo Landman (New York: KTAV Publishing House, 1980), 89–90; Howard J. Jonas, *Anti-Semitica Americana* (New York: American Jewish Committee, 1941).

2. Norman Cohn, *Warrant for Genocide* (London: Pelican, 1970); Heywood Broun and George Britt, *Christians Only: A Study in Prejudice* (New York: Vanguard, 1931).

3. Loucks's *Ku Klux Klan in Pennsylvania* does not even feature index entries for either "Jews" or "anti-Semitism." For the *Public Ledger* incident, see Cohn, *Warrant for Genocide*, 172.

4. Donald S. Strong, *Organized Anti-Semitism in America: The Rise of Group Prejudice during the Decade 1930–1940* (Washington, D.C.: American Council on Public Affairs, 1941), 138–47; "Anti-Semitic Organizations," *Fortune*, February 1936, 142–44.

5. U.S. House of Representatives, Special Committee on Un-American Activities (the Dies Committee), *Investigation of Un-American Propaganda Activities in the United States: Hearings before a Special Committee on Un-American Activities*, 75th Cong., 3d sess., and 76th Cong., 1st sess., on H. Res. 282 (Washington, D.C.: Government Printing Office, 1938–41), 12:7241; David S. Wyman, *Paper Walls: America and the Refugee Crisis, 1938–1941* (Amherst: University of Massachusetts Press, 1968); Wyman, *The Abandonment of the Jews* (New York: Pantheon, 1984). For True, see his newsletter *Industrial Control Reports*.

6. Robert E. Herzstein, *Roosevelt and Hitler* (New York: Wiley, 1994), 171, 264–65; Jewish refugees and immigrants are a constant theme in the Albert M. Greenfield Papers from the mid-1930s onward (Historical Society of Pennsylvania, Philadelphia, Pa.).

7. Klan archives for Pennsylvania, New Jersey, and Delaware, in State

Police Archives, RG 30, Pennsylvania State Archives, Harrisburg, Pa. (hereafter cited as Klan Archives, PSA).

8. Records of the German American Bund, Records of Other Organizations, the American Coalition of Patriotic Societies, RG 131, National Archives, College Park, Md.; "Sinister Whispering Campaigns," *Pittsburgh Post-Gazette*, March 26, 1939; "Deny Refugees Ousted Store Workers Here," *Pittsburgh Sunday Sun-Telegraph*, April 18, 1939; Moseley to Tiffany Blake, March 30, 1939, George Van Horn Moseley Papers, Library of Congress, Washington, D.C.

9. For Jewish communities in Pennsylvania, see Murray Friedman, ed., *When Philadelphia Was the Capital of Jewish America* (Philadelphia: Balch Institute for Ethnic Studies, 1993); Friedman, ed., *Jewish Life in Philadelphia, 1830–1940* (Philadelphia: Institute for the Study of Human Issues, 1983); Maxwell Whiteman, "Philadelphia's Jewish Neighborhoods," in *The Peoples of Philadelphia*, ed. Allen F. Davis and Mark H. Haller (Philadelphia: Temple University Press, 1973), 231–54.

10. Ailon Shiloh, ed., *By Myself, I'm a Book!* (Waltham, Mass.: American Jewish Historical Society, 1972), 156–58; Jacob Feldman, *The Jewish Experience in Western Pennsylvania: A History, 1775–1945* (Pittsburgh: Historical Society of Western Pennsylvania, 1986).

11. Joe Rottenberg, "The Rise of Albert M. Greenfield," in Friedman, *Jewish Life in Philadelphia*, 213–35; Sandra Featherman, "Jewish Politics in Philadelphia," in Friedman, *Jewish Life in Philadelphia*, 276–89.

12. This theme is represented by many letters and pamphlets in the Greenfield Papers.

13. John P. Rossi, "The Kelly-Wilson Mayoralty Election of 1935," *Pennsylvania Magazine of History and Biography* 107 (1983): 171–94.

14. *Jewish World* (Philadelphia), August 2, 1938.

15. Richard Calvin Keller, "Pennsylvania's Little New Deal" (Ph.D. diss., Columbia University, 1960), 355–56.

16. Greenfield Papers, 1937; "No Relief to Aliens, P.O.S. of A. Demands," *Philadelphia Record*, August 24, 1938.

17. "Boost America, P.O.S. of A. Urged," *Philadelphia Record*, August 24, 1939; for the organization's rejection of extreme anti-Semites such as Bessie Burchett, see, for example, "P.O.S. of A. Disavows Attack on Stoddard," *Philadelphia Record*, February 11, 1940.

18. Greenfield Papers.

19. Philip Jenkins and Gary W. Potter, "The Politics and Mythology of Organized Crime: A Philadelphia Case-Study," *Journal of Criminal Justice* 15 (1987): 473–84.

20. Presentments of the Special (October 1937) Grand Jury and Instructions of the Court, Philadelphia County, PA: Investigation of Vice, Crime,

and Law Enforcement, Oct. 1937 to March 1939 (Philadelphia, 1939) (copy in State Police Records, RG 30, Pennsylvania State Archives).

21. Albert Fried, *The Rise and Fall of the Jewish Gangster in America* (New York: Holt, Rinehart, Winston, 1980).

22. *Pennsylvania Manual*; Louis T. McFadden, *Collective Speeches of Congressman Louis T. McFadden* (Hawthorne, Calif.: Omni, 1970).

23. Paul B. Beers, *Pennsylvania Politics Today and Yesterday: The Tolerable Accommodation* (University Park, Pa.: Penn State Press, 1980), 104.

24. McFadden, *Collective Speeches*, 1–52, 44; 298–329.

25. Ibid., 417.

26. Ibid., 227.

27. Ibid., 273–75.

28. Ibid., 299.

29. Ibid., 60–62; Geoffrey S. Smith, *To Save a Nation: American Counter-Subversives, the New Deal, and the Coming of World War II* (New York: Basic Books, 1973), 15; David H. Bennett, *Demagogues in the Depression: American Radicals and the Union Party, 1932–1936* (New Brunswick, N.J.: Rutgers University Press, 1969), 49; Charles Higham, *American Swastika* (New York: Doubleday, 1985), 70.

30. McFadden, *Collective Speeches*, 330.

31. *New York Times*, May 30, 1933; George J. Mintzer and Newman Levy, *The International Anti-Semitic Conspiracy* (New York: American Jewish Committee, 1946), 44; John L. Spivak, *A Man in His Time* (New York: Horizon, 1967), 276–81.

32. *Congressional Record*, May 29, 1933, 4538–41; McFadden, *Collective Speeches*, 382–88.

33. Mintzer and Levy, *International Anti-Semitic Conspiracy*, 44.

34. McFadden, *Collective Speeches*, 349.

35. Ibid., 399.

36. Ibid., 388–94.

37. Ibid., 512.

38. Ibid., 394.

39. Ibid., 518–24.

40. Ibid., 444–46.

41. Ibid., 485.

42. Ibid., 481, 487.

43. Ibid., 493.

44. Ibid., 497.

45. John Roy Carlson, *Under Cover* (New York: World Publishing, 1943), 148.

46. McFadden, *Collective Speeches*, ix.

47. John L. Spivak, *Secret Armies: The New Technique of Nazi Warfare*

(New York: Modern Age Books, 1939), 91; Travis Hoke, *Shirts!* (New York: ACLU, 1934), 25; Carlson, *Under Cover*, 86–87; Robert E. Edmondson, *The Move to Destroy Free Speech* (New York: Privately printed, 1937), 8.

48. Edward Dahlberg, *Nightgown Riders of America* (New York: Commission Investigating Fascist Activities, 1934).

49. Donnell Byerly Portzline, "William Dudley Pelley and the Silver Shirt Legion of America" (Ed.D. diss., Ball State University, 1966); John McIntyre Werly, "The Millenarian Right: William Dudley Pelley and the Silver Legion of America" (Ph.D. diss., Syracuse University, 1972); Leo P. Ribuffo, *The Old Christian Right: The Protestant Far Right from the Great Depression to the Cold War* (Philadelphia: Temple University Press, 1983), 25–79.

50. Hoke, *Shirts!*

51. Michael Barkun, *Religion and the Racist Right* (Chapel Hill: University of North Carolina Press, 1994), 91–96; Suzanne C. Ledeboer, "The Man Who Would Be Hitler," *California History* 65 (1986): 126–36. In February 1940 Pelley was interviewed by the Dies committee; see U.S. House of Representatives (Dies Committee), *Investigation of Un-American Propaganda Activities in the United States*, 12:7201–7333.

52. Werly, "Millenarian Right."

53. Smith, *To Save a Nation*, 56.

54. Portzline, "William Dudley Pelley"; William Dudley Pelley, *The Golden Scripts* (Noblesville, Ind.: Fellowship Press, 1973).

55. Hoke, *Shirts!*, 11–12.

56. *Fascism* (New York: ACLU, 1934), 18. Pelley may also have drawn on the popular media. He decided to form his movement on January 30, 1933, the day that Hitler took power in Germany. It also marked the first radio broadcast of the western series *The Lone Ranger*, with its heroic Rangers and the recurrent "silver" themes.

57. Smith, *To Save a Nation*, 63; Charles A. Beard, *Exposing the Anti-Semitic Forgery about Franklin* (New York: League for Labor Palestine, 1935); *Liberation*, February 3, 1934. General Moseley was one of many who cited the "prophecy" as authoritative; see Moseley to Tiffany Blake, March 30, 1939, Moseley Papers.

58. Strong, *Organized Anti-Semitism*, 40–56; Milton S. Mayer, "Unmasking the Silver Shirts," *Real America*, June 1934, 8–13; Mayer, "Old Klans in New Shirts," *Real America*, July 1934.

59. Portzline, "William Dudley Pelley," 215–18; Werly, "Millenarian Right," 233, 301; Eckard V. Toy Jr., "Silver Shirts in the Northwest: Politics, Prophecies, and Personalities," *Pacific Northwest Quarterly* 80 (1989).

60. American League against War and Fascism, *Facts and Figures on War and Fascism*, August 1, 1937 (emphasis added).

61. Hoke, *Shirts!*, 19. For Sieber, U.S. House of Representatives (Dies Committee), *Investigation of Un-American Propaganda Activities in the United States*, 12:7208, 7314–15. See Chapter 3, above, for Sieber's Klan connections. Beamish was on the liberal wing of the Pinchot coalition and was close to David Stern and many of the state Democratic leaders (Richard Beamish Papers, Pennsylvania State Archives).

62. Hoke, *Shirts!*, 17.

63. U.S. House of Representatives, Special Committee on Un-American Activities (the McCormack-Dickstein Committee), *Investigation of Nazi Propaganda Activities and Investigation of Certain Other Propaganda Activities, 1934–35*, 73d Cong., 2d sess., and 74th Cong., 1st sess. (Washington, D.C.: Government Printing Office, 1935), iv, 79 (May 1934).

64. Ibid., 271, 279 (June 1934).

65. Ibid., 262–87 (June 1934).

66. Ibid., 267 (June 1934).

67. Ibid., 273 (June 1934).

68. Ibid., 271 (June 1934).

69. See Chapter 6, below.

70. Smith, *To Save a Nation*, 59.

71. McFadden, *Collective Speeches*, 86, 167–70.

72. Ibid., 86.

73. Spivak, *A Man in His Time*, 263–64; Spivak, *Anti-Semitism Exposed: Plotting America's Pogroms* (New York: *New Masses*, 1934).

74. Carlson, *Under Cover*, 86; Strong, *Organized Anti-Semitism*, 131–32.

75. Carlson, *Under Cover*, 86–87.

76. Sander A. Diamond, *The Nazi Movement in the United States, 1927–1941* (Ithaca, N.Y.: Cornell University Press, 1974), 88, 110–27.

77. Hoke, *Shirts!*, 15–17; Spivak, *A Man in His Time*, 259–61.

78. U.S. House of Representatives (Dies Committee), *Investigation of Un-American Propaganda Activities in the United States*, 6:4143; Spivak, *Plotting America's Pogroms*, 41–51; Hoke, *Shirts!*, 25.

79. Spivak, *A Man in His Time*, 276–81.

80. Spivak, *Plotting America's Pogroms*, 49–51.

81. Abraham Bernard Magil and Henry Stevens, *The Peril of Fascism: The Crisis of American Democracy* (New York: International, 1938), 217.

82. "Roy Zachary Takes Over Silver Shirts after Pelley's Flight," *The Hour* 22 (December 2, 1939): 4–5 (all references to *The Hour* are from the reprinted edition, Robert Sobel, ed., *The Hour* [Westport, Conn.: Greenwood, 1970]); Strong, *Organized Anti-Semitism*, 48.

83. See Chapter 2, above.

84. U.S. House of Representatives (Dies Committee), *Investigation of Un-American Propaganda Activities in the United States*, 6:4065.

85. "The Defendants in the Washington Sedition Trial," *The Facts* (Anti-Defamation League) 3, no. 1 (January 1948): 29–30.

86. U.S. House of Representatives (Dies Committee), *Investigation of Un-American Propaganda Activities in the United States*, 3:2239. See Chapter 2, above.

87. U.S. House of Representatives (Dies Committee), *Investigation of Un-American Propaganda Activities in the United States*, 2:1215; Werly, "Millenarian Right," 301; Portzline, "William Dudley Pelley," 222. Pelley's Pittsburgh speech is reported in "Bund Assailed by Germans Residing Here," *Pittsburgh Post-Gazette*, April 6, 1939.

88. "Front Group Disbanded as Interest Lags," *Pittsburgh Press*, January 15, 1940.

89. Bessie Rebecca Burchett, *Janus in Roman Life and Cult* (Menasha, Wisc.: Banta, 1913); Richard A. Varbero, "Philadelphia's South Italians in the 1920s," in Davis and Haller, *Peoples of Philadelphia*, 255–76. For Burchett, see now Glen Jeansonne, *Women of the Far Right: The Mothers' Movement and World War II* (Chicago: University of Chicago Press, 1996), 123–25.

90. "Stoddard Defies Anti-Red Blast," *Philadelphia Record*, February 10, 1940.

91. "2000 Rap Radio Ban on Father Coughlin," *Philadelphia Record*, February 13, 1939.

92. "Red Teaching Laid to Philadelphia Schools," *Philadelphia Inquirer*, May 5, 1936; "Education Board Votes Red Probe at Broome Request," *Philadelphia Inquirer*, May 7, 1936; "Strike against Dr. Burchett Fizzles Out at High School," *Philadelphia Record*, April 20, 1937.

93. Bessie Rebecca Burchett, *Education for Destruction* (Philadelphia: Privately printed, 1941), 1–2, 54–56, 72.

94. Ibid., 102.

95. Ibid., 68.

96. Ibid., 18, 119.

97. "Daly Pledges Free Speech before Meeting of 'Antis,' " *Philadelphia Record*, March 17, 1939.

98. "Two-Gun Bessie Foils Lurking Reds Again," *Philadelphia Record*, February 4, 1938; "Union Asks Ouster of Two-Gun Bessie," *Philadelphia Record*, July 12, 1938.

99. Burchett, *Education for Destruction*, 101–3.

100. Ibid., 40–42.

101. Ibid., 12.

102. U.S. House of Representatives, Special Committee on Un-American Activities, *Investigation of Un-American Propaganda Activities in the United States: Executive Hearings*, 77th Cong., 1942, vol. 6 (Washington, D.C.: Government Printing Office, 1942), 2544.

103. Burchett, *Education for Destruction*, 12.

104. "Two-Gun Bessie Foils Lurking Reds Again"; "Now Poor Bessie Has Only Fists to Fight Red Menace," *Philadelphia Record*, February 9, 1938.

105. Samuel Stouch to Philip M. Allen, July 31, 1936, and Samuel Stouch to George Stranahan, September 13, 1936, Klan Archives, PSA; "Mrs. Dilling Charges YMCA is a Nest of Communism," *Philadelphia Record*, February 17, 1939; "13 Held in Bail as Tolerance Rally Raiders," *Philadelphia Record*, March 16, 1939.

106. E. Digby Baltzell, *Puritan Boston and Quaker Philadelphia* (Boston: Beacon, 1979).

107. Richard Hofstadter, *The Paranoid Style in American Politics* (Chicago: University of Chicago Press, 1979), 68–69; Seymour M. Lipset, "Three Decades of the Radical Right: Coughlinites, McCarthyites, and Birchers," in *The New American Right*, rev. ed., ed. Daniel Bell (New York: Anchor, 1964), 382–84.

108. Hoke, *Shirts!*

109. Norman Hapgood, ed., *Professional Patriots* (New York: Albert and Charles Boni, 1927); William Pencak, *For God and Country: The American Legion, 1919–1941* (Boston: Northeastern University Press, 1989), 25–27, for the popularity of veterans' organizations in the United States in this era.

110. Records of the German American Bund, Records of Other Organizations, the American Coalition of Patriotic Societies.

111. Compare Carlson, *Under Cover*, 217–22; "Hundreds of Reactionary Groups Back Anti-Alien Movement," *The Hour* 30 (February 3, 1940): 2; George Seldes, *You Can't Do That* (New York: Da Capo, 1972), 162–70; Arnold Forster and Benjamin R. Epstein, *Cross Currents* (New York: Doubleday, 1956), 159.

112. McFadden, *Collective Speeches*, 42; Margaret Payne Dutton, "The DAR Sees Red," *Forum*, April 1937, 239–44; Seldes, *You Can't Do That*, 144–52; Thomas F. Armstrong, "The Public Educational Programs of Selected Lay Organizations in Pennsylvania" (Ed.D. diss., Temple University 1947), 132–208; "Mustn't Let Children Think, Says Colonial War Daughter," *Philadelphia Record*, February 20, 1940.

113. Armstrong, "Public Educational Programs," 142.

114. Ibid., 184–85.

115. Ibid., 178–82, 200.

116. Ibid., 148.

117. U.S. House of Representatives, *Investigation of Un-American Propaganda Activities in the United States: Executive Hearings*, 1942, 6:2587; Samuel Stouch to Philip M. Allen, July 31, 1936, Klan Archives, PSA; Mrs. Philip M. Allen, "Genealogical Material," typescript, ca. 1952, in State Library of Pennsylvania, Harrisburg, Pa.

118. "Milwaukee Nazi Agent Arrested by FBI Linked to Philadelphia Fifth Columnist," *The Hour* 110 (August 16, 1941): 1; "Nazi Activity in Philadelphia," *The Hour* 113 (September 13, 1941): 1.

119. Donald Janson and Bernard Eismann, *The Far Right* (New York: McGraw Hill, 1963), 142–43.

120. Gordon Sager, "Swastika over Philadelphia," *Equality*, August 1939, 3–8.

121. See Chapter 9, below.

122. Sager, "Swastika over Philadelphia"; U.S. House of Representatives (Dies Committee), *Investigation of Un-American Propaganda Activities in the United States*, 3:2356.

123. Burchett, *Education for Destruction*, 18.

124. Ibid., 19.

125. Ibid., 26.

126. Ibid., 118.

127. U.S. House of Representatives, *Investigation of Un-American Propaganda Activities in the United States: Executive Hearings*, 1942, 6:2552.

128. "Daly Pledges Free Speech before Meeting of 'Antis.'"

129. "Meetings Urge US to Do Something about Hitler Victims," *Philadelphia Record*, November 19, 1938.

130. U.S. House of Representatives, *Investigation of Un-American Propaganda Activities in the United States: Executive Hearings*, 1942, vol. 6.

131. "13 Held in Bail as Tolerance Rally Raiders."

132. U.S. House of Representatives, *Investigation of Un-American Propaganda Activities in the United States: Executive Hearings*, 1942, 6:2551–53.

133. Ibid., 2590.

134. Ibid., 2591.

135. Ibid., 2595.

136. Ibid., 2630.

137. Ibid., 2636.

138. "Daly Pledges Free Speech before Meeting of 'Antis.'" Pelley had popularized the "President Rosenfeld" usage, complete with a spurious genealogy to show the family's descent from Dutch Jews.

139. "13 Held for Grand Jury in Alleged Nazi Effort to Incite Riot Here," *Philadelphia Inquirer*, March 16, 1939.

140. See, for example, U.S. House of Representatives, *Investigation of Un-American Propaganda Activities in the United States: Executive Hearings*, 1942, 6:2538, 2567, 2593, 2619; "Daly Pledges Free Speech before Meeting of 'Antis.'" For Edmondson, see, for example, his tracts *The Move to Destroy Free Speech, Court Dismissal Follows Jewish Backdown* (New York: Privately printed, 1938), and *Jewish Congressman Celler Moves to Kill Free Speech* (Stoddartsville, Pa.: Privately printed, 1939). Robert E. Edmondson, "Adulterating Americanism: Unassimilated Immigration" (invitation address

before the Public Relations Council of the Women's City Club of Philadelphia, April 4, 1940).

141. U.S. House of Representatives, *Investigation of Un-American Propaganda Activities in the United States: Executive Hearings*, 1942, 6:2601; for Deatherage, see also 2537, 2567, 2583; U.S. House of Representatives (Dies Committee), *Investigation of Un-American Propaganda Activities in the United States*, 5:3455–3543 (May 1939).

142. "Two-Gun Bessie Foils Lurking Reds Again"; U.S. House of Representatives (Dies Committee), *Investigation of Un-American Propaganda Activities in the United States*, 3:2356–57.

143. U.S. House of Representatives (Dies Committee), *Investigation of Un-American Propaganda Activities in the United States*, 3:2357.

144. U.S. House of Representatives, *Investigation of Un-American Propaganda Activities in the United States: Executive Hearings*, 1942, vol. 6.

145. "Father Coughlin's Trojan Horse in the Catholic World," *Equality*, March 1940, 31.

146. "Bund Member Held for War upon Jews," *Philadelphia Record*, November 12, 1938.

147. "German Spy Owns Club in Sellersville," *Philadelphia Record*, September 8, 1939.

148. U.S. House of Representatives (Dies Committee), *Investigation of Un-American Propaganda Activities in the United States*, 3:2357; *To Bigotry No Sanction: A Documented Analysis of Anti-Semitic Propaganda*, Prepared by the Philadelphia Anti-Defamation Council and the American Jewish Committee (New York: Industrial Press), 1941.

149. "City Schools Full of Anti-Semitism, Presbytery Finds," *Philadelphia Record*, April 4, 1939.

150. "Documents Seized by FBI in Raid on Nazi Retreat," *Philadelphia Inquirer*, December 13, 1941. Although in fictional form, Lewis Browne's *See What I Mean?* (New York: Random House, 1943) gives a convincing portrait of the anti-Semitic propaganda campaign at this time.

151. "Ex-City Official Accused in Christian Front Probe," *Philadelphia Record*, January 17, 1940. Similar "air attacks" occurred before Christmas 1939 in Washington and Chicago, suggesting an organized campaign.

152. Michael Higger, "Talmud Falsifications," *Equality*, November 1939, 15–18; Mintzer and Levy, *International Anti-Semitic Conspiracy*, 28; Spivak, *Plotting America's Pogroms*, 15; "Kurt Mertig," *The Facts* 2, no. 7/8 (July/August 1947): 23; *Jewish Ritual Murder in San Diego: An American Citizen Pamphlet* (London: Brown and Burrowes, 1933); *To Bigotry No Sanction*. See the collection of anti-Semitic ephemera in the collection of Nathan Katz, Blaufeld-Katz Papers, Historical Society of Western Pennsylvania, Pittsburgh, Pa.

153. Strong, *Organized Anti-Semitism*, 4; Kenneth J. Heineman, "A

Catholic New Deal: Religion and Labor in 1930s Pittsburgh," *Pennsylvania Magazine of History and Biography* 118 (1994): 389.

154. Handbill obtained in Philadelphia and posted to Internet discussion group H-Holocaust by Elsa Wachs, December 1994 (emphasis in original).

155. "Daly Pledges Free Speech before Meeting of 'Antis.' " Though the "Kehillah" idea is derived chiefly from Henry Ford's *International Jew* and the *Dearborn Independent*, Pelley cited conspiracy theorist Nesta Webster as a source; see U.S. House of Representatives (Dies Committee), *Investigation of Un-American Propaganda Activities in the United States*, 12:7245.

156. "13 Held in Bail as Tolerance Rally Raiders"; U.S. House of Representatives, *Investigation of Un-American Propaganda Activities in the United States: Executive Hearings*, 1942, 6:2600.

157. Sager, "Swastika over Philadelphia," 4.

158. U.S. House of Representatives, *Investigation of Un-American Propaganda Activities in the United States: Executive Hearings*, 1942, 6:2592.

159. "Coughlinites in Philadelphia Prepare for Christmas," *The Hour* 23 (December 9, 1939): 4.

160. Postcard postmarked December 20, 1938, Greenfield Papers, 1938–39.

161. "Jews Becoming a Problem in America," typed pamphlet, Greenfield Papers, 1938–39.

CHAPTER SIX

1. Robert E. Herzstein, *Roosevelt and Hitler* (New York: Wiley, 1994); Sander A. Diamond, *The Nazi Movement in the United States 1927–1941* (Ithaca, N.Y.: Cornell University Press, 1974); Susan Canedy, *America's Nazis: A Democratic Dilemma* (New York: Margraf, 1991); Leland V. Bell, *In Hitler's Shadow: The Anatomy of American Naziism* (Port Washington, N.Y.: Kennikat Press, 1973); Geoffrey S. Smith, *To Save a Nation: American Counter-Subversives, the New Deal, and the Coming of World War II* (New York: Basic Books, 1973); O. John Rogge, *The Official German Report* (New York: Yoseloff, 1961); Donald S. Strong, *Organized Anti-Semitism in America: The Rise of Group Prejudice during the Decade 1930–1940* (Washington, D.C.: American Council on Public Affairs, 1941), 21–39. The Bund's internal documents were seized by the federal government in 1942 and are now preserved in the National Archives at College Park, Maryland, as RG 131, Records of the German American Bund. This collection is referred to hereafter as Bund Archives, NA.

2. Bund der Freunde des Neuen Deutschland is the German original of Friends of the New Germany.

3. Rogge, *Official German Report*, 115.

4. Herzstein, *Roosevelt and Hitler*, 136–49, 201–17.

5. Diamond, *Nazi Movement in the United States*; Alson J. Smith, "I Went to a Nazi Rally," *Christian Century* 56 (March 8, 1939): 320–22.

6. LaVern J. Rippley, *The German Americans* (Lanham, Md.: University Press of America, 1984).

7. "Germantown Fete Greeted by Hitler," *Philadelphia Record*, October 7, 1933; "Absence of Swastika Flag Makes Luther Cancel Talk at Germantown Gathering," *Philadelphia Record*, October 8, 1933.

8. Diamond, *Nazi Movement in the United States*, 60, 72–73.

9. Ibid., 200; compare "Pennsylvania-Deutsche Bräuche," *Junges Volk*, December 1939, 5–6.

10. Figures are drawn from the 1930 U.S. Census. "Majority of German Americans Here Oppose Hitler's Invasion of Poland," *Philadelphia Record*, September 3, 1939.

11. For German religious traditions in Pennsylvania, see Robert Grant Crist, ed., *Penn's Example to the Nations: Three Hundred Years of the Holy Experiment* (Harrisburg, Pa.: Pennsylvania Council of Churches, 1987).

12. Oswald Seidensticker, *Geschichte der Deutschen Gesellschaft von Pennsylvanien, 1764–1917*, 2 vols. (Philadelphia: Graf and Brueninger, 1917); Frederick C. Luebke, "The Germans," in *Ethnic Leadership in America*, ed. John Higham (Baltimore: Johns Hopkins University Press, 1978), 64–90.

13. Seidensticker, *Geschichte der Deutschen Gesellschaft*; Rippley, *German Americans*, 180–213; Frank Trommler and Joseph McVeigh, eds., *America and the Germans*, 2 vols. (Philadelphia: University of Pennsylvania Press, 1985); Carl Wittke, *The German-Language Press in the United States* (Lexington: University of Kentucky Press, 1957); Clifton James Child, *The German Americans in Politics, 1914–1917* (Madison: University of Wisconsin Press, 1939).

14. Frederick C. Luebke, *Bonds of Loyalty: German Americans and World War One* (DeKalb: Northern Illinois University Press, 1974); William H. Skaggs, *German Conspiracies in America* (London: Fisher Unwin, 1915).

15. Child, *German Americans in Politics*, 118–23, 168–73.

16. Luebke, *Bonds of Loyalty*; General Correspondence: Wartime Activities, 1917–18, State Police Archives, RG 30, Pennsylvania State Archives, Harrisburg, Pa.; Philip Jenkins, "Spy Mad: Investigating Subversion in Pennsylvania, 1917–18," *Pennsylvania History* 63, no. 2 (1996): 204–31.

17. Henry Landau, *The Enemy Within: The Inside Story of German Sabotage in America* (New York: Putnam's, 1937); Cheryl Miller, "*Der Volksblatt und Freiheits Freund*: The Loyalties of German Americans in Pittsburgh during World War I," *Pittsburgh Undergraduate Review* 5, no. 1 (1985).

18. LaVern J. Rippley, "Ameliorated Americanization," in Trommler and McVeigh, *America and the Germans*, 2:217–31; Luebke, "The Germans."

19. "Germantown Fete Greeted by Hitler"; "Absence of Swastika Flag Makes Luther Cancel Talk at Germantown Gathering."

20. Diamond, *Nazi Movement in the United States*, 57–58; Luebke, "The Germans."

21. Fredric M. Miller, Morris J. Vogel, and Allen F. Davis, *Philadelphia Stories* (Philadelphia: Temple University Press, 1988), 88–89; "Thousands Assail Hitler's Violence in Protests Here," *Pittsburgh Post-Gazette*, March 28, 1933; "2000 Protest Book-Burning by Hitlerites," *Pittsburgh Post-Gazette*, May 11, 1933.

22. U.S. House of Representatives, Special Committee on Un-American Activities (the Dies Committee), *Investigation of Un-American Propaganda Activities in the United States: Hearings before a Special Committee on Un-American Activities*, 75th Cong., 3d sess., and 76th Cong., 1st sess., on H. Res. 282 (Washington, D.C.: Government Printing Office, 1938–41), 14:8252–54.

23. Ibid., 6:3871; Ludwig Lore, "Nazi Politics in America," *Nation*, November 29, 1933, 615–17.

24. U.S. House of Representatives, Special Committee on Un-American Activities (the McCormack-Dickstein Committee), *Investigation of Nazi Propaganda Activities and Investigation of Certain Other Propaganda Activities, 1934–35*, 73d Cong., 2d sess., and 74th Cong., 1st sess. (Washington, D.C.: Government Printing Office, 1935), iv, 17–43 (May 1934); Records of the German American Business League Inc. (Deutscher Konsum Verband—DKV), Bund Archives, NA.

25. U.S. House of Representatives (McCormack-Dickstein Committee), *Investigation of Nazi Propaganda Activities*.

26. Ibid., iv, 26 (May 1934).

27. Ibid., iv, 40 (May 1934).

28. Ibid., iv, 57–79 (May 1934); John L. Spivak, *Anti-Semitism Exposed: Plotting America's Pogroms* (New York: *New Masses*, 1934).

29. U.S. House of Representatives (McCormack-Dickstein Committee), *Investigation of Nazi Propaganda Activities*, 300 (June 1934).

30. Ibid., iv, 68–69 (May 1934); Spivak, *Plotting America's Pogroms*, 78.

31. Spivak, *Plotting America's Pogroms*, 73–83; Philip S. Klein and Ari Hoogenboom, *A History of Pennsylvania*, 2d ed. (University Park, Pa.: Penn State Press, 1980), 454. Compare David M. Oshinsky, *The Case of the Nazi Professor* (New Brunswick, N.J.: Rutgers University Press, 1989).

32. Diamond, *Nazi Movement in the United States*, 338–44; "Leader of Bund Draws Attack in Senate Quiz," *Philadelphia Record*, July 9, 1940.

33. "Kunze to Fill Kuhn's Shoes," *The Hour* 15 (October 14, 1939): 4. All references to *The Hour* are from the reprinted edition, Robert Sobel, ed., *The Hour* (Westport, Conn.: Greenwood, 1970).

34. John Roy Carlson, *Under Cover* (New York: World Publishing, 1943), 46.

35. "Kuhn Confirms Martin as Bund Leader Here," *Philadelphia Record*, October 20, 1939.

36. "Former Philadelphian Is New Bund Führer," *Philadelphia Record*, December 6, 1939.

37. G. W. Kunze, "Race, Youth," in *Free America!: Six Addresses on the Aims and Purposes of the German American Bund* (New York: A. V. Publishing, 1939), 11–14.

38. Herzstein, *Roosevelt and Hitler*, 276.

39. Carlson, *Under Cover*, 46–47.

40. "Milwaukee Nazis Plan New Drive," *The Hour* 11 (September 16, 1939): 5.

41. Rogge, *Official German Report*, 37–38.

42. U.S. House of Representatives (Dies Committee), *Investigation of Un-American Propaganda Activities in the United States*, 6:3738.

43. Herzstein, *Roosevelt and Hitler*, 189.

44. Strong, *Organized Anti-Semitism*, 32.

45. "FBI Given Data on Local Bund," *Philadelphia Record*, September 15, 1939.

46. "German Spy Owns Club in Sellersville," *Philadelphia Record*, September 8, 1939.

47. Miller et al., *Philadelphia Stories*, 104; "Flood of Hitler Propaganda Comes through Air Daily to Organized Followers Here," *Philadelphia Record*, January 7, 1938, 14.

48. U.S. House of Representatives (Dies Committee), *Investigation of Un-American Propaganda Activities in the United States*, 6:3887.

49. "Philadelphia Unit, 1936–1938," Records of the German American Business League Inc., Bund Archives, NA; see also box 7, file 13, Records of the *Deutsch-Amerikanische Berufsgemeinschaft*, Ortsgruppe Philadelphia, 1935–38.

50. Theodore Irwin, "Inside the Christian Front," *Forum and Century* 103, no. 3 (March 1940): 102–8.

51. U.S. House of Representatives (Dies Committee), *Investigation of Un-American Propaganda Activities in the United States*, 10:6094–95 (October 1939); "Local Bund Leader Returns to Germany," *Pittsburgh Post-Gazette*, April 5, 1939; "Reveal City Has Strong Nazi Bund," *Pittsburgh Post-Gazette*, April 5, 1939; "Bund Assailed by Germans Residing Here," *Pittsburgh Post-Gazette*, April 6, 1939; "Nazi Threat Is Made to Moose Chief," *Pittsburgh Post-Gazette*, May 13, 1940; "Nazi Activity in Pittsburgh to be Probed," *Pittsburgh Post-Gazette*, May 15, 1940.

52. U.S. House of Representatives (Dies Committee), *Investigation of Un-American Propaganda Activities in the United States*, 2:1131; "Bund Assailed by Germans Residing Here."

53. *Werbereise des Bundeswerbeleiters*, 1938, Friends of the New Germany, Miscellaneous, General Records of the Bund, box 8, folder 120, Bund Archives, NA.

54. U.S. House of Representatives (Dies Committee), *Investigation of Un-American Propaganda Activities in the United States*, 10:6094; for Seegers as *Ortsgruppenleiter*, see, for example, Severin Winterscheidt, 2 *Jahrbuch des Amerikadeutscher Volksbundes auf das Jahr 1938: Kampfendes Deutschtum* (Philadelphia: Graf und Sohne, 1938).

55. Diamond, *Nazi Movement in the United States*, 249; for the German presence in Reading, see Henry G. Stetler, *The Socialist Movement in Reading, PA, 1896-1936* (Storrs: [University of Connecticut], 1943).

56. "Anti-Union Power of Nazis Bared in Berkshire Strike: Tight Grip Held on Reading," *Philadelphia Record*, January 6, 1938.

57. "Plan for Nazi Camp in Berks Rapped by Sons of Revolution," *Philadelphia Record*, February 14, 1938; "Nazi Camp Opposed by Labor in Reading," *Philadelphia Record*, February 12, 1938.

58. U.S. House of Representatives (Dies Committee), *Investigation of Un-American Propaganda Activities in the United States*, 2:1205.

59. "Fritz Kuhn Arrested Near Reading for Theft of Bund Cash," *Philadelphia Record*, May 26, 1939.

60. See above, Chapter 2.

61. "Anti-Union Power of Nazis Bared in Berkshire Strike."

62. Rogge, *Official German Report*, 38.

63. "Riot Call and a Picket Line Mark a Nazi Celebration Here," *Philadelphia Record*, June 5, 1938.

64. Diamond, *Nazi Movement in the United States*, 212.

65. Bell, *In Hitler's Shadow*, 27-30.

66. U.S. House of Representatives (Dies Committee), *Investigation of Un-American Propaganda Activities in the United States*, 2:1126, 1205-7.

67. "German Spy Owns Club in Sellersville."

68. U.S. House of Representatives (McCormack-Dickstein Committee), *Investigation of Nazi Propaganda Activities*, iv, 69 (May 1934).

69. General Records of the Bund, box 6, folder 73, Camp Siegfried, Bund Archives, NA; Diamond, *Nazi Movement in the United States*, 243; Bell, *In Hitler's Shadow*, 27; and see below for Camp Nordland.

70. Carlson, *Under Cover*, 109.

71. U.S. House of Representatives (Dies Committee), *Investigation of Un-American Propaganda Activities in the United States*, 2:1126.

72. "Nazi Shrine Found by G-Men in Raid on North Philadelphia Home," *Philadelphia Inquirer*, December 14, 1941.

73. "37 Seized in Round-Up of Axis Citizens Here: City's Number One Nazi Held," *Philadelphia Inquirer*, December 10, 1941.

74. U.S. House of Representatives (Dies Committee), *Investigation of Un-American Propaganda Activities in the United States*, 14:8269.

75. Carlson, *Under Cover*, 46.

76. U.S. House of Representatives (Dies Committee), *Investigation of Un-*

American Propaganda Activities in the United States, 10:6196–99. For Kunze's friendship with hard-core Protestant circles, see, for example, H. M. Alexander Hartmann to Samuel Stouch, October 3, 1939, Klan archives for Pennsylvania, New Jersey, and Delaware, in State Police Archives, RG 30, Pennsylvania State Archives, Harrisburg, Pa.

77. "4000 Listen to Earl Browder Attack US Aid to Finland," *Philadelphia Record*, February 10, 1940.

78. Herzstein, *Roosevelt and Hitler* 271–84; General Records of the Bund, box 7, folder 109, Bund Archives, NA.

79. "Daly Pledges Free Speech before Meeting of 'Antis,' " *Philadelphia Record*, March 17, 1939.

80. Gordon Sager, "Swastika over Philadelphia," *Equality*, August 1939, 3–8.

81. U.S. House of Representatives, Special Committee on Un-American Activities, *Investigation of Un-American Propaganda Activities in the United States: Executive Hearings*, 77th Cong., 1942, vol. 6 (Washington, D.C.: Government Printing Office, 1942), 2544–46.

82. "Nazi Activity in Philadelphia," *The Hour* 113 (September 13, 1941): 1.

83. U.S. House of Representatives, *Investigation of Un-American Propaganda Activities in the United States: Executive Hearings*, 1942, 6:2624.

84. Sager, "Swastika over Philadelphia"; Paul B. Beers, *Pennsylvania Politics Today and Yesterday: The Tolerable Accommodation* (University Park, Pa.: Penn State Press, 1980), 30, 91; *Pennsylvania Manual*, 1939; *Annual Proceedings: Pennsylvania Society of Sons of the Revolution, 1934–35, and List of Members* (Philadelphia: Society of Sons of the Revolution, 1935).

85. "German Spy Owns Club in Sellersville"; "New Light on Nazi Effort to Bore into US Armed Forces," *The Hour* 11 (September 16, 1939): 1.

86. "Gen. Brookfield Admits Going to German Rallies," *Philadelphia Record*, September 10, 1939.

87. "German Spy Owns Club in Sellersville"; "Gen. Brookfield Admits Going to German Rallies."

88. "German Spy Owns Club in Sellersville."

89. Diamond, *Nazi Movement in the United States*, 197.

90. Advertisements in the *Philadelphia Herold* provide a copious listing of such clubs and groupings.

91. See, for example, *German Society of Pennsylvania: 175th Annual Report for 1939* (Philadelphia: German Society of Pennsylvania, 1939); Harry W. Pfund, *A History of the German Society of Pennsylvania* (Philadelphia: German Society of Pennsylvania, 1944).

92. Sager, "Swastika over Philadelphia," 5; Diamond, *Nazi Movement in the United States*, 247–48, for the network of Bund affiliates; Records of the German American Business League Inc., Bund Archives, NA.

93. Robert Reiss, "120,000 Anti-Nazi Germans Combat Bund in America," *Philadelphia Record*, October 1, 1939.

94. For the Ross speech, see the advertisement in *Philadelphia Herold*, December 2, 1938.

95. General Records of the Bund, 1926–1942, box 4, folders 14–15, The *Kyffhäuserbund*; also Records of Other Organizations, The *Kyffhäuserbund*, "Correspondence and miscellaneous material regarding relief efforts for prisoners of war held in Canadian camps 1939–1941," Bund Archives, NA.

96. Its home was at 3827 North 13th Street.

97. Diamond, *Nazi Movement in the United States*, 249 n.

98. Geoffrey S. Smith, *To Save a Nation*, 148.

99. *Pennsylvania Manual*, 1941.

100. "Libel Is Charged by Rep. Gartner, Called Pro-Nazi," *Philadelphia Record*, November 5, 1940; Leonard Dinnerstein, *Anti-Semitism in America* (New York: Oxford University Press, 1994), 136; Stefan Heym, *Nazis in USA* (New York: American Committee for Anti-Nazi Literature, 1938), 32.

101. George Britt, *The Fifth Column Is Here* (New York: Wilfred Funk, 1940), 112.

102. Sager, "Swastika over Philadelphia."

103. Mayor Wilson to Fritz Kuhn, November 28, 1938, and A. Russell Phillips to Wilhelm Luedtke, November 22, 1938, Records of the German American Business League Inc., Bund Archives, NA.

104. "No Signs of Bund as 2300 Observe German Day Here," *Philadelphia Record*, October 7, 1939.

105. *German Society of Pennsylvania: 175th Annual Report*, 21.

106. "Senator Davis Main Speaker at Nazis' Rally in Philadelphia," *The Hour* 13 (September 30, 1939): 5; "Senator Davis Heiled in Philadelphia," *The Hour* 15 (October 14, 1939): 3.

107. The other cities were Chicago and Los Angeles.

108. "Kuhn and Bund Face Federal Prosecution," *The Hour* 3 (June 16, 1939): 4a; "Flood of Hitler Propaganda"; see, for example, "Final Report of Samuel McK. Perry, Examiner, Acting as a Representative of the Treasury Department," 1942, Records of the A. V. Publishing Co., Bund Archives, NA; Strong, *Organized Anti-Semitism*, 35.

109. *Anzeigen-Kunden in Philadelphia (Pa.) und dortigen Bezirk*, March 29, 1940, Records of the A. V. Publishing Co., Bund Archives, NA.

110. Graf and Brueninger to the Editor, *Evening Bulletin*, 1941?, Records of the A. V. Publishing Co., Bund Archives, NA.

111. Records of the A. V. Publishing Co., Bund Archives, NA.

112. William B. Graf to A. V. Publishing Co., June 11, 1940, Records of the A. V. Publishing Co., Bund Archives, NA.

113. Graf and Brueninger to the Editor, *Evening Bulletin*.

114. "Final Report of Samuel McK. Perry," 7.

115. See, for example, a characteristic issue in 1934: "Die Saar muss Deutsch bleiben" and "Ist Kongressman Dickstein ein Lügner?," *Philadelphia Herold*, September 1, 1934.

116. "Fascist Boom in Philadelphia," *The Hour* 45 (May 18, 1940).

117. See, for example, "Die Deutsche wieder in der Offensive," *Pittsburgh Sonntagsbote*, January 2, 1942.

118. Records of the A. V. Publishing Co., Bund Archives, NA.

119. "Nazis Plan Chain of Papers in US for Propaganda," *Philadelphia Inquirer*, March 19, 1938; "News Men Praised for Snub to Nazis," *Philadelphia Inquirer*, March 20, 1938; Heym, *Nazis in USA*, 17. One of the journalists who remained to collaborate with the venture was Colonel Emerson; see Chapter 5, above.

120. Henry R. Hoke, *It's a Secret* (New York: Reynal and Hitchcock, 1946), 81–83.

121. *Annual Proceedings*; Ralph Beaver Strassburger, *The Strassburger Family and Allied Families of Pennsylvania* (Gwynedd Valley, Pa.: Privately printed, 1922); Strassburger, *Pennsylvania German Pioneers* (Norristown, Pa.: Pennsylvania German Society, 1934).

122. Quoted in Rogge, *Official German Report*, 221.

123. Charles Higham, *American Swastika* (New York: Doubleday, 1985), 23–25; Rogge, *Official German Report*, 156–58, 219–29.

124. "Dies Links Nazi Diplomats to Spies," *Philadelphia Record*, November 22, 1940; "Dies Committee Charges Admitted by Strassburger," *Philadelphia Record*, November 23, 1940. Bullitt retained his Philadelphia ties and in 1943 ran for the mayoralty on the Democratic ticket; see Will Brownell and Richard N. Billings, *So Close to Greatness: A Biography of William C. Bullitt* (New York: Macmillan, 1987), 298–302.

125. Rogge, *Official German Report*, 157.

126. "Anti-Union Power of Nazis Bared in Berkshire Strike"; "Flood of Hitler Propaganda"; "Local Nazis Play Storm Troopers," *Philadelphia Record*, January 23, 1938.

127. "Flood of Hitler Propaganda."

128. "WPEN Fires Program Chief after Pro-Nazi Propaganda," *Philadelphia Record*, January 8, 1938; "Bars Citizenship to Nazi Radio Propagandist," *Philadelphia Record*, September 26, 1940.

129. Rogge, *Official German Report*, 43–45, 68–69, 317; Spivak, *Plotting America's Pogroms*, 75; "Dies Links Nazi Diplomats to Spies."

130. Rogge, *Official German Report*, 60.

131. "Fascist Boom in Philadelphia."

132. Luebke, "The Germans," 80–82; Herzstein, *Roosevelt and Hitler*, 133, 139; "Ex-Envoy Quits Foundation over Nazi Literature," *Philadelphia*

Record, May 23, 1940; "Schurz Foundation Ends Reich Award," *Philadelphia Inquirer*, September 17, 1940; "Naziism Assailed by Carl Schurz Memorial Group," *Philadelphia Record*, September 17, 1940.

133. "New Pro-Nazi Organization in Philadelphia," *The Hour* 105 (July 12, 1941): 1–2.

134. "Fascist Boom in Philadelphia"; "Majority of German Americans Here Oppose Hitler's Invasion of Poland."

135. "German Consul Here Admits Throwing Heil Hitler Party," *Philadelphia Record*, May 28, 1940; "Consuls Calm in Philadelphia as War Spreads," *Philadelphia Record*, June 12, 1940. Compare *New York Times*, May 28, 1940.

136. U.S. House of Representatives (Dies Committee), *Investigation of Un-American Propaganda Activities in the United States*, 2:1153. Knoepfel later found employment teaching language skills to American officers preparing to undertake occupation duties in conquered Germany; see "The Germans," *Pittsburgh Press Roto*, September 26, 1971.

137. Britt, *Fifth Column Is Here*, 31.

138. "Fortra Merges Nazi Affairs," *Philadelphia Record*, January 24, 1940.

139. "FBI Given Data on Local Bund."

140. "Nazis Accused of State Drive," *Philadelphia Record*, August 21, 1939; "Nazi Propaganda Pours into City," *Philadelphia Record*, November 7, 1939; "Threefold Probe of Nazi Propaganda Hits Legal Snag," *Philadelphia Record*, November 9, 1939; "Nazis Mail New Circulars Here," *Philadelphia Record*, November 11, 1939; "Legion to Probe Nazi Propaganda," *Philadelphia Record*, December 5, 1939; "New Nazi Propaganda Floods US," *Jewish Exponent*, November 15, 1940.

141. "Bundists Join Reds in Sabotage and Strikes, Ex-Nazi Aide Says Here," *Philadelphia Inquirer*, May 21, 1941; Leon G. Turrou, *The Nazi Spy Conspiracy in America* (1939; reprint, Freeport, N.Y.: Books for Libraries, 1972).

142. Ladislas Farago, *The Game of the Foxes* (New York: McKay, 1971).

143. Ibid., 488–89.

144. Ibid., 442.

145. John J. Stephan, *The Russian Fascists: Tragedy and Farce in Exile* (New York: Harper and Row, 1978); Herzstein, *Roosevelt and Hitler*, 276–77.

146. Farago, *Game of the Foxes*, 442–45.

147. See Chapter 8, below.

148. Stephan, *Russian Fascists*; Farago, *Game of the Foxes*, 442–45, 502.

149. Charles Higham, *American Swastika*, 121–33.

150. Ibid., 132.

151. "Theodore Martin's Resignation Leaves Nazis of Pennsylvania in Dismay," *The Hour* 18 (November 4, 1939): 4.

152. Reiss, "120,000 Anti-Nazi Germans Combat Bund in America."

153. "Nazis Quit Here, Raff Declares," *Philadelphia Record*, February 19, 1940.

154. "Bund Dying Here, Martin Asserts," *Philadelphia Record*, October 21, 1939; "Bund Dissolves in Several Localities," *The Hour* 24 (December 16, 1939): 1–2.

155. "Camera Smashed at Bund Meeting," *Philadelphia Record*, January 9, 1938.

156. "Shell Wrecks Philadelphia Nazi Bund," *Philadelphia Record*, February 21, 1938.

157. "Bund Dying Here, Martin Asserts."

158. "Bomb Wrecks Doctor's Home: Family Unharmed by Blast," *Philadelphia Record*, September 20, 1938.

159. "Turngemeinde Alters Name to Avoid Stigma of Nazism," *Philadelphia Record*, December 7, 1938.

160. "Anti-Nazis Plan to Picket Envoy," *Philadelphia Record*, February 5, 1938; "Anti-Nazis Picket German Group Play," *Philadelphia Record*, March 5, 1939.

161. Graf and Brueninger to the Editor, *Evening Bulletin*; "German Consul Is Threatened," *Philadelphia Record*, June 20, 1940.

162. *Philadelphia Record*, September 14, 1938.

163. "2000 March Here in Protest against Czech and Albanian Grabs," *Philadelphia Record*, April 23, 1939.

164. See Chapter 7, below.

165. U.S. House of Representatives, *Investigation of Un-American Propaganda Activities in the United States: Executive Hearings*, 1942, 6:2628, 2645.

166. "Bund Dying Here, Martin Asserts"; "Bund Assailed by Germans Residing Here."

167. U.S. House of Representatives (Dies Committee), *Investigation of Un-American Propaganda Activities in the United States*, 2:1107–80 (September 1938); 6:3705–3889 (August 1939); 10:6043–6124.

168. Herzstein, *Roosevelt and Hitler*, 282–83; Records of Court Cases Involving the German American Bund, Bund Archives, NA.

169. "Bund Club Cited by Liquor Board for Violations," *Philadelphia Record*, November 5, 1939.

170. "Kuhn Successor, Two Others, Seized at Bund Camp," *Philadelphia Record*, July 5, 1940; "Race Hatred Law Ruled Invalid by NJ Court: 9 Bundists to Go Free," *Philadelphia Inquirer*, December 6, 1941.

171. Reiss, "120,000 Anti-Nazi Germans Combat Bund in America." The office of collector had long been one of the plum patronage gifts in the hands of the ruling party, suggesting Raff's ties with the Democratic leadership.

172. "German Spy Owns Club in Sellersville"; "FBI Given Data on Local Bund"; "Nazi Plot to Kill A. R. Raff Bared," *Philadelphia Record*, June 22, 1940.

173. Reiss, "120,000 Anti-Nazi Germans Combat Bund in America."

174. Ibid.

175. "German Americans in City Unite to War on Hitlerism," *Philadelphia Record*, January 17, 1938; "Anti-Nazi Society Reports Big Gains," *Philadelphia Record*, February 13, 1939; "Nazis Accused of State Drive"; "Majority of German Americans Here Oppose Hitler's Invasion of Poland."

176. Reiss, "120,000 Anti-Nazi Germans Combat Bund in America"; "German Americans Cheer at Condemnation of Hitler," *Philadelphia Record*, June 24, 1940.

177. "Schurz Foundation Ends Reich Award."

178. "German Spy Owns Club in Sellersville"; for FBI agents at Bund meetings, see "German Consul Here Admits Throwing Heil Hitler Party."

179. "Bund Camp Stoned," *York Dispatch*, September 6, 1939; "Probe Bund Camp at Sellersville," *Philadelphia Record*, September 7, 1939; "Fire Siren in Sellersville: Is It the Camp?," *Philadelphia Record*, September 12, 1939; "FBI Given Data on Local Bund"; "Two Posts Expose Memorial Day Plans of Bund," *Philadelphia Record*, May 30, 1940.

180. "Mystery Man Pays Cash on Bund Camp," *Philadelphia Inquirer*, September 15, 1940.

181. "Anxious City Shocked by War," *Philadelphia Record*, September 1, 1939.

182. "Majority of German Americans Here Oppose Hitler's Invasion of Poland."

183. "Nazis Quit Here, Raff Declares"; "Bund Assailed by Germans Residing Here." In Pittsburgh the Bund was denounced by established institutions such as the *Volksblatt und Freiheits-Freund*; see "*Volksblatt* Back," *Bulletin Index*, February 1, 1940.

184. Diamond, *Nazi Movement in the United States*, 248 n.

185. Bund Commands nos. 1–50, 1938–1941, box 5, folder 66, and box 5, folder 67, *Bundesbefehl*, General Records of the Bund, Bund Archives, NA.

186. Records of the German American Business League Inc., "Philadelphia Unit 1936–1938," Bund Archives, NA.

187. Records of Other Organizations: the *Kyffhäuserbund*, correspondence and handbills; see, for example, *Philadelphia Herold*, December 3, 1938, Bund Archives, NA.

188. General Records, box 11, folder 167, Bund Archives, NA; also Records of Other Organizations: The *Kyffhäuserbund*, "Correspondence and miscellaneous material regarding relief efforts for prisoners of war held in Canadian camps, 1939–1941"; Ernst H. Boehm, *Unsere Pflicht der Heimat gegenüber*, pamphlet (Philadelphia: Kyffhäuser-Hilfswerk für Deutschland, 1940).

189. "Reich Vets in US Send $32,000 Home," *Philadelphia Inquirer*, September 14, 1940; "37 Seized in Round-Up of Axis Citizens Here."

190. "Fascist Boom in Philadelphia."

191. David Karr, "The Flag-Waving Bund," *Equality*, December 1939, 26–28.

192. "Sez Who?," cartoon, *Philadelphia Inquirer*, September 16, 1940.

193. Herzstein, *Roosevelt and Hitler*.

194. "New Pro-Nazi Organization in Philadelphia."

195. *American Appeal* 1, no. 1 (September 1, 1939): 9.

196. Diamond, *Nazi Movement in the United States*, 149–51, 363.

197. Ibid., 216.

198. Rogge, *Official German Report*, 444.

199. Diamond, *Nazi Movement in the United States*, 338–47.

CHAPTER SEVEN

1. "Coughlin Terror," *Nation*, January 20, 1940, 59–60; "The Brooklyn Beer-Hall Putsch," *New Republic*, January 22, 1940, 99; George Britt, "Coughlin's Christian Front," *New Republic*, January 29, 1940, 142–45; J. H. Carpenter, "Christian Front Accused of Plot," *Christian Century* 57 (January 31, 1940): 154; Edward C. McCarthy, "The Christian Front Movement in New York City, 1938–1940" (master's essay, Columbia University, 1965); Philip Jenkins, "Homegrown Terror," *American Heritage* 46, no. 5 (September 1995): 38–46.

2. "Anybody Know Anything About This?," cartoon, *Pittsburgh Press*, January 17, 1940.

3. For Catholic reactions to labor and radical politics in these years, see Kenneth J. Heineman, "A Catholic New Deal: Religion and Labor in 1930s Pittsburgh," *Pennsylvania Magazine of History and Biography* 118 (1994): 363–94; Heineman, *A Catholic New Deal: Religion, Labor, and Politics in Depression Pittsburgh* (University of Pittsburgh Press, forthcoming).

4. Ibid.; George Q. Flynn, *American Catholics and the Roosevelt Presidency, 1932–1936* (Lexington: University of Kentucky Press, 1968).

5. Thomas H. Coode and John D. Petrarulo, "The Odyssey of Pittsburgh's Father Cox," *Western Pennsylvania Historical Magazine* 55 (1972): 217–38; Douglas P. Seaton, *Catholics and Radicals: The Association of Catholic Trade Unionists and the American Labor Movement from Depression to Cold War* (Lewisburg, Pa.: Bucknell University Press, 1981); Richard Deverall, "Catholic Radical Alliance," *Christian Front* 2, no. 10 (1937): 141–43; Patrick J. McGeever, *Rev. Charles Owen Rice, Apostle of Contradiction* (Pittsburgh: Duquesne University Press, 1989).

6. "What We're Doing," *Christian Front* 4, no. 1 (1939): 8–9; John L. Lewis, "Industrial Unionism—CIO," *Christian Front* 2, no. 4 (1937): 52–54; Philip Murray, "Control Technology," *Christian Social Action* 4, no. 7 (1940).

7. For the political odyssey of Father Coughlin, see Alan Brinkley, *Voices of Protest: Huey Long, Father Coughlin, and the Great Depression* (New York: Knopf, 1982); Seymour M. Lipset and Earl Raab, *The Politics of Unreason: Right Wing Extremism in America, 1790–1970,* 2d ed. (Chicago: University of Chicago Press, 1978), 150–202; Sheldon Marcus, *Father Coughlin: The Tumultuous Life of the Priest of the Little Flower* (Boston: Little Brown, 1973); Geoffrey S. Smith, *To Save a Nation: American Counter-Subversives, the New Deal, and the Coming of World War II* (New York: Basic Books, 1973); Charles J. Tull, *Father Coughlin and the New Deal* (Syracuse, N.Y.: Syracuse University Press, 1965); James P. Shenton, "The Coughlin Movement and the New Deal," *Political Science Quarterly* 82 (1958); John L. Spivak, *Shrine of the Silver Dollar* (New York: Modern Age Books, 1940); Raymond Swing, *Forerunners of American Fascism* (New York: Messner, 1935).

8. David H. Bennett, *Demagogues in the Depression: American Radicals and the Union Party, 1932–1936* (New Brunswick, N.J.: Rutgers University Press, 1969).

9. George Q. Flynn, *Roosevelt and Romanism: Catholics and American Diplomacy, 1937–1945* (Westport, Conn.: Greenwood, 1976); Schuyler C. Marshall, "Editorial Comment on the Spanish Civil War in the Pittsburgh Papers," *Western Pennsylvania Historical Magazine* 35 (1952): 123–32.

10. McCarthy, "The Christian Front Movement in New York City"; Edward Lodge Curran, "The Christian Front," *Social Justice,* April 4, 1938, 14.

11. Theodore Irwin, "Inside the Christian Front," *Forum and Century* 103, no. 3 (March 1940): 102–8.

12. Donald S. Strong, *Organized Anti-Semitism in America: The Rise of Group Prejudice during the Decade 1930–1940* (Washington, D.C.: American Council on Public Affairs, 1941), 57–70; John Roy Carlson, *Under Cover* (New York: World Publishing, 1943), 317; Geoffrey S. Smith, *To Save a Nation,* 191, n. 18. For the anti-Coughlin polemic at this time, see, for example, Alson J. Smith, *The Case against the Christian Front: Coughlin's Storm Troopers* (New York: American League for Peace and Democracy, 1939), or *Father Coughlin—His Facts and Arguments* (New York: American Jewish Congress, 1939).

13. "Coughlin Traces Persecution to Hate of Communism," *Pittsburgh Press,* November 21, 1938; "Coughlin Rebuked by Radio Station," *Philadelphia Record,* November 22, 1938; "Coughlin Defends His Radio Sermon," *Philadelphia Record,* November 25, 1938; "US Sleuth Denies Father Coughlin Story," *Philadelphia Record,* November 29, 1938; "Rev. Charles E. Coughlin fasst Bock bei den Hornen," *Philadelphia Herold,* December 3, 1938; George Sylvester Viereck, "The Messiah in the Sealed Car," *Social Justice,* May 23, 1938, 3–4. Compare Denis Fahey, *The Rulers of Russia* (1938; American ed., Royal Oak, Mich.: Social Justice Publishing, 1940).

14. McCarthy, "The Christian Front Movement in New York City";
J. Wechsler, "Coughlin Terror," *Nation*, July 22, 1939, 92–97; Alson J. Smith, "Christian Terror," *Christian Century* 56 (August 23, 1939): 1017–19; "New York Meeting," *Commonweal*, September 1, 1939, 428–29.

15. Carlson, *Under Cover*. From 1939 to 1941 there is extensive (if partisan) coverage of the Christian Front movement in the New York–based journal *Equality*.

16. See, for example, Carlson, *Under Cover*, 216–17, 450–55.

17. Bennett, *Demagogues in the Depression*, 71.

18. Swing, *Forerunners of American Fascism*, 60.

19. Ibid., 52; Marcus, *Father Coughlin*, 291; Amos Pinchot, "Open Letter to the President," *Social Justice*, March 28, 1938, 10–11.

20. Wayne S. Cole, *America First: The Battle against Intervention, 1940–1941* (Madison: University of Wisconsin Press, 1953); Amos Pinchot, *History of the Progressive Party, 1912–1916* (New York: New York University Press, 1958).

21. Electoral statistics derived from the *Pennsylvania Manual*, 1937. The 34th and 40th Wards both included strong concentrations of Italian support; see Hugo V. Maiale, "The Italian Vote in Philadelphia between 1928 and 1946" (Ph.D. diss., University of Pennsylvania, 1950).

22. For Catholic support in this campaign, see Seymour M. Lipset, "Three Decades of the Radical Right: Coughlinites, McCarthyites, and Birchers," in *The New American Right*, rev. ed., ed. Daniel Bell (New York: Anchor, 1964), 382–84.

23. "Fuehrer of Front Spoke Here Twice," *Philadelphia Inquirer*, January 15, 1940.

24. See also Chapter 6, above.

25. "Seventeen Leaders Here Arrange Prayers for Jewish Victims," *Philadelphia Record*, November 16, 1938; "Speakers Demand Break with Reich; Burn Hitler Effigy," *Philadelphia Record*, November 18, 1938; "Meetings Urge US to Do Something about Hitler Victims," *Philadelphia Record*, November 19, 1938.

26. "Picketing of Stores Selling Nazi Goods Planned Here," *Pittsburgh Press*, November 15, 1938.

27. "Veterans Rout Silver Shirts," *Pittsburgh Press*, November 18, 1938; Donnell Byerly Portzline, "William Dudley Pelley and the Silver Shirt Legion of America" (Ed.D. diss., Ball State University, 1966), 142–43.

28. See for example "Anti-Nazis Picket German Group Play," *Philadelphia Record*, March 5, 1939.

29. "Roving CIO Pickets Urge Nazi Boycott," *Philadelphia Record*, November 24, 1938.

30. "Pastors Denounce German Policies," *Pittsburgh Press*, November 21, 1938; "Churches of City Unite in Decrying Nazi Persecution," *Philadelphia*

Record, November 21, 1938; "Pastors Denounce Jewish Outrages in Thanksgiving Talks," *Philadelphia Record*, November 25, 1938; "Church Federation and Council Assail Nazi Drive on Jews," *Philadelphia Record*, November 26, 1938; "Churches Continue Protests against Nazi Persecution," *Philadelphia Record*, November 28, 1938; "Anti-Semitism Hit as Churches Mark Second Advent Sunday," *Philadelphia Record*, December 5, 1938.

31. Stations still carrying the Coughlin programs were listed weekly in *Social Justice*; see, for example, February 12, 1940.

32. "1000 Picket Station to Protest Radio Ban on Father Coughlin," *Philadelphia Record*, December 5, 1938.

33. *Social Justice*, January 2, 1939, 15.

34. "2000 Protest Ban on Father Coughlin," *Philadelphia Record*, December 14, 1938.

35. "2000 Rap Radio Ban on Father Coughlin," *Philadelphia Record*, February 13, 1939.

36. "5000 Picket Radio Station to Protest Father Coughlin Ban," *Philadelphia Record*, December 12, 1938; "Pickets Again Hit Father Coughlin Ban," *Philadelphia Record*, December 19, 1938; "1200 Picket WDAS in Father Coughlin Ban," *Philadelphia Record*, January 2, 1939; "1200 Renew Picketing at Radio Station Here," *Philadelphia Record*, January 9, 1939.

37. "St. Patrick Gets Royal Welcome," *Philadelphia Record*, March 18, 1939.

38. "1000 Picket Station to Protest Radio Ban on Father Coughlin"; "Dr. Harr Assails Radio Censorship of Father Coughlin," *Philadelphia Record*, December 7, 1938.

39. "Pickets Again Hit Father Coughlin Ban."

40. "Keep Frankfurter Out, Pickets at WDAS Urge," *Philadelphia Record*, January 16, 1939.

41. "1000 Picket Station to Protest Radio Ban on Father Coughlin."

42. Dennis J. Clark, "Irish-Jewish Relations in Philadelphia," in *Jewish Life in Philadelphia, 1830–1940*, ed. Murray Friedman (Philadelphia: Institute for the Study of Human Issues, 1983), 253–75, at pp. 259–61.

43. "1200 Renew Picketing at Radio Station Here."

44. U.S. House of Representatives, Special Committee on Un-American Activities, *Investigation of Un-American Propaganda Activities in the United States: Executive Hearings*, 77th Cong., 1942, vol. 6 (Washington, D.C.: Government Printing Office, 1942), 2560, 2632.

45. "1200 Renew Picketing at Radio Station Here."

46. Gordon Sager, "Swastika over Philadelphia," *Equality*, August 1939, 3–8; "2000 Rap Radio Ban on Father Coughlin"; Edward F. Brophy, *The Christian Front* (1940; reprint, Metairie, La.: Sons of Liberty, 1978).

47. "Father Coughlin's Trojan Horse in the Catholic World," *Equality*,

March 1940, 31–33; Bessie Rebecca Burchett, *Education for Destruction* (Philadelphia: Privately printed, 1941), 29–30.

48. "Daly Pledges Free Speech before Meeting of 'Antis,'" *Philadelphia Record*, March 17, 1939.

49. "Philadelphia Coughlinites Hold Mass Meeting," *The Hour* 19 (November 11, 1939): 4 (all references to *The Hour* are from the reprinted edition, Robert Sobel, ed., *The Hour* [Westport, Conn.: Greenwood, 1970]); U.S. House of Representatives, *Investigation of Un-American Propaganda Activities in the United States: Executive Hearings*, 1942, 6:2644.

50. U.S. House of Representatives, *Investigation of Un-American Propaganda Activities in the United States: Executive Hearings*, 1942, 6:2647.

51. Burchett, *Education for Destruction*, 15.

52. "New Anti-Catholic Society Established," *The Register* (Altoona-Johnstown diocesan paper), June 25, 1939.

53. Irwin, "Inside the Christian Front," 103.

54. "13 Held for Grand Jury in Alleged Nazi Effort to Incite Riot Here," *Philadelphia Inquirer*, March 16, 1939.

55. "Daly Pledges Free Speech before Meeting of 'Antis.'"

56. "13 Held for Grand Jury in Alleged Nazi Effort to Incite Riot Here."

57. "Daly Pledges Free Speech before Meeting of 'Antis.'"

58. "Protestant Action League Formed to Teach Democracy," *Philadelphia Record*, May 15, 1939.

59. "Father Coughlin's Trojan Horse," 31.

60. "11 Seized in Fear of Riot at Y Rally for Race Tolerance," *Philadelphia Record*, March 15, 1939; "13 Held in Bail as Tolerance Rally Raiders," *Philadelphia Record*, March 16, 1939; "Daly Pledges Free Speech before Meeting of 'Antis.'" For Jones, see Elizabeth Vining, *Friend of Life: The Biography of Rufus M. Jones* (Philadelphia: Lippincott, 1958).

61. U.S. House of Representatives, *Investigation of Un-American Propaganda Activities in the United States: Executive Hearings*, 1942, 6:2622–23.

62. "13 Held in Bail as Tolerance Rally Raiders."

63. "13 Held for Grand Jury in Alleged Nazi Effort to Incite Riot Here"; "It's Time to Disband the Bund," *Philadelphia Inquirer*, March 17, 1939.

64. "FBI to Receive Report Today on Activities of Anti-Semites Here," *Philadelphia Inquirer*, January 17, 1940; "Christian Front Watched Here for Eight Months," *Philadelphia Record*, January 16, 1940.

65. Leonard Dinnerstein, *Anti-Semitism in America* (New York: Oxford University Press, 1994), 116–24, remarks on the extensive nature of anti-Semitic violence during 1939.

66. "West Philadelphia Called a Stronghold of Fascism," *Philadelphia Record*, March 24, 1939.

67. "Police Aid Sought against Nazi Thugs," *Philadelphia Record*, May 28,

1939; "Peace Council Sets Protest Meeting," *Philadelphia Record*, May 30, 1939.

68. "Academy President Says Nazi Pressure Can't Stop Forums," *Philadelphia Record*, July 2, 1939.

69. "Father Coughlin's Trojan Horse," 33.

70. "City Group to Aid Front Members," *Philadelphia Record*, January 20, 1940.

71. Presentments of the Special (October 1937) Grand Jury and Instructions of the Court, Philadelphia County, PA: Investigation of Vice, Crime, and Law Enforcement, Oct. 1937 to March 1939 (Philadelphia, 1939), 14–18, 115–16, 165 (copy in State Police Records, RG 30, Pennsylvania State Archives).

72. "Daly Pledges Free Speech before Meeting of 'Antis,' "

73. See, for example, Irwin, "Inside the Christian Front."

74. Ibid., 102.

75. *Social Justice*, July 24, 1939; "Christian Front Carries Fight into More States," *Social Justice*, July 31, 1939; "200 Police Guard Coughlin Rallies against Picketing," *Philadelphia Record*, July 15, 1939; "Rev. Coughlin Speaks to 5000 in Philadelphia in Phone Broadcast," *Philadelphia Inquirer*, July 15, 1939; "Fuehrer of Front Spoke Here Twice." The July rallies were met with protests by Communist groups denouncing "the fascist gangs of Nazi Bunds and Coughlin . . . the Coughlinites and their mobster hooligans [with] their labor-hating Jew-baiting slime" (leaflet addressed to "Workers of Philadelphia," July 1939, George Van Horn Moseley Papers, Library of Congress, Washington, D.C.).

76. "200 Police Guard Coughlin Rallies against Picketing."

77. Strong, *Organized Anti-Semitism*, 65–67.

78. *Social Justice*, July 24, 1939; "Christian Front Carries Fight into More States."

79. "200 Police Guard Coughlin Rallies against Picketing."

80. Sager, "Swastika over Philadelphia," 6; Curran, "Christian Front"; Brophy, *Christian Front*.

81. Strong, *Organized Anti-Semitism*, 65–67.

82. "Revolt Body Here Small in Number," *Philadelphia Inquirer*, January 16, 1940; "Christian Front Watched Here for Eight Months."

83. "Ex-City Official Accused in Christian Front Probe," *Philadelphia Record*, January 17, 1940.

84. Irwin, "Inside the Christian Front," 103; "Christian Front Watched Here for Eight Months"; "G-Men Seek Christian Front Link Here," *Philadelphia Record*, February 11, 1940.

85. U.S. House of Representatives, *Investigation of Un-American Propaganda Activities in the United States: Executive Hearings*, 1942, 6:2636.

86. "Revolt Body Here Small in Number."

87. "Ex-City Official Accused in Christian Front Probe."

88. "Father Coughlin Knows He Lies," *Equality*, February 1940, 12.

89. U.S. House of Representatives, *Investigation of Un-American Propaganda Activities in the United States: Executive Hearings*, 1942, 6:2638; "New Pro-Nazi Organization in Philadelphia," *The Hour* 105 (July 12, 1941): 1–2.

90. Irwin, "Inside the Christian Front."

91. George J. Mintzer and Newman Levy, *The International Anti-Semitic Conspiracy* (New York: American Jewish Committee, 1946), 53.

92. Annette Thackwell Johnson, "Christ or Coughlin?," *Equality*, August 1939, 9–12; Johnson, "The Christian Front in Pittsburgh," *Equality*, November 1939, 30–31.

93. Irwin, "Inside the Christian Front," 104; Johnson, "Christian Front in Pittsburgh"; "Red Students Routed by Bricks, Stench Bombs," *Pittsburgh Post-Gazette*, May 23, 1939.

94. Johnson, "Christian Front in Pittsburgh"; Leon G. Turrou, *The Nazi Spy Conspiracy in America* (1939; reprint, Freeport, N.Y.: Books for Libraries, 1972).

95. Frank Walsh, *Sin and Censorship: The Catholic Church and the Motion Picture Industry* (New Haven: Yale University Press, 1996); Gregory D. Black, *Hollywood Censored: Morality Codes, Catholics, and the Movies* (Cambridge: Cambridge University Press, 1994); James M. Skinner, *The Cross and the Cinema: The Legion of Decency and the National Catholic Office for Motion Pictures, 1933–1970* (Westport, Conn.: Praeger, 1993).

96. "Front Group Disbanded as Interest Lags," *Pittsburgh Press*, January 15, 1940.

97. Irwin, "Inside the Christian Front," 106.

98. Johnson, "Christ or Coughlin?"

99. George Britt, *The Fifth Column Is Here* (New York: Wilfred Funk, 1940), 97–99.

100. Henry Landau, *The Enemy Within: The Inside Story of German Sabotage in America* (New York: Putnam's, 1937), 8, 275–78.

101. The account of Joe McGarrity (1874–1940) is drawn from the following sources: Tim Pat Coogan, *Eamonn De Valera: The Man Who Was Ireland* (New York: HarperCollins, 1995); Dennis J. Clark, *The Irish of Philadelphia* (Philadelphia: Temple University Press, 1973), 148–58; J. Bowyer Bell, *The Secret Army* (London: Sphere, 1972); and Coogan, *The IRA* (London: Fontana, 1971).

102. "Irish Republicans Revolting, Leader McGarrity Says Here," *Philadelphia Record*, December 1, 1938.

103. Bowyer Bell, *Secret Army*.

104. Clark, *Irish of Philadelphia*, 148–56.

105. "Irish Army Vets to Mark Rising," *Philadelphia Record*, April 9, 1939; Bowyer Bell, *Secret Army*, 76.

106. Britt, *Fifth Column Is Here*, 97–98; see Chapter 8, below.

107. Charles Higham, *American Swastika* (New York: Doubleday, 1985), 115.

108. Though this does not necessarily indicate McGranery's own political views, he had earlier served as attorney for Khaki Shirt leader Art J. Smith; see "Big Shirt Smith Ready to Give Up, His Attorney Says," *Philadelphia Record*, October 16, 1933.

109. Bowyer Bell, *Secret Army*, 196; Coogan, *The IRA*.

110. Irwin, "Inside the Christian Front."

111. "Irish Here Ask US Aid against Britain," *Philadelphia Record*, January 23, 1939.

112. "5000 Irish Demand War Debts Be Paid," *Philadelphia Record*, February 20, 1939.

113. Carlson, *Under Cover*, 227–40; "Front Claimed Link to Congress," *Philadelphia Record*, April 30, 1940; Victor Riesel, "Two Pro-Fascist US Senators Aid Nationwide Vigilante Drive," *Reading Labor Advocate*, February 10, 1939. Reynolds is mentioned in admiring tones in the correspondence of the Pennsylvania Klan leadership, in General Correspondence, 1939, Klan archives for Pennsylvania, New Jersey, and Delaware, in State Police Archives, RG 30, Pennsylvania State Archives, Harrisburg, Pa.

114. "IRA Vets Here Pledge Support," *Philadelphia Record*, March 25, 1940; "Irish Group Hits Trust of British," *Philadelphia Record*, August 4, 1940; "Eire Envoy Says Britain Doesn't Need Irish Bases," *Philadelphia Record*, December 9, 1940; "Irish Denounce British Propaganda in Rally Here," *Pittsburgh Sun-Telegraph*, February 8, 1941.

115. Irwin, "Inside the Christian Front."

116. Ibid., 104; Dennis J. Clark, "The Philadelphia Irish: Enduring Presence," in *The Peoples of Philadelphia*, ed. Allen F. Davis and Mark H. Haller (Philadelphia: Temple University Press, 1973), 135–54.

117. Dennis Clark, "Urban Blacks and Irishmen," in *Black Politics in Philadelphia*, ed. Miriam Ershkowitz and Joseph Zikmund (New York: Basic Books, 1973), 15–30.

118. Thomas F. Armstrong, "The Public Educational Programs of Selected Lay Organizations in Pennsylvania" (Ed.D. diss., Temple University, 1947), 292.

119. Sager, "Swastika over Philadelphia."

120. "13 Held in Bail as Tolerance Rally Raiders."

121. "St. Patrick Gets Royal Welcome."

122. "Fascist Boom in Philadelphia," *The Hour* 45 (May 18, 1940).

123. Sager, "Swastika over Philadelphia."

124. "Fascists Active among Philadelphia Negroes," *The Hour* 19 (November 11, 1939): 4.

125. "Flood of Hitler Propaganda Comes through Air Daily to Organized Followers Here," *Philadelphia Record*, January 7, 1938.

126. U.S. House of Representatives, Special Committee on Un-American Activities (the Dies Committee), *Investigation of Un-American Propaganda Activities in the United States: Hearings before a Special Committee on Un-American Activities*, 75th Cong., 3d sess., and 76th Cong., 1st sess., on H. Res. 282 (Washington, D.C.: Government Printing Office, 1938–41), 3:2340–41.

127. *Jewish World* (Philadelphia), August 2, 1938.

128. Carlson, *Under Cover*, 158–63, 268–69; General Records, box 12, folder 184, Records of the German American Bund, RG 131, National Archives, College Park, Md. (referred to hereafter as Bund Archives, NA); Robert A. Hill, ed., *The FBI's RACON: Racial Conditions in the United States during World War II* (Boston: Northeastern University Press, 1995), 211, 233–35, 498–507.

129. Dinnerstein, *Anti-Semitism in America*, 203–9.

130. Quoted in ibid., 204.

131. The comparison with Jewish conditions is quoted in Charles Pete T. Banner-Haley, *To Do Good and to Do Well: Middle Class Blacks and the Depression in Philadelphia, 1929–1941* (New York: Garland, 1993), 162–64; for wartime conditions, see Dinnerstein, *Anti-Semitism in America*, 207.

132. Banner-Haley, *To Do Good and to Do Well*, 163–67; Brenda Gayle Plummer, *Rising Wind: Black Americans and U.S. Foreign Affairs, 1935–1960* (Chapel Hill: University of North Carolina Press, 1996); see Chapter 4, above, for conflicts between blacks and Italians.

133. "Meetings Urge US to Do Something about Hitler Victims."

134. Sager, "Swastika over Philadelphia," 7.

135. See above, Chapter 3; "New Anti-Catholic Society Established."

136. Heineman, "Catholic New Deal."

137. "The Christian Front and the Catholic Church," *Equality*, October 1939.

138. Ibid., 14.

139. Carlson, *Under Cover*, 60.

140. "Spain in Holy War, Msgr. Hawks Says," *Philadelphia Record*, October 21, 1938.

141. "2000 Rap Radio Ban on Father Coughlin."

142. "Father Coughlin's Trojan Horse," 33.

143. "Two Lectures Planned in K of C Campaign," *Philadelphia Record*, March 5, 1939.

144. "Jews Back Radio Drive against Father Coughlin," *The Register*, August 6, 1939.

145. Letter of Charles Coughlin to Bishop Hugh Boyle, September 1939, and letter of Bishop Boyle to Rev. A. G. Cicognani, Apostolic Delegate, Sep-

tember 1939, Papers Relating to Father James Cox, Archives of the Diocese of Pittsburgh, Pittsburgh, Pa.

146. Joseph R. Barr, "Choose Your Poison," *Christian Front* 4, no. 1 (1939): 10–11.

147. Higham, *American Swastika*, 74–75; "13 Held for Grand Jury in Alleged Nazi Effort to Incite Riot Here"; "Father Coughlin Backs Front: Catholic Paper Rebukes Him," *Philadelphia Record*, January 22, 1940; John A. Ryan, "Catholics and Anti-Semitism," *Current History* 49 (1939): 25–26.

148. "I Hate Jews!," *Christian Front* 4, no. 1 (1939): 2.

149. *Equality*, October 1939, 13.

150. McGeever, *Rev. Charles Owen Rice*; "Anti-Semitism Called Mortal Sin for Catholics by Priest on Air," *Catholic Standard and Times* (Philadelphia), August 18, 1939; Papers Relating to Father James Cox, Archives of the Diocese of Pittsburgh.

151. James R. Cox, "Hitler's Hatchet Man" (speech delivered to Dormont Rotary Club, Pittsburgh, July 1939?); Cox, "Father Coughlin: Hitler's Hatchet Man," *Equality*, July 1939, 30–31, reprinted in *American Appeal* 1, no. 1 (September 1, 1939). Rice's radio address was delivered on August 17, 1939, on station WWSW.

152. Letter of Charles E. Coughlin to Bishop Hugh Boyle, September 1939, Papers Relating to Father James Cox, Archives of the Diocese of Pittsburgh.

153. See, for example, "Pope Flays Racism," *Catholic Standard and Times* (Philadelphia), November 3, 1939; Heineman, "Catholic New Deal," 387–90; "Aid of Catholics to Negroes Lauded," *Philadelphia Record*, May 29, 1940.

154. Joe Rottenberg, "The Rise of Albert M. Greenfield," in Friedman, *Jewish Life in Philadelphia*, 213–35. Dougherty's good relations with Jewish leaders predated his friendship with Greenfield; see "Dr. Krauskopf Lauds Cardinal," 1924, newscutting in scrapbook, Archives of the Archdiocese of Philadelphia, Philadelphia, Pa.

155. "Cardinal Dougherty Praised by Mayor, Clerics, and Laity," *Philadelphia Record*, November 26, 1938; "Aid of Catholics to Negroes Lauded." For coverage of Nazism, see, for example, "Former Prisoner Describes Nazi Concentration Camp," *Catholic Standard and Times*, June 30, 1939.

156. "Nazi Atrocities against Subjugated Poland," *Catholic Standard and Times*, February 9, 1940. The Altoona-Johnstown diocesan paper, *The Register*, February 4, 1940, headlined, "Polish Persecution Called Worst in History." For Scranton, see *Republika-Górnik*, January 5, 1940, statement of Bishop W. J. Hafey.

157. "The Christian Front," editorial in *Catholic Standard and Times* (Philadelphia), January 26, 1940.

158. James F. Connally, ed., *The History of the Archdiocese of Philadelphia* (Philadelphia: Archdiocese of Philadelphia, 1976).

159. "G-Men Arrest 17 in Plot to Overthrow Government," *Pittsburgh Press*, January 15, 1940; "G-Men Smash Plot to Overthrow US, Murder Congressmen," *Philadelphia Inquirer*, January 15, 1940; "Hoover Reports 18 Arrests Nipped Plot to Overthrow US," *Philadelphia Record*, January 15, 1940.

160. Carlson, *Under Cover*, 253.

161. Higham, *American Swastika*, 85–101; Carlson, *Under Cover*.

162. "Christian Front Watched Here for Eight Months"; "Revolt Body Here Small in Number"; "FBI to Receive Report Today on Activities of Anti-Semites Here"; "G-Men Seek Christian Front Link Here"; James B. True, "Phony War against Christian Front," *Industrial Control Reports*, January 27, 1940, no. 298.

163. "Dynamite, Caps, Stolen from National Guard," *Pittsburgh Press*, January 17, 1940; "Dynamite Theft Rouses Fear of More Sabotage," *Philadelphia Record*, December 3, 1940.

164. Bund Commands, January 15, 1940, General Records of the Bund, box 5, folder 66, Bund Archives, NA.

165. Henry R. Hoke, *It's a Secret* (New York: Reynal and Hitchcock, 1946), 136; Charles E. Coughlin, *I Take My Stand, and Discussing "A" Christian Front* (Royal Oak, Mich.: Social Justice Publishing, 1940); *An Answer to Father Coughlin's Critics* (Royal Oak, Mich.: Radio League of the Little Flower, 1940).

166. "City Group to Aid Front Members"; "G-Men Seek Christian Front Link Here."

167. "Christian Front Watched Here for Eight Months."

168. "City Group to Aid Front Members."

169. "G-Men Seek Christian Front Link Here."

170. American Civil Liberties Union, "Report on Prosecutions Allegedly for Political Purposes," March 29, 1940, Records of Other Organizations, Bund Archives, NA; "FBI Tactics Protested by Defense Attorney," *Social Justice*, February 5, 1940; "Trial Is Vindication of Christian Fronters," *Social Justice*, July 8, 1940; "Christian Front Emerges More Potent Than Ever," *Christian Century* 57 (July 17, 1940): 892–93.

CHAPTER EIGHT

1. Robert E. Herzstein, *Roosevelt and Hitler* (New York: Wiley, 1994); Geoffrey S. Smith, *To Save a Nation: American Counter-Subversives, the New Deal, and the Coming of World War II* (New York: Basic Books, 1973).

2. U.S. House of Representatives, Special Committee on Un-American Activities (the Dies Committee), *Investigation of Un-American Propaganda Activities in the United States: Hearings before a Special Committee on Un-American Activities*, 75th Cong., 3d sess., and 76th Cong., 1st sess., on H. Res. 282 (Washington, D.C.: Government Printing Office, 1938–41), 2:1215.

3. Ibid., e.g., 2:1192, 1210.

4. John Roy Carlson, *Under Cover* (New York: World Publishing, 1943).

5. Leonard Dinnerstein, *Anti-Semitism in America* (New York: Oxford University Press, 1994).

6. H. M. Alexander Hartmann to Samuel Stouch, October 3, 1939, Klan archives for Pennsylvania, New Jersey, and Delaware, in State Police Archives, RG 30, Pennsylvania State Archives, Harrisburg, Pa. (hereafter cited as Klan Archives, PSA).

7. O. John Rogge, *The Official German Report* (New York: Yoseloff, 1961), 208; "The Defendants in the Washington Sedition Trial," *The Facts* (Anti-Defamation League) 3, no. 1 (January 1948).

8. Donald S. Strong, *Organized Anti-Semitism in America: The Rise of Group Prejudice during the Decade 1930–1940* (Washington, D.C.: American Council on Public Affairs, 1941), 133–37.

9. Herzstein, *Roosevelt and Hitler*, 262–70.

10. Charles Higham, *American Swastika* (New York: Doubleday, 1985), 83. The George Van Horn Moseley Papers in the Library of Congress, Washington, D.C., contain a substantial corpus of anti-Semitic ephemera as well as extensive evidence of Moseley's connections with far-Right theorists such as Winrod, Edmondson, Deatherage, and Reynolds, ties that endured well into the 1950s.

11. "Legion Leader Asks Patriotic Group to Repudiate Moseley," *Philadelphia Record*, March 30, 1939.

12. *Annual Proceedings: Pennsylvania Society of Sons of the Revolution, 1934–35, and List of Members* (Philadelphia: Society of Sons of the Revolution, 1935).

13. U.S. House of Representatives (Dies Committee), *Investigation of Un-American Propaganda Activities in the United States*, 5:3584–85, 3634–38.

14. Ibid., 5:3634–35.

15. Ibid., 5:3636.

16. Ibid., 5:3637. George Van Horn Moseley to Tiffany Blake, March 30, 1939, Moseley Papers.

17. Rogge, *Official German Report*, 285; H. L. Trefousse, *Germany and American Neutrality, 1939–1941* (New York: Octagon Books, 1969), 46–49.

18. U.S. House of Representatives (Dies Committee), *Investigation of Un-American Propaganda Activities in the United States*, 5:3553–60.

19. General Records, box 18, folder 247, Records of the German Ameri-

can Bund, RG 131, National Archives, College Park, Md. (referred to here- 315
after as Bund Archives, NA); U.S. House of Representatives (Dies Commit-   *Notes*
tee), *Investigation of Un-American Propaganda Activities in the United States,*   *to Pages*
5:3545–3704.   *197–200*

20. "Legion Leader Asks Patriotic Group to Repudiate Moseley."

21. Annette Thackwell Johnson, "The Christian Front in Pittsburgh,"
Equality, November 1939, 30–31.

22. "Klan-Bund Rally Addressed by Coughlin's Friend," *The Hour* 59
(August 24, 1940): 1–2. All references to *The Hour* are from the reprinted
edition, Robert Sobel, ed., *The Hour* (Westport, Conn.: Greenwood, 1970).

23. Carlson, *Under Cover*, 153; Sheldon Marcus, *Father Coughlin: The
Tumultuous Life of the Priest of the Little Flower* (Boston: Little Brown, 1973),
150; "A Wedding at Wedding of Klan and Bund," *Philadelphia Record*, Au-
gust 20, 1940; "The Klan Meets the Bund," *Free America and Deutscher
Weckruf*, August 1, 1940; "The Klan Strikes at Its Enemies," *Free America
and Deutscher Weckruf*, August 15, 1940. For Arthur Bell, see U.S. House of
Representatives (Dies Committee), *Investigation of Un-American Propaganda
Activities in the United States*, 14:8307–13.

24. Carlson, *Under Cover*, 152–53.

25. Kenneth S. Davis, *FDR: Into the Storm, 1937–1940* (New York: Random House, 1993); Herzstein, *Roosevelt and Hitler*.

26. Gordon Sager, "Swastika over Philadelphia," *Equality*, August
1939, 6.

27. "Coughlinites in Philadelphia Prepare for Christmas," *The Hour* 23
(December 9, 1939): 4.

28. "G-Men Smash Plot to Overthrow US, Murder Congressmen,"
Philadelphia Inquirer, January 15, 1940.

29. Bessie Rebecca Burchett, *Education for Destruction* (Philadelphia: Privately printed, 1941), 151.

30. Ibid., 33.

31. Ibid., 144.

32. Ibid., 28–30.

33. Ibid., 168.

34. Ibid., 58.

35. J. Roffe Wike, *The Pennsylvania Manufacturers' Association* (Philadelphia: University of Pennsylvania Press, 1960), 94.

36. Ibid., 173.

37. "Gartner's Mail 100 to 1 for Ban," *Philadelphia Record*, September 27,
1939.

38. "Navy Pioneer Honored," *York Dispatch*, September 11, 1939; "No
Signs of Bund as 2300 Observe German Day Here," *Philadelphia Record*,
October 7, 1939.

39. "Isolationist Organizations," Records of Other Organizations, Bund Archives, NA; Henry R. Hoke, *It's a Secret* (New York: Reynal and Hitch-cock, 1946).

40. Gordon Brooks, "The Church *vs.* War Hysteria," *Equality*, September 1940, 11.

41. Terry Radtke, *The History of the Pennsylvania American Legion* (Mechanicsburg, Pa.: Stackpole, 1993), 55–56.

42. *Congressional Record*, May 1, 1941, 3488.

43. William Pencak, *For God and Country: The American Legion, 1919–1941* (Boston: Northeastern University Press, 1989), 306; compare "Veterans Parade to Freedom Rally," *Philadelphia Inquirer*, May 29, 1941.

44. Justus Doenecke, *In Danger Undaunted: The Anti-Interventionist Movement of 1940–41* (Stanford, Calif.: Hoover Institution Press, 1990); Bill Kauffman, *America First!: Its History, Culture, and Politics* (Amherst, N.Y.: Prometheus, 1995); compare "William A. White Forms Group to Aid Allies," *Philadelphia Record*, May 20, 1940.

45. Wayne S. Cole, *America First: The Battle against Intervention, 1940–1941* (Madison: University of Wisconsin Press, 1953), 109.

46. Herzstein, *Roosevelt and Hitler*, 385–88.

47. Gifford Pinchot supported repeal of the Neutrality Act; see Gifford Pinchot, "We Are Neutral, We Must Stay Neutral," *Philadelphia Record*, November 3, 1939.

48. Cole, *America First*, 22, 31.

49. Jules Archer, *The Plot to Seize the White House* (New York: Hawthorn, 1973); "War Is a Racket, Says Gen. Butler in Armistice Talk," *Philadelphia Record*, November 11, 1939.

50. Cole, *America First*, 171; "War and Peace," *Bulletin Index* (Pittsburgh), May 22, 1941. Pittsburgh leftists produced an isolationist paper titled the *Peace-Gazette*, a parody on the well-known *Post-Gazette*.

51. U.S. House of Representatives, Special Committee on Un-American Activities, *Investigation of Un-American Propaganda Activities in the United States: Executive Hearings*, 77th Cong., 1942, vol. 6 (Washington, D.C.: Government Printing Office, 1942), 2517–26; Michael Sayers and Albert E. Kahn, *Sabotage: The Secret War against America* (New York: Harper, 1942), 203; George Britt, *The Fifth Column Is Here* (New York: Wilfred Funk, 1940), 113.

52. Cole, *America First*, 264.

53. "Academy Bars Lindbergh: Flier Will Speak at Arena," *Philadelphia Inquirer*, May 21, 1941; "Lindy Is Refused Use of Academy for Anti-Aid Talk," *Philadelphia Record*, May 21, 1941.

54. "Academy President Says Nazi Pressure Can't Stop Forums," *Philadelphia Record*, July 2, 1939. For earlier conflicts at this venue, see Chapter 7,

above. The academy also stands adjacent to the Bellevue Stratford, scene of
Moseley's rally in 1939.

55. *Social Justice* noted the Jewish name of the WCAU executive who refused the advertisements at that station; see "Colonel Lindbergh: A Challenge to Philadelphia," *Social Justice*, June 2, 1941, 6; "Anti-Lindbergh Rally Issues More Tickets Than Isolation Group," *Philadelphia Inquirer*, May 28, 1941.

56. Sayers and Kahn, *Sabotage*, 197–99; "Lindbergh to Speak in America First Rally at Arena Here Tonight," *Philadelphia Inquirer*, May 29, 1941.

57. George M. Mawhinney, "British Flee Crete, Nazis Say; 16,000 Hail Lindbergh Here; Says Roosevelt Seeks World Rule by US," *Philadelphia Inquirer*, May 30, 1941.

58. "LaGuardia and Bullitt to Address Big Rally against Appeasement," *Philadelphia Record*, May 24, 1941; George M. Mawhinney, "12,000 at Rally Here Roar for US Aid to Defeat Axis Powers," *Philadelphia Inquirer*, May 29, 1941; Will Brownell and Richard N. Billings, *So Close to Greatness: A Biography of William C. Bullitt* (New York: Macmillan, 1987).

59. Dinnerstein, *Anti-Semitism in America*, 129; Trefousse, *Germany and American Neutrality*, 46–49.

60. Cole, *America First*, 179.

61. Sayers and Kahn, *Sabotage*, 197–98.

62. "16,000 Hear Flyer Condemn FDR, Boo Churchill," *Philadelphia Record*, May 30, 1941.

63. Sayers and Kahn, *Sabotage*, 197–98.

64. Mawhinney, "British Flee Crete" (emphasis added).

65. "An Appreciative Audience," *Philadelphia Record*, May 30, 1941.

66. Rogge, *Official German Report*, 274–83. Amos Pinchot stirred intense controversy by his defense of Lindbergh following the Des Moines speech; see correspondence, September/October 1941, Amos Pinchot Papers, Library of Congress. The affair had local ramifications: In Williamsport, Pennsylvania, for example, one active isolationist engaged in a "heated argument" with a local rabbi about the degree to which war fever was whipped up by American Jews (L. Shannon to Amos Pinchot, October 15, 1941, Pinchot Papers).

67. "Academy Bars Lindbergh"; Philip M. Allen to Amos Pinchot, September 8, 1941, Pinchot Papers.

68. Sayers and Kahn, *Sabotage*, 219; compare Cole, *America First*, 131–54.

69. U.S. House of Representatives, *Investigation of Un-American Propaganda Activities in the United States: Executive Hearings*, 1942, 6:2543–4 (October 16, 1941); Sayers and Kahn, *Sabotage*, 219.

70. "Save Freedom Rally Tickets Going Fast," *Philadelphia Record*, May 27, 1941.

71. "Women for the United States of America," *The Facts* 2, no. 1 (January 1947): 7–12.

72. Cole, *America First*, 138.

73. Dinnerstein, *Anti-Semitism in America*, 129; Carlson, *Under Cover*, 253.

74. Hoke, *It's a Secret*, 113.

75. U.S. House of Representatives, *Investigation of Un-American Propaganda Activities in the United States: Executive Hearings*, 1942, 6:2544–46.

76. Ibid., 2619.

77. Ibid., 2548.

78. Ibid., 2521–26.

79. "Milwaukee Nazi Agent Arrested by FBI Linked to Philadelphia Fifth Columnist," *The Hour* 110 (August 16, 1941): 1; "Nazi Activity in Philadelphia," *The Hour* 113 (September 13, 1941): 1.

80. U.S. House of Representatives, *Investigation of Un-American Propaganda Activities in the United States: Executive Hearings*, 1942, 6:2610.

81. Herzstein, *Roosevelt and Hitler*, 364–65.

82. Sayers and Kahn, *Sabotage*, 164 n.

83. Correlli Barnett, *Engage the Enemy More Closely* (New York: Norton, 1991).

84. Philip Jenkins, "The Ku Klux Klan in Pennsylvania, 1920–1940," *Western Pennsylvania Historical Magazine* 69 (1986), quoting Pennsylvania Klan archives.

85. Lewis W. Button to Samuel Stouch, October 7, 1940, Klan archives for Pennsylvania, New Jersey, and Delaware, in State Police Archives, RG 30, Pennsylvania State Archives, Harrisburg, Pa. (hereafter cited as Klan Archives, PSA).

86. U.S. House of Representatives, *Investigation of Un-American Propaganda Activities in the United States: Executive Hearings*, 1942, 6:2588.

87. For example, "Rescue Klan #311 to J. A. Colescott," August 1940, Klan Archives, PSA.

88. U.S. House of Representatives (Dies Committee), *Investigation of Un-American Propaganda Activities in the United States*, 14:8251–8331; "Dictators Dissolve Masonic Lodges in Conquered Lands," *Fiery Cross*, September–October 1940.

89. "Klan Officials Removed from Office Following Alleged Klan-Bund Meet," *Fiery Cross*, September–October 1940; J. A. Colescott to Samuel Stouch, letters of August 20, 21, 28, 1940, Klan Archives, PSA.

90. U.S. House of Representatives, *Investigation of Un-American Propaganda Activities in the United States: Executive Hearings*, 1942, 6:2925.

91. Dinnerstein, *Anti-Semitism in America*, 134. The damning remarks are from Olive Ewing Clapper, *Washington Tapestry* (New York: Whittlesey House, 1946), 250–52, and from Carlson, *Under Cover*. There is a fine ac-

count of Mothers' organizations in Glen Jeansonne, *Women of the Far Right: The Mothers' Movement and World War II* (Chicago: University of Chicago Press, 1996).

92. "Daly Pledges Free Speech before Meeting of 'Antis,' " *Philadelphia Record*, March 17, 1939; Paul Lyons, *Philadelphia Communists, 1936–1956* (Philadelphia: Temple University Press, 1982), 87; for women in extremist groups, compare Kathleen M. Blee, *Women of the Klan: Racism and Gender in the 1920s* (Berkeley: University of California Press, 1991); Jeansonne, *Women of the Far Right.*

93. Trefousse, *Germany and American Neutrality*, 46–49; Clapper, *Washington Tapestry*, 250–52.

94. "More about the Mothers' March on Washington," *The Hour* 67 (October 19, 1940): 2; U.S. House of Representatives, *Investigation of Un-American Propaganda Activities in the United States: Executive Hearings*, 1942, 6:2648–52; "Pacifist Women Stage a Hanging," *Philadelphia Record*, August 22, 1940.

95. U.S. House of Representatives, *Investigation of Un-American Propaganda Activities in the United States: Executive Hearings*, 1942, vol. 6.

96. Emmanuel A. Piller, *Time Bomb* (New York: Arco, 1945), 109–20.

97. "More about the Mothers' March on Washington"; Glen Jeansonne, *Gerald L. K. Smith: Minister of Hate* (New Haven: Yale University Press, 1988), 85; Jeansonne, *Women of the Far Right.*

98. Piller, *Time Bomb*; Carlson, *Under Cover*, 509.

99. The group's usual venue was the POS of A Hall, North Broad Street.

100. Hoke, *It's a Secret*, 172–73; Jeansonne, *Women of the Far Right*, 138–51.

101. Piller, *Time Bomb*, 110.

102. Carlson, *Under Cover*, 509.

103. U.S. House of Representatives, *Investigation of Un-American Propaganda Activities in the United States: Executive Hearings*, 1942, 6:2652.

104. Hoke, *It's a Secret*, 172–74, 182.

105. Piller, *Time Bomb*, 112.

106. Ibid., 113–15.

107. Ibid., 113.

108. Britt, *Fifth Column Is Here*, 1.

109. Higham, *American Swastika*, 102–16.

110. Records of Special Duty Involving Visiting Dignitaries: Visit of the King and Queen of England, Pennsylvania State Police, Bureau of Crime and Traffic Law Enforcement, RG 30, Pennsylvania State Archives. One dangerous section of the route lay between Philadelphia and Trenton, "particularly in and through Bristol, PA. Aliens and foreign-born residents are numerous through the entire area and reside in the vicinity of the railroad." Bristol had a sizable Italian presence.

111. Philip S. Klein and Ari Hoogenboom, *A History of Pennsylvania*, 2d ed. (University Park, Pa.: Penn State Press, 1980), 469; compare "York Pounds Plowshares into Swords and Becomes Major Munitions Center," *Philadelphia Record*, June 6, 1940.

112. Henry Landau, *The Enemy Within: The Inside Story of German Sabotage in America* (New York: Putnam's, 1937); Britt, *Fifth Column Is Here*, 5–7.

113. Britt, *Fifth Column Is Here*, 5–7; Sayers and Kahn, *Sabotage*.

114. "Sears to Head G-Men in City," *Philadelphia Record*, December 2, 1939; "Waterfront Guarded against Sabotage Here: All of US on Alert," *Philadelphia Inquirer*, May 31, 1941.

115. "Sabotage Suspected," *York Dispatch*, September 7, 1939; "Troopers Guarding Penna Super-Road," *Philadelphia Inquirer*, December 10, 1941; "Railway Official Bares Sabotage along Its Lines," *Philadelphia Record*, June 5, 1940. For vigilantism, see A. J. Foglietta, "2500 Volunteers in State Hunting Fifth Columnists," *Philadelphia Record*, May 24, 1940; A. J. Foglietta, "State Session of Legion to Ask Draft Speedup," *Philadelphia Record*, August 16, 1940; "John Pew Backs Vigilantes Here," *Philadelphia Inquirer*, September 6, 1940; "Hyatt Claims 65,000 Members in Vigilantes," *Philadelphia Record*, Oct. 11, 1940.

116. Piller, *Time Bomb*.

117. "Probe Bund Camp at Sellersville," *Philadelphia Record*, September 7, 1939; "Sellersville Plant Warns It Will Fire All Bund Members," *Philadelphia Record*, September 26, 1939; "Dies Agents Find Nazis and Reds in Navy Yard Here," *Philadelphia Record*, November 16, 1940.

118. "Two Workers Fired at Arsenal for Bund Activities," *Philadelphia Record*, October 9, 1940; "37 Seized in Round-Up of Axis Citizens Here; City's Number One Nazi Held," *Philadelphia Inquirer*, December 10, 1941.

119. "Mysterious Tie-Up at Arsenal Halts Shell Fuse Output," *Philadelphia Record*, October 16, 1938.

120. Sayers and Kahn, *Sabotage*.

121. "Evidence of Sabotage Uncovered after Blasts in Three Plants Kill Fifteen," *Philadelphia Record*, November 13, 1940; Sayers and Kahn, *Sabotage*, 110; "Survivors Talk of Bund's Hand in Jersey Blast," *Philadelphia Inquirer*, September 13, 1940.

122. "Ship-Sinking Plot Bared at Chester," *Philadelphia Record*, January 30, 1940; "Vessels Set Afire, Pipes Cut in Sabotage at Sun Shipyard," *Philadelphia Record*, October 2, 1940.

123. Sayers and Kahn, *Sabotage*, 112–19.

124. "Father Coughlin Knows He Lies," *Equality*, February 1940, 9.

125. Ladislas Farago, *The Game of the Foxes* (New York: McKay, 1971), 445.

126. John J. Stephan, *The Russian Fascists: Tragedy and Farce in Exile* (New York: Harper and Row, 1978); Sayers and Kahn, *Sabotage*, 122–24.

127. "City Slovaks Hope for Peace: Pledge Loyalty to America," *Philadelphia Record*, August 27, 1939.

128. "Arrest of Doshen," *The Hour* 114 (September 27, 1941): 3.

129. "Vonsiatsky and International Nazism," *The Hour* 8 (August 15, 1939): 4–5; Stephan, *Russian Fascists*.

130. Alexander Lushnycky, Nadia Diakun, and Lew Shankowsky, *Ukrainians in Pennsylvania: A Contribution to the Growth of the Commonwealth* (Philadelphia: Ukrainian Bicentennial Committee, 1976).

131. Ibid., 53, 60.

132. U.S. House of Representatives (Dies Committee), *Investigation of Un-American Propaganda Activities in the United States*, 9:5259–5322; Higham, *American Swastika*, 117–33; Britt, *Fifth Column is Here*, 101–3.

133. Sayers and Kahn, *Sabotage*, 78–94; U.S. House of Representatives (Dies Committee), *Investigation of Un-American Propaganda Activities in the United States*, 9:5314.

134. "Ukrainian Fascists Meet in New York and New Jersey," *The Hour* 55 (July 27, 1940): 2–4; "Ukrainian Fascists in Midwestern Drive," *The Hour* 57 (August 10, 1940): 2–3; "Nazi Agent Katamay," *The Hour* 104 (July 5, 1941): 3.

135. U.S. House of Representatives (Dies Committee), *Investigation of Un-American Propaganda Activities in the United States*, 2:1209.

136. Sayers and Kahn, *Sabotage*, 70–73; Stephan, *Russian Fascists*, 248–302.

137. Higham, *American Swastika*, 125–27; Sayers and Kahn, *Sabotage*, 73; "Vonsiatsky and International Nazism."

138. Sayers and Kahn, *Sabotage*, 3–4.

139. Ibid., 81.

140. Higham, *American Swastika*, 120; "Nazi-Ukrainians Photograph US Industrial Centers," *The Hour* 112 (August 30, 1941): 1; "Ukrainian Fifth Columnists," *The Hour* 121 (December 13, 1941): 4.

141. Higham, *American Swastika*, 119.

142. Sayers and Kahn, *Sabotage*, 3–4; "Ukrainian Fascists and Pennsylvania Train Wreck," *The Hour* 91 (April 5, 1941): 1–2; "Career of Kalina Lissiuk," *The Hour* 93 (April 19, 1941): 2–3.

143. "Buchko Criticized by His Superior," *The Hour* 63 (September 21, 1940): 2–3.

144. "Buchko Leaves US," *The Hour* 120 (November 29, 1941): 3.

145. "Letter from Ukrainian Churchman," *The Hour* 62 (September 14, 1940): 2–3; "Ukrainian Fascists Troubled," *The Hour* 63 (September 21, 1940): 2.

146. "Buchko Criticized by His Superior," 2–3.

147. "Ukrainian-Americans Fight Fascist Elements," *The Hour* 67 (October 19, 1940): 2.

148. "ODWU and Hetman in Retreat," *The Hour* 68 (October 26, 1940): 2; "US Hetman to Disband," *The Hour* 89 (March 22, 1941): 1; "Government Freezes Funds of Ukrainian National Association," *The Hour* 122 (December 30, 1941).

149. Farago, *Game of the Foxes*, 488; "Germans, Italians, Seized along with Japanese Here," *Philadelphia Inquirer*, December 9, 1941; "37 Seized in Round-Up of Axis Citizens Here"; "115 Aliens Interned at Gloucester Include Professor at U of P," *Philadelphia Inquirer*, December 12, 1941; "Nazi Shrine Found by G-Men in Raid on North Philadelphia Home," *Philadelphia Inquirer*, December 14, 1941; "Japanese, German, Italian Nationals Rounded Up Here," *Pittsburgh Press*, December 9, 1941; "Professor, Attorney, Held in Axis Alien Roundup," *Pittsburgh Press*, December 10, 1941.

150. Radtke, *History of the Pennsylvania American Legion*, 56.

151. "Documents Seized by FBI in Raid on Nazi Retreat," *Philadelphia Inquirer*, December 13, 1941.

152. Records of the German American Business League Inc. (Deutscher Konsum Verband — DKV), Bund Archives, NA; letter of Willi Gruenenberg, *Philadelphia Deutscher Weckruf*, December 11, 1941.

153. Russell F. Weigley, Nicholas B. Wainwright, and Edwin Wolf, *Philadelphia: A Three Hundred Year History* (New York: Norton, 1982), 639; "Italians, Germans, Vow US Loyalty," *Philadelphia Inquirer*, December 12, 1941.

154. "German, Italian, Papers Continue," *Philadelphia Inquirer*, December 12, 1941.

155. Sayers and Kahn, *Sabotage*, 121–22; Higham, *American Swastika*, 130–32.

156. Stephan, *Russian Fascists*, 299–302.

157. "The Defendants in the Washington Sedition Trial," *The Facts* 3, no. 1 (January 1948): 29–30; Hoke, *It's a Secret*, 197.

158. Higham, *American Swastika*, 63; Hoke, *It's a Secret*, 294.

159. Rogge, *Official German Report*, 310; Constance Drexel, *Armament Manufacture and Trade* (Worcester, Mass.: Carnegie Endowment for International Peace, Division of Intercourse and Education, 1933); "Gertie on Berlin Radio Is Former Local Resident," *Pittsburgh Post-Gazette*, August 24, 1943; "Former Chum, WAVE, Aided Exposé of Gertie," *Pittsburgh Post-Gazette*, August 24, 1943.

160. "New Issue of *Herold* Allowed in Mails: Paper Still Faces Action," *Philadelphia Inquirer*, May 6, 1942; "Final Report of Samuel McK. Perry, Examiner, Acting as a Representative of the Treasury Department," 1942,

Records of the A. V. Publishing Co., Bund Archives, NA; "Attorney General 323
to Crack Down on *Social Justice*," *Social Justice*, April 6, 1942.

161. "Defendants in the Washington Sedition Trial"; Carlson, *Under
Cover*, 484–86; Hoke, *It's a Secret*; Leo P. Ribuffo, *The Old Christian Right:
The Protestant Far Right from the Great Depression to the Cold War* (Philadel-
phia: Temple University Press, 1983), 178–224; Higham, *American Swastika*.

162. Rogge, *Official German Report*, esp. 173–218.

163. Hoke, *It's a Secret*; Rogge, *Official German Report*.

164. Hoke, *It's a Secret*; Higham, *American Swastika*.

165. Maximilian St. George and Lawrence Dennis, *A Trial on Trial: The
Great Sedition Trial of 1944* (New York: National Civil Rights Committee,
1946).

166. Neal Gabler, *Winchell: Gossip, Power, and the Culture of Celebrity*
(New York: Knopf, 1994), 333–36; Higham, *American Swastika*; *The Sedition Case* (Lowell, Ariz.: Lutheran Research Society, 1953). For Rogge, see
Joseph P. Kamp, *The Fifth Column in Washington* (New Haven: Constitutional Educational League, 1940). For Rankin and Hoffman as anti-Semites,
see "The Political Scene," *The Facts* 3, no. 10 (October 1948).

167. Hoke, *It's a Secret*, 294–95.

168. Albert E. Kahn, *High Treason: The Plot against the People* (New York:
Lear, 1950), 256–60.

CHAPTER NINE

1. Philip S. Klein and Ari Hoogenboom, *A History of Pennsylvania*, 2d
ed. (University Park, Pa.: Penn State Press, 1980), 472; J. Roffe Wike, *The
Pennsylvania Manufacturers' Association* (Philadelphia: University of Pennsylvania Press, 1960), 214; Seymour M. Lipset and Earl Raab, *The Politics
of Unreason: Right Wing Extremism in America, 1790–1970*, 2d ed. (Chicago:
University of Chicago Press, 1978), 214–24; Elizabeth A. Fones-Wolf, *Selling Free Enterprise: The Business Assault on Labor and Liberalism, 1945–60*
(Urbana: University of Illinois Press, 1994).

2. David H. Bennett, *The Party of Fear*, 2d ed. (New York: Vintage, 1995),
286–315.

3. Donald F. Crosby, "The Politics of Religion," in *The Specter*, ed. Robert
Griffith and Athen Theoharis (New York: Franklin Watts, 1974), 18–39.

4. Les K. Adler and Thomas G. Paterson, "Red Fascism: The Merger
of Nazi Germany and Soviet Russia in the American Image of Totalitarianism, 1930s–1950s," *American Historical Review* 75 (1970): 1046–64; Joel
Kovel, *Red Hunting in the Promised Land: Anti-Communism and the Making
of America* (New York: Basic Books, 1994); Richard Gid Powers, *Not without*

Honor: The History of American Anti-Communism (New York: Free Press, 1995).

5. John Cogley, *Catholic America* (New York: Doubleday Image, 1974), 92–93; compare Richard Hofstadter, *The Paranoid Style in American Politics* (Chicago: University of Chicago Press, 1979), 68–69; David M. Oshinsky, *A Conspiracy So Immense: The World of Joe McCarthy* (New York: Free Press, 1983).

6. David Caute, *The Great Fear* (New York: Simon and Schuster, 1978), 216–23; Jeffrey Zaslow, "When the Red Scare Hit Pittsburgh," *Pittsburgher Magazine*, March 1980, 61–72. Anti-Red street violence was orchestrated by local veterans' groups: "Reds Claim Police Shirked Duty at Rally," *Pittsburgh Post-Gazette*, April 4, 1949.

7. Ronald L. Filippelli and Mark McColloch, *Cold War in the Working Class: The Rise and Decline of the United Electrical Workers* (Albany: State University of New York Press, 1995); Kenneth J. Heineman, "A Catholic New Deal: Religion and Labor in 1930s Pittsburgh," *Pennsylvania Magazine of History and Biography* 118 (1994); Filippelli, "Pittsburgh Power Strike of 1946," in *Labor Conflict in the United States: An Encyclopedia*, ed. Filippelli (New York: Garland, 1990), 421–23; Filippelli, "Steel Strike of 1946," in Filippelli, *Labor Conflict*, 509–10; Patrick J. McGeever, *Rev. Charles Owen Rice, Apostle of Contradiction* (Pittsburgh: Duquesne University Press, 1989); Michael P. Weber, *Don't Call Me Boss* (Pittsburgh: University of Pittsburgh Press, 1988), 218–27; Douglas P. Seaton, *Catholics and Radicals: The Association of Catholic Trade Unionists and the American Labor Movement from Depression to Cold War* (Lewisburg, Pa.: Bucknell University Press, 1981); David M. Oshinsky, "Labor's Cold War," in Griffith and Theoharis, *The Specter*, 116–51.

8. Francis Eugene Walter, *Chronicle of Treason: Reprint of Series of Articles Appearing in the Philadelphia Inquirer. Committee on Un-American Activities, House of Representatives, 85th Congress, second session* (Washington, D.C.: Government Printing Office, 1958); Paul B. Beers, *Pennsylvania Politics Today and Yesterday: The Tolerable Accommodation* (University Park, Pa.: Penn State Press, 1980), 69; Caute, *Great Fear*, 92–95, 377, 386.

9. Beers, *Pennsylvania Politics Today and Yesterday*, 136; Weber, *Don't Call Me Boss*, 282–86, 378–80.

10. Caute, *Great Fear*, 218; Michael A. Musmanno, *Across the Street from the Courthouse* (Philadelphia: Dorrance, 1954); Steve Nelson, James R. Barrett, and Rob Ruck, *Steve Nelson: American Radical* (Pittsburgh: University of Pittsburgh Press, 1981).

11. Musmanno, *Across the Street from the Courthouse*, 181–85, 268–74, 290–91.

12. Ibid.; Weber, *Don't Call Me Boss*.

13. Musmanno, *Across the Street from the Courthouse*, 53.

14. Daniel J. Leab, "Anti-Communism, the FBI, and Matt Cvetic," *Pennsylvania Magazine of History and Biography* 115 (1991): 554–56.

15. Terry Radtke, *The History of the Pennsylvania American Legion* (Mechanicsburg, Pa.: Stackpole, 1993), 71–73.

16. Ernest A. Biagi, *The Italians of Philadelphia* (New York: Hearthstone, 1967), 155–57.

17. Paul Lyons, *Philadelphia Communists, 1936–1956* (Philadelphia: Temple University Press, 1982), 149.

18. Crosby, "Politics of Religion," 25.

19. Albert E. Kahn, *High Treason: The Plot against the People* (New York: Lear, 1950), 285–86.

20. Crosby, "Politics of Religion," 32.

21. Caute, *Great Fear*, 203–5; Lyons, *Philadelphia Communists*, 159.

22. Bessie Rebecca Burchett, *Education for Destruction* (Philadelphia: Privately printed, 1941), 25.

23. Caute, *Great Fear*, 419; Lyons, *Philadelphia Communists*, 158.

24. Beers, *Pennsylvania Politics Today and Yesterday*, 175–76; Radtke, *History of the Pennsylvania American Legion*, 71–73.

25. Caute, *Great Fear*, 38, 586; Richard M. Fried, "Electoral Politics and McCarthyism," in Griffith and Theoharis, *The Specter*, 208–9.

26. Klein and Hoogenboom, *History of Pennsylvania*, 478.

27. Musmanno, *Across the Street from the Courthouse*, 185.

28. Klein and Hoogenboom, *History of Pennsylvania*, 478; Caute, *Great Fear*, 72–75; Musmanno, *Across the Street from the Courthouse*, 1954; Beers, *Pennsylvania Politics Today and Yesterday*, 176; Statement by Albert R. Pechan, State Senator from Butler and Armstrong Counties, ca. 1953, Papers of Governor John Fine (William W. Wheaton Collection), MG 206, Pennsylvania State Archives, Harrisburg, Pa.

29. Thomas C. Reeves, *The Life and Times of Joe McCarthy* (New York: Stein and Day, 1982), 644.

30. Radtke, *History of the Pennsylvania American Legion*, 75–76.

31. Daniel Bell, ed., *The New American Right*, rev. ed. (New York: Anchor, 1964); Lipset and Raab, *Politics of Unreason*; Leo P. Ribuffo, *The Old Christian Right: The Protestant Far Right from the Great Depression to the Cold War* (Philadelphia: Temple University Press, 1983); Bennett, *Party of Fear*; Carey McWilliams, *A Mask for Privilege: Anti-Semitism in America* (Boston: Little Brown, 1948).

32. Ruth G. Weintraub, *How Secure These Rights?* (Garden City: Doubleday, 1949), 94–98.

33. O. John Rogge, *The Official German Report* (New York: Yoseloff, 1961), 370.

34. "What's the Story in Philadelphia?," *ADL Bulletin*, February 1952, 1–8.

35. Weintraub, *How Secure These Rights?*, 94–98; "A Survey of the Anti-Semitic Scene in 1946," *The Facts* (Anti-Defamation League) 2, no. 4 (April 1947): 36; "National Progress," *The Facts* 2, no. 6 (June 1947): 19–20. Some MacFarland pamphlets survive in the George Van Horn Moseley Papers in the Library of Congress, Washington, D.C.: see, for example, MacFarland to "Dear Friend," June 12, 1950, and MacFarland to "Dear fellow patriot," July 15, 1954; *American Flag Committee* newsletter, June–July 1954.

36. Arnold Forster and Benjamin R. Epstein, *Cross Currents* (New York: Doubleday, 1956), 250–52.

37. Emmanuel A. Piller, *Time Bomb* (New York: Arco, 1945), 102; Glen Jeansonne, *Gerald L. K. Smith: Minister of Hate* (New Haven: Yale University Press, 1988); David H. Bennett, *Demagogues in the Depression: American Radicals and the Union Party, 1932–1936* (New Brunswick, N.J.: Rutgers University Press, 1969), 284–86; Ribuffo, *Old Christian Right*; U.S. Congress, *Investigation of Un-American Activities in the United States: Gerald L. K. Smith* (Washington, D.C.: Government Printing Office, 1946).

38. Benjamin R. Epstein and Arnold Forster, *The Radical Right* (New York: Vintage, 1967), 104–5.

39. "A Survey of the Anti-Semitic Scene in 1946," 5–6.

40. Ibid., 36; "National Progress," 19–20; "Conde J. McGinley," *The Facts* 3, no. 4 (April 1948): 10–14.

41. "The Eastern Region," *The Facts* 1, no. 1 (May 1946): 13–17; "Kurt Mertig," *The Facts* 2, no. 7/8 (July/August 1947): 23.

42. "Women for the United States of America," *The Facts* 2, no. 1 (January 1947): 7–12; Glen Jeansonne, *Women of the Far Right: The Mothers' Movement and World War II* (Chicago: University of Chicago Press, 1996), 221.

43. U.S. Congress, Committee on Un-American Activities, *Preliminary Report on Neo-Fascist and Hate Groups* (Washington, D.C.: Government Printing Office, 1954); Donald Janson and Bernard Eismann, *The Far Right* (New York: McGraw Hill, 1963), 142–43.

44. "The Political Scene," *The Facts* 7, no. 6 (October 1952): 1.

45. Forster and Epstein, *Cross Currents*, 55–60. General Moseley was close to General MacArthur, who once remarked that Moseley was "always my strongest supporter, my wisest adviser, and my most loyal friend" (MacArthur to Moseley, September 30, 1935, Moseley Papers).

46. "Philadelphia Coughlinites Hold Mass Meeting," *The Hour* 19 (November 11, 1939): 4 (from the reprinted edition, Robert Sobel, ed., *The Hour* [Westport, Conn.: Greenwood, 1970]); Gordon Sager, "Swastika over Philadelphia," *Equality*, August 1939, 3; U.S. House of Representatives, Special Committee on Un-American Activities (the Dies Committee), *Investigation of Un-American Propaganda Activities in the United States: Hearings before a*

Special Committee on Un-American Activities, 75th Cong., 3d sess., and 76th Cong., 1st sess., on H. Res. 282 (Washington, D.C.: Government Printing Office, 1938–41), 5:3559.

47. Henry R. Hoke, *It's a Secret* (New York: Reynal and Hitchcock, 1946), 190–91.

48. Compare Jeansonne, *Gerald L. K. Smith*, 85; "The Defendants in the Washington Sedition Trial," *The Facts* 3, no. 1 (January 1948).

49. John Roy Carlson, *Under Cover* (New York: World Publishing, 1943), 414; Hoke, *It's a Secret*, 28, 180.

50. Forster and Epstein, *Cross Currents*, 147, 159; "Reading, 'Riting—and Retreat," *ADL Bulletin*, December 1950, 3–4; Hoke, *It's a Secret*, 72; Piller, *Time Bomb*, 34; Carlson, *Under Cover*, 48–50, 64, 458–61; "House Set to OK Dies Committee," *Philadelphia Record*, January 23, 1940.

51. Forster and Epstein, *Cross Currents*, 158–59. General Moseley was a fierce partisan of Joe McCarthy: "I am for him just 100 percent" (file "Senator McCarthy," Moseley Papers).

52. Seymour M. Lipset, "Three Decades of the Radical Right: Coughlinites, McCarthyites, and Birchers," in Bell, *New American Right*; Bennett, *Party of Fear*.

53. Epstein and Forster, *Radical Right*, 208.

54. J. Harry Jones Jr., *A Private Army* (New York: Collier, 1969), 108, cf. p. 60.

55. Epstein and Forster, *Radical Right*, 198, 202.

56. Pennsylvania State Society, Daughters of the American Revolution, *Sixty-Third Annual State Conference* (Pittsburgh: Daughters of the American Revolution, 1959); Mark Sherwin, *The Extremists* (New York: St. Martin's Press, 1963), 112–27; Hofstadter, *Paranoid Style*, 75–77; Bennett, *Party of Fear*, 328–31.

57. Epstein and Forster, *Radical Right* 65; Frank P. Mintz, *The Liberty Lobby and the American Right* (Westport, Conn.: Greenwood, 1985).

58. Gary Allen, *None Dare Call It Conspiracy* (Rossmoor, Calif.: Concord Press, 1972); William P. Hoar, *Architects of Conspiracy* (Belmont, Mass.: Western Islands, 1984).

59. Unfortunately, surviving Pennsylvania Klan archives do not cover this period. See Ronald L. Filippelli, "Philadelphia Transit Strike of 1944," in Filippelli, *Labor Conflict*, 419–21; Allan M. Winkler, "The Philadelphia Transit Strike of 1944," *Journal of American History* 59 (1972): 73–89; Pennsylvania State Police, Bureau of Crime and Traffic Law Enforcement, Special Duty, 1914–1964, "Strike Reports": Philadelphia Transit Strike 1944—Report of PFC John C. Friedrich, August 11, 1944, RG 30, Pennsylvania State Archives. In 1945 Pittsburgh experienced racial confrontations; see Weber, *Don't Call Me Boss*, 279.

60. Piller, *Time Bomb*, 113; Alvin J. Paine to Governor Martin, August 1, 1944, Governor Edward Martin, Official Papers, Philadelphia Transport Strike, 1944, MG156, Pennsylvania State Archives.

61. Dennis J. Clark, *The Irish of Philadelphia* (Philadelphia: Temple University Press, 1973), 161.

62. "A Survey of the Anti-Semitic Scene in 1946," 5.

63. S. A. Paolantonio, *Frank Rizzo: The Last Big Man in Big City America* (Philadelphia: Camino, 1994).

64. Jones, *Private Army*; *Extremism on the Right: A Handbook* (New York: Anti-Defamation League, 1983), 66, 84–85; U.S. House of Representatives, *Activities of Ku Klux Klan Groups in the United States: Hearings before the Committee on Un-American Activities*, 89th Cong., 2d sess., February 1966, part 4 (Washington, D.C.: Government Printing Office, 1966), 3342–63; Judy Rakowsky, "Klansman Convicted in Hate Crime Case," *Boston Globe*, February 17, 1995; "Hate Group Membership on Increase," *Centre Daily Times* (State College, Pa.), April 16, 1995.

65. Kevin Flynn and Gary Gerhardt, *The Silent Brotherhood* (New York: Signet, 1990), 157–59, 195–96.

66. Peter Binzen, *Whitetown, USA* (New York: Random House, 1970).

67. Michael Barkun, *Religion and the Racist Right* (Chapel Hill: University of North Carolina Press, 1994); Brent L. Smith, *Terrorism in America* (Albany: State University of New York Press, 1994); Peter H. Merkl and Leonard Weinberg, *Encounters with the Contemporary Radical Right* (Boulder, Colo.: Westview, 1993); Vince Rause, "The State of Hate," *Philadelphia Magazine*, August 1994, 66–71.

68. Kenneth S. Stern, *A Force upon the Plain: The American Militia Movement and the Politics of Hate* (New York: Simon and Schuster, 1996); Morris Dees, *Gathering Storm: America's Militia Threat* (New York: HarperCollins, 1996); Rause, "State of Hate," 66–71; Janet Bukovinsky, "New Hope Is Burning," *Philadelphia Magazine*, November 1993, 92–97; Suzanne Cassidy, Teresa Candori, and Adam Bell, "Militias in State Keep Low Profile" and "State Has Militia Activity in Eight Counties, Source Says," both in *Harrisburg Patriot News*, April 30, 1995; Michael A. Giarusso, "Militia Leaders Say Pennsylvania Is Fertile Recruiting Ground," *Centre Daily Times*, May 1, 1995; James William Gibson, *Warrior Dreams: Paramilitary Culture in Post-Vietnam America* (New York: Hill and Wang, 1994).

69. Pennsylvania Human Relations Commission, *52 White Supremacist Groups Active in Pennsylvania since January 1, 1991* (Harrisburg, Pa.: Pennsylvania Human Relations Commission, 1994); Mark S. Hamm, *American Skinheads: The Criminology and Control of Hate Crime* (New York: Praeger, 1993); Susan Miller, "One Family's Nightmare," *Newsweek*, March 13, 1995, 27; "Hate Group Membership on Increase."

70. Jeannette Krebs and Barry Fox, "Skeptics Bristle at Klan's Bid for Respectability," *Harrisburg Patriot News*, February 4, 1990.

71. "Klan Is in Charge in Mount Union," *Centre Daily Times*, September 16, 1990; Marty Nathan, "Skinheads in Huntingdon County," *Voices of Central Pennsylvania* (State College, Pa.), April 1994, 5–6.

72. "NAACP Protesters Outnumber Klan Ralliers in Uniontown," *Centre Daily Times*, July 21, 1986; "Protests Planned against Klan Rally in Ephrata," *Evening News* (Harrisburg, Pa.), October 2, 1987; Jim Strader, "Short Marches Newest Attempt for Publicity," *York Sunday News* (York, Pa.), December 1, 1991; "Officials Take Wait and See Attitude on Klan Request to March," *Daily Item* (Sunbury, Pa.), January 19, 1992; Strader, "Klan, Opponents, Battling for Hearts and Minds," *Centre Daily Times*, May 25, 1992.

73. Nathan, "Skinheads in Huntingdon County."

74. Jack Levin and Jack McDevitt, *Hate Crimes: The Rising Tide of Bigotry and Bloodshed* (New York: Plenum, 1993); Jeannette Krebs, "Hate Crimes Rise in State, Panel Reports," *Harrisburg Patriot News*, July 29, 1992; "Hate Crimes Grow in County," *Centre Daily Times*, February 24, 1995; "Hate Group Membership on Increase."

75. Bennett, *Party of Fear*; Philip Jenkins, *Pedophiles and Priests: Anatomy of a Social Crisis* (New York: Oxford University Press, 1996); Debbie Nathan and Michael Snedeker, *Satan's Silence: Ritual Abuse and the Making of a Modern American Witch Hunt* (New York: Basic Books, 1995); Philip Jenkins and Daniel Maier-Katkin, "Satanism: Myth and Reality in a Contemporary Moral Panic," *Crime, Law and Social Change* 17 (1992): 53–75.

76. Pat Robertson, *The New World Order* (Dallas: Word, 1991), 6, 126; Gustav Niebuhr, "Olive Branch to Jews from Conservative Christians," *New York Times*, April 4, 1995.

77. Michael Kazin, *The Populist Persuasion: An American History* (New York: Basic Books, 1995); Alan Crawford, *Thunder on the Right* (New York: Pantheon, 1980).

78. Dallas A. Blanchard, *The Anti-Abortion Movement and the Rise of the Religious Right* (New York: Twayne, 1994).

79. Niebuhr, "Olive Branch to Jews." However, the contemporary Christian Right attracts Jewish ire for analogies often drawn between abortion and the Holocaust.

CHAPTER TEN

1. Geoffrey S. Smith, *To Save a Nation: American Counter-Subversives, the New Deal, and the Coming of World War II* (New York: Basic Books, 1973), 3.

2. See Chapter 9, above.

3. Les K. Adler and Thomas G. Paterson, "Red Fascism: The Merger of Nazi Germany and Soviet Russia in the American Image of Totalitarianism, 1930s–1950s," *American Historical Review* 75 (1970): 1046–64; Richard Gid Powers, *Not without Honor: The History of American Anti-Communism* (New York: Free Press, 1995).

4. Richard Hofstadter, *The Paranoid Style in American Politics* (Chicago: University of Chicago Press, 1979); Seymour M. Lipset and Earl Raab, *The Politics of Unreason: Right Wing Extremism in America, 1790–1970*, 2d ed. (Chicago: University of Chicago Press, 1978); Daniel Bell, ed., *The New American Right*, rev. ed. (New York: Anchor, 1964).

5. Frank Kitson, *Low Intensity Operations* (London: Faber, 1971).

6. Robert E. Herzstein, *Roosevelt and Hitler* (New York: Wiley, 1994); David S. Wyman, *The Abandonment of the Jews* (New York: Pantheon, 1984).

7. Hofstadter, *Paranoid Style*; David H. Bennett, *The Party of Fear*, 2d ed. (New York: Vintage, 1995); John Higham, *Strangers in the Land: Patterns of American Nativism, 1860–1925* (New Brunswick, N.J.: Rutgers University Press, 1955).

8. David Brion Davis, *The Slave Power Conspiracy and the Paranoid Style* (Baton Rouge: Louisiana State University Press, 1969); Davis, "Some Themes of Counter-Subversion: An Analysis of Anti-Masonic, Anti-Catholic, Anti-Mormon Literature," in *From Homicide to Slavery* (New York: Oxford University Press, 1986), 137–54; Davis, *Fear of Conspiracy: Images of Un-American Subversion from the Revolution to the Present* (Ithaca, N.Y.: Cornell University Press, 1971); Michael Kazin, *The Populist Persuasion: An American History* (New York: Basic Books, 1995); Philip Jenkins and Daniel Maier-Katkin, "Satanism: Myth and Reality in a Contemporary Moral Panic," *Crime, Law and Social Change* 17 (1992): 53–75.

9. Hofstadter, *Paranoid Style*; Bennett, *Party of Fear*.

10. U.S. House of Representatives, *Investigation of Un-American Propaganda Activities in the United States: Executive Hearings*, 77th Cong., 1942, vol. 6 (Washington, D.C.: Government Printing Office, 1942), 2533–34.

11. Ibid., 2648.

12. Bessie Rebecca Burchett, *Education for Destruction* (Philadelphia: Privately printed, 1941), 142–43; "Authority Halts Two Housing Plans," *Philadelphia Record*, February 3, 1940.

13. Burchett, *Education for Destruction*, 144.

14. Richard Hofstadter, *Anti-Intellectualism in American Life* (New York: Vintage, 1966); Leonard Dinnerstein, *Anti-Semitism in America* (New York: Oxford University Press, 1994).

15. Hofstadter, *Paranoid Style*.

16. Smith, *To Save a Nation*, 87–100.

17. Walter Laqueur, ed., *Fascism: A Reader's Guide* (London: Pelican, 1979); Francis L. Carsten, *The Rise of Fascism* (London: Methuen, 1967); Hans Rogger and Eugen Weber, eds., *The European Right* (London: Weidenfeld and Nicholson, 1965).

18. William Preston Jr., *Aliens and Dissenters*, 2d ed. (Urbana: University of Illinois Press, 1994); Blair Coán, *The Red Web* (Belmont, Mass.: Western Islands, 1969); Norman Hapgood, ed., *Professional Patriots* (New York: Albert and Charles Boni, 1927).

19. Porter Versfelt III, "Behind the White Mask: The Ku Klux Klan in Pennsylvania," television script of a program broadcast on WPSX-TV, 1993.

20. "Former Philadelphian Is New Bund Führer," *Philadelphia Record*, December 6, 1939.

21. Philip Jenkins, "Eugenics, Crime, and Ideology," *Pennsylvania History* 51, no. 1 (1984): 64–78.

22. Manuscripts, pamphlets, and radio scripts ca. 1925–40, Elwyn schools library, Media, Delaware County, Pa.; James W. Trent Jr., *Inventing the Feeble Mind: A History of Mental Retardation in the United States* (Berkeley: University of California Press, 1994).

23. Philip Jenkins, "A Progressive Revolution?: Pennsylvania Penology, 1900–1950," *Criminal Justice History* 6 (1985): 177–99.

24. William T. Root and G. T. Giardini, *A Psychological and Educational Survey of 1916 Prisoners in the Western Penitentiary of Pennsylvania* (Pittsburgh: Board of Trustees of the Western Penitentiary, 1927).

25. The suggestion that Nazi ruthlessness was in part a defensive response to Communist practice and rhetoric was deeply controversial in the Germany of the 1980s, during the so-called *Historikerstreit*.

26. This was in part a consequence of Communist Party policies during the Nazi-Soviet detente. See, for example, the antiwar coverage in the antifascist journal *Equality* between 1939 and 1941.

27. Thomas Robbins, *Cults, Converts, and Charisma* (Newbury Park, Calif.: Sage, 1991).

28. Leo P. Ribuffo, *The Old Christian Right: The Protestant Far Right from the Great Depression to the Cold War* (Philadelphia: Temple University Press, 1983).

29. Hofstadter, *Paranoid Style*, 69.

30. George Britt, *The Fifth Column Is Here* (New York: Wilfred Funk, 1940), 63.

31. Apart from the Silver Shirt presence, this had also been White Shirt territory in the early 1930s, and Seattle was one of the regional centers proposed for a new Bund newspaper. See Eckard V. Toy Jr., "Silver Shirts in the Northwest: Politics, Prophecies, and Personalities," *Pacific Northwest Quarterly* 80 (1989); Toy, "The Ku Klux Klan in Oregon," in *Experiences in a*

Promised Land: Essays in Pacific Northwest History, ed. J. Edward Thomas and Carlos Schwantes (Seattle: University of Washington Press, 1986), 269–86.

32. George Seldes, *Lords of the Press* (New York: Blue Ribbon, 1941), 34–35; Paul Blanshard, *American Freedom and Catholic Power* (Boston: Beacon, 1949), 195–98.

Index